T0295918

Global Mobility and the Management of Expatriates

With approximately 66 million people across the globe considered expatriates (persons living and working abroad for a limited time), global mobility is an important issue for individuals, organisations and national governments. Written by a team of internationally renowned scholars from around the world, this volume summarises what is known about the management of global mobility and sets an agenda for future research. It also offers comprehensive overview of the practical implications for organizations that manage expatriates, and individuals who are currently or aspiring expatriates. Providing an accessible and globally relevant introduction to the subject of expatriation and global mobility, this book will appeal to postgraduate, MBA and EMBA students studying global mobility or international human resource management. It will also be of interest to practitioners, such as human resource managers and global mobility managers, who would like to gain a better understanding of the expatriation process.

Jaime Bonache is Professor of Management at University Carlos III of Madrid (Spain) and Visiting Professor of Esade Business School (Barcelona, Spain). His academic production includes around thirty articles in international peer-reviewed academic journals and three books, including *Managing the Global Workforce* (co-authored with Paula Caligiuri and David Lepak, 2010).

Chris Brewster is Professor of International Human Resource Management at Henley Business School, University of Reading. He has been involved as author or editor in the publication of more than 30 books, including *Working Internationally: Expatriation, Migration and Other Global Work* (co-authored with Yvonne McNulty, 2019), as well as more than 100 book chapters and over 200 articles.

Fabian Jintae Froese is Professor of Human Resource Management at the University of Goettingen, Germany, Editor-in-Chief of *Asian Business & Management*, and Associate Editor of the *International Journal of Human Resource Management*. His research has been published in more than 50 journal articles.

CAMBRIDGE COMPANIONS TO MANAGEMENT

Cambridge Companions to Management provide an essential resource for academics, graduate students and reflective business practitioners seeking cutting-edge perspectives on managing people in organizations. Each *Companion* integrates the latest academic thinking with contemporary business practice, dealing with real-world issues facing organizations and individuals in the workplace, and demonstrating how and why practice has changed over time. World-class editors and contributors write with unrivalled depth on managing people and organizations in today's global business environment, making the series a truly international resource.

TITLES PUBLISHED

Brief *Diversity at Work*
Cappelli *Employment Relations*
Cooper, Pandey and Quick *Downsizing*
Pearce *Status in Management and Organizations*
Reb and Atkins *Mindfulness in Organizations*
Saunders, Skinner, Dietz, Gillespie and Lewicki *Organizational Trust*
Sitkin, Cardinal and Bijlsma-Frankema *Organizational Control*
Smith, Bhattacharya, Vogel and Levine *Global Challenges in Responsible Business*
Sparrow, Scullion and Tarique *Strategic Talent Management*
Tjosvold andWisse *Power and Interdependence in Organizations*
Bonache, Brewster and Froese *Global Mobility and the Management of Expatriates*

Global Mobility and the Management of Expatriates

Edited by

JAIME BONACHE
Carlos III University of Madrid
CHRIS BREWSTER
University of Reading
FABIAN JINTAE FROESE
University of Goettingen

CAMBRIDGE
UNIVERSITY PRESS

University Printing House, Cambridge CB2 8BS, United Kingdom

One Liberty Plaza, 20th Floor, New York, NY 10006, USA

477 Williamstown Road, Port Melbourne, VIC 3207, Australia

314–321, 3rd Floor, Plot 3, Splendor Forum, Jasola District Centre, New Delhi – 110025, India

79 Anson Road, #06–04/06, Singapore 079906

Cambridge University Press is part of the University of Cambridge.

It furthers the University's mission by disseminating knowledge in the pursuit of education, learning, and research at the highest international levels of excellence.

www.cambridge.org
Information on this title: www.cambridge.org/9781108492225
DOI: 10.1017/9781108679220

First published 2021

A catalogue record for this publication is available from the British Library.

Library of Congress Cataloging-in-Publication Data
Names: Bonache, Jaime, editor. | Brewster, Chris, editor.
Title: Global mobility and the management of expatriates / edited by Jaime Bonache, Carlos III University of Madrid, Chris Brewster, University of Reading, Fabian Jintae Froese, University of Goettingen.
Description: New York, NY : Cambridge University Press, 2021. | Series: Cambridge companions to management | Includes index.
Identifiers: LCCN 2020035995 (print) | LCCN 2020035996 (ebook) | ISBN 9781108492225 (hardback) | ISBN 9781108729130 (paperback) | ISBN 9781108679220 (ebook)
Subjects: LCSH: Occupational mobility. | Employment in foreign countries.
Classification: LCC HD5717 .G575 2021 (print) | LCC HD5717 (ebook) | DDC 658.30086/91–dc23
LC record available at https://lccn.loc.gov/2020035995
LC ebook record available at https://lccn.loc.gov/2020035996

ISBN 978-1-108-49222-5 Hardback

Contents

Figures

Tables

Contributors

Thomas A. Birtch is Associate Professor in the SITE Department at Exeter Business School and Adjunct Associate Professor at the University of South Australia. His research interests currently revolve around leadership and strategic decision-making; the performance and behaviour of individuals and organisations across borders; and innovation, creativity, and knowledge management. His background in industry is extensive and includes holding senior executive level and management positions in both the private sector and government spanning three continents.

Jaime Bonache is Professor of Management at Carlos III University of Madrid, Spain, and Esade Business School, Spain. He has also been Full Professor at Cranfield School of Management, United Kingdom, and Visiting Professor at the University of Goettingen, Germany. He has lived and worked in Canada, Spain, the United Kingdom, and Germany. His research interest lies in global mobility, expatriate compensation, cross-cultural management, and epistemology.

Chris Brewster is Professor of International Human Resource Management, Henley Business School, United Kingdom, and Swinburne University of Technology, Australia. He researches international and comparative human resource management (HRM) and has published over thirty books and more than 200 articles.

Pawan Budhwar is the 50th Anniversary Professor of International HRM at Aston Business School, United Kingdom. He is Associate Pro-Vice Chancellor International, Aston University, and Co-Editor-in-Chief of the *British Journal of Management*. Pawan's research interests are in the field of strategic HRM, international HRM, and emerging markets with a specific focus on India.

Flora F. T. Chiang is Professor of Management at the China Europe International Business School (CEIBS). Her current research interests primarily focus on factors influencing employee behaviour and performance; how different forms of leadership affect both individual and organisational outcomes; the dynamics of managing people and organisations across borders; and how knowledge is created, managed, and diffused. Prior to her academic career, Professor Chiang held senior management and directorate positions in large private organisations and government.

Helen De Cieri (PhD, University of Tasmania) is Professor of Management at Monash Business School, Monash University, Australia. Her current research interests are in international HRM, employee health and well-being, and inclusive organisations. Helen is an associate editor for *Human Resource Management* and serves on several editorial boards.

Michael Dickmann's research focuses on human resource strategies, structures and processes of multinational organisations, cross-cultural management, international mobility, and global careers. He is the Senior Editor-in-Chief of *The International Journal of Human Resource Management* and the lead author/editor of several books on international HRM and global careers.

Fabian Jintae Froese is Professor of Human Resource Management at the University of Goettingen, Germany, Editor-in-Chief of *Asian Business & Management*, and Associate Editor of the *International Journal of Human Resource Management*. Previously, he worked for more than ten years in China, Japan, and Korea. His research interests lie in expatriation, diversity, and talent management.

Arno Haslberger is Senior Research Fellow at Middlesex University in London, United Kingdom. He researches on cross-cultural adjustment and expatriate management. Having grown up in Austria, he has over two decades' experience as an assigned and as a self-initiated expatriate as well as a trailing partner in the United States, the United Kingdom, Germany, and Spain. Currently, he divides his time between Austria and Luxembourg. Besides working in academia, he has held human resource management positions in multinational corporations for a total of ten years.

Anne Lessle (PhD) is a global HR professional specialising in organisational change and leadership development in multiple industries, including automotive, government, and the United Nations. Having lived and worked in five countries across three continents, her research focuses on expatriate adjustment.

Vesa Peltokorpi is Professor of Management at Hiroshima University, Japan. He received his PhD at Hanken School of Economics in Helsinki, Finland. His research interests include various international HRM-related issues, such as expatriation, recruitment, and language policies and practices, especially in subsidiaries of foreign multinational corporations in Japan. He has published more than fifty papers in journals such as the *Journal of Applied Psychology*, *Journal of International Business Studies*, *Journal of Management Studies*, and *Journal of Organizational Behavior*.

Margaret A. Shaffer is the Michael F. Price Chair of International Business at the Price College of Business, the University of Oklahoma. Her research interests are in the areas of global mobility, expatriation, and work–life interplay. Her publications have appeared in the *Academy of Management Review*, *Academy of Management Journal*, *Journal of Applied Psychology*, *Personnel Psychology*, *Journal of Management*, and *Journal of International Business Studies*.

Sebastian Stoermer is Junior Professor at the Technical University Dresden, Germany. His research primarily revolves around expatriation management and diversity management. Having a background in psychology, he approaches his research mainly from an individual-level perspective. Sebastian serves as an associate editor for the *Journal of Global Mobility*.

Vesa Suutari is Professor of International Management, University of Vaasa, Finland. His research has focused on expatriation, self-initiated expatriation, and global careers.

Emmy van Esch is Assistant Professor of Management at The Open University of Hong Kong. Her major research interests include expatriate management, international HRM, and knowledge management.

Arup Varma (PhD, Rutgers University) is Professor of Human Resource Management at Loyola University Chicago's Quinlan

School of Business. His research has been published in several leading journals, including the *Academy of Management Journal*, *Personnel Psychology*, *Journal of Applied Psychology*, and *Human Resource Management Review*. He is co-founder and past president of the Indian Academy of Management.

Viktoriya Voloshyna (PhD candidate at the School of Human Resources Management, York University, Canada) focuses on the area of career transitions, professional identity transformation, and identity threat.

Min (Maggie) Wan is Assistant Professor at the McCoy College of Business Administration, Texas State University. Her research interests include work–life issues, employee self-regulation, and international HRM.

Chun-Hsiao Wang is Associate Professor and Director of the Graduate Institute of Human Resource Management, National Central University. He received his PhD from McMaster University. His research interests include international assignments, organisational citizenship behaviour, and strategic HRM.

Marie-France Waxin is Associate Professor of Management at the American University of Sharjah. Her current research interests include international HRM; expatriation management; and different aspects of sustainability, such as diversity, workforce localisation, and sustainable development.

Celia Zárraga-Oberty is Associate Professor of Organization Studies at the Department of Business Administration of Carlos III University of Madrid. She holds a degree in Industrial Engineering and a PhD in Business Administration from the University of Las Palmas de Gran Canaria (Spain). Her research interests are in the areas of knowledge management, international compensation, and work teams. She has published her research in a number of international journals, including *Organization Studies*, *The International Journal of Human Resource Management*, and *Journal of World Business*.

Jelena Zikic (PhD, Associate Professor at the School of Human Resources Management, York University, Canada) focuses on career transitions, stress, and coping of diverse populations (e.g., skilled migrants), combining the individual as well as organisational perspective.

1 Global Mobility

Reasons, Trends, and Strategies

JAIME BONACHE, CHRIS BREWSTER, FABIAN JINTAE FROESE

1.1 Introduction

According to a PwC report (PwC, 2019), '80% of the future workforce will be mobile, and many want to work anywhere, anytime'. Global mobility, that is, the relocation of people across countries, has and will continue to be a major trend. The total number of expatriates, that is, employees who live and work abroad for a limited period of time, is estimated to amount to around 66.2 million worldwide and has been on a steady rise (Finaccord, 2019). Taking a wider perspective, the Organisation for Economic Co-operation and Development (OECD) estimates that there are currently around 250 million people living outside their home country, amounting to 3.3 per cent of the world's population, and with 70 per cent of them of working age (OECD, 2017).

The coronavirus crisis that the world suffered in the final stages of us putting this book together has and will have a substantial influence on global mobility in the short run, and then several possible long-term effects, though as we write we cannot say what they may be. However, we are certain that in the long run global mobility will remain important because, as we explain in this chapter, it has a key role for the development of both individuals and organizations.

Global mobility presents both opportunities and challenges for organisations and individuals. Organisations despatch expatriates to transfer knowledge, for control and coordination, and management development (Edström & Galbraith, 1977), with the ultimate goal of improving innovation and organisational performance (Bebenroth & Froese, 2020; Chang, Gong, & Peng, 2012). In terms of management development, international experience is the most effective way for individuals to acquire new knowledge and skills and boost their careers (Froese, Kim, & Eng, 2016; Sarabi, Froese, & Hamori, 2017). Despite these merits, and the high cost of assigned expatriates, many assignments fail to meet organisational, individual, and family expectations, which is very disappointing (Black & Gregersen, 1999).

In response, research and practice have investigated the reasons for success and failure (for a review, see Bhaskar-Shrinivas, Harrison, Shaffer, & Luk, 2005). Large consulting companies such as PwC, KPMG and Mercer have dedicated business units, and smaller specialised consulting companies have emerged to support companies in managing their expatriates. Larger multinational enterprises (MNEs) also have their own dedicated teams to prepare and support their expatriates. Despite all this wealth of knowledge and expertise, some expatriates continue to struggle and fail to meet organisational objectives. Economic shifts, demographic changes, and digitalisation have created a more diverse landscape in global mobility and new challenges (Bonache et al., 2018). For instance, MNEs increasingly utilise self-initiated expatriates (Froese & Peltokorpi, 2013; Furusawa & Brewster, 2018), international business travellers, and short-term assignees (Mäkelä, Saarenpää, & McNulty, 2017). While expatriate research has produced great insights, many questions remain unanswered. In particular, research has had difficulties in keeping pace with recent trends in global mobility.

Thus, this book provides a comprehensive and up-to-date overview of the topic. This book is a reader on international working. We asked some of the leading scholars in international human resource management to bring together, to synthesise, and to comment on what is known about key aspects of current debates on global mobility. This book will help professionals, scholars, and students to comprehend the complexity and diversity of international work.

This chapter will introduce background information and recent trends in expatriation. We will begin by briefly reviewing the early literature on expatriation, from the 1960s to the late 1980s. We will then describe some changes that occurred in the 1990s that transformed radically the field of global mobility. Finally, we will outline key trends in global mobility that define its current landscape. The chapter concludes by summarising the contents and key contributions that the reader will find in each chapter of this book.

1.2 Early Research: The Prototypical Expatriate

In early research, the term 'global mobility' was restricted to expatriation and that in turn was restricted to refer to those work experiences in which individuals, and oftentimes their families, are relocated from one country to another by an employer, generally from a context of familiarity (a home country) to one of greater novelty (a host country) for a limited period of time (Caligiuri & Bonache, 2016). These globally mobile employees were typically known as 'expatriates' or 'international assignees', and their existence had grown in importance as firms expanded their global reach.

From the 1960s through the late 1980s, then, researchers studying expatriates were examining a relatively homogeneous group within organisations: senior executives from developed-country headquarters of large MNEs sent abroad for a period of two to five years. They were mostly married men who were sent to be 'in charge' of a host-country subsidiary. This prototypical expatriate of the past brought with him his non-working wife – and the company's way of doing things. He would enjoy a generous compensation and benefits package for the 'hardship' of living in another country. This homogenous group enabled numerous macro-level and micro-level studies that came to build and define a fascinating literature on the expatriation experience.

1.2.1 *When and Why Assigned Expatriates Are Used*

At the macro level, early global mobility research focused on when and how expatriates foster a firm's strategic growth globally. In the 1970s, as companies began to accelerate their global reach, there was an interest in understanding the strategic reasons for expatriate assignments. To this end, Edström and Galbraith (1977), in their seminal article, identified three key functions or reasons for expatriation: for control, organisational development, and for management development.

The first potential function of expatriates, the control role, is for expatriates to represent the parent company's interests in the subsidiary. Headquarters send expatriates to liaise between the home- and host-country interests, safeguard the organisation's overall interests, and ensure that the decisions made in the subsidiary do not compromise the organisation as a whole (Boyacigiller, 1990; Brewster, 1991). Edström and Galbraith (1977) noted that the control function also tends to involve an element of coordination, especially in firms from industries with a high overall integration of their operations (e.g., automobiles). Expatriates are familiar with the firm's international network; they are aware of the impact a subsidiary's decisions may have on the rest of the corporation; and they develop numerous contacts, which thereby permit them to act as go-betweens across interdependent units (Boyacigiller, 1990). In this organisational development role, expatriates have formal position power to give them control, are socialising agents to impart culture, and can use informal communication to foster network ties (Harzing, 2001).

The second function identified by Edström and Galbraith (1977) is to transfer knowledge from headquarters to the subsidiary in order to develop the organisation. This knowledge may be of a general nature (e.g., corporate culture) or more technical and specific, such as that referring to the processes of purchasing inputs (e.g., purchasing or negotiating skills), transformation (e.g., product design, process engineering), or outputs (e.g., marketing skills). Much of this knowledge is tacit, as it cannot be coded or set out in manuals, but instead is steeped in the experience and skills of the organisation's members (Polanyi, 1962). This means that its global dissemination can best be achieved by posting staff abroad (Bonache & Brewster, 2001; Mäkelä & Brewster, 2009). It should be noted that Edström and Galbraith (1977) do not refer to knowledge transfer, per se; it was later, especially after the knowledge-based view of the firm was introduced in the management literature (Barney, 1991), that the expatriates performing this function became known as 'knowledge agents' (e.g., Bonache & Brewster, 2001; Beaverstock, 2004; Bonache & Zárraga-Oberty, 2008).

The final expatriate function identified by Edström and Galbraith (1977) is management development. Through international assignments, high-potential executives become immersed in a wide array of new and challenging intercultural situations (Black, Gregersen, & Mendenhall, 1992), which will enable them to develop a holistic approach and global business acumen. This experience will lead to greater career opportunities for those executives seeking professional growth (Brewster, 1991), as well as provide the MNE with a competitive advantage (Spreitzer, McCall, & Mahoney, 1997).

Far from having a merely historical interest, the contribution made by Edström and Galbraith (1977) is one of the topics in expatriate literature that is deemed to be widely accepted, appearing in practically every study that seeks to explain the deployment of expatriates in MNEs (Tan & Mahoney, 2006). However, as will be highlighted later, while the three expatriate functions that they identified are still valid in organisations today, the mix and relative importance of these functions have changed dramatically.

1.2.2 Traditional Challenges for the Assigned Expatriates

Early micro-research on expatriation focused on the main issues and challenges that people performing these strategic functions had to face. Two main challenges came to dominate the literature. One refers to the high rates of expatriate failure, particularly among US expatriates (Tung, 1988). It was estimated that 20–40 per cent of US expatriates returned prematurely without completing their assignments. This is three to four times higher than the failure rates experienced by European and Asian companies, although the US rate was almost certainly an overestimate (Harzing, 1995). Apart from early return, prior research also identified that around a third of expatriates performed below expectations abroad (Black & Gregersen, 1999). Expatriation assignments are costly, and when they fail, because they have to be brought back early or because they under-perform, the cost to all involved is high. Research has investigated the reasons for such failures. In particular, prior research identified cross-cultural adjustment (Church, 1982; Mendenhall & Oddou, 1985, 1986), training (Fiedler, Mitchel, & Triandis, 1971; Tung, 1981), selection (Caligiuri, 2000), and family problems (Stephens & Black, 1991) as the main reasons for success or failure. Accordingly, this book will tackle these challenges in Chapters 2, 3, and 4 to help us better understand the causes of expatriation success.

The other 'star' challenge in this era was that of repatriation, again highlighted for over thirty years (Caligiuri & Bonache, 2016; Lazarova & Cerdin, 2007; Suutari & Brewster, 2003;Yan, Zhu, & Hall, 2002). Early research reported that many repatriates leave their organisation within two years after repatriation, limiting the return on any developmental gain the expatriate might have brought to the globalisation efforts of the company in the future (Black et al., 1992; Harvey, 1982). And they generally stay in the same occupational field, working for competitors. Given the costs of expatriate assignments, this is poor human resource management. One study found that 42 per cent of repatriates had seriously considered leaving the company and 26 per cent were actively searching for an alternative employer (Black et al., 1992).

Some of the primary reasons repatriates often gave for leaving their organisation are also typical today (Festing & Maletzky, 2011; Kraimer et al., 2012; Ren et al., 2013). They include a lack of respect for the acquired skills (Gómez Mejía & Balkin, 1987), loss of status (Harvey, 1982), poor planning for return position (Gómez Mejía & Balkin, 1987), and reverse culture shock (Black & Gregersen, 1991). The extensive research on the 'repatriation problem' clearly highlighted how offering expatriate career advancement opportunities that are consistent with expatriates' new internationally oriented identities are critical to increase repatriation retention. Thus, Chapter 6 will discuss in detail repatriation and career development.

1.3 Changes in the Context

The aforementioned macro and micro issues and challenges in relation to assigned expatriates, introduced before 1990, provided a solid foundation for the field of expatriation by revealing high-level issues (e.g., strategic alignment, selection, cross-cultural adjustment, repatriation) in the field of global mobility. However, a number of economic, technological, organisational, and demographic changes in the business population from the 1990s onwards have had significant influence on the research and practice in global mobility. Such changes are summarised in Table 1.1.

1.3.1 Changes Affecting the Deployment of Expatriates

From the 1990s onwards, there were a number of major transformations that led to greater globalisation (Dunning, 2009). First, the fall of the Berlin Wall led to a transition to a market economy in many former Soviet-bloc countries. An alternative model, retaining a single-party state government, would also be followed by China, with the ensuing impact this has had on the global economy. Second, the liberalisation of cross-border markets encouraged regional economic integration (e.g., NAFTA, AFTA, APEC, and the European Union) and stimulated economic growth and accelerated international commercial transactions among businesses and private individuals. Third, the digital revolution and the advances made in information technology and computing systems paved the way for all firms (large and small) to embark upon greater innovation, and launch into markets that had, in prior years, been inaccessible. Fourth, there was a dynamic increase in the international operations of firms from every part of the world. Large MNEs, which not only reinforced their international

Table 1.1 *The changing nature of global mobility*

	Traditional expatriation (1960s to the late 1980s)	Type of change	Modern global mobility approach (1990s to the present)
a. Deployment of expatriates			
Reason for expatriation emphasised in the literature	• Control of subsidiaries • Fill skill gaps unavailable in host countries	*Increased globalisation* • Fall of the Berlin Wall • Liberalisation of cross-border markets • Digital revolution • Increase in international operations	• Knowledge transfer around MNEs • Professional development of global leaders
Typical mobility flow	• One-directional flow from headquarters to subsidiaries • Mostly from large US, European, and Japanese headquarters		• Mobility in all directions (e.g., lateral moves, reverse expatriations) and different periods • MNEs from emerging markets and developing countries
b. Demographic changes			
Gender	• Male expatriates	*Demographic and societal changes* • Number of households with dual-career couples	• More female expatriates
Age and level	• Middle-aged • Senior-level managers and executives		• All ages • From all levels in the organisation

Table 1.1 (*cont.*)

	Traditional expatriation (1960s to the late 1980s)	Type of change	Modern global mobility approach (1990s to the present)
Other family issues	• Single-income families • Non-working spouse	• Number of women working internationally • Increased lifespan of people globally	• Dual-career couples • Elderly parents • Non-traditional families
c. Changes in careers and working conditions			
Duration of assignments	• Relatively long assignments (two- to four-year period)	*Communication and labour market changes* • Advances in communications and the easy of global travel	• More travelling, short-term and project-oriented forms of global mobility
Employment modes	• Relational contracts	• Changes in employment modes	• Relational and transactional contracts
Initiating the global experience	• The company requests employees to relocate	• Increase number of global careers	• The company posts open requisitions for international assignments • The employees request opportunities for international assignments

Dominant perspective	• Headquarters' perspective was dominant		• Multiple perspectives (headquarters, regional, local) are considered
Prototypical expatriate	• Senior male executives from developed-country headquarters of large multinational corporations sent abroad for a period of two to five years	*As a result of the above changes* →	• A diverse landscape of expatriation experiences (e.g., corporate long- and short-term assignments, international commuters, self-initiated expatriates, migrants)

transactions, also increased their direct investment abroad, either through joint ventures or through wholly owned subsidiaries. New players also appeared on the economic scene, such as new MNEs from emerging countries, particularly in Asia, and small- and medium-sized enterprises, some being 'born global'.

These factors led to a redistribution of power around the world and the emergence of some countries (particularly China) as new world economic champions. This had obvious implications for the home country of expatriates. Before the 1990s era of globalisation, international assignments were the domain of US and European firms (Brewsteret al., 2014). The huge investment in Japan following the Second World War enabled it to become a leader in the automobile and electronics industries, with it being commonplace at the time to wonder how to respond to the Japanese challenge (Ouchi, 1981). It is not surprising, therefore, that expatriation in Japanese firms was studied closely (e.g., Tsurumi, 1978). Along with the Japanese, European and American expatriates monopolised the expatriation landscape. This is no longer the case. By 2007, emerging market countries had seventy firms in Fortune's ranking of the world's five hundred largest corporations, when a decade earlier this same figure was only twenty (Guillén & García-Canal, 2009).

So, large MNEs began appearing in emerging countries, such as Samsung in South Korea, China Mobile Limited, and Reliance Industries Limited in India. The rapid growth of emerging economies also meant that these countries became the typical destination for MNEs from developed countries. China's case is a particularly noteworthy one. As Bruning, Sonpar, and Wang (2012) have reported, in this new millennium China now hosts the highest number of expatriates per year, only behind the United States. It stands to reason that since the end of the 1990s, many studies have sought to understand the predictors of expatriate success in China (e.g., Selmer, 1999). Other studies have focused on different environments that may also be challenging for western expatriates, such as Japan (Froese & Peltokorpi, 2011; Peltokorpi & Froese, 2009) and Korea (Bader, Froese, & Kraeh, 2018; Stoermer et al., 2018). While firms in the past had posted talent from headquarters to other parts of the world, with the developed countries being the main destinations, some authors note that '[e]xpatriation no longer implies relocation to a glamorous site' (Groysberg, Nohria, & Herman, 2011: 11); it could include countries such as Nigeria (Okpara & Kabongo, 2011) and Iran (Soltani & Wilkinson, 2011).

A third implication the post-1990s era of globalisation had on global mobility was that more individuals being sent on expatriate assignments were from countries other than just the headquarters' country. This change was a major transition in leaders' mindset and organisational culture – one which has its own interesting history. We started seeing a greater use of 'inpatriate' assignments, an ethnocentric term for individuals from foreign subsidiaries who relocate for an expatriate assignment into the headquarters country (Froese et al., 2016; Portniagin & Froese, 2019; Sarabi et al., 2017), and third-country national assignments, individuals from one subsidiary who are relocated to another (Tarique, Schuler, & Gong, 2006). The diversity of 'to' and 'from' locations for international assignments has strategic implications for how – and how successfully – firms compete globally (Colakoglu, Tarique, & Caligiuri, 2009; Collings, Scullion, & Morley, 2007; Sarabi, Hamori, & Froese, 2019).

The more competitive and globalised business reality post 1990 required a new managerial mindset (Levy et al., 2007), labelled as a 'transnational' mentality (Ghoshal & Bartlett, 1990). The transnational mentality requires the simultaneous achievement of three different but complementary goals. The first is local responsiveness where MNEs differentiate their products and services to suit the preferences of their clients, the characteristics of the sector, and the cultural and legal environment of each one of the national markets in which they operate. The second goal or capability is the global integration of each MNE's operations in order to take advantage of different national factors of production, leverage economies of scale in all activities, and share costs and investments across different markets and business units. The third capability to be developed by a company competing across borders is innovation and a "learning organisation", which requires the different units (headquarters or subsidiaries) to learn from each other and exchange innovations in management systems and processes.

These strategic capabilities (and, in particular, the third one) have a clear impact on the deployment of expatriates. Although the three expatriate functions identified by Edström and Galbraith (1977) are still valid in the new context, it is also true that the mix of these functions has changed dramatically. Through the late 1980s the control function dominated. Today, many firms are reported as identifying knowledge transfer and acquisition as the primary reason for sending expatriates on assignment (Brookfield, 2016; Stoermer, Davies, & Froese, 2017). This is an important change. Rather than expatriates as control-oriented subsidiary leaders (positions that are now more likely held by local managers), expatriates today are more strategically oriented towards knowledge transfer/organisational development (Beaverstock, 2004; Harzing, 2001; Welch, 2003) and management development (Spreitzer et al., 1997; Shaffer et al., 2012).

Reflecting this change from the control function to a broader organisational development function (Harzing, 2001), we have seen burgeoning research to understand the relationship between expatriation and knowledge transfer (e.g., Bonache & Brewster, 2001; Furuya et al., 2009; Lazarova & Tarique, 2005; Mäkelä & Brewster, 2009; Reiche, Harzing, & Kraimer, 2009). This focus is consistent with the strategic literature on the difficulties of knowledge transfer within a firm's international network (Kostova, 1999; Szulanski, 1996) and has been flagged as a more arduous task than was predicted by the models of transnational firms where information flowed freely (Ghoshal & Bartlett, 1990).

In addition to knowledge transfer, managerial development has received increased attention as an essential reason to send people abroad. Today, consultants report 23 per cent of firms identify management development as a primary objective of international assignments (Brookfield, 2015). Recent research has brought to the fore the importance of international experience for people's professional development and their career possibilities (Cerdin & Pargneux, 2009; Sarabi et al., 2017). Expatriation is good for your marketability (Mäkelä et al., 2016) and for your career (Schmid & Wurster, 2017; Sarabi et al., 2017; Suutari et al, 2017). Further, the international experience of top management has a positive impact on the firm's performance (Daily, Certo, & Dalton, 2000; Carpenter, Sanders, & Gregersen, 2001), the level of presence in global markets (Carpenter & Fredrickson, 2001), and access to valuable knowledge with a view to formulating more effective global strategies (Athanassiou & Nigh, 2000).

1.3.2 Demographic Changes

Three demographic trends have had a great impact on the composition of the population of expatriates and the availability of expatriate candidates (Caligiuri & Bonache, 2016): (1) the number of households with dual-career couples, (2) the increased number of women on international assignments, and (3) the increased lifespan of people globally. Regarding the first of these trends, families, once traditionally, in the West at least, having a male primary income earner and a female homemaker, have now changed. At the time of early research, in the 1970s and 1980s, expatriates tended to be married men, likely with a wife who did not work outside of the home. Today, consultancies find married men comprise around half of expatriates (Brookfield, 2016). These changing demographics have shifted the focus of support practices. For example, organisations are now focused on providing expatriate partners' career support and offer provision for unmarried and same-sex partners.

The issue of dual-career couples in the expatriate context goes even deeper than changing demographics. It has long been understood that global mobility affects the expatriate employee and all of his or her loved ones, whether directly or indirectly (Caligiuri & Bonache, 2016). Partners and children have had their lives disrupted for the sake of the expatriates' relocation, and their experiences in the host country can often have profound influence on the expatriates' sense of work–life balance and, subsequently, on the outcome of the assignment. These changes associated with the relocation may be even more pronounced for the accompanying partner compared to the expatriate employee; while the expatriate has the routine and the social network of his or her new position, the partner needs to re-establish a personal and professional identity and a social network (Shaffer & Harrison, 2001).

Considering women on international assignments, the number of expatriate women apparently rose from 3 per cent in the 1980s (Adler, 1984), to 10–14 per cent in the 1990s, and to 16–20 per cent in the new millennium (see Salamin & Hanappi, 2014 for a review). The under-representation of female expatriates was not due to the lack of interest among women in pursuing an international career (Adler, 1987). Rather, it was due to prejudice on the part of managers, who believed that women were not viable candidates for international assignments because of dual-career marriages, host country nationals' (HCN) unwillingness to work with women, and an assumed lack of interest in expatriation (Adler, 1984; Stroh ,Varma, & Valy-Durbin 2000). Today, more than half of female expatriates think that they face greater obstacles in getting accepted for assignments than men

(Brookfield, 2016). In most organisations, selection processes are informal, which allows such prejudices more scope (Harris & Brewster, 1999; Varma, Stroh, & Schmitt, 2001). Women do face unique issues related to their adjustment and success in different positions and host-country locations (Caligiuri & Bonache, 2016).

The last of the above demographic trends is also very relevant. As lie expectancy increases globally, there is a greater number of professionals who are part of the 'sandwich generation'; sandwiched between caring for children they have had later in life and caring for elderly parents living longer. Recent decades have seen a dramatic increase in average life expectancy. Global life expectancy in the 1950s was 48 years and is predicted to rise to 75 years by 2050 (Chand & Tung, 2014). Life expectancy in the developed world is now 82 years (Chand & Tung, 2014). Increased longevity has had an impact on global mobility, with organisations extending relocation benefits to elderly parents who are dependent on their adult children for care (Brookfield, 2016). A number of firms (small percentage) that did so even paid for provision for elder care in the assignment location.

Taken together, these changes in the demography of expatriates have resulted in major challenges for women expatriates and global families. Accordingly, this book has two chapters on these topics: Chapter 10 on women and global mobility and Chapter 11 on global families.

1.3.3 Changes Affecting Careers and Working Conditions

Given the advances in communications and the ease of global travel, not only the number of traditional long-term managerial assignments continues to grow, but other less costly and more project-oriented forms of international staffing are growing faster (Beaverstock, 2004; Tharenou & Harvey, 2006). One different form of international mobility is short-term assignments (Collings, McDonnell, & McCarter, 2015; Suutari & Brewster, 2009; Mäkelä et al., 2017). Short-term assignments are usually defined (Collings et al. 2015) as work in another country lasting less than 12 months, although in practice the fiscal and residency issues that arise after six months means that six months is the usual maximum period. Another form of short-term assignments is international business travel, by people who do not relocate but engage in multiple short-term business trips. Short-term assignments have always been present in organisations, but they are being used at a far greater level in response to both cost and strategic pressures (Collings et al., 2007). This trend is also an outcome of an ever-increasing share of the labour force in some places expressing a resistance to international mobility (Colling et al., 2007; Harvey, Buckley, & Novicevic, 2000) and a desire to solve or, at least, reduce a major organisational concern: the high cost of expatriate compensation packages (Bonache, 2006; Collings et al., 2007; Bonache & Stirpe, 2012).

The nature and type of expatriate assignments is also widening. Globalisation has brought with it greater flexibility (geographic, temporal) and a wider variety of contractual relations (Banai & Harry, 2004). In particular, it has led to the displacement of relational contracts – those based on loyalty and long-term service – with transactional ones – those based on projects (Herriot & Pemberton, 1995). It has been argued that organisation-based careers are being replaced by more 'protean careers' (Hall, 2004), careers that are self-managed rather than organisation-directed and defined by greater inter-organisational mobility. The driving forces behind these careers are people's own values; career success is determined by professional satisfaction rather than the number of organisational promotions.

While traditional careers continue to exist for many people (Cappelli, 1999), there is more organisational mobility in professional careers – a change mirrored in today's mobile expatriate population. Fifty years ago one could correctly assume that corporate expatriates were bound to their organisations by a long-term relational contract (Rousseau, 2004), a tacit agreement whereby expatriates agreed to live and work abroad for two to five years in exchange for a generous pay package and future career opportunities. This has changed, with research suggesting that not all expatriates had a relational connection; rather, some expatriate assignments have a transactional purpose (Pate & Scullion, 2010; Yan et al., 2002). For the organisation, the task to be performed by the expatriate may be technical or routine in nature and have a well-defined temporal horizon. Individuals, in turn, may look upon the position as a good opportunity for learning, developing new contacts, or applying their own knowledge in an international context. In such cases, their continuity with the organisation once the project has been completed is not an option for them, which means that staff turnover should not then be seen as a failure from either the individual or the firm's perspective (Cerdin & Pargneux, 2009; Yan et al., 2002).

The need to incorporate additional perspectives in the discussion of careers and working conditions has also become increasingly clear. Although there are many people living and working outside their home countries as corporate expatriates, in relative terms they make up a very small number of employees, particularly when they are compared to HCNs (i.e., local employees who work in the various countries in which MNEs operate). The relative proportion of each one of these groups is very uneven. Some surveys (e.g., Bonache, Sánchez, & Zárraga-Oberty, 2009) affirm that expatriates comprise just 0.8 per cent of the workforce of US and European MNEs, and up to 2.7 per cent in the case of Japanese MNEs, where it is customary to employ a larger number of expatriates (Bartlett & Yoshihara, 1988; Kopp, 1994). Despite being quantitatively far more numerous, the perspective of HCN employees in relation to the expatriate experience was practically ignored by research in the 1970s and 1980s (cf Adler, 1987, for a notable exception). This changed in the past few decades as the HCN-expatriate relationships became a focus of investigation (Bader et al., 2017; Chen, Choi, & Chi, 2002; Toh & Denisi, 2003; Bruning et al., 2012).

Leading this research on host nationals' perspectives was an examination of the salary gap between HCN and expatriate staff (Chen et al., 2002; Oltra, Bonache, & Brewster, 2013; Toh & Denisi, 2003), a topic that will be dealt with in Chapter 5. Another area of focus is the role HCN play as socialising agents, sources of social support, assistance and friendship for expatriates (Bader et al., 2017; Mahajan & Toh, 2014; Toh & Denisi, 2003; Varma, Budhwar, & Pichler, 2011). For example, some research has identified how expatriates' individual characteristics, such as ethnocentrism, can affect HCNs' willingness to offer expatriates information and support (Varma, Pichler, & Budhwar, 2011) and be socialising agents for them (Toh & Denisi, 2007).

The specific influence of HCNs on expatriate assignment outcomes is just starting to be understood. For example, Bruning et al. (2012) found a relationship between expatriate relationships with HCN colleagues and adjustment. In any case, it is important to note that the host national perspective is not a homogeneous one. In an ethnographic study on the Romanian subsidiaries of US corporations, HCNs constitute a cultural group with values influenced by their headquarters or home cultures (Caprar, 2011). Similar to what the next section will highlight for the case of expatriates, HCN are not identical in their roles, positions, or perspectives.

1.3.4 A New and More Diverse Landscape in Global Mobility

We have reviewed the expatriate issues that have changed as a function of economic, competitive, and demographic trends in the post-1990. Each one of the changes analysed highlights how the scope of expatriation has become much more complex and heterogeneous. Specifically, we have seen – and continue to see – a broader plurality of reasons and employment modes for expatriation, a broader diversity in the assignments location and nationalities, a higher complexity of family and gender issues, and increasing interest in host country nationals' perspectives.

In addition to corporate expatriates, the traditional focus of mainstream expatriation literature, there are even more forms of international working, such as self-employed consultants, and those from another country with short-term employment (not unknown amongst academics, actors or musicians, for example). International commuters are people who live in one country and work in another. There are many of these in Europe, where the packing together of lots of small countries, and the automatic working rights of all EU citizens makes cross-border working very easy, but there are also cases where expatriates are working in dangerous locations and their family is housed in a nearby safer country, so that they can more easily be together in between periods of work. These different types of expatriation are discussed in more depth in Chapter 7.

Todays' literature on global mobility does not restrict its attention to long and short-term assigned expatriates. Following the first identification of self-initiated expatriates (SIEs) (Suutari and Brewster 2000), the literature on SIEs has expanded enormously (Cerdin & Selmer, 2014; Froese & Peltokorpi, 2013; Peltokorpi & Froese, 2009). SIEs are foreign professionals who find employment in a foreign country on their own. Unlike assigned expatriates, SIE receive no or little expatriate benefits. Chapter 8 provides a comprehensive update of the burgeoning SIE literature.

Despite attempts to restrict this group to the elite (Cerdin & Selmer 2014), this field in turn expanded so that there have recently been studies focusing not only on highly skilled-migrants (Tharenou,

2015) but also on low status expatriates (Haak-Saheem and Brewster 2017; Özçelik et al., 2019). In the past, the sociological literature focused on migrants and low status expatriates, while the business literature focused on corporate, high-status expatriates. Organisations and business researchers have identified the importance of migrants as a source capable of filling the demand for labour. Thus, Chapter 9 provides insights into the careers of migrants.

1.4 Summary and Outline of the Book

This chapter has elaborated on what expatriates are, what they do, and why they are important. Moreover, we have explained how economic shift, digitalisation, and globalisation have led to major changes in global mobility. We have seen how the diversity of ways of working internationally has created an important need for conceptual clarity in research and practice on global mobility. All these new forms of global mobility may create a set of additional and different challenges from the ones typically analysed in traditional expatriation literature. To obtain a comprehensive overview and further our understanding of the current situation and future trends, we have compiled this up-to-date book on global mobility, with contributions from world-renowned experts from four different continents. Interestingly, many of the contributors had lived or are currently living outside their home country. All chapters of the book review the extant literature and provide implications for research and practice.

Considering both organisational needs and current trends in global mobility, we have organised our book into two parts. Part 1 deals with the expatriation process of corporate expatriates. We offer five chapters that depict the typical expatriation cycle of assigned expatriates covering important aspects before, during, and after the expatriate assignments. Chapter 2, written by Marie-France Waxin, based in the United Arab Emirates, and Chris Brewster, UK, discusses selection and training, important yet often neglected issues, before the international assignment. The following three chapters deal with important aspects during the international assignment. Chapter 3, authored by Anne Lessle, Australia, Arno Haslberger, Austria, and Chris Brewster, UK, critically assess cross-cultural adjustment, which has been identified in prior expatriate research as a core variable explaining expatriate success. Chapter 4, written by Arup Varma, USA, Chun-Hsiao Wang,

China, and Pawan Budwhar, UK, introduces performance management for expatriates, an important but often neglected function. Chapter 5, written by Jaime Bonache, Spain, and Celia Zarraga-Oberty, Spain, deals with an important topic for both expatriates and employing organizations, that is, compensation. Chapter 6, authored by Flora F. T. Chiang, China, Emmy van Esch, China, and Thomas Birtch, UK, focuses on the critical time after the international assignments, that is, repatriation, and pays particular attention to career development.

Considering the changing trends in global mobility, Part 2 of our book looks at the different types of expatriates and stakeholders. Three chapters focus on different types of expatriates, two chapters focus on the changing roles of women and family, and Chapter 12 focuses on the global mobility department. Chapter 7, written by Chris Brewster, UK, Michael Dickmann, UK, and Vesa Suutari, Finland, introduces different types of expatriates, including international business travellers, short-term assignees, and international commuters. Chapter 8, authored by Sebastian Stoermer, Germany, Fabian Jintae Froese, Germany, and Vesa Peltokorpi, Japan, provides insights into self-initiated expatriates, a group of expatriates that has received substantial research attention in recent years. Chapter 9, written by Jelena Zikic, Canada and Viktoria Voloshya, Canada, directs our attention to skilled migrants, a group that has been largely neglected in international business research until recently. Chapter 10, written by Helen De Cieri, Australia, reinforces awareness of the changing role of women in global mobility. Chapter 11, written by Margaret A. Shaffer, USA and Min (Maggie) Wan, USA, provides an overview of the important role of the family. Chapter 12, written by Michael Dickmann, UK, completes our book by explaining the role of the global mobility department.

References

Adler, N. J. 1984. Expecting international success: female managers overseas. *Columbia Journal of World Business*, 19(3): 79–85.

Adler, N. J. 1987. Pacific basin managers: a gaijin, not a woman. *Human Resource Management*, 26(2): 169–191.

Athanassiou, N. & Nigh, D. 2000. Internationalization, tacit knowledge and the top management teams of MNCs. *Journal of International Business Studies*, 31(3): 471–487.

Bader, A. K., Froese, F. J, Achteresch, A., & Behrens, S. 2017. Expatriates' influence on the organizational commitment of host country nationals in China. The moderating role of individual values and status characteristics. *European Journal of International Management*, 11(2): 181–200.

Bader, K., Froese, F. J., & Kraeh, A. 2018. Clash of cultures? German expatriates' work-life boundary adjustment in South Korea. *European Management Review*, 15: 357–374.

Banai, M. & Harry, W. 2004. Boundaryless global careers: the international itinerants. *International Studies of Management & Organization*, 34(3): 96–120.

Barney, J. 1991. Firm resources and sustained competitive advantage. *Journal of Management*, 15: 175–190.

Bartlett, C. A. & Yoshihara, H. 1988. New challenges for Japanese multinationals: is organization adaptation their Achilles heel? *Human Resource Management*, 27(1): 19–43.

Beaverstock, J. V. 2004. Managing across borders: knowledge management and expatriation in professional service legal firms. *Journal of Economic Geography*, 4(2), 157–179.

Bebenroth, R. & Froese, F. J. 2020. Consequences of expatriate top manager replacement on foreign subsidiary performance. *Journal of International Management*, in press.

Bhaskar-Shrinivas, P., Harrison, D. A., Shaffer, M. A., & Luk, D. M. 2005. Input-based and time-based models of international adjustment: meta-analytic evidence and theoretical extensions. *Academy of Management Journal*, 48(2): 257–281.

Black, J. S. & Gregersen, H. B. 1991. When Yankee comes home: factors related to expatriate and spouse repatriation adjustment. *Journal of International Business Studies*, Vol. 22(4): 671–694.

Black, J. S. & Gregersen, H. B. 1999. The right way to manage expats. *Harvard Business Review,* March–April, 52–63.

Black, J. S., Gregersen, H. B., & Mendenhall, M. E. 1992. Toward a theoretical framework of repatriation adjustment. *Journal of International Business Studies*, 23(4): 737–760.

Bonache, J. 2006. The compensation of expatriates: a review and a future research agenda. In G. Stahl & I. Bjorkman (eds.), *Handbook of Research in International Human Resource Management*: 58–175. Cheltenham: Edward Elgar Publishing.

Bonache, J. & Brewster, C. 2001. Knowledge transfer and the management of expatriation. *Thunderbird International Business Review*, 43(1): 145–168.

Bonache, J., Brewster, C., Suutari, V., & Cerdin, J. L. 2018. The changing nature of expatriation. *Thunderbird International Business Review*, 60(6): 815–821.

Bonache, J., Sánchez, J., & Zárraga-Oberty, C. 2009. The interaction of expatriate pay differential and expatriate inputs on host country nationals pay unfairness. *International Journal of Human Resource Management*, 20(10): 2135–2149.

Bonache, J. & Stirpe, L. 2012. Compensating global employees. In G. K. Stahl, I. Björkman, & S. Morris (eds.), *Handbook of Research in International Human Resource Management* (2nd ed.): 162–182. Cheltenham: Edward Elgar Publishing.

Bonache, J. & Zárraga-Oberty, C. 2008. Determinants of the success of international assignees as knowledge transferors: a theoretical framework. *International Journal of Human Resource Management*, 19 (1): 1–18.

Boyacigiller, N. 1990. The role of expatriates in the management of interdependence complexity and risk in multinational corporations. *Journal of International Business Studies*, 21(3): 357–381.

Brewster, C. 1991. *The Management of Expatriates*. London: Kogan Page.

Brewster, C., Bonache, J., Cerdin, J. L., & Suutari, V. 2014. Exploring expatriate outcomes. *International Journal of Human Resource Management*, 25(14): 1921–1937.

Brookfield. 2015. Global Relocation Trends Survey Report. Woodridge.

Brookfield. 2016. Global Mobility Trends Survey. Woodridge.

Bruning, N. S., Sonpar, K., & Wang, X. 2012. Host-country national networks and expatriate effectiveness: a mixed-methods study. *Journal of International Business Studies*, 43: 444–450.

Caligiuri, P. M. 2000. Selecting expatriates for personality characteristics: a moderating effect of personality on the relationship between host national contact and cross-cultural adjustment. *Management International Review*, 40(1): 61–80.

Caligiuri, P. M. & Bonache, J. 2016. Evolving and enduring challenges in global mobility. *Journal of World Business*, 51(1): 127–141.

Cappelli, P. 1999. *The New Deal at Work: Managing the Market-driven Workforce*. Boston: Harvard Business Press.

Caprar, D. V. 2011. Foreign locals: a cautionary tale on the culture of MNE local employees. *Journal of International Business Studies*, 42(5): 608–628.

Carpenter, M. A. & Fredrickson, J. W. 2001. Top management teams, global strategic posture, and the moderating role of uncertainty. *Academy of Management Journal*, 44(3): 533–545.

Carpenter, M. A., Sanders, W. G., & Gregersen, H. B. 2001. Bundling human capital with organizational context: the impact of international assignment experience on multinational firm performance and CEO pay. *Academy of Management Journal*, 44(3): 493–511.

Cerdin, J. L. & Pargneux, M. L. 2009. Career and international assignment fit: toward an integrative model of success. *Human Resource Management*, 48(1): 5–25.

Cerdin, J. L. & Selmer, J. 2014. Who is a self-initiated expatriate? Towards conceptual clarity of a common notion. *The International Journal of Human Resource Management*, 25(9): 1281–1301.

Chand, M. & Tung, R. 2014. The aging of the world's population and its effects on global business. *Academy of Management Perspectives*, 28(4): 409–429.

Chang, Y. Y., Gong, Y., & Peng, M. W. 2012. Expatriate knowledge transfer, subsidiary absorptive capacity, and subsidiary performance. *Academy of Management Journal*, 55(4): 927–948.

Chen, C. C., Choi, J., & Chi, S. C. 2002. Making justice sense of local-expatriate compensation disparity: mitigation by local referents, ideological explanations, and interpersonal sensitivity in China-foreign joint ventures. *Academy of Management Journal*, 45(4): 807–826.

Church, A. T. 1982. Sojourner adjustment. *Psychological Bulletin*, 91(3): 540.

Colakoglu, S., Tarique, I., & Caligiuri, P. 2009. Towards a conceptual framework for the relationship between subsidiary staffing strategy and subsidiary performance. *International Journal of Human Resource Management*, 20(6): 1291–1308.

Collings, D. G., McDonnell, A., & McCarter, A. 2015. Types of international assignees. In D. Collings, G. Wood, & P. Caligiuri (eds.), *The Routledge Companion to International Human Resource Management*: 259–275. London: Routledge.

Collings, D. G., Scullion, H., & Morley, M. J. 2007. Changing patterns of global staffing in the multinational enterprise: challenges to the conventional expatriate assignment and emerging alternatives. *Journal of World Business*, 42(2): 198–213.

Daily, C. M., Certo, S. T., & Dalton, D. R. 2000. International experience in the executive suite: the path to prosperity? *Strategic Management Journal*, 21(4): 515–523.

Dunning, J. H. 2009. Location and the multinational enterprise: John Dunning's thoughts on receiving the Journal of International Business Studies 2008 Decade Award. *Journal of International Business Studies*, 40(1): 20–34.

Edström, A. & Galbraith, J. R. 1977. Transfer of Managers as a Coordination and Control Strategy in Multinational Organizations. *Administrative Science Quarterly*, 22(2): 248.

Festing, M. & Maletzky, M. 2011. Cross-cultural leadership adjustment – A multilevel framework based on the theory of structuration. *Human Resource Management Review*, 21(3): 186–200.

Fiedler, F. E., Mitchel, T., & Triandis, H. C. 1971. The culture assimilator: an approach to cross-cultural training. *Journal of Applied Psychology*, 55 (2): 95–102.

Finaccord 2019. *Global Expatriates: Size, Segmentation and Forecast for the Worldwide Market*. Singapore.

Froese, F. J., Kim, K., & Eng, A. 2016. Language, cultural intelligence, and inpatriate turnover intentions: leveraging values in multinational corporations through inpatriates. *Management International Review*, 56: 283–301.

Froese, F. J. & Peltokorpi, V. 2011. Cultural distance and expatriate job satisfaction. *International Journal of Intercultural Relations*, 35: 49–60.

Froese, F. J. & Peltokorpi, V. 2013. Organizational expatriates and self-initiated expatriates: differences in cross-cultural adjustment and job satisfaction. *International Journal of Human Resource Management*, 24: 1953–1967.

Furusawa, M. & Brewster, C. 2018. Japanese self-initiated expatriates as boundary-spanners in Chinese subsidiaries of Japanese MNEs: antecedents, social capital, and HRM practices. *Thunderbird International Business Review*, 60(6): 911–919.

Furuya, N., Stevens, M. J., Bird, A., Oddou, G., & Mendenhall, M. 2009. Managing the learning and transfer of global management competence: antecedents and outcomes of Japanese repatriation effectiveness. *Journal of International Business Studies*, 40(2): 200–215.

Ghoshal, S. & Bartlett, C. A. 1990. The multinational corporation as an interorganizational network. *Academy of Management Review*, 15(4): 603–626.

Gómez Mejía, L. & Balkin, D. B. 1987. The Determinants of Managerial Satisfaction with the Expatriation and Repatriation Process. *Journal of Management Development*, 6(1): 7–17.

Groysberg, B., Nohria, N., & Herman, K. 2011. *Solvay Group: International Mobility and Managing Expatriates*. HBSP 9–409–079.

Guillén, M. F. & García-Canal, E. 2009. The American model of the multinational firm and the 'new' multinationals from emerging economies. *Academy of Management Perspectives*, 23(2): 23–35.

Haak-Saheem, W. & Brewster, C. 2017. 'Hidden' expatriates: international mobility in the United Arab Emirates as a challenge to current understanding of expatriation. *Human Resource Management Journal*, 27(3): 423–439.

Hall, D. T. 2004. He protean career: a quarter-century journey. *Journal of Vocational Behavior*, 65(1): 1–13.

Harris, H. & Brewster, C. 1999. The coffee machine system: how international resourcing really works. *International Journal of Human Resource Management*, 10(3): 488–500.

Harvey, M. G. 1982. The other side of foreign assignments: dealing with the repatriation dilemma. *Columbia Journal of World Business*, 17(1): 53–59.

Harvey, M. G., Buckley, M. R., & Novicevic, M. M. 2000. Strategic global human resource management: a necessity when entering emerging markets. *Research in Personnel and Human Resources Management*, 19: 175–242.

Harzing, A.-W. K. 1995. The persistent myth of high expatriate failure rates. *International Journal of Human Resource Management*, 6(2): 457–474.

Harzing, A.-W. K. 2001. Who's in Charge? An empirical study of executive staffing practices in foreign subsidiaries. *Human Resource Management*, 40(2): 139–158.

Herriot, P. & Pemberton, C. 1995. *New deals: The revolution in managerial careers*. John Wiley.

Kopp, R. 1994. International human resource policies and practices in Japanese, European, and United States multinationals. *Human Resource Management*, 33(4): 81–599.

Kostova, T. 1999. Transnational transfer of strategic organisational practices: a contextual perspective. *Academy of Management Review*, 24 (2): 308–324.

Kraimer, M. L., Shaffer, M. A., Harrison, D. A., & Ren, H. 2012. No place like home? An identity strain perspective on repatriate turnover. *Academy of Management Journal*, 55(2): 399–420.

Lazarova, M. B. & Cerdin, J.-L. 2007. Revisiting repatriation concerns: organizational support versus career and contextual influences. *Journal of International Business Studies*, 38(3): 404–429.

Lazarova, M. B. & Tarique, I. 2005. Knowledge transfer upon repatriation. *Journal of World Business*, 40(4): 361–373.

Levy, O., Beechler, S., Taylor, S., & Boyacigiller, N. A. 2007. What we talk about when we talk about 'global mindset': Managerial cognition in multinational corporations. *Journal of International Business Studies*, 38 (2): 231–258.

Mahajan, A. & Toh, S. M. 2014. Facilitating expatriate adjustment: the role of advice-seeking from host country nationals. *Journal of World Business*, 49(4): 476–487.

Mäkelä, K. & Brewster, C. 2009. Interunit interaction contexts, interpersonal social capital, and differing levels of knowledge sharing. *Human Resource Management*, 48(4): 591–614.

Mäkelä, L., Saarenpää, K., & McNulty, Y. 2017. International business travellers, short-term assignees and international commuters. In Y. McNulty & J. Selmer (eds.).*Research Handbook of Expatriates*: 276–294. London: Edward Elgar Publishing.

Mäkelä, L., Suutari, V., Brewster, C., Dickmann, M., & Tornikoski, C. 2016. The impact of career capital on expatriates' marketability. *Thunderbird International Business Review*, 58(1): 29–40.

Mendenhall, M. & Oddou, G. 1985. The dimensions of expatriate acculturation: a review. *Academy of Management Review*, 10(1): 39–47.

Mendenhall, M. & Oddou, G. 1986. Acculturation profiles of expatriate managers: implications for cross-cultural training programs. *Columbia Journal of World Business*, 21(4): 73–79.

OECD. 2017. *International Migration Outlook*. Paris: Organisation for Economic Co-operation and Development.

Okpara, J. O. & Kabongo, J. D. 2011. Cross-cultural training and expatriate adjustment: a study of western expatriates in Nigeria. *Journal of World Business*, 46(1): 22–30.

Oltra, V., Bonache, J., & Brewster, C. 2013. A new framework for understanding inequalities between expatriates and host country nationals. *Journal of Business Ethics*, 115(2): 291–310.

Ouchi, W. 1981. Theory Z: how American business can meet the Japanese challenge. *Business Horizons*, 24(6): 82–83.

Özçelik, G., Haak-Saheem, W., Brewster, C., & McNulty, Y. 2019. Hidden inequalities amongst the international workforce. In S. Nachmias & V. Caven (eds.), *Palgrave Explorations in Workplace Stigma. Inequality and organizational practice* (Vol. 2): 221–251. Cham: Palgrave Macmillan.

Pate, J. & Scullion, H. 2010. The changing nature of the traditional expatriate psychological contract. *Employee Relations*, 32(1): 56–73.

Peltokorpi, V. & Froese, F. J. 2009. Organizational expatriates and self-initiated expatriates: who adjusts better to work and life in Japan? *International Journal of Human Resource Management*, 20(5): 1095–1111.

Polanyi, M. 1962. *Personal Knowledge: Towards a Post-critical Philosophy*. Chicago: University of Chicago Press.

Portniagin, F. & Froese, F. J. 2019. Inpatriation management: a literature review and recommendations for future research. In Liu, Y (ed.) *Research Handbook of International Talent Management*: 186–212. Cheltenham: Edward Elgar Publishing.

PwC. 2019. PwC Global Mobility Vision of the Future. www.PwC.com/gx/en/services/people-organisation/global-employee-mobility.html, accessed 10 January 2020.

Reiche, B. S., Harzing, A. W., & Kraimer, M. L. 2009. The role of international assignees' social capital in creating inter-unit intellectual capital: a cross-level model. *Journal of International Business Studies*, 40 (3): 509–526.

Ren, H., Bolino, M. C., Shaffer, M. A., & Kraimer, M. L. 2013. The influence of job demands and resources on repatriate career satisfaction: a relative deprivation perspective. *Journal of World Business*, 48(1): 149–159.

Rousseau, D. M. 2004. Research edge: psychological contracts in the workplace: understanding the ties that motivate. *Academy of Management Executive*, 18(1): 120–127.

Salamin, X. & Hanappi, D. 2014. Women and international assignments: a systematic literature review exploring textual data by correspondence analysis. *Journal of Global Mobility*, 2(3): 343–374.

Sarabi, A., Froese, F.J., & Hamori, M. 2017. Is international assignment experience a ticket to the top of a foreign subsidiary? The moderating effect of subsidiary context. *Journal of World Business*. 52: 680–690.

Sarabi, A., Hamori, M., & Froese, F. J. 2019. Managing global talent flows. In Collings, D., Scullion, H., & Caligiuri, P. (eds.) *Global Talent Management*: 59–74. London: Routledge.

Schmid, S. & Wurster, D. J. 2017. International work experience: is it really accelerating the way to the management Board of MNCs? *International Business Review*, 26(5): 991–1008.

Selmer, J. 1999. Effects of coping strategies on sociocultural and psychological adjustment of Western expatriate managers in the PRC. *Journal of World Business*, 34(1): 41–51.

Shaffer, M. A. & Harrison, D.A. 2001. Forgotten partners of international assignments: development and test of a model of spouse adjustment. *Journal of Applied Psychology*, 86: 238–254.

Shaffer, M. A., Kraimer, M. L., Chen, Y., & Bolino, M. C. 2012. Choices, challenges, and career consequences of global work experiences: a review and future agenda. *Journal of Management*, 38(4): 1282–1327.

Soltani, E. & Wilkinson, A. 2011. The Razor's edge: managing MNC affiliates in Iran. *Journal of World Business*, 46(4): 462–475.

Spreitzer, G. M., McCall, M. W., & Mahoney, J. D. 1997. Early identification of international executive potential. *Journal of Applied Psychology*, 82(1): 6.

Stephens, G. K. & Black, S. 1991. The impact of spouse's career-orientation on managers during international transfers. *Journal of Management Studies*, 28(4): 417–428.

Stoermer, S., Davies, S., & Froese, F. J. 2017. Expatriate cultural intelligence, embeddedness and knowledge sharing: a multilevel analysis. *Academy of Management Best Paper Proceedings*. 2017(1): 16294.

Stoermer, S., Haslberger, A. Froese, F. J., & Kraeh, A. 2018. The influence of cross-cultural adjustment on expatriate job satisfaction: a person-environment fit perspective. *Thunderbird International Business Review*, 60: 851–860.

Stroh, L. K., Varma, A., & Valy-Durbin, S. J. 2000. Why are women left at home: are they unwilling to go on international assignments? *Journal of World Business*, 35(3): 241.

Suutari, V. & Brewster, C. 2000. Making their own way: international experience through self-initiated foreign assignments. *Journal of World Business*, 35(4): 417–436.

Suutari, V. & Brewster, C. 2003. Repatriation: empirical evidence from a longitudinal study of careers and expectations among Finnish expatriates. *International Journal of Human Resource Management*, 14 (7): 1132–1151.

Suutari, V. & Brewster, C. 2009. Beyond expatriation: different forms of international employment. In P. Sparrow (ed.) *Handbook of International Human Resource Management: Integrating People, Process and Context*: 131–150. Chichester: Wiley.

Suutari, V., Brewster, C., Dickmann, M., Mäkelä, L., Tanskenan, J., & Tornikoski, C. 2017. The effect of international work experience on the career success of expatriates: a comparison of assigned and self-initiated expatriates. *Human Resource Management*, 57(1): 37–54.

Szulanski, G. 1996. Exploring internal stickiness: impediments to the transfer of best practice within the firm. *Strategic Management Journal*, 17: 27–43.

Tan, D. & Mahoney, J. T. 2006. Why multinational firm chooses expatriates: integrating resource-based, agency and transaction costs perspectives. *Journal of Management Studies*, 43(3): 457–484.

Tarique, I., Schuler, R., & Gong, Y. 2006. A model of multinational enterprise subsidiary staffing composition. *International Journal of Human Resource Management*, 17(2): 207–224.

Tharenou, P., 2015. Researching expatriate types: the quest for rigorous methodological approaches. *Human Resource Management Journal*, 25 (2): 149–165.

Tharenou, P. & Harvey, M. 2006. Examining the overseas staffing options utilized by Australian headquartered multinational corporations. *International Journal of Human Resource Management*, 17(6): 1095–1114.

Toh, S. M. & Denisi, A. S. 2003. Host country national reactions to expatriate pay policies: a model and implications. *Academy of Management Review*, 28(4): 606–621.

Toh, S. M. & Denisi, A. S. 2007. Host country nationals as socializing agents: a social identity approach. *Journal of Organizational Behavior*, 28(3): 281–301.

Tsurumi, Y. 1978. Best of times and worst of times – Japanese management in America. *Columbia Journal of World Business*, 13(2): 56–61.

Tung, R. L. 1981. Selection and training of personnel for overseas assignments. *Columbia Journal of World Business*, 16(1): 68–78.

Tung, R. L. 1988. Career issues in international assignments. *Academy of Management Perspectives*, 2(3): 241–244.

Varma, A., Budhwar, P., & Pichler, S. 2011. Chinese host country nationals' willingness to help expatriates: the role of social categorization. *Thunderbird International Business Review*, 53(3): 353–364.

Varma, A., Pichler, S., & Budhwar, P. 2011. The relationship between expatriate job level and host country national categorization: an investigation in the UK. *International Journal of Human Resource Management*, 22(1): 103–120.

Varma, A., Stroh, L. K., & Schmitt, L. B. 2001. Women and international assignments: the impact of supervisor–subordinate relationships. *Journal of World Business*, 36(4): 380.

Welch, D. 2003. Globalisation of staff movements: beyond cultural adjustment. *Management International Review*, 43(2): 149–199.

Yan, A., Zhu, G., & Hall, D. T. 2002. International assignments for career building: a model of agency relationships and psychological contracts. *Academy of Management Review*, 27(3): 373–391.

PART I

The Expatriation Process of Corporate Expatriates

2 The Recruitment, Selection, and Preparation of Expatriates

MARIE-FRANCE WAXIN, CHRIS BREWSTER

2.1 Introduction

Effective recruitment and selection is "the most critical human resource function for organizational survival and success" (Collins & Kehoe, 2009, p. 209). For organisations and for individuals, effective recruitment, selection, and preparation of new workers or workers in new circumstances are always important: get these crucial issues wrong, get people involved in the organisation who are not able to or do not want to do the work and everything involved in their management becomes more difficult – and the individuals are unlikely to get satisfaction from their work. This issue is exacerbated in the case of international work, where issues of cross-national adjustment complicate the picture even further (see Chapter 3). Although most expatriates cope well, are able to do a good job and able to advance their careers, the cases where this does not happen, where the wrong person has been selected for that position, or where they cannot adjust to the new circumstances can create misery for the expatriate, for their co-workers and their families, and can severely damage an organisation's reputation.

Effective recruitment, selection, and preparation can significantly impact expatriate performance (Cheng & Lin, 2009; Harrison & Shaffer, 2005; Littrell et al., 2006; Mol et al., 2005). Unsurprisingly, therefore, there has been extensive research on the selection and preparation of assigned expatriates (Feitosa et al., & Salas, 2014; Kim, Brewster, & Chung, 2019; McNulty & Brewster, 2019). Research on self-initiated expatriates' (SIEs) recruitment, selection, and training is, however, sparse. The objective of this chapter is to examine and summarise the extant research on international assignees' recruitment, selection, and preparation. Since, nearly all the research on selection and preparation has examined long-term assigned expatriates (AEs), we will focus on these and only refer to the other options where appropriate.

The chapter is structured as follows: First, we discuss expatriate recruitment sources, methods, and the expatriates' motivations to work abroad. Second, we examine expatriate selection criteria, methods, and how expatriates are selected in practice. Third, we present the variety of expatriate preparation methods, discuss expatriate training effectiveness, and expatriate preparation in practice. We conclude by considering future avenues of research. Overall, in the area of selection and preparation for international assignments there is good material for researchers to build on and to grow understanding of the key issues. Nevertheless, there remains here a rich field for exciting research in the future.

2.2 Recruitment of Expatriates

The recruitment process can begin as soon as the strategic planning of the international assignment has been done, and when (1) the goals of the international assignments, (2) the job description, (3) the job specification, and (4) the ownership for the responsibility of managing the full expatriation/repatriation cycle have been established (Waxin, 2007, 2008a).

The main objectives of international recruitment are (1) elaborating ways and techniques that will allow the organisation to attract a sufficient number of motivated and qualified international candidates; (2) identifying candidates, at the lowest possible cost, who are capable of filling foreign positions; and (3) increasing, at the lowest possible cost, the pool of international candidates, anticipating the organisation's future needs in personnel (Waxin, 2008a, 2008b). At the recruitment stage, the major issues are the sources and the methods of recruitment, and the employee's motivations to accept an international assignment.

2.2.1 Recruitment Sources

The first decision to be made is whether to recruit internally or externally. In the case of AEs there is often not such a clear connection with recruitment, because most multinational enterprises (MNEs) depend almost exclusively on internal recruitment for their expatriate positions (Shen & Lang, 2009): the candidates are already organisational employees before they are selected. According to KPMG (2019), 89 per cent of the MNEs' international assignees were sourced by internal recruitment by the relevant business unit. This preferred recruitment option can be found even in local markets where there is plenty of skilled labour. This is largely because of the strategic value of these international assignments, and the importance for the expatriates of understanding the organisation's culture and systems. AEs are largely used to fill skills gaps, to control subsidiaries, and to develop the organisation and themselves (Edström & Galbraith, 1977): although there have been subsequent taxonomies and amendments to this original list, these continue to be the main reasons for the use of expatriates. Logic implies that for control and development purposes internal candidates have significant advantages over external recruits.

This does not necessarily apply to skills issues, so the external recruitment of specialists in the oil and gas, high tech., sports and cultural, and other sectors, is common. In many of these cases the expatriate works in an isolated (oil and gas) or very controlled (sports and culture) circumstance, where they may come into little contact with local people, certainly not with ones who are not connected to their work. And in such sectors, it seems that the skill requirement is the crucial criterion for recruitment. Other issues (such as ability to cope in the new context) are rarely considered.

2.2.2 Recruitment Methods

The second decision to be made concerns the choice of recruitment methods. For larger organisations, the major internal recruitment method for AEs is the use of internal databases, including data on potential candidates, their work experience, performance, skills, availability, and their preferences regarding a potential international assignment: where he or she would be interested in working, in what capacity and on what sort of projects (Harris & Brewster, 1999). This international mobility database could be linked to a company's talent management database to keep track of internationally mobile talents (Cerdin & Brewster, 2014; Collings, 2014; Tarique & Schuler, 2010). For example, Tetrapack developed their 'Management Planning and Development' centralised database, which contains the profile of thousands of high potential employees and which is up-dated once a year. This database can be consulted at any time by the human resource management (HRM) specialist community and can be used to support the expatriates' recruitment process (Marchon, 2004).

According to KPMG (2019), MNEs are developing a stronger integration between global mobility and talent management policies throughout the employment lifecycle (Cerdin & Brewster, 2014; Collings, 2014). For the MNEs that have aligned their global mobility and talent management programmes, nearly half see global assignments as a formal part of their organisation's talent development, succession, and retention initiatives. We note, however, that for smaller and newer internationalised businesses, systems are often more informal (Harris & Brewster, 1999).

When suitable candidates for international assignments cannot be found internally, companies turn to the external market. External recruitment methods for international positions include Internet job posting, campaigns in international media, and using the services of recruitment agencies or international head-hunters (Waxin, 2007). Some SIEs are also recruited internationally. Key posts in organisations such as the United Nations and European Union, and in organisations such as Universities, are advertised online and in outlets such as the Economist and candidates have to go through rigorous application procedures. Most SIEs, however, are recruited locally, by local managers against local criteria. For low-status SIEs the recruitment and selection processes are almost always outsourced to agencies (Haak-Saheem & Brewster, 2017).

2.2.3 *What Motivates Expatriates to Accept Work Abroad?*

It is useful to examine the recruitment issue from the point of view of the employee. 'Expatriation willingness' is defined as the likelihood of accepting a job offer that requires living and working in a foreign country for a temporary period (Mol et al., 2009). 'Expatriation willingness' is an important predictor for expatriate success: employees with higher expatriation willingness are more likely to accept expatriate assignments (Tharenou, 2008), more likely to remain in the host country until the end of their initial contract, and adjust better to the host-country environment than unwilling candidates (Peltokorpi & Froese, 2009).

Why should an employee accept an assignment that will mean they have to uproot themselves and their families, where they have a nuclear family, and move to another country? Research has examined a wide range of antecedents of expatriation willingness. Globally, the main motivations to accept an expatriation are the opportunity for a wider and more exciting kind of work, sometimes referred to as cosmopolitanism (Froese, Jommersbach, & Klautsch, 2013), the attractiveness of particular locations, and the personal and developmental career opportunities the assignment offers (Dickmann et al., 2008; Doherty, Dickmann, & Mills, 2011; Richardson & McKenna, 2002; Stahl, Miller, & Tung, 2002). The financial packages that tend to go with expatriate assignment also play a part, but national differences in the significance of a financial incentive need to be viewed in relation to the other factors considered important to the decision to move (Dickmann et al., 2008). It seems that global HRM experts, compared to the expatriates themselves, tend to overestimate the importance of the salary component and underestimate the importance of work-related and developmental opportunities.

Individual and family factors matter. There has been research focused specifically on the individual and family related antecedents of willingness to expatriate. Dupuis, Haines, and Saba (2008) examined willingness to accept an international assignment in employed MBA graduates from dual-earner couples in Canada. They found that the perceived willingness of partners to relocate, beliefs regarding their partners' and the couples' mobility, relative income, and the presence of children are all associated with willingness to accept an international assignment. They also found significant gender differences in willingness to expatriate, across low and high cultural distance country destinations.

Host country characteristics matter too. Kim & Froese (2012) examine the direct and moderating effects of host-country characteristics (economic level and language) and employee's role commitments (work and family) on the expatriation willingness of Korean employees. They show that host-country characteristics and occupational role commitment have direct effects on employees' expatriation willingness and that host-country economic level interacts with occupational role commitment: for Korean employees, working in advanced or English-speaking countries was more attractive than working elsewhere. Generally, proficiency in the host country language, the host country's perceived level of safely, and cultural attraction were important factors explaining decisions to work in emerging economies (de Eccher & Duarte, 2018).

Finally, Doherty, Dickmann, and Mills (2011) compared AEs and SIEs' motivation to go abroad and found that location concerns and host country reputation were more important to SIEs, while AEs placed significantly more emphasis on career development motives.

The question for the organisation then is how they can encourage these employees to accept a foreign assignment? In order to enlarge the pool of candidates for international assignments, companies develop, implement, and communicate their international mobility policy, and link their international mobility to their talent development programmes (Waxin 2008a), as discussed earlier.

Improving alignment between business objectives, mobility policy types and assignees' selection continues to play a part in supporting the talent agenda (KPMG 2019).

However, according to Brookfield (2016), while 61 per cent of the MNEs communicated the importance of international assignments to employees' careers, only 23 per cent of them had a formal process for identifying potential international assignees, and 73 per cent of them did not maintain a candidate pool for future international assignments. Only 23 per cent have a specific process for career planning from assignment acceptance. When we remember that these are consultancy reports, drawn from the consultants' databases and therefore probably including businesses that are most concerned about these issues, it is clear that there is a considerable distance to go.

2.2.4 Selection of Expatriates

The main objectives of the expatriate selection process are as follows: (1) enabling the company and the employee to determine whether candidates possess the competencies and motivation to successfully accomplish their international assignments; (2) minimising the risk of assignment failure and the related costs; and (3) assigning candidates to suitable positions, thus maximising the posting to the organisation's and the candidate's benefit (Waxin, 2008b). Because of the specificity and importance of the tasks the expatriate will have to perform, multinational companies try to ensure that they have an appropriate selection process for international assignments. In section 2.2.5, we review the selection criteria and methods.

2.2.5 Expatriate Selection Criteria

In theory, the choice of selection criteria for international employees should be based on an analysis of the characteristics of the multinational (internationalisation stage, business strategy, staffing policy, international HRM orientation, organisational culture), the subsidiary (ownerships mode, role), host-country characteristics (culture, regulations), and the position to fill (function of the international assignment, duration, job description, and specification) (Waxin, 2008a, 2008b).

Many researchers have examined the individual characteristics of expatriates that predict success in the assignment: these include job factors, personal traits (flexibility/tolerance for ambiguity, self-efficacy), relational abilities/cross cultural competencies, motivational state, language skills, family situation, (Anderson, 2005; Reiche, Harzing, & Kraimer, 2009; Waxin, Brewster, & Ashill, 2019), and previous international work experience (Caligiuri, Tarique, & Jacobs, 2009, Culpan & Wright, 2002; Kimet al., 2019). These criteria have been found to be critically related to expatriate performance in international assignments and their consideration depends on the role of the expatriates (Tungli & Peiperl, 2009) and the expatriates' country of origin (Waxin et al., 2019).

Job-related selection criteria are based on the international assignment's job description and competency profile and knowledge, skills and competencies necessary to perform the job role (Waxin, 2008a, 2008b; Avril & Magnini, 2007). Confidence in technical skills has been found to predict work adjustment and reduce expatriates' time to proficiency, or TTP (Bhaskar-Shrinivas et al., 2005; Waxin et al., 2019), and previous international experience to predict expatriates' success (Caligiuri et al., 2009). Green (2012), focusing on American expatriate officials, found that the length of previous international experience was positively related to adjustment scores. Some SIEs are deliberately selected for their international experience, as boundary-spanners between the local environment and the country of origin, for example (Furusawa & Brewster, 2018), or for their language skills and knowledge of their home country, as often happens in airline sales offices. Most of them, however, are simply additional members of the workforce, employed based on the same criteria as local staff.

Based on the works of Mendenhall and Oddou (1985), Cerdin, Chandon, and Waxin (1999), identified six dimensions of the expatriate's adjustability that positively impact the expatriates' work, interaction, and general adjustment, (Campoy et al., 2005; Waxin, 2006; Waxin & Chandon, 2002) and reduced their time to proficiency (Waxin et al., 2019): confidence in their own technical competencies, social orientation, willingness to communicate, substitution capacity, cultural openness, and stress resistance. These individual determinants of expatriate success significantly varied across country of origin.

Other studies show that a proactive personality (i.e., high extraversion, conscientiousness, emotional stability, agreeableness, and openness) predicts proactive behaviour (e.g., social networking and information seeking) which, in turn, reduces turnover intention and re-adjustment problems (Lazarova & Cerdin, 2007). Active stress resistance has been found to reduce expatriates' TTP (Waxin et al., 2019). Research also suggests that a repatriate with a higher level of motivation is more likely to marshal personal resources to overcome challenges and is found to be positively related to desirable repatriation outcomes, such as knowledge transfer (Hyder & Lövblad, 2007).

Foreign language ability has also been noted as a key criterion, particularly in studies of European MNEs (Ling & Harzing, 2017). Among non-US expatriates, foreign language competence was found to be significantly correlated with adjustment (Peltokorpi, 2008; Puck, Kittler, & Wright, 2008). Green (2012) found that when host language fluency increased among official American expatriates, so did their general and their work adjustment.

So, based on these research' results, MNEs' selection criteria for international assignments should not only include job related criteria, but also cross-cultural skills, the right mix of personality traits (e.g., proactive personality), motivations (e.g., extrinsic or intrinsic), and attitudes (e.g., highly motivated, willingness to learn). However, in practice, organisations tend, when selecting expatriates, not to look far beyond technical expertise and previous performance in the country of origin (Brookfield, 2015). They are beginning to include other criteria. Tungli & Peiperl (2009) found that globally, the most used selection criteria for international assignments were technical/professional skills, expatriates' willingness to go, and experience in the organisation. The next most cited selection criteria were personality factors, leadership skills, ability to work in teams, and previous performance appraisals. The importance of these criteria in the selection process varied with country. As ever, most of our research comes from developed western countries. Other factors may be significant elsewhere.

2.2.6 Expatriate Selection Methods

Linehan, Morley, & Walsh (2002), found that interviews were the most common selection method – and seen as the most effective method to select overseas assignees. According to Finn and Morley (2002), cultural awareness and adaptability tests were almost never used because they were expensive and difficult to construct and interpret. More recently, Tungli & Peiperl (2009) examined international staffing practices in four countries, and found that references, structured interviews, and self-nominations were, globally, the most used selection methods. Then came cultural awareness assessments, more used in Germany and Japan, and behavioural assessment, also more used in Germany than the other countries, but still to a much lower extent. Cognitive and psychological tests were very rarely used, except in UK organisations, but even there their use was still low.

Harris and Brewster (1999) proposed a typology of selection methods for international assignees comprising four categories, organised on two axes: (1) open/closed procedure, and (2) formal/informal procedure. First, the selection process can be open or closed. In an open system, all vacancies are advertised. All the candidates are interviewed with greater or lesser degrees of formalised testing, and selection decisions are made by consensus amongst selectors. In contrast, in a closed system, selectors at corporate headquarter choose or nominate 'suitable' candidates, who are informed once the decision has been made between headquarters personnel and the line manager. The selection interview consists of a negotiation about the terms and conditions of the assignment. The selection process can also be either formal or informal. In formal systems, vacancies are advertised internally, job related selection criteria are specified, psychometric tests are likely to be used, and selectors need to agree among themselves about the best candidates. In informal systems, selection criteria are often not defined, selectors assume that personality characteristics are already known: networking, reputation, and team fit play a great role, and individual preferences of selectors can predominate.

	Formal	Informal
Open	• Clearly defined criteria • Clearly defined measures • Training for selectors • Open advertising of vacancy (Internal/External) • Panel discussions	• Less defined criteria • Less defined measures • Limited training for selectors • No panel discussions • Open advertising of vacancy • Recommendations
Closed	• Clearly defined criteria • Clearly defined measures • Training for selectors • Panel discussions • Nominations only (networking/reputation)	• Selectors'individual preferences determine criteria and measures • No panel discussions • Nominations only (networking/reputation)

Figure 2.1 Typology of expatriate selection processes (Harris and Brewster, 1999)

Closed and informal selection systems present three major disadvantages (Harris and Brewster, 1999). First, they limit the degree to which interpersonal and intercultural skills are taken into account when selecting international managers. Second, they restrict the pool of potential candidates to those who are appreciated by the selectors. Third, they prevent the strategic management of international assignments, as the role of the HR Manager is limited to dealing with the financial, physical and social aspects of international selection, instead of strategically managing international assignments.

2.2.7 Selection of International Assignees in Practice

In 1999, the majority of organisations operated predominantly closed and informal selection systems, and many AEs were selected according to what has been called the 'coffee machine' system (Harris & Brewster, 1999). In other words, the key criterion was being known to a senior manager. Twenty years later, this happened much less in major multinationals but this method was still commonly used: according to KPMG (2019), the applicable business unit drives the selection process for sourcing the prospective international assignees in 89 per cent of the MNEs surveyed. While

38 per cent of MNEs assess an international assignee's suitability for a transfer through an informal review by line management/ human resource management specialists or via self-assessments, the majority of participants (60 per cent) do not use any kind of process at all to assess an assignee's global skills suitability. Overall, management of the assignment planning process is lacking, with 35 per cent of the respondents saying it is not well managed and 25 per cent having a neutral point of view. According to Mercer (2015), poor candidate selection was the first reason why international assignments fail. Again, let us remind ourselves that these consultants' reports are likely to be based upon the larger, more formalised, organisations – the majority will be a lot more informal and personal contacts will be the only thing that matters.

In conclusion here, although the researchers unanimously agree about the significance of an objective selection system for international assignees, there is still a big gap between their suggestions and the MNE's practices.

Against common assumptions, this is different for the recruitment and selection of public sector expatriates (Waxin & Brewster, 2018). Public sector expatriates are employees who have signed up to a career that they know will involve international transfer. In the different parts of the public sector, employees are selected after careful screening and their contracts include an international mobility clause.

In any case, the objectives of the position, the job description and specification, and the details about the management of the expatriation/repatriation processes should be explained to the candidate by the end of the selection process. Expatriates should know the exact purposes of their assignment before the beginning of the assignment. Several studies have showed that job clarity was a significant predictor of expatriate' work adjustment (Bhaskar-Shrinivas et al., 2005; Waxin, 2000), and reduced time to proficiency (Waxin et al., 2016).

2.3 Preparation for Expatriation

The purpose of international assignees' preparation is to provide them with the necessary elements that will help them perform and succeed during the assignment (Waxin, 2008a; Morey & Waxin, 2008).

2.3.1 The Different Expatriate Preparation Methods

To prepare international assignees before their assignment, MNEs can provide pre-assignment visits, practical assistance, language, cross-cultural training, coaching, and partner's training.

Pre-assignment visit. The organisation offers a trip to the host country to the assignee so that they can get an idea of their future work and living environment. This option is sometimes used at the end of the selection process so that the candidate can confirm their acceptance of the position. During this trip, the assignee finalises the contract and settles some issues like finding accommodation or a school for the children (Waxin, 2000, 2008a, 2007).

According to KPMG (2019), 87 per cent of MNEs provided a formal pre-assignment visit to the host location, and the majority (57 per cent) included both the assignee and their partner in the trip.

Practical assistance. This includes arranging for the visas, transportation, finding new accommodation for the family, and new schools for the children, if it has not been done during the preliminary visit. Many MNEs use the services of relocation specialists to provide this practical assistance. The goal is to facilitate the expatriate's transfer and settling in the host location. Waxin (2000, 2006) found that the home country's logistical support facilitates expatriate general adjustment. According to KPMG (2019), pre-assignment consultations and tax briefings are widely provided as core policy benefits (81 per cent and 87 per cent, respectively) to thoroughly review the prospective assignment terms and conditions prior to relocation.

Language training. The assignee is taught at least the basics of the language of the region where they will be sent. According to Ashamalla (1998), language ability facilitates adjustment in the local environment and enhances effectiveness in dealing with foreign counterpart groups including government officials, bankers, labour organisations, suppliers, and customers. The rigour of the training should depend on the relational aspect of the expatriate's job.

Cross-cultural training (CCT). CCT is defined as the educative processes used to improve intercultural learning via the development of the cognitive, affective, and behavioural competencies needed for successful interactions in diverse cultures (Morris & Robie, 2001). CCT programmes can be analysed in terms of training content, process and elements (Feitosa et al., 2014). In terms of content, there are two possible orientations: either the training focuses on the notion of culture in general and aims at sensitising participants to the notion of culture, or it focuses on one specific culture in particular (Gudykunst, Guzley, & Hammer, 1996; Gertsen, 1990). In terms of process, Brislin (1979) identifies three methods of cross-cultural training: cognitive, affective, and behavioural. The cognitive method corresponds to a diffusion of information, using conferences or non-participative sessions, on a foreign cultural environment. The affective method aims at provoking individual reactions, so the subject can learn to deal with critical cultural incidents. The behavioural method aims at improving participants' capacity to adapt their communication style, and to establish positive relationships with members of another culture. The training process can be broadly categorised as either intellectual/conventional or experiential (Bennett, 1986; Gertsen, 1990). With conventional training, the trainee is passive, information is transmitted through a unidirectional communication, while with experimental training, the trainee actively participates in 'real life' situations. Littrell & Salas' (2005) framework identified six training approaches, in ascending level of rigour: attribution, culture awareness, interaction, language, didactic, and experiential. The most rigorous, experiential, training programmes are based on simulations, role playing, field trips, and intercultural workshops. Finally, information, demonstration, practice, and feedback (IDPF) are the basic four elements of any training programme, and Feitosa et al. (2014) extrapolate this logic to expatriate training.

According to KPMG (2019), language training and CCT are offered by the majority of their client MNEs with an observable trend of these training programmes beginning before arrival in the host country to support a quicker transition and integration. The assignee's partner and children are likely to be included in training.

Expatriate coaching. Some MNEs offer home-country sponsors or mentors to help international assignees remain visible to the organisation and to prepare for their return (Carraher, Sullivan, & Crocitto, 2008). Other MNEs offer the social support of a local coach or tutor (Andreason, 2008). Jassawalla, Asgary, and Sashittal (2006) examined the functions of both types of expatriates' mentors, and found that while host-country mentors typically helped the expatriates with cross-cultural adjustment, home-country mentors linked the expatriates to the global organisation and assisted with repatriation issues. Carraher et al. (2008) examined the impact of home- and host-country mentors on eight measures of expatriate effectiveness, in a large service MNE that had a formal mentoring programme. They found that having a host-country mentor had a positive effect on five measures of effectiveness (organisational knowledge, knowledge-sharing, team work, performance, and promotability), and having a home-country mentor had a positive effect on three measures of effectiveness (promotability, performance, and organisational knowledge) showing that both kinds of mentors are beneficial to a successful international assignment. They suggested that if their organisation did not provide formal mentoring programmes, expatriates should be encouraged to develop such a relationship in order to improve their own international experience.

Partner Training and Support. Inclusion of all family members in cross-cultural training is important (Webb, 1996) because of the strong impact of their global adjustment on the expatriate's adjustment (Andreason, 2008; Haslberger & Brewster, 2008; Merignac & Roger 2012). In particular, specific training programmes need to be developed for the unique challenges faced by expatriate partners (e.g., how to get work permits and develop personal careers in the other country) and children (e.g., education-related issues). While organisational support has been associated with enhanced partner personal (Simeon & Fujiu, 2000) and cultural (Abdul Malek, Budhwar, & Reiche, 2015) adjustment, as well as well-being (Gupta, Banerjee, & Gaur, 2012; McNulty, 2012), there is no indication that such support facilitates partner interaction adjustment. Perhaps organisations do not offer training that targets the development and maintenance of effective relationships with host country nationals, or such relationships require more time than is generally allotted to expatriate assignments.

2.3.2 *Expatriate Training Effectiveness*

There is a continuing need for valid and reliable methods to assess cultural learning outcomes, and to identify the most efficient training methods. Research results on the effectiveness of expatriate training are mixed, however: while some researchers find that pre-departure preparation is important and effective (Black & Mendenhall, 1990; Waxin & Panaccio, 2005); others find no evidence that it works (Kealey & Protheroe, 1996; Puck et al., 2008).

Waxin and Panaccio (2005) studied the impact of the four types of pre-departure CCT on expatriates' cross-cultural adjustment. They found that: (1) pre-departure CCT had a positive impact on adjustment (with the smallest effect on work adjustment); (2) experimental types of CCT were the most effective; (3) the larger the cultural distance between the home and host countries, the more significant were the effects; and (4) CCT's effectiveness was stronger for managers with less international experience. Another study showed CCT effectiveness was also influenced by the expatriate's self-efficacy: higher self-efficacy was related to a stronger relation between CCT and adjustment (Osman-Gani & Rockstuhl, 2009). However, a meta-analysis by Morris and Robie (2001) shows that CCT effectiveness is not as high as expected and that result vary widely. Puck, Kittler, and Wright (2008) analysed the impact of pre-departure CCT on expatriate adjustment, taking into account variations in participation, length, and comprehensiveness of training, for expatriates from twenty German MNEs sent to a broad range of host countries. They found that CCT had little, if any, effect on expatriates' adjustment. However, they found a significant impact of foreign language competence on expatriate adjustment.

The findings on the effectiveness of partners' CCT are also mixed, with Black and Gregersen (1991) reporting a negative relationship between CCT and partner cultural adjustment and Gupta et al. (2012) suggesting that such training will facilitate partner well-being. Cole (2011) found that employment assistance offered by companies related to partner interaction adjustment. Insofar as training and organisational support help to reduce the uncertainty and stress of adjusting to a foreign culture, organisations that offer assistance to expatriate partners will support a positive experience and enhanced adjustment.

To conclude on the effectiveness of preparation, since the training programmes vary widely, and are not systematically evaluated, it is difficult to ascertain which programmes are effective and which are not. McNulty and Brewster (2018) identified four reasons for the lack of consistency in expatriate training effectiveness: first, researchers are studying different kinds of preparation and training; second, expensive preparation programmes might be less effective than informal learning from former expatriates and their families; third, most MNEs make their CCT and other training programmes voluntary/non-mandatory, resulting in a perception that preparation is 'not needed'; and, fourth, thanks to technology, changing the way preparation and training are delivered (Wankel, 2016), it is possible to discover many aspects of a host country without moving away from your screen.

2.3.3 Expatriate Preparation in Practice

Although the consultancy surveys of the larger companies show that in some cases there is an extensive preparation for international assignments, beyond these companies it seems clear that, in most cases, most expatriates get very little preparation. This is largely because of the very short time between the decision to send them and them leaving for the new country (McNulty & Brewster, 2019): this is a period when the new expatriate has to finish up the work they are doing and pass it on, to decide what to do about their house or apartment at home (sell, rent, or leave it empty?), to find new accommodation in their new location, to sort out their children's schooling, and to get round to see all their friends and relatives before they leave – and a host of practical issues concerned with the move itself. Trying to squeeze preparation or training into a very crowded few weeks is almost impossible. Most expatriates are reduced to informal methods of preparation – speaking to people who have been to that country, reading company reports, checking the websites or reading the Rough Guide to Wherever on the plane!

SIEs, in comparison to AEs, receive little organisational training and support from their employers: in most cases they have to find out about the institutional, social and cultural characteristics of the host country by themselves. They will get little training about the host country and have to navigate by themselves their work contract issues, and the specific local employment and immigration laws (Waxin & Brewster, 2020).

Public sector organisations usually provide better preparation for their international assignees than private MNEs. International assignees are often given training specific to their region of destination, including language training, cultural familiarity training, or political area studies (Honley, 2005). The US Department of State, for example, offers several publications and courses to families with the aim of mitigating culture shock and maximising successful adjustment (Green, 2012). Although the US Department of Defense provides

Cultural Training at the US Department of Defense

The US Department of Defense established cultural centres to develop and deliver training. Special Forces personnel always had a cultural and regional element in their roles and training.

For the US Department of Defense, providing effective training to large numbers of personnel within a short period of time is a big challenge. The US military services adopt both culture specific and culture general content: while professional military education covers regional or culture-specific elements, and more general principles and skills, pre-deployment cultural training tends to be highly tailored to the country and cultures that personnel will encounter on their upcoming deployment. A wide range of pedagogical methods are used: readings, lectures, critical incidents, case and problem-solving based instruction, and opportunities to apply cultural knowledge and skills, through different media. Live role play is still commonly used at training centres, but the use of computer-based simulations is increasing.

While substantial resources have been deployed to develop and implement cultural instruction, the evaluation of its impact on learning or performance has been neglected. The US military services developed instruments to assess the effectiveness of cultural training on performance and relevant competencies, but these instruments have not been implemented for institutional use. Training effectiveness has been evaluated in some cases, showing that training had a positive effect on cultural learning in the short-term, but its impact on performance was even less often assessed.

Figure 2.2 Case study
Source: adapted from Abbe & Gouge (2012).

more extensive programmes (Abbe & Gouge, 2012), even here expatriates want more (Fenner & Selmer, 2008).

Trochowska (2014) examined the implementation of cultural training in pre-deployment and operational training and activities by NATO (including Canada, the UK, Germany, Poland, and Turkey) and other armies (such as Australia, South Korea, Pakistan, Singapore, and Nepal). They found that in most of the armies studied (except the United Kingdom, Canada, and Germany), cultural training and support only consists of a few hours lecturing during the pre-deployment preparation for the mission, and the use of cultural advisors during the operation. Moreover, training involving universal cultural skills that could facilitate the adjustment process and the gaining of regional knowledge during the vocational education of soldiers, commands, staff, and reserve officers are not carried out in a systematic manner in any of the armies studied.

2.4 Conclusions

Research has given us considerable information about the recruitment, selection, and preparation of AEs, in large MNEs from developed countries. We see that most assigned expatriates, apart from subject specialists, are recruited from already existing employees; the question for the organisation then is how they can encourage these individuals to accept a foreign assignment. Some, the cosmopolitans, need little encouragement, while others will weigh issues of salary and career, location and family to reach a decision. When it comes to selecting expatriates, MNEs tend to have rather informal systems and to privilege performance in previous, non-expatriate roles. But there is some evidence of MNEs beginning to understand the weaknesses of such an approach and to develop criteria that include cultural adaptability and to operate more formal selection systems. We also reviewed the preparation that MNEs offer for those selected. We found that most expatriates get very little in the way of preparation, because of the lack of time, in most instances, between them being selected and having to leave for the new location. However, those that do receive training are very positive about its value and those that receive the most intensive training are the most positive.

But there is still much that we do not know: the field remains a rich source of potential research. We know much more about long-term expatriation than we do about other types of international work (McNulty & Brewster, 2019). The biggest gap concerns SIEs: how do they get their jobs? How are they recruited, selected? What preparation do they undertake for themselves prior to moving?

There is a dearth of research into public sector expatriates (Waxin & Brewster, 2018). There are millions of people working as public sector expatriates around the world, in governmental armed and diplomatic services, and also in inter-governmental organisations. We need more research on the different types of international assignments in the public sector and how these international assignments are managed.

Other research gaps reflect the common lacunas in expatriate research. There is a major dearth of research into the practices of emerging economy multinationals. It seems likely that the selection systems and preparation practices may not be the same for international workers from less-studied countries, in less-studied cultures and for less-studied jobs. There may, for example, in some cases, be a significant influence of extended family and a significant impact from religion in Asia-Pacific, Muslim country-based MNEs. There is an almost entire absence of research into the management of international assignees in smaller businesses.

Overall, in the area of selection and preparation for international assignments there is good material for researchers to build on and to grow understanding of the key issues. Nevertheless, there remains here a rich field for exciting research in the future.

References

Abbe, A. & Gouge, M. 2012. Cultural training for military personnel. *Military Review*, 92(4): 9–17.

Abdul Malek, M., Budhwar, P., & Reiche, B. S. 2015. Sources of support and expatriation: a multiple stakeholder perspective of expatriate adjustment and performance in Malaysia. *International Journal of Human Resource Management*, 26(2): 258–276.

Anderson, B. 2005. Expatriate selection: good management or good luck? *International Journal of Human Resource Management*, 16(4): 567–583.

Andreason, A. W. 2008. Expatriate adjustment of spouses and expatriate managers: an integrative research review. *International Journal of Management*, 25: 382–393.

Ashamalla, M. 1998. International human resources practices: the challenge of expatriation. *Competitiveness Review*, 8(2): 54–65.

Avril, A. B. & Magnini, V. P. 2007. A holistic approach to expatriate success, *International Journal of Contemporary Hospitality Management*, 19 (1): 53–64.

Bennett, J. M. 1986. Modes of cross-cultural training: conceptualizing cross-cultural training as education. *International Journal of Intercultural Relations*, 10: 117–134.

Bhaskar-Shrinivas, P, Harrison, DA, Shaffer, MA., & Luk, DM. 2005. Input-based and time-based models of international adjustment: meta-analytic evidence and theoretical extensions. *The Academy of Management Journal*, 48(2): 257–281.

Black, J. S. & Mendenhall, M. 1990. Cross-cultural training effectiveness: a review and a theoretical framework for future research. *Academy of Management Review*, 15(1): 113–136.

Black, J. S. & Gregersen, H. B. 1991. Antecedents to cross-cultural adjustment for expatriates in Pacific Rim assignments. *Human Relations*, 44(5): 497–515.

Brislin, R. W. 1979. Orientation programs for cross-cultural preparation. *Perspectives on Cross-cultural Psychology*: 287–304.

Brookfield, 2015. *Global mobility trends survey*. Brookfield Global Relocation Services 2015. https://docplayer.net/15337612–2015-global-mobility-trends-survey-report-mindful-mobility.html.

Brookfield. 2016. *Global mobility trends survey*. Brookfield Global Relocation Services 2016. http://globalmobilitytrends.bgrs.com/.

Caligiuri, P., Tarique, I., & Jacobs, R. 2009, Selection for international assignments. *Human Resource Management Review*, 19(3): 252–262.

Campoy, E., Waxin, M., Davoine, E., Charles-Pauvers, B., Commeiras, N., & Goudarzi, K. 2005. La socialisation organisationnelle en contexte. In N. Delobbe, O. Herrbach, D. Lacaze & K. Mignonac (eds.), *Comportement organisationnel, Vol. 1 : Contrat psychologique, émotions au travail, socialisation organisationnelle, De Boeck* : 341–393. Bruxelles.

Carraher, S. M., Sullivan, S. E., & Crocitto, M. M. 2008. Mentoring across global boundaries: an empirical examination of home- and host-country mentors on expatriate career outcomes. *Journal of International Business Studies*, 39: 1310–1326.

Cerdin J-L., Chandon J-L. & Waxin, M-F. 1999. The adaptability of the French expatriates, a confirmatory analysis, September, 1999. Centre d'études et de Recherche sur les Organisations et la Gestion CEROG: WP 575. IAE Aix-en-Provence: France.

Cerdin, J-L. & Brewster, C. 2014. Talent management and expatriation: bridging two streams of research and practice *Journal of World Business* 49 (2): 245–252.

Cheng, H. L. & Lin, C. Y. Y. 2009. Do as the large enterprises do? Expatriate selection and overseas performance in emerging markets: the case of Taiwan SMEs. *International Business Review*, 18(1): 60–75.

Cole, N. D. 2011. Managing global talent: solving the spousal adjustment problem. *International Journal of Human Resource Management*, 22(07): 1504–1530.

Collings, D. G. 2014. Integrating global mobility and talent management: exploring the challenges and strategic opportunities. *Journal of World Business*, 49(2): 253–261.

Collins, C. J. & Kehoe, R. R. 2009. Recruitment and selection. In J. Storey, P. M. Wright, & D. Ulrich (eds.), *The Routledge Companion to Strategic Human Resource Management*: 209–223. New York: Routledge.

Culpan, O. & Wright, G. H. 2002. Women abroad: getting the best results from women managers. *International Journal of Human Resource Management*, 13(5): 784–801.

Dickmann, M., Doherty, N., Mills, T., & Brewster, C. 2008. Why do they go? Individual and corporate perspectives on the factors influencing the decision to accept an international assignment. *International Journal of Human Resource Management*, 19(4): 731–751.

Doherty, N., Dickmann, M., & Mills, T. 2011. Exploring the motives of company-backed and self-initiated expatriates *International Journal of Human Resource Management*, 22(3): 595–611.

Dupuis, M. J., Haines, V. Y. III, & Saba, T. 2008. Gender, family ties, and international mobility: cultural distance matters. *International Journal of Human Resource Management*, 19(2): 274–295.

de Eccher, U. & Duarte, H. 2018. How images about emerging economies influence the willingness to accept expatriate assignments. *International Journal of Human Resource Management*, 29(4): 637–663.

Edström, A. & Galbraith, J. 1977. Transfer of managers as a coordination and control strategy in multinational organizations. *Administrative Science Quarterly*, 22(2): 248–263.

Feitosa, J., Kreutzer C., Kramperth A., Kramer W. S., & Salas, E. 2014. Expatriate adjustment: considerations for selection and training. *Journal of Global Mobility*, 2(2): 134–159.

Fenner Jr., C. R. & Selmer, J. 2008. Public sector expatriate managers: psychological adjustment, personal characteristics and job factors. *International Journal of Human Resource Management*, 19(7): 1237–1252.

Finn, L. & Morley, M. 2002. Expatriate selection: The case of an Irish multinational. In M. Linehan, M. Morley, & J. Walsh. (eds.), *International Human Resource Management and Expatriate Tranfers*: 101–131. Dublin, Ireland: Irish Experiences, Blackhall Press.

Froese, F. J., Jommersbach, S., & Klautsch, E. 2013. Cosmopolitan career choices: a cross-cultural study of job candidates' expatriation willingness. *International Journal of Human Resource Management*, 24 (17): 3247–3261.

Furusawa, M. & Brewster, C. 2018. Japanese self-initiated expatriates as boundary spanners in Chinese subsidiaries of Japanese MNEs: antecedents, social capital, and HRM practices. *Thunderbird International Business Review*, 60(6), 911–919.

Gertsen, M. C. 1990. Intercultural competence and expatriates. *International Journal of Human Resource Management*, 1(3): 341–362.

Green, J. M. 2012. *The relationship between adjustment and personal and work variables among American government employees and their spouses stationed abroad*. Dissertation, Northcentral University, Graduate Faculty of the School of Behavioral and Health Sciences, Prescott Valley.

Gudykunst, W. B., Guzley, R. M., & Hammer, M. R. 1996. Designing intercultural training. In Landis, D. and Bahgat, R. S. (eds.), *Handbook of Intercultural Training*. Thousand Oaks: Sage.

Gupta, R., Banerjee, P., & Gaur, J. 2012. Exploring the role of the spouse in expatriate failure: a grounded theory-based investigation of expatriate's spouse adjustment issues from India. *International Journal of Human Resource Management*, 23(17): 3559–3577.

Haak-Saheem, W. & Brewster, C. 2017. 'Hidden' expatriates: international mobility in the United Arab Emirates as a challenge to current understanding of expatriation. *Human Resource Management Journal*, 27(3): 423–439.

Harris, H. & Brewster, C. 1999. The coffee machine system: how international selection really works. *International Journal of Human Resource Management*, 10(3): 488–500.

Harrison, D. A. & Shaffer, M. A. 2005. Mapping the criterion space for expatriate success: task- and relationship-based performance, effort and adaptation. *International Journal of Human Resource Management*, 16 (8): 1454–1474.

Haslberger, A. & Brewster, C. 2008. The expatriate family: an international perspective. *Journal of Managerial Psychology*, 23(3): 324–346.

Honley, S. A. 2005. Focus on FSI/FS training: FSI settles into Arlington Hall. *Foreign Service Journal, Jul-Aug*, 17–31.

Hyder, A. S. & Lövblad, M. 2007. The repatriation process–a realistic approach. *Career Development International*, 12(3): 264–281.

Jassawalla, A., Asgary, N., & Sashittal, H. 2006. Managing expatriates: the role of mentors. *International Journal of Commerce and Management*, 16 (2): 130–140.

Kealey, D. J. & Protheroe, D. R. 1996. The effectiveness of cross-cultural training for expatriates: an assessment of the literature on the issue. *International Journal of Intercultural Relations*, 20(2):141–165.

Kim, C., Brewster, C., & Chung, C. 2019. Beyond nationality: international experience as a key dimension for subsidiary staffing choices in MNEs? *Journal of Global Mobility* 7 (3): 269–284.

Kim, J. & Froese, F. J. 2012. Expatriation willingness in Asia: the importance of host-country characteristics and employees' role commitments. *International Journal of Human Resource Management*, 23 (16): 3414–3433.

KPMG. 2019. Global assignment policies and practices survey. https://home.kpmg/xx/en/home/insights/2016/10/global-assignment-policies-and-practices-survey-2016.html, Accessed on 27 November 2019.

Lazarova, M. B. & Cerdin, J. L. 2007. Revisiting repatriation concerns: organizational support versus career and contextual influences. *Journal of International Business Studies*, 38(3): 404–429.

Linehan, M., Morley, M., & Walsh, J. (eds.). 2002. *International Human Resource Management and Expatriate Transfers: Irish Experiences*, Dublin, Blackhall: 108–109.

Ling, E. Z. & Harzing, A.-W. 2017. Language as a local practice: why English as a corporate language won't work in China. *European Academy of Management (EURAM) Conference*, 21–24 June, Glasgow, Scotland.

Littrell, L. N. & Salas, E. 2005. A review of cross-cultural training: best practices, guidelines, and research needs. *Human Resource Development Review*, 4(3): 305–334.

Littrell, L. N., Salas, E., Hess, K. P., Paley, M., & Riedel, S. 2006. Expatriate preparation: a critical analysis of 25 years of cross-cultural training research. *Human Resource Development Review*, 5(3): 355–388.

Marchon, J. 2004. *Expatriation management: Theoretical principles and practices in suiss-based multinational companies.* Master's thesis, Economics and Social Sciences Faculty, University of Fribourg, Switzerland.

McNulty, Y. 2012. Being dumped in to sink or swim: an empirical study of organizational support for the trailing spouse. *Human Resource Development International*, 15(4): 41–434.

McNulty, Y. & Brewster, C. 2018. Management of (business) expatriates. In *Organizational Behaviour and Human Resource Management*: 109–137. Springer, Cham.

McNulty, Y. & Brewster, C. 2019. *Working Internationally: Expatriation, Migration and Other Global Work*, Cheltenham, Edward Elgar.

Mendenhall M. & Oddou G. 1985. The dimensions of expatriate acculturation. *Academy of Management Review*, 10; 39–47.

Mercer, 2015. *Worldwide Survey of International Assignment Policies and Practices*. Mercer. www.mercer.com. Accessed 20 September 2019.

Merignac, O. & Roger, A. 2012. Comprendre les préoccupations du conjoint qui doit suivre un expatrié à l'étranger. *Gestion*, 37 (2): 23–33.

Mol, S. T., Born, M. P., Willemsen, M. E., & Van der Molen, H. T. 2005. Predicting expatriate job performance for selection purposes: a quantitative review. *Journal of Cross-Cultural Psychology*, 36(5): 590–620.

Mol, S. T., Born, M. P., Willemsen, M. E., Henk, T. V. D. M., & Derous, E. 2009. When selection ratios are high: predicting the expatriation willingness of prospective domestic entry-level job applicants, *Human Performance*, 22(1): 1–22.

Morey, S. & Waxin, M-F. 2008. Le développement managérial à l'international. In M.-F. Waxin & C. Barmeyer (eds.), *Gestion des Ressources Humaines Internationales* 7: 291–334. Paris, France : Éditions de Liaisons.

Morris, M. A. & Robie, C. 2001. A meta-analysis of the effects of cross-cultural training on expatriate performance and adjustment. *International Journal of Training and Development*, 5(2): 112–125.

Osman-Gani, A. M. & Rockstuhl, T. 2009. Cross-cultural training, expatriate self-efficacy, and adjustments to overseas assignments: an empirical investigation of managers in Asia. *International Journal of Intercultural Relations*, 33(4): 277–290.

Peltokorpi, V., 2008. Cross-cultural adjustment of expatriates in Japan. *International Journal of Human Resource Management*, 19(9): 1588–1606.

Peltokorpi, V. & Froese, F. J. 2009. Organizational expatriates and self-initiated expatriates: who adjusts better to work and life in Japan? *International Journal of Human Resource Management*, 20(5): 1096–1112.

Puck, J. F., Kittler, M. G., & Wright, C., 2008. Does it really work? Re-assessing the impact of pre-departure cross-cultural training on expatriate adjustment. *International Journal of Human Resource Management*, 19 (12): 2182–2197.

Reiche, B., Harzing. A-W., & Kraimer, M. 2009. The role of international assignees' social capital in creating inter-unit intellectual capital: a cross-level model. *Journal of International Business Studies*, 40(3): 509–526.

Richardson, J. & McKenna, S. 2002. Leaving and experiencing: why academics expatriate and how they experience expatriation. *Career Development International*, 7(2): 67–78.

Shen, J. & Lang, B. 2009. Cross-cultural training and its impact on expatriate performance in Australian MNEs. *Human Resource Development International*. 12(4): 371–386.

Simeon, R. & Fujiu, K. 2000. Cross-cultural adjustment strategies of Japanese spouses in Silicon Valley. *Employee Relations*, 22(6): 594–611.

Stahl, G., Miller, D. J., & Tung, R. L. 2002. Towards the boundaryless career: a closer look at the expatriate career concept and the perceived implications of an international assignment. *Journal of World Business*, 37 (3): 216–227.

Tarique, I. & Schuler, R. S. 2010. Global talent management: literature review, integrative framework, and suggestions for further research. *Journal of World Business*, 45(2): 122–133.

Tharenou, P. 2008.Disruptive decisions to leave home: gender and family differences in expatriation choices. *Organizational Behavior and Human Decision Processes*, 105(2): 183–200.

Trochowska, K., 2014. International experiences in the operationalization of culture for military operations–field research results. *Connections*, 13(3): 83–104.

Tungli, Z. & Peiperl, M. 2009. Expatriate practices in German, Japanese, UK, and US multinational companies: a comparative survey of changes. *Human Resource Management*: 48(1), 153–171.

Wankel, C. 2016. Developing cross-cultural managerial skills through social media. *Journal of Organizational Change Management*, 29(1), 116–124.

Waxin, M-F. 2000. *L'adaptation des cadres expatriés en Inde: Ses déterminants et l'effet de la culture d'origine*, Thèse de doctorat, Unpublished PhD Dissertation, Université Aix-Marseille III, IAE Aix-en-Provence, France.

Waxin, M-F. 2006. The effect of culture of origin on the adjustment process. In M. Morley, N. Heraty & D. Collings (eds.), *New Directions in Expatriate Research*: 120–142. London, England: Palgrave Macmillan.

Waxin, M-F. 2007. Strategic HRM management of international assignments", in M. Katsioloudes & S. Hadjidakis (eds.), *International Business*, 12: 387–438. London: Elsevier.

Waxin, M-F. 2008a. La gestion stratégique des affectations internationales. In M-F. Waxin & C. Barmeyer (eds.), *Gestion des Ressources Humaines Internationales, problématiques, stratégies et pratiques* (3): 103–146. Paris, France: Éditions de Liaisons.

Waxin, M-F. 2008b. Le recrutement et la sélection à l'international. In M-F. Waxin & C. Barmeyer (eds.), *Gestion des Ressources Humaines Internationales, problématiques, stratégies et pratiques (4)*: 151–204. Paris, France: Éditions de Liaisons.

Waxin, M-F. & Brewster, C. 2018. Public sector expatriation. In A. Farazmand (ed.), *Global Encyclopedia of Public Administration, Public Policy, and Governance*: 41–49. *Springer International Publishing Switzerland.*

Waxin, M-F. & Brewster, C. 2020. The impact of host country characteristics on SIEs' career success. In Andresen, M., Brewster, C., & Suutari, V. (eds.), *Mastering the Context of Self-Initiated Expatriates' Careers: Recognizing Space, Time and Institutions* (3). London: Routledge.

Waxin, M-F. & Chandon J-L. 2002. L'adaptation à l'interaction des expatriés en Inde, *Revue Internationale de Gestion*, 27 (1), 56–64.

Waxin, M-F. & Panaccio, A. J. 2005. Cross-cultural training to facilitate expatriate adjustment: it works! *Personnel Review*, 34 (1): 51–67.

Waxin, M-F., Brewster, C., Ashill, N., & Chandon, J-L. 2016. The impact of expatriates' home country culture on their time to proficiency: empirical evidence from the Indian context. *Journal of Developing Areas*, 50(4): 401–422.

Waxin, M-F., Brewster, C. & Ashill, N. 2019. Expatriate time to proficiency: individual antecedents and the moderating effect of home country, *Journal of Global Mobility*, doi:10.1108/JGM-12-2018-0060.

Webb, A. 1996. The expatriate experience: implications for career success. *Career Development International*, 1(5): 38–44.

3 *Expatriate Adjustment*

ANNE LESSLE, ARNO HASLBERGER, CHRIS BREWSTER

3.1 Introduction

Adjustment is the process of changing behaviour, feelings, and cognitions to achieve a balance with the environment (Black, Mendenhall, & Oddou 1991; Lofquist & Dawis, 1991). Adjustment is needed whenever an individual transfers from a familiar setting to an unfamiliar setting, if they want to live comfortably and perform effectively (Jackson & Manderscheid, 2015). However, the needed change might be upsetting to the individual because it includes new routines and uncertainty. As adjustment is essential for expatriation success, a book such as this one would be incomplete without explaining the concept.

There is now an extensive body of literature on expatriate adjustment examining what it is that people have to adjust to, how they do it, who is likely to do it best, and what the outcomes of adjustment are likely to be. Although most of our research into expatriation so far has been focused on high-status assigned expatriates in leadership roles or as key technical players (Dabic, González-Loureiro, & Harvey, 2015; McPhail et al., 2012), there has been increasing attention to different categories of expatriates: low status expatriates (Haak-Saheem & Brewster, 2017) and military expatriates (Fisher, Hutchings, & Pinto, 2015); those in the aid and NGO sectors (Claus et al., 2015; Ritchie et al., 2015; Wechtler, Koveshnikov, & Dejoux, 2017), the LGBTQ community (McPhail & McNulty, 2015), and female expatriates (Shortland, 2016).

In this chapter we examine what we have learned from the literature. We discuss antecedents to adjustment and critically reflect on the most common approaches to analysing expatriate adjustment. Furthermore, new alternatives on how to understand adjustment that mitigate the limitations of previous models will be highlighted and we will share insights on how to apply a holistic assessment. Finally, we will provide our readers with some practical and research implications.

3.2 The Notion and Importance of Adjustment

For the organisation sending the expatriate, rapid adjustment means that the expatriate can take on their new role and do their job effectively. The sooner they can perform at a level of proficiency, the sooner the organisation begins to recoup its substantial investment in their transfer (Waxin et al., 2017). As assigned expatriates are expensive, they are monitored closely (Armstrong & Yan, 2017; McNulty & De Cieri, 2013; Nowak & Linder, 2016). Although host nationals' stereotypes of expatriates might impact performance (Bonache, Langinier, & Zárraga-Oberty, 2016; Kang & Shen, 2018), the ability of expatriates to adjust rapidly will help local colleagues to operate effectively, too. The willingness of the expatriate to ask for advice and follow through will positively affect their subsequent adjustment (Mahajan & Toh, 2014).

Adjustment issues that result in the premature departure of the expatriate can lead to serious problems for the organisation. These can range from extensive transfer expenses, the difficulty of replacing the individual, the loss of reputation amongst customers and employees, and to problems of credibility in the host location where the choice of expatriate might be seen as poor decision-making (Hemmasi, Downes, & Varner, 2010; Jackson & Manderscheid, 2015). In the more common case where adjustment is poor but not so bad as to require the ending of the assignment, the organisation will have to deal with an unhappy expatriate and family members, unhappy co-workers and possible reputational damage from poor performance.

For the expatriates themselves, and for the accompanying families (Bayraktar, 2019; Haslberger & Brewster, 2008; and see Chapter 11), short-term adjustment is crucial. Their well-being and their comfort are dependent upon their ability to operate effectively in the new environment. Rapid adjustment will be positive for all family members, allowing them to transition into a 'routine stage' (Buechele, 2018), or to a 'feeling at home' stage (Lessle, 2019), where they can feel settled in their new environment, form new networks (Mao & Shen, 2015; Wang, 2002), and acquire the host language. Slow adjustment or a failure to adjust, either by the expatriate themselves or members of their family, will create stress, misery, and might even lead to health issues. Further, if expatriates are completely unable to adjust, they are likely to have to leave the assignment, with the need for the family to make ad-hoc plans and a possible unfavourable knock-on for the expatriates' careers that could be permanent.

In the longer-term, successive well-adjusted expatriates can help local colleagues to understand the global organisations' objectives, policies and requirements, transfer organisational culture, enhance their own learning and development, and can create an international mindset in the local staff making them more competitive in the labour market. Well-adjusted expatriates are also more likely to accept subsequent international assignments, which furthers their career prospects and earning potential in the long run (Dickmann et al., 2016; Ramaswami, Carter, & Dreher, 2016; Suutari, Tornikoski, & Mäkelä, 2012; Suutari et al., 2017). In brief, then, both immediately and in the longer term, the adjustment of expatriates has significant upside and downside implications. The more we understand it, the better for all stakeholders.

3.3 Antecedents of Adjustment

Traditional models of expatriate adjustment such as Black et al.'s (1991) model pointed out a series of antecedents which are expected to facilitate expatriate adjustment. Antecedents to adjustment, such as (1) previous expatriation experience (Bhaskar-Shrinivas et al., 2005; Moon, Choi, & Jung, 2012; Zhu, Wanberg, Harrison, & Diehn, 2016), (2) language fluency (Bhaskar-Shrinivas et al., 2005; Krishnaveni & Arthi, 2015; Ravasi, Salamin, & Davoine, 2015), (3) personality factors (Shaffer et al., 2006; Zimmermann & Neyer, 2013), (4) cultural distance (Cho, Hutchings, & Marchant, 2013; Hemmasi & Downes, 2013), (5) organisational support (Black & Gregersen, 1991; McNulty, 2012; Rosenbusch & Cseh, 2012; Wu & Ang, 2011), and (6) dual-career issues and social identity (Cole, 2011; Gupta, Banerjee, & Gaur, 2012; McNulty, 2012; Ward & Searle, 1991), have been examined in regard to their value in supporting adjustment. However, although extensively researched, these factors could not reliably predict successful adjustment. Therefore, only some of them will be discussed here (for an extensive evaluation see Bhaskar-Shrinivas et al., 2005; Takeuchi, 2010).

3.3.1 Previous Expatriation Experience

Researchers asserted that individuals learn from past experience to make inferences about the future and therefore previous experience should have a positive effect on adjustment (Black et al., 1991). Consequently, several studies explored the influence of previous international experience on expatriation adjustment, but the results are meagre at best. Bhaskar-Shrinivas et al. (2005) and Moon et al., (2012) found no impact of previous expatriation experience on adjustment while Zhu et al. (2016) relied on limited data to show an effect. However, a more detailed view provided by Lessle (2019) suggested that previous expatriation experience does have a positive effect on cognitive adjustment in the first and last stage during an assignment.

3.3.2 Language Proficiency

Being able to effectively communicate shows positive effects on social relationships and has a powerful impact on adjustment (Bhaskar-Shrinivas et al., 2005; Krishnaveni & Arthi, 2015). Language fluency allows social interaction with host nationals and facilitates adjustment (Lazarova, Westman, & Shaffer, 2010). Language ability also influences identity reconstruction by allowing individuals to express themselves (McNulty, 2012). However, English is widely accepted as a business language and the motivation to learn the host language might vary. Furthermore, mastering the foreign language does not necessarily mean being understood. For example, the same words may have different meanings depending on local specifics or accents. This might have a detrimental effect on adjustment when expatriates assess their cognitive skills as sufficient, whereas the environment misinterprets their attempts at communication. This divergence of individual competency and external expectations might lead to negative feelings and therefore adjustment declines (Rosenbusch, Cerny II, & Earnest, 2015).

3.3.3 Personality

Personality factors also impact adjustment, although there is dissent as to whether the most important factor is open mindedness (van Erp et al., 2014), self-efficacy (Bhaskar-Shrinivas et al., 2005), emotional stability, (Shaffer et al., 2006) or extroversion (Zimmermann & Neyer, 2013). An extroverted personality, for example, might assist with connecting to host country nationals in one culture and be perceived as offensive in a different culture (Ward, Leong, & Low, 2004). Therefore, as person-environment fit depends on the person as much as the environment, the situational context needs to be considered when assessing the impact of personality factors on expatriate adjustment.

Researchers found that some traits fit a particular culture better than others (Peltokorpi & Froese, 2014). An interesting twist was the attempt to create and clarify a construct of 'cultural intelligence'. At this point, there is a lack of consensus about the definition of the construct and it risks becoming tautological as cultural intelligence is acquired by coping with different cultures and also assessed by checking how one can cope with different cultures. Nevertheless, it has become a lively topic, with a range of different contributions (Ang & Van Dyne, 2015; Bücker et al., 2014; Lorenz, Ramsey, & Richey, 2018; Presbitero & Quita, 2017). Given the uncertainty surrounding the concept, it is not surprising that the results are equivocal.

3.3.4 Cultural Distance

Each destination is bound by its own culture, manifested in beliefs, cultural artefacts and values, and social interaction (Fu, Morris, & Hong, 2015). Depending on the expatriate's home culture, the differences in the host culture may be small or large, so the cultural distance, conceptualised as the perceived difference between home-culture and host-culture, varies depending on the cultures involved (Fu et al., 2015). In general, cultures that have a common denominator such as language, seasons, or political systems are perceived as closer than cultures without a common base.

Researchers who have examined cultural distance as a factor impacting adjustment confirm the importance of direction in the context of cultural distance and concluded that a transition from collectivistic cultures to individualistic cultures is less stressful (Cho et al., 2013; Hemmasi & Downes, 2013). Although large cultural distance is related to adjustment difficulties, in such situations organisations tend to fill management positions with home-country nationals rather than local talent (Hemmasi & Downes, 2013). The reasons for that decision are frequently trust issues concerning the unfamiliar culture, as well as the goal of distributing the organisational culture, processes, and regulations from the headquarters to subsidiaries (Hemmasi & Downes, 2013; Mayrhofer & Brewster, 1996).

3.3.5 Organisational Support

Organisations may provide formal support programmes, ranging from moving goods, assistance in finding a new home, providing language or cultural classes, up to informal support systems to help expatriates to adjust (Cho et al., 2013; Teague, 2015). Research shows that organisational support is received by about 80 per cent of assigned expatiates and typically favourably perceived (McNulty, 2012). Organisational support can influence adjustment to an unfamiliar environment by bridging the gap between individual needs and environmental requirements by providing the resources to interact more effectively. However, the timing of organisational support is essential for its effectiveness and Lessle (2019) as well as Rosenbusch and Cseh (2012) have highlighted the changing support demands over time.

3.3.6 Dual-Career Issues

Historically, researchers perceived the expatriate-partner as the female spouse accompanying her husband and tending to her duties as homemaker. This situation has changed dramatically with female expatriate partners often integrated into the workforce and an increasing number of male expatriate partners, almost always in employment themselves (Cole, 2011). Modern expatriate partners are an important part of the decision-making process about whether or not to accept an international assignment. The literature suggests that about four fifths of expatriate partners are employed before departure and a third are able to continue their career in the new location; which means many partners have to pause their career in favour of the expatriate's advancement (Gupta, Banerjee, & Guar 2012; McNulty, 2012). The opportunity to stay in the workforce has a substantial impact on expatriate partner adjustment, considering the high levels of education of many of the travelling partners (Cho et al., 2013; Cole, 2011). Spouses who are able to transfer their professional career into the new life are more likely to adjust well (Cole, 2011; Teague, 2015; and see Chapter 11).

The current state of research shows largely mixed results about what antecedents support expatriate adjustment. The inconsistency of the findings might be the result of overusing models which are not able to assess adjustment in its complexity and over time. This means that most existing studies failed to examine which factors are most relevant at certain times over the course of the assignment (Lessle, 2019). Therefore, we need to discuss the 'traditional' models to analyse adjustment and see how new approaches might provide us with a more realistic understanding of what happens when.

3.4 The Most Common Approaches to Analysing Expatriate Adjustment

Some of the first modern analyses of adjustment to a new culture, and repatriation adjustment, come from the sociologist Alfred Schütz (1944, 1945). He analysed adjustment from a phenomenological point of view, describing in detail the mental development of sojourners as they change their mental reference frame to fit with the new environment. His two articles gave a preview of some of the main themes featured in adjustment research to this day: underlying cultural assumptions and their influence on the cognitive reference frames of people, the uncertainty felt because of the unreliability of one's thinking and acting as usual, and the overcoming of the resulting crisis that leads to a level of renewed comfort and hence adjustment.

The two decades following Schütz' articles saw the development of the persistent idea of a common U-curved path to adjustment and the notion of a culture shock experienced in international moves (Gullahorn & Gullahorn, 1963; Lysgaard, 1955; Oberg, 1960). Although the veracity of these ideas was questioned early on and then over the years (e.g. Church, 1982; David, 1972; Kim & Ruben, 1988; Lundstedt, 1963; Ward, Bochner, & Furnham, 2001), they remain influential (Bhaskar-Shrinivas, et al., 2005; Wechtler, 2015). This is not the only example of the field holding on to old ideas in spite of well-founded, long-running criticism of a theoretical as well as empirical nature. The most common conceptualisation of cross-cultural adjustment as consisting of three facets is over thirty years old (Black, 1988). Developed by Black et al. (1991), the Comprehensive Model of

Adjustment (CMA) is today's most influential model of expatriate adjustment. The wealth of studies it triggered has resulted in several meta-analyses (Bhaskar-Shrinivas et al., 2005; Harari et al., 2018; Hechanova, Beehr, & Christiansen, 2003).

The core concept of the CMA (Black et al., 1991) rests on the assumption that adjustment takes place in two stages (anticipatory adjustment and in-country adjustment) and three adjustment domains: (1) the work domain which includes job related adjustments, (2) the interactional domain that relates to interaction with host-nationals, and (3) a 'catch-all' general domain that includes cultural norms as well as the general environment (Black et al., 1991).

Although numerous researchers have adopted the simple and easy-to-use 14-item scale (Chen & Shaffer, 2018; Claus et al., 2015; Dabic et al., 2015; Davies, Kraeh, & Froese, 2015; Jing et al., 2016; Ravasi et al., 2015; Richardson & Wong, 2018; Salamin & Davoine, 2015; Sousa et al., 2017; Wechtler et al., 2017, for some recent examples), there is extensive debate about the model (Dabic et al., 2015; Haslberger, Brewster, & Hippler, 2013; Hippler, Caligiuri, & Johnson, 2014a; Hippler, Brewster, & Haslberger, 2015; Ravasi et al., 2015; Thomas & Lazarova, 2006). Researchers have argued that the scale refers the term adjustment exclusively to the psychological well-being of the expatriate and have criticised the scale for being drawn from a small number of responses to a flawed questionnaire with no theoretical underpinning. Studies based on the CMA (Black et al., 1991) have been largely cross-sectional and do not reflect the impact of time. Furthermore, the individual importance of external factors perceived by the expatriate has been neglected (Hippler et al., 2015).

Nevertheless, the CMA (Black et al., 1991) inspired and advanced expatriate research for over two decades (Ravasi et al., 2015). It is based on the notion that adjustment takes place in the interaction between the individual and the environment, as suggested in Dawis and Lofquist's (1984) theory of work adjustment (TWA). Leaning on systems theory and as an application of P-E-fit, Dawis and Lofquist (1984) conceptualised work adjustment as the interaction between the employee and the work environment. As shown in Figure 3.1, differences between individual's needs and environmental requirements can be tolerated to a certain level (Dawis & Lofquist, 1984). Non-correspondence that cannot be tolerated might be bridged by actively

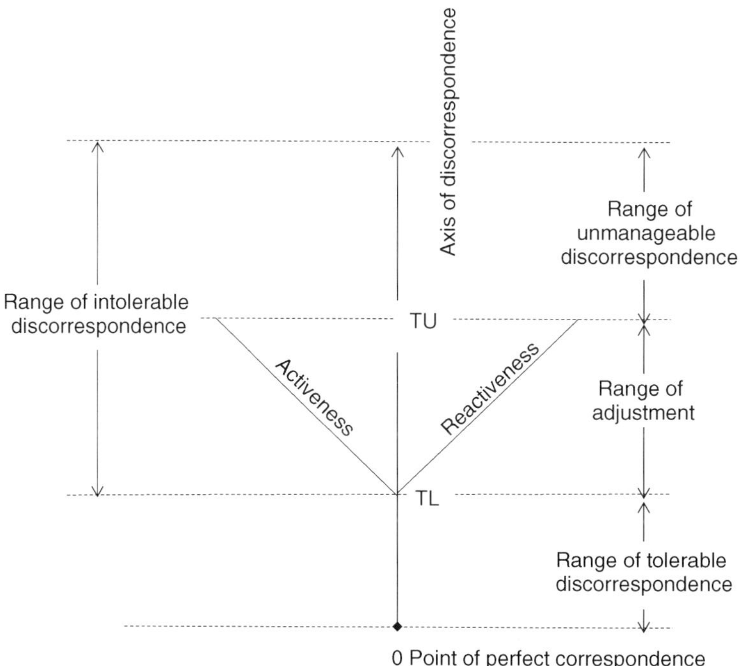

Figure 3.1 Theory of work adjustment model
Note: The theory of work adjustment model, adapted from Dawis & Lofquist, 1984, p. 64. Point 0 signifies the point of perfect correspondence between individual needs and environmental requirements. TL signifies the lower threshold up to which the discorrespondence is tolerable. TU signifies the upper threshold up to which the individual might adjust. Activeness signifies the change of the environment to support adjustment whereas reactiveness signifies changing of self (Haslberger, Brewster, & Hippler 2014).

changing the environment or by changing the individual's own behaviour. Non-correspondence that is beyond the person's flexibility and cannot be mended will lead to the individual leaving the situation or trigger a crisis (McNulty et al. 2019). TWA (Dawis & Lofquist, 1984) has influenced research on expatriate adjustment, highlighting the context-dependency of adjustment (Black & Gregersen, 1991; Haslberger & Dickmann, 2016).

Building upon P E fit, Kim's (2001) Integrative Communication Theory of Cross-cultural Adjustment stresses the importance of recognising adjustment within the poles of individual needs. The three central dimensions include the cognitive, affective, and behavioural adjustment (Kim & McKay-Semmler, 2013). This theory explains how expatriates are required to shift from their home culture towards their host-culture. Personal communication is presented as the engine that drives adjustment in the cognitive, affective, and behavioural dimensions.

Maertz, Takeuchi and Chen (2016) on the other hand offer a psychological framework that views adjustment as a change process that is driven by interaction episodes between expatriates and their hosts. It explores adjustment through different lenses, such as stress management, identity development, and learning, to arrive at an overall process model of adjustment. The model takes the perspective of the adjusting individual only, that is, in Dawis and Lofquist's (1984) terms, 'satisfaction'.

3.5 Criticisms of the Most Common Approaches and Alternative Frameworks

Each of these various theories of adjustment has been subjected to critique. Well over a decade ago, Thomas and Lazarova (2006: 248) argued that there had been an 'overwhelming focus on adjustment that is not necessarily warranted by the nature of the phenomenon itself'. Their main arguments were that such research was poorly served by existing measures (for an agreeing and more detailed review see Haslberger, Brewster, & Hippler, 2014) and that's because adjustment could not be directly connected to performance, such studies had little practical value.

The CMA, for example, has been shown to have serious shortcomings of both a theoretical and an empirical nature (Hippler, 2000; Hippler et al., 2014a; Lazarova & Thomas, 2012; Stahl & Caligiuri, 2005; Suutari & Brewster, 1999; Thomas & Lazarova, 2006) that, it seems, many current researchers just ignore in favour of the expediency of using a simple questionnaire. One particular concern is the failure of most of the research that uses these models to take account of the implications of time (Hippler et al., 2015). Presumably because of the difficulty of collecting enough data to allow the researcher to divide their sample into those who have been in the location for various periods of time, expatriates who have been there for years are conflated with expatriates who have only been there for a few weeks.

Fortunately, there are some recent conceptualisations that attempt to capture adjustment in a more comprehensive fashion (Haslberger et al. 2013; Haslberger et al., 2014; Maertz et al., 2016). Maertz et al. (2016) though, do not take into account the environmental perspective, that is, the satisfactoriness of the expatriate in the eyes of the hosts. And there have been recent efforts to measure adjustment more validly (Hippler et al., 2014b).

3.6 A Comprehensive Approach: The 3-D Model of Adjustment

If the current state of research has shown one thing, it is that past models (although convenient and easy to use) are not suitable for dealing with the complexities of adjustment, even less allowing for testable hypotheses (Hippler et al., 2015). A model recognising the situational context, dimensions, and dynamics is needed; and the 3D-Model of adjustment (Haslberger et al., 2014) is a good starting point. The three Ds of Haslberger and colleague's (2014) 3-D model of adjustment stand for dimensions, domains, and dynamics. The adjustment cube, as shown in Figure 3.2, illustrates the interaction between dimensions, domains, and time according to the findings of Lessle (2019).

The following sections will explain in detail the dimensions of adjustment, the domains in which adjustment takes place, and how dimensions and domains may influence each other by cross-over and spill-over effects. Furthermore, we will elaborate on how far time has an effect on adjustment and how the 3-D model of adjustment (Haslberger et al., 2014) accounts for time.

3.6.1 Dimensions of Adjustment

The first D refers to the cognitive, affective, and behavioural dimensions of adjustment as conceptualised by most current theories of adjustment (Haslberger et al., 2014; Hippler et al., 2015; Shaffer et al., 2006). Cognitive adjustment in the 3-D model of adjustment refers to the individual's knowledge and understanding of the new environment; affective adjustment refers to their feelings towards the situation; and behavioural adjustment describes the actions an individual takes to be effective in the new environment (Haslberger et al., 2014; Hippler et al., 2015). Historically, research examined each dimension individually (Black et al., 1991; McNulty, 2012; Shaffer

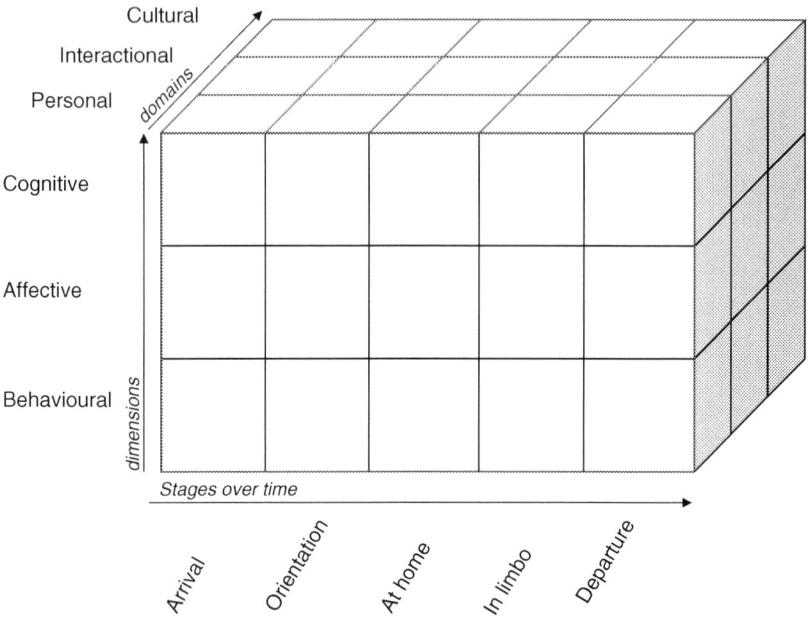

Figure 3.2 Adjustment cube
Note: The model reflects the domains and stages of adjustment, adapted from Lessle (2019).

et al., 2006). However, assessing adjustment in only one dimension allows only limited insight into the process as adjustment follows an individual trajectory in each dimension (Haslberger et al., 2014). This concept explains the mixed results of the effectiveness of antecedents on adjustment. Someone who is cognitively well adjusted but doesn't agree with the cultural values might behave completely unadjusted. A model that analyses adjustment one-dimensionally would not recognise this effect as the positive cognitive adjustment and the negative behavioural adjustment would cancel each other out.

3.6.2 Domains of Adjustment

The second D in the 3-D model of adjustment (Haslberger et al., 2014) refers to the domains or situational contexts in which an individual interacts and to which the expatriate needs to adjust.

The need to assess adjustment in individual domains was identified early on; however, researchers had diverging ideas of which specific domains are to be examined (Black et al., 1991; Haslberger et al., 2014; Hippler et al., 2014b). Haslberger et al. (2014), for example, suggested distinguishing adjustment domains by their focus such as on a macro level work and non-work domains, whereas on the micro-level the domains might include freedom of decision making or job content. They adopted the Navas et al. (2005) framework of domains that get increasingly more difficult, and less likely, for the expatriate to adjust to: regulation, work, economic systems, family relations, social relations, and their world-view (Weltanschauung). Hippler et al. (2015) on the other hand, suggested a more manageable frame of domains that proposed a distinction into economic, social, and family domains. Whichever domains are examined, one has to be aware that domains and dimensions might impact each other through spill-over and cross-over effects (Haslberger et al., 2014; Malek, Budhwar, & Reiche, 2015). Spill-over effects explain the transfer of adjustment between domains. Individuals who have positive emotions in one part of life are typically more likely to be content in other domains (Carlson et al., 2019). Cross-over effects, however, suggest the transfer between the shared domains of two individuals, for example, the expatriate and their partner (Wurtz, 2018) as illustrated in Figure 3.3.

For example, withdrawal cognitions of the expatriate might be amplified by negative cognitions of the partner. These spill-over and cross-over effects are important to consider as they make clear that adjustment needs to be researched in its complexity and domain-specific research might be misleading.

3.6.3 *Dynamics of Adjustment*

The third D of the 3-D model of adjustment refers to the dynamics of adjustment. Adjustment is a process that needs to be assessed over time (Haslberger et al., 2014; Haslberger et al., 2013; Hippler et al., 2015; Maertz et al., 2016). However, very little research has taken the dynamics of adjustment into account (Bhaskar-Shrinivas et al., 2005; Haslberger et al., 2014). The time dimension adds to the 3-D model's complexity and individual adjustment-trajectories will never be accurately predictable

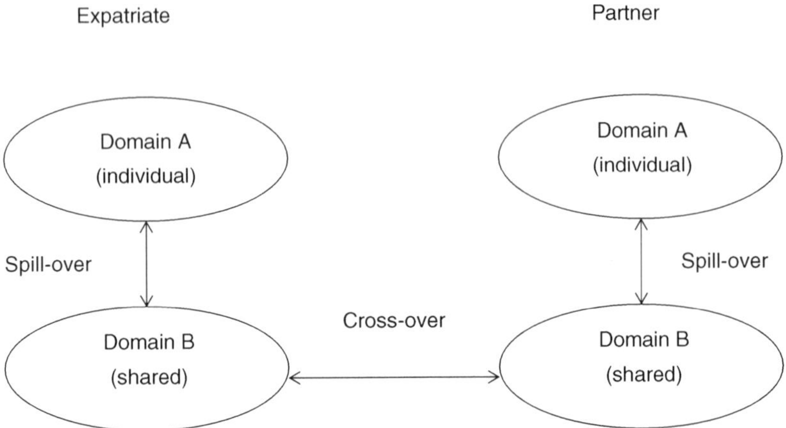

Figure 3.3 Spill-over and cross-over
Note: Spill-over effects explain the transfer of cognitions, feelings, and behaviour between the domains of one individual whereas cross-over effects explain the transfer between the shared domains of two individuals, adapted from Haslberger et al., 2014: 117.

3.7 Some Practical and Research Implications

The practical implications of better understanding of adjustment are enormous for all parties: for the expatriate and their family, for co-workers and for the organisation. If expatriates could be advised what the process of adjustment might look like, they might be able to adjust better. Appreciating how people adjust to a new country could be a value input to selection of potential expatriates (see Chapter 2).

Organisations could use expatriations more effectively to support globalisation and employee development. By making expatriation a positive experience, employees are more likely to accept foreign assignments in the future. This benefits the organisation by attracting talent and supporting strategic HRM activities such as building a global management pool. Additional supportive measures such as language training, cultural or location-specific training, home visits, and psychological support might be made more effective by aligning them with adjustment trajectories.

But to reach such a position we need better research. To obtain a current picture of the state of research on adjustment, we conducted a search of the topic in the EBSCO database. However, except for some studies conceptualising adjustment as a multidimensional phenomenon developing over time (Lessle, 2019), most research has been based on the Black et al. (1991) model. The inadequacy of which explains the inconsistent findings, as the model neither accounts for time nor examines the cognitive, affective, and behavioural dimension of adjustment individually.

3.8 Conclusions

In conclusion, we would like to emphasise two key points. First, for researchers we see it as imperative that adjustment is examined with rigour, depth and detail in order to provide valuable insights which can translate to support globally mobile workers in their adjustment. The phenomenon of expatriate adjustment has been acknowledged as critical for expatriation success for several decades. However, there is still much to do. Most of the existing studies use cross-sectional designs which neglect the fact that adjustment develops in multiple dimensions over time: most people are cognitively and behaviourally more adjusted after six months than they are after six weeks or six days. They may affectively be less adjusted after six months than after six days though, as the strain of coping with the new environment may have taken a toll on their emotional resources. Because this has been ignored, we have an abundant trove of contradictory findings with limited value to our understanding. To allow for real insights, and there is still plenty to know, research needs to accept the fact that simple models are limited. We therefore strongly encourage future researchers to abandon shortcuts in favour of valid results.

Second, we would like to encourage the assigning organisations and global mobility providers to seek a better understanding of context dependency and how adjustment develops over time to avoid unnecessary costs and failed assignments. Valuable research has started to acknowledge the need to examine context variables and expatriate communities that have been underrepresented in our research to date. Future researchers might also want to examine how far traditional global mobility concepts of moving an individual and his or her family abroad might be replaced by other forms of global collaboration especially in recognising political shifts and increasingly closed borders. It will be interesting to see how the global order has an impact on global mobility.

References

Ang, S. & Van Dyne, L. 2015. *Handbook of Cultural Intelligence*. Hoboken: Taylor and Francis.

Armstrong, S. J. & Yan, L. 2017. A study of Anglo expatriate managers' learning, knowledge acquisition, and adjustment in multinational companies in China. *Academy of Management Learning & Education*, 16(1): 1–22.

Bayraktar, S. 2019. A diary study of expatriate adjustment: collaborative mechanisms of social support. *International Journal of Cross Cultural Management*, 19(1): 47–70.

Bhaskar-Shrinivas, P., Harrison, D. A., Shaffer, M. A., & Luk, D. M. 2005. Input-based and time-based models of international adjustment: meta-analytic evidence and theoretical extensions. *Academy of Management Journal*, 48(2): 257–281.

Black, S. J. 1988. Work role transitions: a study of American expatriate managers in Japan. *Journal of International Business Studies*, 19(2): 277–294.

Black, S. J. & Gregersen, H. B. 1991. The other half of the picture: antecedents of spouse cross-cultural adjustment. *Journal of International Business Studies*, 22(3): 461–477.

Black, S. J., Mendenhall, M., & Oddou, G. 1991. Toward a comprehensive model of international adjustment: an integration of multiple theoretical perspectives. *Academy of Management Review*, 16(2): 291–317.

Bonache, J., Langinier, H. & Zárraga-Oberty, C. 2016. Antecedents and effects of host country nationals negative stereotyping of corporate expatriates. A social identity analysis. *Human Resource Management Review*, 26(1): 59–68.

Buechele, J. 2018. 'We live a life in periods': perceptions of mobility and becoming an expat spouse. *Migration Letters*, 15(1): 45–54.

Bücker, J., Furrer, O., Poutsma, E., & Buyens, D. 2014. The impact of cultural intelligence on communication effectiveness, job satisfaction and anxiety for Chinese host country managers working for foreign multinationals. *International Journal of Human Resource Management*, 25(14): 2068–2087.

Carlson, D., Kacmar, K., Thompson, M., & Andrews, M. 2019. Looking good and doing good: family to work spillover through impression management. *Journal of Managerial Psychology*, 34(1): 31–45.

Chen, Y.-P. & Shaffer, M. 2018. The influence of expatriate spouses' coping strategies on expatriate and spouse adjustment. *Journal of Global Mobility*, 6(1): 20–39.

Cho, T., Hutchings, K., & Marchant, T. 2013. Key factors influencing Korean expatriates' and spouses' perceptions of expatriation and repatriation. *International Journal of Human Resource Management*, 24(5): 1051–1075.

Church, A. T. 1982. Sojourner Adjustment. *Psychological Bulletin*, 91(3): 540–572.

Claus, L., Maletz, S., Casoinic, D., & Pierson, K. 2015. Social capital and cultural adjustment of international assignees in NGOs: do support networks really matter? *International Journal of Human Resource Management*, 26(20): 2523–2542.

Cole, N. 2011. Managing global talent: solving the spousal adjustment problem. *The International Journal of Human Resource Management*, 22(7): 1504–1530.

Dabic, M., González-Loureiro, M., & Harvey, M. G. 2015. Evolving research on expatriates: what is 'known' after four decades (1970–2012). *International Journal of Human Resource Management*, 26(3): 316–337.

David, K. H. 1972. *Intercultural Adjustment and Applications of Reinforcement Theory to Problems of 'Culture Dhock'*. Hilo: Center for Cross-Cultural Training and Research. University of Hawaii at Hilo.

Davies, S., Kraeh, A., & Froese, F. 2015. Burden or support? The influence of partner nationality on expatriate cross-cultural adjustment. *Journal of Global Mobility*, 3(2): 169–182.

Dawis, R. V. & Lofquist, L. H. 1984. *A Psychological Theory of Work Adjustment*. Minneapolis: University of Minnesota Press.

Dickmann, M., Suutari, V., Brewster, C., Mäkelä, L., Tanskanen, J. & Tornikoski, C. 2016. The career competencies of self-initiated and assigned expatriates: assessing the development of career capital over time. *International Journal of Human Resource Management*, 29(16): 2353–2371.

Fisher, K., Hutchings, K., & Pinto, L. H. 2015. Pioneers across war zones: the lived acculturation experiences of US female military expatriates. *International Journal of Intercultural Relations*, 49(Supplement C): 265–277.

Fu, J., Morris, M. W., & Hong, Y. 2015. A transformative taste of home: home culture primes foster expatriates' adjustment through bolstering relational security. *Journal of Experimental Social Psychology*, 59: 24–31.

Gullahorn, J. T. & Gullahorn, J. E. 1963. An extension of the U-curve hypothesis. *Journal of Social Issues*, 19(3): 33–47.

Gupta, R., Banerjee, P., & Gaur, J. 2012. Exploring the role of the spouse in expatriate failure: a grounded theory-based investigation of expatriate' spouse adjustment issues from India. *International Journal of Human Resource Management*, 23(17): 3559–3577.

Haak-Saheem, W. & Brewster, C. 2017. 'Hidden' expatriates: international mobility in the United Arab Emirates as a challenge to current understanding of expatriation. *Human Resource Management Journal*, 27(3): 423–439.

Haslberger, A. & Brewster, C. 2008. The expatriate family: an international perspective. *Journal of Managerial Psychology*, 23(3): 324–346.

Haslberger, A., Brewster, C., & Hippler, T. 2013. The dimensions of expatriate adjustment. *Human Resource Management*, 52(3): 333–351.

Haslberger, A., Brewster, C., & Hippler, T. 2014. *Managing Performance Abroad: A New Model for Understanding Expatriate Adjustment*. London: Routledge.

Haslberger, A. & Dickmann, M. 2016. The correspondence model of cross-cultural adjustment: exploring exchange relationships. *Journal of Global Mobility*, 4(3): 276–299.

Harari, M. B., Reaves, A. C., Beane, D. A., Laginess, A. J., & Viswesvaran, C. 2018. Personality and expatriate adjustment: a meta analysis. *Journal of Occupational & Organisational Psychology*, 91(3): 486–517.

Hechanova, R., Beehr, T. A., & Christiansen, N. D. 2003. Antecedents and consequences of employees' adjustment to overseas assignment: a meta–analytic review. *Applied Psychology: An International Review*, 52(2): 213–236.

Hemmasi, M., Downes, M., & Varner, I. I. 2010. An empirically-derived multidimensional measure of expatriate success: reconciling the discord. *International Journal of Human Resource Management*, 21(7): 982–998.

Hemmasi, M. & Downes, M. 2013. Cultural distance and expatriate adjustment revisited. *Journal of Global Mobility*, 1(1): 72–91.

Hippler, T. 2000. European assignments: international or quasi-domestic? *Journal of European Industrial Training*, 24(9): 491–504.

Hippler, T., Caligiuri, P., & Johnson, J. 2014a. Revisiting the construct of expatriate adjustment – implications for theory and measurement. *International Studies of Management & Organisation*, 44(3): 8–24.

Hippler, T., Caligiuri, P. M., Johnson, J. E., & Baytalskaya, N. 2014b. The development and validation of a theory-based expatriate adjustment scale. *International Journal of Human Resource Management*, 25(14): 1938–1959.

Hippler, T., Brewster, C., & Haslberger, A. 2015. The elephant in the room: the role of time in expatriate adjustment. *International Journal of Human Resource Management*, 26(15): 1920–1935.

Jackson, D. & Manderscheid, S. V. 2015. A phenomenological study of Western expatriates' adjustment to Saudi Arabia. *Human Resource Development International*, 18(2): 131–152.

Jing, Z., Wanberg, C. R., Harrison, D. A., Diehn, E. W., & Zhu, J. 2016. Ups and downs of the expatriate experience? Understanding work adjustment trajectories and career outcomes. *Journal of Applied Psychology*, 101(4): 549–568.

Kang, H. & Shen, J. 2018. Antecedents and consequences of host-country nationals' attitudes and behaviors toward expatriates: what we do and do not know. *Human Resource Management Review*, 28(2): 164–175.

Kim, Y. Y. 2001. *Intercultural Transformation. On becoming Intercultural: An Integrative Theory of Communication and Cross-cultural Adaptation*: 183–200. Thousand Oaks: Sage.

Kim, Y. Y. & Ruben, B. D. 1988. Intercultural transformation – A systems theory. In Y. Y. Kim & W. B. Gudykunst (eds.), *Theories in Intercultural Communication*: 299–321. Newbury Park: Sage.

Kim, Y. Y. & McKay-Semmler, K. 2013. Social engagement and cross-cultural adaptation: an examination of direct- and mediated interpersonal communication activities of educated non-natives in the United States. *International Journal of Intercultural Relation*, 37: 99–112.

Krishnaveni, R. & Arthi, R. 2015. An overview of multidimensional factors influencing effective performance of expatriates. *Management: Journal of Contemporary Management Issues*, 20(2): 135–147.

Lazarova, M. B. & Thomas, D. C. 2012. Expatriate adjustment and performance revisited. In G. K. Stahl, I. Björkman, & S. Morris (eds.), *Handbook of Research in International Human Resource Management*: 271–292. Cheltenham: Edward Elgar.

Lazarova, M., Westman, M., & Shaffer, M. A. 2010. Elucidating the positive side of the work-family interface on international assignments: a model of expatriate work and family performance. *Academy of Management Review*, 35(1): 93–117.

Lessle, A. D. 2019. *The Cognitive, Affective, and Behavioral Adjustment of Expatriate Spouses. A case study*. PhD dissertation, Grand Canyon University, Phoenix AZ. Available from ProQuest Dissertations and Theses database.

Lofquist, L. H. & Dawis, R. V. 1991. *Essentials of Person-Environment-Correspondence Counseling*. Minneapolis: University of Minnesota Press.

Lorenz, M. P., Ramsey, J. R., & Richey, R. G. 2018. Expatriates' international opportunity recognition and innovativeness: the role of metacognitive and cognitive cultural intelligence. *Journal of World Business*, 53(2): 222–236.

Lundstedt, S. 1963. An introduction to some evolving problems in cross-cultural research. *Journal of Social Issues*, 19(3): 1–9.

Lysgaard, S. 1955. Adjustment in a foreign society: Norwegian Fulbright grantees visiting the United States. *International Social Science Bulletin*, 7 (1): 45–51.

Mahajan, A. & Toh, S. M. 2014. Facilitating expatriate adjustment: the role of advice-seeking from host country nationals. *Journal of World Business*, 49(4): 476–487.

Maertz, C. P., Takeuchi, R., & Chen, J. 2016. An episodic framework of outgroup interaction processing: integration and redirection for the expatriate adjustment research. *Psychological Bulletin*, 142(6): 623–654.

Malek, A. M., Budhwar, P., & Reiche, S. B. 2015. Sources of support and expatriation: a multiple stakeholder perspective of expatriate adjustment and performance in Malaysia. *International Journal of Human Resource Management*, 26(2): 258–276.

Mao, J. & Y. Shen 2015. Cultural identity change in expatriates: a social network perspective. *Human Relations*, 68(10): 1533–1556.

Mayrhofer, W. & Brewster, C. 1996. In Praise of Ethnocentricity: expatriate policies in European multinationals *International Executive*, 38(6): 749–778.

McNulty, Y. 2012. 'Being dumped in to sink or swim': an empirical study of organisational support for the trailing spouse. *Human Resource Development International*, 15(4): 417–434.

McNulty, Y. & De Cieri, H. D. 2013. Measuring expatriate return on investment with an evaluation framework. *Global Business & Organisational Excellence*, 32(6): 18–26.

McNulty, Y., Lauring, J., Jonasson, C., & Jan, S. 2019. Highway to hell? Managing expatriates in crisis. *Journal of Global Mobility*. 10.1108/JGM-10–2018–0054.

McPhail, R. & McNulty, Y. 2015, 'Oh, the places you won't go as an LGBT expat!' A study of HRM's duty of care to lesbian, gay, bisexual and transgender expatriates in dangerous locations. *European Journal of International Management*, 9(6): 737–765.

McPhail, R., Fisher, R., Harvey, M. G., & Moeller, M. 2012. Staffing the global organisation: 'Cultural nomads'. *Human Resource Development Quarterly*, 23(2): 259–276.

Moon, H. K., Choi, B. K., & Jung, J. S. 2012. Previous international experience, cross-cultural training, and expatriates' cross-cultural adjustment: effects of cultural intelligence and goal orientation. *Human Resource Development Quarterly*, 23(3): 285–330.

Navas, M., Garcia, M. C., Sánchez, J., Rojas, A. J., Pumares, P., & Fernández, J. S. 2005. Relative Acculturation Extended Model (RAEM): new contributions with regard to the study of acculturation. *International Journal of Intercultural Relations*, 29: 21–37.

Nowak, C. & Linder, C. 2016. Do you know how much your expatriate costs? An activity-based cost analysis of expatriation. *Journal of Global Mobility*, 4(1): 88–107.

Oberg, K. 1960. Cultural shock: adjustment to new cultural environments. *Practical Anthropology*, 7(4): 177–182.

Peltokorpi, V. & Froese, F. 2014. Expatriate personality and cultural fit: the moderating role of host country context on job satisfaction. *International Business Review*, 23(1): 293–302.

Presbitero, A. & Quita, C. 2017. Expatriate career intentions: links to career adaptability and cultural intelligence. *Journal of Vocational Behavior*, 98: 118–126.

Ramaswami, A., Carter, N. M., & Dreher, G. F. 2016. Expatriation and career success: a human capital perspective. *Human Relations*, 69(10): 1959–1987.

Ravasi, C., Salamin, X., & Davoine, E. 2015. Cross-cultural adjustment of skilled migrants in a multicultural and multilingual environment: an explorative study of foreign employees and their spouses in the Swiss context. *International Journal of Human Resource Management*, 26(10): 1335–1359.

Richardson, C. & Wong, H.-W. 2018. Expatriate academics in Malaysia: motivation, adjustment, and retention. *Journal of Management Development*, 37(3): 299–308.

Ritchie, W., Brantley, B. I., Pattie, M., Swanson, B., & Logsdon, J. 2015. Expatriate Cultural Antecedents and Outcomes. *Nonprofit Management & Leadership*, 25(3): 325–342.

Rosenbusch, K. & Cseh, M. 2012. The cross-cultural adjustment process of expatriate families in a multinational organisation: a family system theory perspective. *Human Resource Development International*, 15(1): 61–77.

Rosenbusch, K., Cerny II, L. J., & Earnest, D. R. 2015. The impact of stressors during international assignments. *Cross Cultural Management*, 22(3): 405–430.

Salamin, X. & Davoine, E. 2015. International adjustment of female vs male business expatriates. A replication study in Switzerland. *Journal of Global Mobility*, 3(2): 183–212.

Schütz, A. 1944. The stranger: an essay in social psychology. *American Journal of Sociology*, 49(6): 499–507.

Schütz, A. 1945. The homecomer. *American Journal of Sociology*, 50(5): 369–376.

Shaffer, M. A., Harrison, D. A., Gregersen, H. B., Black, S. J., & Ferzandi, L. A. 2006. You can take it with you: individual differences and expatriate effectiveness. *Journal of Applied Psychology*, 91(1): 109–125.

Shortland, S. 2016. The purpose of expatriation: why women undertake international assignments. *Human Resource Management*, 55(4): 655–678.

Sousa, C., Gonçalves, G., Santos, J., & Leitão, J. 2017. Organisational practices for the expatriates' adjustment: a systematic review. *Journal of Global Mobility*, 5(3): 251–274.

Stahl, G. K. & Caligiuri, P. M. 2005. The effectiveness of expatriate coping strategies: the moderating role of cultural distance, position level, and time on the international assignment. *Journal of Applied Psychology*, 90(4): 603–615.

Suutari, V. & Brewster, C. 1999. International assignments across European borders: no problems? In C. J. Brewster & H. Harris (eds.), *International Human Resource Management: Contemporary Issues in Europe*: 183–202. London: Routledge.

Suutari, V., Brewster, C., Mäkelä, L., Dickmann, M., & Tornikoski, C. 2017. The effect of international work experience on the career success of expatriates: a comparison of assigned and self-initiated expatriates. *Human Resource Management*, 57(1): 37–54.

Suutari, V., Tornikoski, C., & Mäkelä, L. 2012. Career decision making of global careerists. *International Journal of Human Resource Management*, 23(15–16): 3455–3478.

Takeuchi, R. 2010. A critical review of expatriate adjustment research through a multiple stakeholder view: progress, emerging trends, and prospects. *Journal of Management*, 36(4): 1040–1064.

Teague, J. 2015. Corporate preparation for the cross-cultural adaptation experience of the accompanying expatriate spouse. *Journal of International Business Research*, 14(2): 139–151.

Thomas, D. C. & M. Lazarova 2006. Expatriate adjustment and performance: a critical review. In G. K. Stahl & I. Bjorkman (eds.), *Handbook of Research in International Human Resource Management*. G. K. Cheltenham: Edward Elgar.

van Erp, K. J., van der Zee, K. I., Giebels, E., & van Duijn, M. A. 2014. Lean on me: the importance of one's own and partner's intercultural personality for expatriate's and expatriate spouse's successful adjustment abroad. *European Journal of Work and Organisational Psychology*, 23(5): 706–728.

Wang, X. 2002. Expatriate adjustment from a social network perspective: theoretical examination and a conceptual model. *International Journal of Cross-Cultural Management*, 2(3): 321–337.

Ward, C. & Searle, W. 1991. The impact of value discrepancies and cultural identity on psychological and sociocultural adjustment of sojourners. *International Journal of Intercultural Relations*, 22(3): 209–224.

Ward, C., Leong, C., & Low, M. 2004. Personality and sojourner adjustment: an exploration of the Big Five and the cultural fit proposition. *Journal of Cross-Cultural Psychology*, 35(137): 137–151.DOI:10.1177/0022022103260719.

Ward, C., Bochner, S., & Furnham, A. 2001. *The Psychology of Culture Shock* (2nd ed.). London: Routledge.

Waxin, M.-F., Brewster, C., Ashill, N., & Chandon, J. 2017. Antecedents of expatriates' time to proficiency; does home country culture have an effect? *Journal of Developing Areas*, 50(4): 401–422.

Wechtler, H. 2015. Cross-cultural adjustment of female self-initiated expatriates: a longitudinal diary study. *Academy of Management Annual Meeting Proceedings, 2015*(1).

Wechtler, H., Koveshnikov, A., & Dejoux, C. 2017. Career Anchors and Cross-Cultural Adjustment Among Expatriates in a Non-Profit Organisation. *Management International Review (MIR)*, 57(2): 277–305.

Wu, P. & Ang, S. 2011. The impact of expatriate supporting practices and cultural intelligence on cross-cultural adjustment and performance of expatriate in Singapore. *International Journal of Human Resource Management*, 22(13): 2683–2702.

Wurtz, O. 2018. Expatriation, alcohol and drugs: antecedents and consequences of substance use in expatriation. *Journal of Global Mobility*, 6 (3/4): 16–334.

Zhu, J., Wanberg, C. R., Harrison, D. A., & Diehn, E. W. 2016. Ups and downs of the expatriate experience? Understanding work adjustment trajectories and career outcomes. *Journal of Applied Psychology*, 101(4): 549–568.

Zimmermann, J. & Neyer, F. J. 2013. Do we become a different person when hitting the road? Personality development of sojourners. *Journal of Personality & Social Psychology*, 105(3): 515–530.

4 *Performance Management for Expatriates*

ARUP VARMA, CHUN-HSIAO WANG, PAWAN S. BUDHWAR

4.1 Introduction

In a recent article summarizing 100 years of research in performance appraisal and performance management, DeNisi and Murphy (2017) make a rather pertinent observation – that performance appraisal and performance management are related but different. They further clarify that while performance appraisal specifically refers to the periodic evaluation of an employee's performance, performance management refers to a whole range of activities designed to help manage an employee's performance, such as goal setting, feedback, and training (see, e.g., Varma, Budhwar, & McCusker, 2014; Varma & Tung, 2020).

This distinction between performance management and performance appraisal is critical, as one of the reasons many organisations fail to do a good job of managing employee performance is that they believe that conducting annual (or semi-annual) evaluations is sufficient. Through performance appraisal, an organisation is able to determine the degree to which an employee is successfully meeting his or her assigned objectives successfully. In other words, a proper performance appraisal process is often the only means to determine whether an organisation strategy is succeeding to the degree which the organisation desires (Schuler & Jackson, 1987). As such, it is critical that each employee's performance is evaluated on a regular basis. In addition to letting the organisation know how well an employee is doing, an effective performance appraisal process would also be equipped to let employees know how they are doing on the job and whether they need to change course. However, as is obvious, a number of activities need to happen before and after the actual appraisal.

As an example, in order to evaluate employee performance, supervisors should provide specific objectives at the beginning of the evaluation period, followed by any relevant and necessary training or guidance. In order to develop an appraisal instrument and select the appropriate dimensions for each job, organisations must conduct job analyses (see, e.g., DeNisi & Gonzalez, 2017) and assess the required KSAOs (knowledge, skills, abilities, and other characteristics required to perform the job successfully) for each job. Once job descriptions are developed from the job analyses, organisations must then develop standards so that employees know, or at least have a very good idea of, how their performance will be evaluated. In other words, if an organisation wants to enable and empower employees to do their best, they must communicate to employees what would constitute (1) acceptable performance, (2) unacceptable performance, and (3) outstanding performance (see, e.g., Bobko & Colella, 1994). Next, organisations must set short- and long-term goals in consultation with all employees so that the employees can clearly understand what is expected and plan their performance accordingly. As noted earlier, it is critical that organisations provide appropriate and timely training so that employees are fully equipped to do their jobs. Once an employee is on the job, he/she needs to have access to his/her supervisor in order to clarify any doubt or to seek guidance. Clearly, a lot goes into getting an employee ready for his/her assignment.

4.2 Expatriate Performance Management Systems

In the case of expatriates, the process of managing performance becomes even more complex and critical, given that expatriates typically operate at locations far from headquarters and will not have access to a supervisor as easily as domestic employees have (Varma, Budhwar, & Yu, 2018). In addition, the contextual realities of the host location can further complicate an expatriate's ability to do his/her job (see, e.g., Toh & DeNisi, 2007). From having to deal with living in a new country, new rules, new norms, new colleagues, and a new way of doing work, expatriates also have to deal with numerous issues outside of the workplace (e.g., see the three dimensions of expatriate adjustment by Black, Mendenhall, & Odour, 1991). These could include searching for the right school for their children, for a good neighbourhood to live in, and for social and cultural activities for themselves and their families. Not surprisingly, many scholars have argued that adjustment to the new location is a critical determinant of individual performance (see, e.g., Silbiger et al., 2017). These authors report that expatriate work adjustment at the host location leads to lower withdrawal cognitions and burnout, and higher job satisfaction. In other words, the sooner an expatriate feels adjusted at the new host location, the sooner he/she will be able to dedicate his/her time and energies to work and productivity, and the lower the chances the expatriate will withdraw from the assignment – a key concern for organisations that assign expatriates to various global locations. In the following section, we discuss unique elements of expatriate performance management. This is followed by a detailed discussion of an over-arching seven-factor model of a performance management system (PMS) specifically for expatriate assignments.

4.2.1 Unique Elements of an Expatriate PMS

4.2.1.1 Soft Skills vs. Hard Skills in a PMS

Several scholars have argued that the soft skills involved in an expatriate assignment can be much more critical in determining potential success than the hard skills (Fee, McGrath-Champ, & Yang, 2011). In other words, having technical knowledge and being able to meet targets is necessary, but not sufficient. For example, studies have found expatriate tasks and contextual performance to be distinct and have different neurological bases (e.g., Kraimer, Wayne, & Jaworski, 2001; Malek & Budhwar, 2013). Moreover, in a sample of several multinational hotel companies, Shay and Tracey (2009) found that expatriate managers' role in innovation (e.g., making significant changes in how a job is carried out) is positively related to local subordinates' satisfaction with the expatriates. An expatriate must also successfully adjust to the new location to perform efficiently in the new cultural and social context. The flip side of this equation is that simply evaluating expatriates based on traditional KPIs (key performance indicators) would be rather unfair, only capturing a part of his/her contextual reality. As Deming (1986) notes, an individual's performance must be evaluated in the context of his/her contextual realities, making allowances and adjustments for what he calls 'system factors', or factors beyond an individual's control.

4.2.1.2 Adapting vs. Developing PMSs for Expatriates

A review of the relevant literature (see, e.g., Kang & Shen, 2016; Suutari & Tahvanainen, 2002; Tahvanainen, 2000) shows that most organisations that assign expatriates to their various global locations do not develop dedicated PMSs for expatriates. Instead, they simply adapt or adopt existing PMSs (often just performance appraisal systems) developed at their home location. As part of his Fulbright project in 2018, the first author spent six months in India meeting with 62 senior executives of multinational enterprises (MNEs). He was specifically interested in understanding how these MNEs, headquartered in different parts of the world, managed expatriate performance. In almost every case, he found that the MNEs simply used existing PMSs or performance appraisal systems to manage/evaluate expatriates working in India (see also Varma, Budhwar, & Singh, 2015).

When asked why these organisations had not spent the time or resources to develop dedicated performance appraisal systems or processes for expatriates, the most common responses offered were (1) the expatriates would only be there for a limited, specified period, and (2) the expatriates were being compensated handsomely for any hardships they may face while on assignment. We believe this is a critical finding which needs further discussion. After all, additional monetary compensation cannot account for the contextual realities or roadblocks experienced by expatriates on assignment. For example, an expatriate who is unable to make connections at his/her new location because local colleagues did not help make those connections would be unable to meet targets on time. This could result in feeling frustration and could potentially result in the expatriate withdrawing from the assignment. In such a case, simply evaluating the expatriate on his/her ability (or inability) to meet targets would be counter-productive, at best.

Indeed, given that expatriate assignments are performed under unique contexts and can cost organisations huge amounts of money, it is critical that organisations measure the return on investment (Nowak & Linder, 2016). As noted above, an organisation cannot conduct an effective performance appraisal without having a corresponding PMS (Suutari & Tahvanainen, 2002; Tung & Varma, 2008; Varma & Budhwar, 2020), that incorporates all relevant features – e.g., goal setting, training, feedback. Thus, it is critical that MNEs develop and implement dedicated PMSs for expatriates, to ensure that expatriates clearly understand what is expected of them along with related boundary conditions such as deadlines, cost restrictions, and the like.

4.2.1.3 Type of Performance and Role Clarity

Next, organisations must take into account both technical and contextual performance. They must also ensure that the expatriate's individual performance is linked to his/her career goals and that the goals of the expatriate's individual assignment are aligned with the organisation's strategic goals (e.g., Martin & Bartol, 2003). Regarding this connection, scholars (e.g., Aycan, 1997; Selmer & Fenner, 2009; Tung & Varma, 2008; Varma & Tung, 2020) have argued that given their unique situation (e.g., distance from home location), expatriates should be provided with high levels of 'role clarity' and their evaluations and rewards should be directly determined by their performance on tasks. This would ensure little to no confusion about expectations, otherwise they may experience difficulties with adjustment and demonstrate lower levels of commitment to assignments (see Kraimer & Wayne, 2004).

In addition to evaluating an expatriate's performance for a specific period under review, it is important that the developmental aspect of an individual's performance is also evaluated (Wang & Varma, 2019). Indeed, scholars (see, e.g., Mezias & Scandura, 2005) have argued that expatriates have 'different needs across different assignment stages' and thus should be provided with both home and host country mentors to help facilitate their adjustment and performance, as confirmed by empirical evidence (also see, e.g., Carraher, Sullivan, & Crocitto, 2008; Feldman & Bolino, 1999).

4.2.1.4 Knowledge Transfer

MNEs have traditionally used expatriate assignments to engage in one-way knowledge transfer to ensure that the headquarters' perspective is fully implemented in host countries. Increasingly, MNEs are using expatriate assignments to engage in *two-way* knowledge transfer between headquarters and host countries to ensure that the organisation as a whole benefits from having *multiple* perspectives. This multiple perspectives framework (Caligiuri & Bonache, 2016) argues that, as the nature of the global business environment grows increasingly uncertain and dynamic, researchers and practitioners need to pivot from a headquarters-centered ethnocentric perspective to an organisational-strategic perspective. Here, MNEs place greater emphasis on (1) local responsiveness (i.e., differentiation of products and services to suit local preferences), (2) global integration (i.e., taking advantage of different national factors of production), (3) innovation, and (4) a learning organisation (i.e., encouraging separate units to learn from each other). Indeed, scholars (e.g., Chang, Gong, & Peng, 2012; Kawai & Chung, 2019) have also emphasized the critical role played by expatriates in knowledge transfer and creation in MNEs. Thus, for the performance management of expatriates, MNEs would once again need to focus on both hard and soft elements of expatriate performance. More specifically, an expatriate would need to build a trusting relationship with host country nationals (HCNs) for them to see him/her as a reliable source of knowledge (the soft side of knowledge transfer). Once the expatriate has been able to establish a trusting relationship with HCNs, he/she can proceed to share knowledge (the hard side of knowledge transfer). Such a relationship between trust-in-expatriate and HCNs' willingness to share knowledge with expatriates has been verified by Toh and Srinivas (2012). Here, the expatriate must also ensure that the knowledge being transferred is relevant, timely, and applicable to each individual HCN's assignment.

4.2.1.5 Long-term Talent Management

According to the literature, most MNEs treat expatriation with a short-term perspective, whereby employees are sent to overseas units to fill skill gaps, rather than thinking of expatriation as a means to develop employees for long-term organisational needs. Indeed, scholars (see, e.g., Cerdin & Brewster, 2014) have specifically noted that the concepts of expatriation and talent management have mostly been considered separately in both research and practice. However, we argue it is critical that the developmental aspect of expatriate assignments be given utmost priority, as most expatriates are typically being prepared for additional future expatriate assignments or more senior roles. Indeed, the performance criteria of expatriate assignments should be tailored to long-term individual developmental needs (Wang & Varma, 2019). Further, supervisors and coworkers should provide constructive and instructional feedback for expatriates to learn from their behaviours. As such, performance criteria should also include more developmental elements such as intercultural skills and social capital building. For instance, Vance et al. (2014) suggest that HCNs become expatriates' trainers and mentors both for the local operation and for beyond repatriation.

4.2.1.6 Prior International Experience

It is critical that the possible confounding effects of international experience in expatriate performance management be acknowledged and accounted for when managing expatriate performance, as there are bound to be significant differences in the performance of expatriates depending on prior international experience (Takeuchi et al., 2005). In other words, expatriates who have had prior international experience will bring this to bear in their current assignment – and this could play itself out in various ways due to differences in prior experience. Factors that could impact future performance include, but are not limited to, (1) length of prior international experience(s), (2) number of prior international postings, (3) the degree to which the expatriate felt prior stints were successful, and (4) the level of difficulty experienced by the expatriate in previous international assignments.

Making this connection, Zhu et al. (2016) find that those with greater levels of previous international experience had higher levels of adjustment to new assignments within the first six months, thereby allowing them to become productive much sooner than those with fewer previous international experiences. Hippler, Brewster, and Haslberger (2015) discuss a U-curve adjustment framework, which reminds managers and HR departments that the most fair and suitable timing to evaluate expatriates should be based on prior experience and current adjustment rather than being based on a blanket date for all.

4.2.1.7 The Impact of Cultural Distance

In connection with expatriate experiences, the notion of cultural distance has gained currency, as cultural differences seem to be a huge stumbling block in many an international venture. When it comes to PMSs, once again, it is critical that organisations make adjustments for the potential impact of cultural distance between home country and host country. For example, individuals from individualistic countries such as the USA would be much more likely to expect and react well to individual rewards than those from collectivistic countries such as Japan or Korea (Kim, Park, & Suzuki, 1990). Similarly, individuals from countries like China are much more likely to be receptive to group-focused feedback (Van de Vliert et al., 2004) than individuals from individualistic countries, who would prefer individual-focused feedback. Accordingly, PMSs for expatriates should be designed to make allowances and adjustments for differences between home and host country. More specifically, it is quite likely that the expatriate and his/her host country manager and colleagues define the concept of work and achievement in different terms, creating situations where the same level and quality of work may be interpreted and evaluated differently (see, e.g., Kossek et al., 2017).

4.2.1.8 Supervisor-subordinate Relationships

One topic that rarely finds mention in performance management systems, yet has a significant impact on the process and outcome of expatriate assignments, is the relationship an individual develops with his/her supervisor. Indeed, this relationship can often determine the individual's overall workplace experience. The leader–member exchange theory (Graen & Uhl-Bien, 1995) studies this relationship in great detail and argues that supervisor-subordinate relationships are not static nor of the same quality. Indeed, supervisors may form differential quality relationships with different subordinates based on personal characteristics of the subordinates such as race, gender, age, etc. When it comes to expatriate assignments, the nuances of these relationships can get further complicated, especially as the supervisor and the subordinate in these dyads most likely hail from different countries.

In order to ensure that the elements noted previously are incorporated into expatriate PMSs and both individual and organisational objectives are paid due attention, we present below a seven-factor overarching model that can be used by MNEs to design, develop, and implement PMSs for their expatriates.

4.2.2 The Seven-Factor Model of Expatriate PMS

In their thesis on a strategic contingency approach to expatriate assignment management, Caligiuri and Colakoglu (2007) identify seven overarching factors (see Figure 4.1) which are essential to developing effective PMSs for expatriates. Wang and Varma (2019) test these seven factors in their comprehensive study of expatriate performance management in Taiwan, and find support for these factors. We discuss each of these seven factors in the coming sections in some detail and provide examples.

Figure 4.1 The seven-factor model of expatriate PMS (Source: Caligiuri & Colakoglu, 2007)

4.2.2.1 Accurately Capture the Strengths and Developmental Areas of Expatriate Assignees

In essence, an organisation's PMS must clearly and accurately capture an individual expatriate's strengths and areas for development. Given that expatriates move to organisations' global locations to perform specific tasks or assignments which are usually time-bound, it is critical that the organisation properly define the job's scope and required KSAOs and match the expatriate for the assignment based on their strengths and areas for development. Failure to do so would result in a situation whereby the expatriate is unable to achieve his/her goals because he/she lacks the KSAOs required for successful completion of the task/assignment. For example, if the specific assignment requires the expatriate to coordinate with government departments in a new country, he/she must have demonstrated the ability to build relationships and make friends as one of his/her strengths. On the other hand, if the individual expatriate needs language training (areas for development) but is sent to the location without the requisite training, he/she would be unable to communicate in the host country's language beyond basic greetings. Thus, logically, his or her negotiation skills may not be up to task, as he/she would be unable to communicate in the local language, let alone negotiate. Given the time pressures and expected return on investment on expatriate assignments, it is absolutely critical that the strengths and areas for development are assessed (and training provided) before an expatriate begins an assignment and at regular intervals throughout the assignment as necessary.

4.2.2.2 Offer Opportunities for Returning Expatriates to Use Knowledge and Skills Learned on Assignment

One major issue with expatriation has been that expatriates often have no job to go back to, or are assigned to inappropriate jobs when they return from the expatriate assignment. Ironically, in many cases, expatriates are promised unrealistic future assignments to convince them to accept the assignment overseas (Bossard & Peterson, 2005). Very often the expatriate suffers from the 'out of sight out of mind' syndrome whereby once he/she leaves for assignment, the emphasis shifts to ensuring that they do a good job while on assignment. Not surprisingly, when expatriates do a good job, the chances that their assignment will be extended increase, either at the same location or to another similar assignment. In most cases, an expatriate who is doing a good job is not likely able to come back to their home base immediately upon completion of the first assignment. This prevents the expatriate from sharing the knowledge he/she has acquired at the host country with colleagues and superiors at home.

In cases where expatriates do return to their home location after the completion of an assignment, it is critical that the organisation provide opportunities for them to practice and/or implement any knowledge and skills acquired while on the expatriate assignment (Ren et al., 2013). Sadly, very often they are either put back in the same job that they left (sometimes with a change in title), or promoted without specific attention to their need to practice newly acquired skills. Not surprisingly, many expatriates leave the organisation upon return or join a competitor at the host location. As a result, it is critical that a dedicated career path be designed and implemented for each expatriate, depending on his/her specific assignment (Cerdin & Brewster, 2014).

4.2.2.3 Establish Mentoring Relationships between Expatriates and Executives from the Host Organisation

As several scholars (e.g., Toh & DeNisi, 2007) have argued, expatriates need help from HCNs in order to successfully adjust and perform at new locations. Indeed, Varma has studied HCN-expatriate interactions in various countries (see, e.g., Varma, Toh, & Budhwar, 2006; Varma et al., 2016), and argues that expatriates require information from HCNs both inside and outside the office. Further, these authors argue that expatriates who receive relevant support adjust and perform much more quickly and efficiently than those who do not receive support. Specifically, outside the workplace, expatriates often need help and guidance adjusting into the local community, including finding the right neighbourhoods to live in and identifying schools and hospitals as necessary. At the workplace, expatriates often require help understanding and interpreting both written and unwritten rules and norms that are accepted in the new location. While most research examining HCN support of expatriates has emphasized the role of HCNs as expatriates' peers, there has been increasing interest in analysing the help that expatriates receive from HCNs at different levels, that is, from supervisors and/or subordinates. Indeed, research on the role of social networks (e.g., Liu & Shaffer, 2005) in expatriation has argued that the supervisors' mentoring relationship can be critical in helping expatriates adjust to a new location and perform assignments successfully (see also Varma, Tallapragada, & Shi, 2019).

While HCN peers can provide information on how to behave appropriately, the host country national supervisor can play the role of a mentor and guide expatriates in a rather different fashion. As a mentor, the HCN supervisor or a HCN coworker assigned this task can take on the dual roles of guide and protector. This can go a long way in helping the expatriate adjust and successfully navigate the new location (Vance, et al., 2014).

4.2.2.4 Align Incentives with Expatriate Assignment Objectives

An interesting reality of an expatriate assignment is that not everyone who is qualified to do an expected job is always willing to go on an expatriate assignment (Wang, 2018). This might be because of the individual's family or personal situation or, at other times, the location itself. For example, an expatriate may go to a first-world location willingly, but have reservations about going on assignment to a third-world country or a hardship location. What is clear is that organisations cannot select expatriates based on an individual's willingness to go on assignment – rather, the individual sent on assignment must be qualified, willing, and a good fit for the role. In many such cases, the organisation has to resort to offering incentives to get qualified expatriates to agree to go on assignment. What is important here is that the incentives offered are aligned with the goals of the assignment. This helps ensure that the organisation's strategic objectives are implemented and that the expatriate's performance is geared towards the organisation's strategic objectives. As an example, if an expatriate is being sent to a new location to set up production facilities (e.g., the expatriate must have the production rolling within six months of arriving at the new location), the incentives must be based on this critical factor, with a bonus built in for every day that production begins before the deadline. On the other hand, if the incentive is based simply on how long he/she stays at the new location, the expatriate may be inclined to delay the launch of production at the facility that he/she is setting up.

4.2.2.5 The Performance Goals of Expatriate Assignments Must Be Clearly Understood by the Expatriates

For any assignment, it is important that the employee clearly understands what is expected of him/her, as this helps the individual to perform accordingly and to ask for help if needed. When it comes to expatriate assignments this becomes much more critical, as in this case the expatriate may not have immediate access to someone who can explain the requirements of the assignment once they've begun. Given the cost of expatriate assignments, any time spent trying to understand the assignment while already on the job can prove to be extremely expensive for the organisation. Furthermore, any time the expatriate spends at the new location without being able to perform because the objectives are unclear is not just time lost – the delay could have severe repercussions on the organisation's objectives and ability to compete in the host location. For instance, it is quite likely that there are other MNEs competing in the same market.

4.2.2.6 Establish Mentoring Relationships between Expatriates and Executives from the Home Organisation

In point 3, above, we note the importance of establishing mentoring relationships between expatriates and host-country mentors. It is equally important that the organisation provides a mentor for the expatriate at the home office location to ensure that the expatriate does not feel disconnected from the home office. Sadly, this is quite common given the physical distance and potential time difference between the expatriate's host location and home office. Moreover, having someone at the home location mentoring and guiding the expatriate will allow the expatriate to access any information or guidance that he or she is in need of from the home office (Carraher et al., 2008). In addition, any policy or strategic changes at the home office that impact the expatriate can be communicated to him/her right away, along with boundary conditions and guidance on how to interpret such changes. Expatriates often feel cut off from home base and may not have access to other expatriates from their home country, making them feel even more isolated. Having a mentor at home who is available to the expatriate when needed can alleviate feelings of loneliness and go a long way in assisting the expatriate in performing successfully.

4.2.2.7 Have Varied Performance Goals or Objectives for Different Types of Expatriate Assignments

Finally, it is important that organisations design incentives that correspond with the type of assignment for which the organisation has deputed the expatriate. For instance, an expatriate responsible for knowledge transfer to HCNs should not be evaluated only on how many people attended his or her classes or how much time is spent on the classes. Instead, an objective assessment of the change in HCN employees' knowledge levels is critical to measure transfer of knowledge and/or learning and the degree to which the expatriate has successfully achieved this in the required time. Time is of the essence, so in addition to ensuring that HCNs have acquired the relevant knowledge, it is also critical that this process is completed within a reasonable amount of time. On the other hand, an expatriate who is responsible for culture transformation at the host country location should not be evaluated on the same basis as the expatriate in our earlier example. Appropriate knowledge transfer and technical learning is time bound, but transforming and creating culture may be a continuous task or effort which is never truly completed, and thus cannot be evaluated by traditional performance evaluation methods alone.

4.3 Conclusions

Scholars of the expatriate experience (e.g., Tung & Varma, 2008; Varma & Tung, 2020) have repeatedly called upon HR practitioners and researchers to ensure that expatriate PMSs are designed specifically for expatriates and not simply adopted (or adapted) from an organisation's existing systems. Indeed, these PMSs should accommodate and emphasize relevant contextual factors such as the culture of the host country (Hofstede, 1980), the level of assignment difficulty (Odour, Mendenhall, & Ritchie, 2000), and the specific task/assignment of the expatriate (Suutari & Tahvanainen, 2002).

In this chapter, we have discussed some key issues involved in developing and implementing PMSs (Varma & Budhwar, 2020) for expatriates. We also offer specific suggestions for how to develop effective PMSs for expatriates. First and foremost, global organisations need to ensure that they create a culture where both raters and ratees understand the organisation's philosophy as it relates to PMSs. So, if the PMS is primarily driven by developmental goals, then both raters and ratees would need to be trained to emphasize the developmental aspects of the ratees' performance. On the other hand, if the organisation's PMS emphasizes administrative outcomes, raters (and, sometimes, ratees) would be called upon to track, record, measure, and evaluate performance outcomes. In the case of expatriates, the goals are often specific and unique. While one expatriate may have been sent on assignment to establish a new manufacturing facility, another may be called upon help transform the culture of the host country office. In both cases, the performance of the expatriates would have to be managed and evaluated with uniquely tailored PMSs.

When it comes to expatriate assignments, contextual realities become much more significant than in the case of domestic assignments. As discussed above, expatriates need to overcome a number of adjustment-related barriers before they can be fully effective with their assignments. Depending on the level of support provided by headquarters and HCNs, the time taken by the expatriate to adjust will vary significantly. Clearly, the evaluation of the expatriate needs to account and adjust for the level of support received. In other words, the ratee cannot be held responsible when system factors (see Deming, 1986) prevent him/her from being fully effective.

One factor that is often overlooked but can have a significant impact on the expatriate's experience and performance at the host country location is the quality of relationship that he/she develops with (a) supervisor(s) at the host country location. As noted earlier, this relationship plays a significant role in determining the ratees' overall experience(s). In the case of expatriates, it is all the more critical that organisations pay close attention to the relationships that develop between supervisors and subordinates, as the quality of the relationship has the potential to significantly alter an expatriate's experience at the host country location. If the supervisor at the host country location has a good (or, high quality) relationship with the expatriate subordinate, he/she is likely to offer the expatriate the required role information and social support. On the other hand, if the relationship that develops between the two is not positive, the HCN supervisor might withhold information from the expatriate subordinate, which would negatively affect his/her ability to be effective.

Of course, many expatriates have a dual reporting relationship whereby they report to one supervisor at headquarters and another at the host country location. In such cases, very often, expatriates will have/develop relationships of different qualities with the two different supervisors, making it necessary for him/her to maintain both relationships. Of course, if the supervisors give conflicting directions or present different expectations, the expatriate will end up spending a lot of his/her time trying to balance conflicting and confusing demands. Thus, it is very important that supervisors share a common vision and understanding of the organisation's strategic objectives. Where possible, the organisation should ensure that supervisors jointly develop goals for the expatriate, as this would ensure the expatriate has clear, consistent objectives. Further, when supervisors collaborate (rather than compete), expatriates have the opportunity to receive guidance and feedback from both locations, thus improving the chances that their performance will be on target.

In summary, if MNEs are to effectively assign expatriates and create conditions so that expatriates can perform at optimal levels, they must ensure that their PMSs (1) capture the strengths and developmental needs of individuals being sent on expatriate assignments, (2) ensure that repatriates have opportunities to use knowledge and skills acquired while on assignment, (3) help establish mentoring relationships between expatriates and host country executives, (4) align incentives with assignment objectives, (5) ensure that performance goals are shared with and understood by expatriates, (6) establish mentoring relationships between expatriates and executives from the home organisation, and finally (7) have varied performance objectives and goals for different assignments.

In essence, it is clear that organisations must develop dedicated PMSs for expatriates which take into account the contextual realities of the host country location as well as the strategic objectives of the organisation and the adjustment needs of expatriates. Only then can global organisations hope to draw the best from expatriate employees and achieve optimal performance. Simply implementing domestic PMSs at the new location is not likely to be successful, even when these are adapted.

References

Aycan, Z. 1997. Expatriate adjustment as a multifaceted phenomenon: individual and organizational level predictors. *International Journal of Human Resource Management*, 8(4): 434–456.

Black, J. S., Mendenhall, M., & Odour, G. 1991. Toward a comprehensive model of international adjustment: an integration of multiple theoretical perspectives. *Academy of Management Review*, 16(2): 291–317.

Bobko, P. & Colella, A. 1994. Employee reactions to performance standards: a review and research propositions. *Personnel Psychology*, 47(1): 1–29.

Bossard, A. B. & Peterson, R. B. 2005. The repatriate experience as seen by American expatriates. *Journal of World Business*, 40(1): 9–28.

Caligiuri, P. & Bonache, J. 2016. Evolving and enduring challenges in global mobility. *Journal of World Business*, 51(1): 127–141.

Caligiuri, P. M. & Colakoglu, S. 2007. A strategic contingency approach to expatriate assignment management. *Human Resource Management Journal*, 17(4): 393–410.

Carraher, S. M., Sullivan, S. E., & Crocitto, M. M. 2008. Mentoring across global boundaries: an empirical examination of home-and host-country mentors on expatriate career outcomes. *Journal of International Business Studies*, 39(8): 1310–1326.

Cerdin, J. L. & Brewster, C. 2014. Talent management and expatriation: bridging two streams of research and practice. *Journal of World Business*, 49(2): 245–252.

Chang, Y.-Y., Gong, Y., & Peng, M. W. 2012. Expatriate knowledge transfer, subsidiary absorptive capacity, and subsidiary performance. *Academy of Management Journal*, 55(4): 927–948.

Deming, W. E. 1986. *Out of Crisis, Centre for Advanced Engineering Study*. Cambridge: Massachusetts Institute of Technology.

DeNisi, A. S. & Gonzalez, J. A. 2017. Design performance appraisal systems to improve performance. *The Blackwell Handbook of Principles of Organizational Behaviour*, 63–75.

DeNisi, A. S. & Murphy, K. R. 2017. Performance appraisal and performance management: 100 years of progress? *Journal of Applied Psychology*, 102 (3): 421.

Fee, A., McGrath-Champ, S., & Yang, X. 2011. Expatriate performance management and firm internationalization: australian multinationals in China. *Asia Pacific Journal of Human Resources*, 49(3): 365–384.

Feldman, D. C. & Bolino, M. C. 1999. The impact of on-site mentoring on expatriate socialization: a structural equation modelling approach. *International Journal of Human Resource Management*, 10(1): 54–71.

Graen, G. B. & Uhl-Bien, M. (1995). Relationship-based approach to leadership: development of leader-member exchange (LMX) theory of leadership over 25 years: applying a multi-level multi-domain perspective. *The Leadership Quarterly*, 6(2), 219–247.

Hippler, T., Brewster, C., & Haslberger, A. 2015. The elephant in the room: the role of time in expatriate adjustment. *The International Journal of Human Resource Management*, 26(15): 1920–1935.

Hofstede, G. 1980. Culture and organizations. *International Studies of Management & Organization*, 10(4): 15–41.

Kang, H. & Shen, J. 2016. International performance appraisal practices and approaches of South Korean MNEs in China. *The International Journal of Human Resource Management*, 27(3): 291–310.

Kawai, N. & Chung, C. 2019. Expatriate utilization, subsidiary knowledge creation and performance: the moderating role of subsidiary strategic context. *Journal of World Business*, 54(1): 24–36.

Kim, K. I., Park, H. J., & Suzuki, N. 1990. Reward allocations in the United States, Japan, and Korea: a comparison of individualistic and collectivistic cultures. *Academy of Management Journal*, 33(1): 188–198.

Kossek, E. E., Huang, J. L., Piszczek, M. M., Fleenor, J. W., & Ruderman, M. 2017. Rating expatriate leader effectiveness in multisource feedback systems: cultural distance and hierarchical effects. *Human Resource Management*, 56(1): 151–172.

Kraimer, M. L. & Wayne, S. J. 2004. An examination of perceived organizational support as a multidimensional construct in the context of an expatriate assignment. *Journal of Management*, 30(2): 209–237.

Kraimer, M. L., Wayne, S. J., & Jaworski, R. A. A. 2001. Sources of support and expatriate performance: the mediating role of expatriate adjustment. *Personnel Psychology*, 54(1): 71–99.

Liu, X. & Shaffer, M. A. 2005. An investigation of expatriate adjustment and performance. A social capital perspective. *International Journal of Cross-Cultural Management*, 5(3): 235–253.

Malek, M. A. & Budhwar, P. 2013. Cultural intelligence as a predictor of expatriate adjustment and performance in Malaysia. *Journal of World Business*, 48(2): 222–231.

Martin, D. C. & Bartol, K. M. 2003. Factors influencing expatriate performance appraisal system success: an organizational perspective. *Journal of International management*, 9(2): 115–132.

Mezias, J. M. & Scandura, T. A. 2005. A needs-driven approach to expatriate adjustment and career development: a multiple mentoring perspective. *Journal of International Business Studies*, 36(5): 519–538.

Nowak, C. & Linder, C. 2016. Do you know how much your expatriate costs? An activity-based cost analysis of expatriation. *Journal of Global Mobility*, 4(1): 88–107.

Odour, G., Mendenhall, M. E., & Ritchie, J. B. 2000. Leveraging travel as a tool for global leadership development. *Human Resource Management*, 39(2–3): 159–172.

Ren, H., Bolino, M. C., Shaffer, M. A., & Kraimer, M. L. 2013. The influence of job demands and resources on repatriate career satisfaction: a relative deprivation perspective. *Journal of World Business*, 48(1): 149–159.

Schuler, R. S. & Jackson, S. E. 1987. Linking competitive strategies with human resource management practices. *Academy of Management Perspectives*, 1(3): 207–219.

Selmer, J. & Fenner, Jr, C. R. 2009. Job factors and work outcomes of public sector expatriates. *Human Resource Management Journal*, 19(1): 75–90.

Shay, J. P. & Tracey, J. B. 2009. Expatriate adjustment and effectiveness: the mediating role of managerial practices. *Journal of International Management*, 15(4): 401–412.

Silbiger, A., Berger, R., Barnes, B. R., & WS Renwick, D. 2017. Improving expatriation success: the roles of regulatory focus and burnout. *British Journal of Management*, 28(2): 231–247.

Suutari, V. & Tahvanainen, M. 2002. The antecedents of performance management among Finnish expatriates. *The International Journal of Human Resource Management*, 13: 55–75.

Tahvanainen, M. 2000. Expatriate performance management: the case of Nokia telecommunications. *Human Resource Management*, 39: 267–275.

Takeuchi, R., Tesluk, P. E., Yun, S., & Lepak, D. P. 2005. An integrative view of international experience. *Academy of Management Journal*, 48(1): 85–100.

Toh, S. M. & DeNisi, A. S. 2007. Host country nationals as socializing agents: a social identity approach. *Journal of Organizational Behavior*, 28(3): 281–301.

Toh, S. M. & Srinivas, E. S. 2012. Perceptions of task cohesiveness and organizational support increase trust and information sharing between host country nationals and expatriate coworkers in Oman. *Journal of World Business*, 47(4): 696–705.

Tung, R. L. & Varma, A. 2008. Expatriate selection and evaluation. In P. B. Smith, M. F. Peterson, & D. C. Thomas (eds.), *Handbook of Cross-Cultural Management Research*; 367–378. Thousand Oaks, CA: Sage.

Van De Vliert, E., Shi, K., Sanders, K., Wang, Y., & Huang, X. 2004. Chinese and Dutch interpretations of supervisory feedback. *Journal of Cross-Cultural Psychology*, 35(4): 417–435.

Vance, C. M., Andersen, T., Vaiman, V., & Gale, J. 2014. A taxonomy of potential contributions of the host country national local liaison role in global knowledge management. *Thunderbird International Business Review*, 56(2): 173–191.

Varma, A. & Budhwar, P. 2020. Introduction – Performance management in context. In A. Varma & P. Budhwar (eds.), *Performance Management Systems: An Experiential Approach*, 1–14 London: Sage.

Varma, A. & P. Budhwar. 2020. Implementing a performance management system. In A. Varma & P. Budhwar (eds.), *Performance Management Systems: An Experiential Approach*. 165–180 London: Sage.

Varma, A., Budhwar, P., & McCusker, C. 2014. Performance management in global organizations. In D. Collings, P. Caligiuri, & G. Wood, (eds.), *Companion to International Human Resource Management*: 172–189. Abingdon: Routledge.

Varma, A., Budhwar, P., Katou, A., & Mathew, J. 2016. Interpersonal affect and host country national support of expatriates: an investigation in China. *Journal of Global Mobility*, 4(4): 476–495.

Varma, A., Budhwar, P., & Singh, S. 2015. Performance management and high-performance work practices in emerging markets. In F. Horwitz & P. Budhwar (eds.), *Handbook of Human Resource Management in Emerging Markets*: 316–334. Cheltenham: Edward Elgar.

Varma, A., Budhwar, P., & Yu, M. (2018). Global performance management. In A. Harzing & S. Reiche (eds.), *International Human Resource Management* (5th ed.), Thousand Oaks, CA: Sage.

Varma, A., Toh, S. M., & Budhwar, P. 2006. A new perspective on the female expatriate experience: the role of host country national categorization. *Journal of World Business*, 41: 112–120.

Varma, A., Tallapragada, R., & Shi, Y. 2019. Expatriate networks in host countries: a recipe for successful adjustment. Paper presented at the IBS Mumbai International HR Conference, Mumbai, India.

Varma, A. & Tung, R. 2020. Performance management for expatriates. In A. Varma & P. Budhwar (eds.), *Performance Management: An Experiential Approach*. 153–164 London: Sage.

Wang, C. H. 2018. To relocate internationally or not to relocate internationally: a Taiwanese case study. *Journal of Global Mobility*, 6(2): 226–240.

Wang, C. H. & Varma, A. 2019. Cultural distance and expatriate failure rates: the moderating role of expatriate management practices. *The International Journal of Human Resource Management*, 30(15): 2211–2230.

Zhu, J., Wanberg, C. R., Harrison, D. A., & Diehn, E. W. 2016. Ups and downs of the expatriate experience? Understanding work adjustment trajectories and career outcomes. *Journal of Applied Psychology*, 101(4): 549–568.

5 *Compensating Global Mobility*

JAIME BONACHE, CELIA ZÁRRAGA-OBERTY

5.1 Introduction

Human resource professionals working in multinational corporations (MNCs) report that the problems associated with the design and management of expatriates' pay packages take up most of their time and energy (Bonache & Zárraga-Oberty, 2020; Caligiuri & Bonache, 2016; Festing & Perkins, 2008). This is logical due to the complexity of the matter, the impact this remuneration has on corporate expenditure and, above all, its influence on the firm's ability to attract, retain, and galvanise the talent it requires to successfully undertake its international operations. It is relatively easy to find studies in the academic literature that analyse topics such as the goals to be pursued by a sound policy on the compensation of global mobility, the challenges and difficulties to be addressed in its design and implementation, the options available and the advantages and drawbacks each one poses, the changes and tendencies that may be observed in this policy, and the key contingency factors (e.g., the type of expatriate and the organisational context) that influence this policy.

This chapter focuses on this research stream, and reviews the relevant literature on the issue. Our aim is to update and contextualise the predominant method used by MNCs to compensate global mobility. To do so, we begin by briefly explaining the traditional way of compensating expatriates, namely, the balance sheet system, discussing its strengths and weaknesses. We then analyse two alternative approaches to this system: local-plus and localisation, and note that although they resolve some of the problems involved in the traditional system, there are still problems. Finally, we will describe the current landscape of international compensation, and highlight some research gaps to be filled in future research.

5.2 The Traditional Approach: The Balance Sheet System

When employees are assigned for a long-term posting (e.g., one to five years), the process of designing the compensation package is especially complex and challenging (Bonache, 2006; Harvey, 1993a, 1993b; Suutari & Tornikoski, 2000, 2001). Within this ambit, there is a whole series of factors or critical elements that need to be taken into careful consideration, and which, nonetheless, tend to be omitted when the aim is to set the salary for local employees or host-country nationals (HCNs). We are referring here to elements such as the employee's home country, their family circumstances (e.g., number and ages of children and partner's employment status), the quality and size of their home, floating exchange rates, differences in living costs, taxes and inflation rates, the need to reconcile home and host-country compensation laws and regulations, and the geographically imposed problems of communication and control. These issues increase both the complexity of the situation and the information needed with regard to individuals and their postings (Suutari & Tornikoski, 2001; Bonache, 2006).

In order to tackle these difficulties, the balance sheet system has become extremely popular in the professional field. The system was designed by a group of economists in the 1950s and 1960s, with one of the leading lights being G. F. Dickover, who is considered to be its foremost champion (Dickover, 1957). His work was probably naïve on a theoretical level, but original and full of potential on a practical level. The system's point of departure involves five goals to which an international remuneration system should aspire (Bonache, 2006; Bonache & Stirpe, 2012), namely: (1) to ease the transfer of international employees in the most cost-effective manner, (2) to be consistent and fair in the treatment of all its employees, (3) to attract (and satisfy) personnel in the areas where the MNC has its greatest needs and opportunities, (4) to facilitate the retention of international assignees in the home country at the end of the foreign assignment, and (5) to foster the expatriate behaviours required for implementing effective global strategies.

With these goals in mind, the balance sheet approach begins with the employee's salary (i.e., the reference salary), and divides it into four items or categories of expenditure: goods and services, housing, taxes, and savings. The amount allocated to each one of these items will depend largely on the level of income and the size of the household. It is fair to say that the more we earn and the larger our household, the more we spend, for example, on goods and services (i.e., transport, food, clothing, and entertainment). Therein lies the need for tables that specify what people with different income levels and personal circumstances spend on each one of the four blocks of expenditure.

In terms of reference salary, there are several options, which define the three basic approaches the system may adopt:

1. First is the *home-country balance sheet approach*. The salary is referred to the expatriate's home country. The idea of this approach is to provide expatriates with equivalent purchasing power abroad in order to maintain the standard of living they enjoyed in their home country.
2. The *host-country balance sheet approach*. This approach is used when the levels of pay for a given position are significantly higher in the host country (O'Really, 1996). It involves taking the salary in the host country as the point of departure for the subsequent calculations.
3. The *global balance sheet approach*. This approach is most relevant when the MNC has numerous employees from different countries who are expected to move to more than one foreign country, thereby losing direct connection with the grading and pay structure in either their home country or their host country (O'Really, 1996). The intention is to pay on an international scale, with allowances derived from that base. An international basket of goods and services would be used across all expatriates regardless of their home country.

The home-country balance sheet approach is the most popular of the three. Consultancies report that this is the common practice among 79 per cent of MNCs (KPMG, 2016). The advantage of this approach is that by keeping expatriates in line with conditions at home they can seamlessly slot back into their lives after their overseas posting.

Once the reference salary has been chosen, the system makes a series of calculations and adjustments to specify the host-country salary (See Figure 5.1). These include differentials or allowances designed to guarantee expatriates' purchasing power (i.e., cost of living differential, housing allowance, and tax differential), or to compensate them for the 'inconveniences' of living abroad (Phillips & Fox, 2003). These

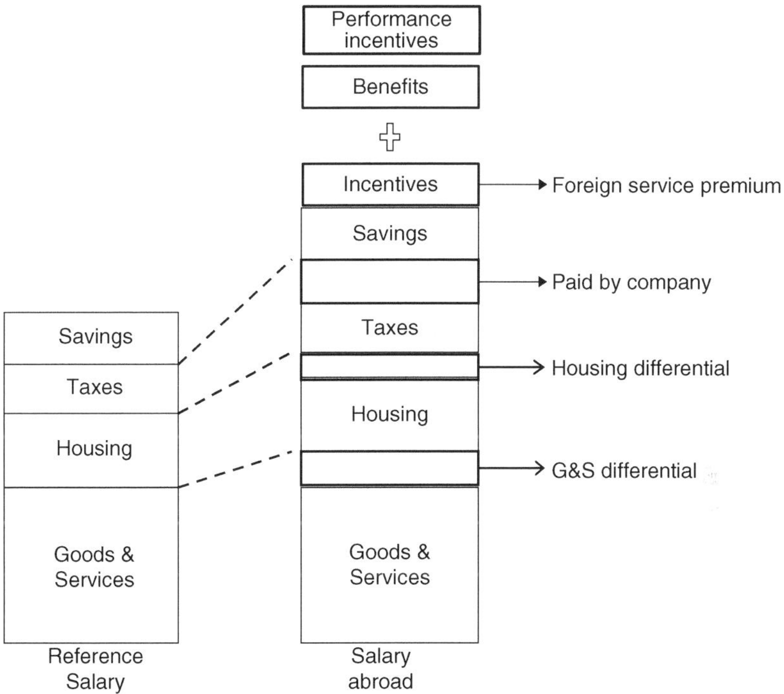

Figure 5.1 Balance-sheet system

latter allowances have different technical terms, such as 'overseas premiums' (Reynolds, 1997), which are a percentage of the reference salary paid monthly during expatriation, or 'mobility premiums', which are lump-sum payments made at the beginning and end of an assignment (Phillips & Fox, 2003).

Why is there a need to include an 'assignment premium'? Traditionally, before the onset of globalisation in the 1990s, the need to incentivise mobility through assignment premiums seemed obvious (Caligiuri & Bonache 2016). In the 1960s, Dickover, the system's pioneer mentioned earlier, provided us with a very clear explanation:

> A construction worker, nomadic by background, may be enticed by high wages to undertake a two-year stint in Iceland or Patagonia, but career employment in Cuba or Venezuela holds little attraction for this year's graduating chemical engineer- or his wife or sweetheart- or even less for the

married man with three or five or 12 years of domestic service with the company. (Dickover, 1957: cited by Reynolds, 1997)

If we overlook the text's sexist tone, it is this type of reasoning that is still used today to justify premium incentives. In addition to family and personal issues (such as the growing importance of quality of life considerations; Shaffer, Harrison, & Gilley, 1999), and the continued uncertainty regarding international terrorism and the political and social unrest in certain destinations (Welch, Welch, & Tahvanainen, 2008), it is frequently mentioned that the career implications of international assignments are often frustrating. A lack of respect for acquired skills, loss of status, and reverse culture shock upon return are recurring problems in many companies (Stahl, Miller, & Tung, 2002). For these reasons, or barriers to international mobility, many individuals will not agree to move unless they are offered a generous compensation system.

On top of the reference salary and the differentials, one should add the benefits of welfare programmes (e.g., education, shipping and storage, travel and club membership, and assistance for the partner). An analysis of the content of these benefits reveals that international remuneration entails a much greater involvement in the expatriate's private life (Bonache, 2006), examining issues that in a purely domestic ambit might well be regarded as invasions of privacy, such as the type of schools chosen for children or a partner's employment status.

5.2.1 Criticisms of the Traditional Approach

The traditional way of remunerating international mobility, structured within the conceptual framework of the balance sheet approach, is an excellent arrangement for avoiding a strictly individual negotiation and having to calculate the salaries in different host locations. This explains its popularity and the fact that it continues to be used for setting the salary of many employees posted abroad. Nevertheless, it also has significant shortcomings. Indeed, as we shall discuss in due course, it has ceased to be 'the system' for paying staff on international assignments to become just one more of the approaches that are now part of the landscape or furniture of global mobility remuneration. For the time being, however, let us focus on some of the key criticisms of the balance sheet system.

5.2.2 Is the System Cost-effective?

This is the most common criticism, and also the most obvious one. The traditional way of remunerating global mobility within the balance sheet approach identifies and includes a whole series of salary items (i.e., bonuses, allowances, and benefits) that make international assignments a very expensive option (Bonache, Sanchez, & Zárraga-Oberty, 2009; Tornikoski, Suutari, & Festing, 2014). The cost of international staff is considerably higher than that of their equivalent HCNs of the same level and category (Mercer, 2015).

In addition to direct costs, there are also indirect ones, such as administrative costs, which although lower are not insignificant (Nowak & Linder, 2016). The traditional system requires at least regular attention and updating, but this may sometimes need to be continuous. Let us take, for example, the cost of living allowance, which offsets the difference in the shopping basket (for the same range and quantity of products that include transport, food, clothing, household items, and entertainment) in the host country compared to the home country. Depending on the host country's stability, this allowance is usually reviewed on a yearly, half-yearly or even monthly basis by a specialised outside firm with which regular contact needs to be maintained. All this requires staff time and effort (Nowak & Linder, 2016). The increasingly more common practice of subcontracting the collection and calculation (including cost estimates) of assignment compensation, which now extends to 45 per cent of organisations working with a particular consultancy, as an example (KPMG, 2016), is a good reflection of the indirect costs associated with this activity.

5.2.3 Is it Fair to HCNs?

In order to be motivating, the rewards need to be perceived as fair. According to equity theory (Festinger, 1954; Adams, 1965), this perception arises in a social medium, as the result of comparing the ratio of our contributions and rewards with that same ratio among other individuals, who thereby act as referents for comparison purposes. Dissimilar ratios lead to perceptions of inequity. This proposition implies that the same organisational circumstance may be perceived as fair or unfair depending on which individual or group of individuals the worker chooses for the comparison. Accordingly, a major concern when analysing people's satisfaction with their compensation system involves identifying the referent used in the individual's comparisons.

The problem faced by expatriate employees is that there are multiple potential referents (Bonache, 2005). They may compare themselves not only to other expatriates within the same company and host country, but also to expatriates within the same company in other host countries, expatriates from other companies within their host country, HCNs, and so forth. The home-country balance sheet approach, which is the most widely used system for remunerating expatriates, insists on the need to refer to a person's peers in the home country (Phillips & Fox, 2003). The assumption is that as expatriates will be repatriated after a relatively short period of time (three to five years), it is more appropriate to compare them to employees in their home country (Phillips, & Fox, 2003).

Unfortunately, prioritising a sense of fairness has the drawback in salary terms of discriminating against HCNs, as they are very likely to consider this situation to be unfair. This is regrettable because HCNs are valuable socialising agents, sources of social support, assistance, and friendship for expatriates (Toh & DeNisi, 2003). The disparity in pay may induce HCNs to become uncooperative or antagonistic, which could even compromise the expatriate's performance (Oltra, Bonache, & Brewster, 2013).

The issues of unfairness with regard to HCNs are so important that many studies have sought to identify the factors that may offset or attenuate the negative influence a pay differential has on the inequity perceived among HCNs (e.g., Chen, Choi, & Chi, 2002; Bonache et al., 2009; Leung, Zhu, & Ge, 2009; Paik, Parboteeah, & Shim, 2007). Thanks to these studies, we know that this perception is especially marked when, for instance, an HCN does not perceive a salary advantage over locals in other companies, when they do not see logical reasons for high expatriate compensation, and when expatriates do not have the appropriate interpersonal skills.

5.2.4 Does it Motivate Cross-cultural Development?

In the balance sheet approach, an expatriate's salary continues to be linked to the living conditions at headquarters or in the home country, thus favouring or fostering a type of experience in which expatriates live in cultural bubbles or relatively isolated and well 'sheltered' communities, with globally neutral shops, language, schools, and activities. Needless to say, this is not the best way of encouraging enculturation or an understanding of what it is like to live and work in another country. Instead, what it does is stop the expatriate from facing a new situation and adjusting to local salary conditions and standards. Engaging in work challenges in cultures that differ from the predominant societal values of expatriates' home culture are the hallmark of what makes these global mobility experiences truly developmental (Gupta & Govindarajan, 2002), and compensation should not be an exception.

What's more, it is not simply that the balance sheet approach does not favour development, but that its very approach negates it. For example, the differential of goods and services assumes that expatriates and their families wish to maintain the same lifestyle. They are not expected to change their shopping habits, yet this is highly debatable. People change as a result of their international experience, and part of the intercultural learning process actually involves assimilating habits and products from beyond one's own frontiers.

5.2.5 Does the System Help to Retain International Assignees?

Although people may accept an international assignment for a variety of reasons (e.g., career development, a more satisfactory position in the host country or upon repatriation, a spirit of adventure, the enjoyment of a cosmopolitan lifestyle, the opportunity for children to become proficient in another language), money is one of the more tangible assets and is easier to quantify, which explains why organisations, in full awareness of the significant role money plays in the decision to accept an international assignment, have made generous salary packages the simplest and most widely used strategy for attracting talent to foreign postings (Bonache, 2006).

It is arguable whether this emphasis on the monetary component is equally effective when the aim is to retain talent once the person is working in the host country. The turnover of expatriates in host countries is not a topic that has been widely studied, although there is circumstantial evidence to show that it might be significant. Existing evidence shows that when analysing the factors that induce people to stay with the organization, money does not play a key role (Reiche, Kraimer, & Harzing, 2011). The decisive factors are career openings or perspectives, recognition, support from and relationships with supervisors, or emotional ties with the organization's management or members. If an expatriate lacks these elements, and only has financial reasons for staying with the company, other companies will not find it difficult to attract them through an equal salary offer. Likewise, competitors will find it very difficult to recruit expatriates if they are content and satisfied (Yan, Zhu, & Hall, 2002).

The problem, nevertheless, is not that generous salary packages may help to attract but not retain staff during the assignment period, but that they may even be the trigger for turnover once the posting has ended. Research has consistently reported the high turnover rates among repatriates, which some studies place at between 20 per cent and 50 per cent (Reiche et al., 2011). Although there are numerous reasons for this high turnover (e.g., greater opportunities elsewhere, new contacts, lack of recognition), compensation has its role to play. The incentives and allowances designed to encourage employees to take up a foreign assignment are not sustained when the expatriate returns home, leading to a substantial loss of income. In fact, such a loss of income is cited as one of the main difficulties upon return (Bonache, 2005).

The possible downside of generous salary packages on the retention of repatriates is not so paradoxical when we analyse it in the light of more recent research into job turnover (Chen et al., 2011). This has highlighted how the essential trigger for job turnover is the nature of the change in satisfaction, rather than overall levels of satisfaction. Let us take as an example the situation depicted in Figure 5.1. It shows two individuals, α and β, who at the time of repatriation have identical levels of job satisfaction. According to the standard literature on job turnover, and all other things being equal (openings in other companies, recognition of their experience within the company, etc.), they will be equally likely to accept a job in another company. Nevertheless, as Figure 5.2 shows, α has held a foreign posting, a situation that was very satisfactory because of the generous incentives received. By contrast, β was subject to local employment conditions, which were not nearly as favourable. α sees this opportunity as a change for the worse, while β considers it an improvement. Let us assume that α loses out by 10 per cent and β gains by that same 10 per cent. By applying the logic of prospect theory (Kahneman and Tversky, 1984) formulated by Daniel Kahneman, a Nobel Prize winner, the more likely scenario is

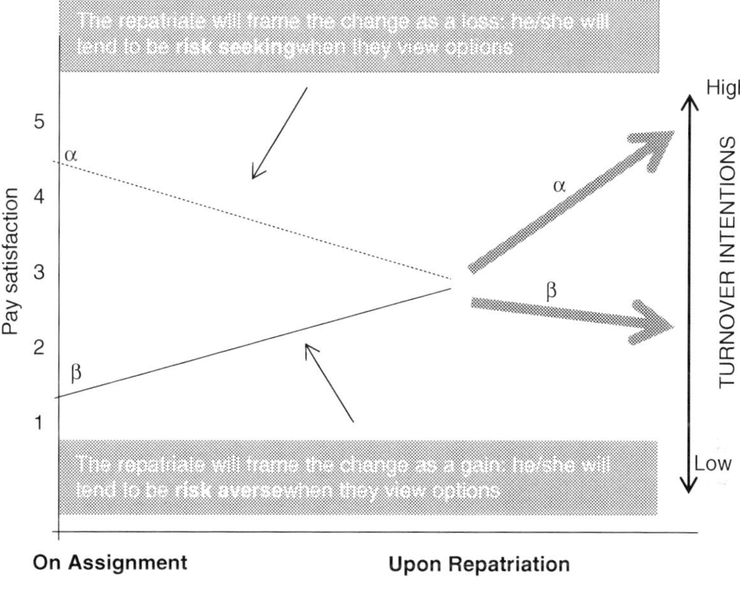

Figure 5.2 Pay satisfaction change and turnover intentions

that the loss of that percentage by α will generate more dissatisfaction than the satisfaction gained by β from that same figure (10 per cent). As posited within the framework of this theory, the problem is that we hate losing more than we love winning. This will make α more inclined than β to accept exactly the same job offer. While the former will be risk-seeking, the latter will be more risk averse. If this is indeed the case, an attractive pay package abroad may drive global mobility but reduce a company's ability to retain employees upon their return.

5.2.6 Is it Consistent with the New Forms of Global Mobility?

As shown in Chapter 7, we now have a huge variety of profiles and situations that fall within the category of international mobility. We can no longer simply assume, as the balance sheet approach does, that expatriates will return to their country of origin after a relatively short period of time (3–5 years), that interest in the deployment lies above all with the company, that repatriation will always take place or be planned, or that equity with employees in the home country is essential (Phillips & Fox, 2003). We require greater variety in the nature of compensation to accommodate the different types of global mobility.

So far, we have seen that the balance sheet system is the traditional approach to expatriate compensation, and that it is not without its problems. As seen below, there are other systems for compensating global mobility, but it is debatable whether they constitute a 'best-practice' in this matter.

5.3 Local-Plus and Localisation

The compensation systems that have emerged as an alternative to the traditional home-country balance sheet approach are referred to as local-plus and localisation (McNulty, 2015). With the local-plus system, an expatriate receives a salary that is consistent with the pay scales in the host country, but it is increased by a series of allowances, such as those for transport, housing, and children's schooling. The package of allowances is not the same for all expatriates. The decision is made by the firm, being determined largely by the assignment's location (i.e., the location's degree of hardship), among other factors.

The local-plus compensation system seems very similar to the host-country balance sheet. We might therefore infer that local-plus is not an innovative compensation system. Yet, while the host-country balance sheet was used as a system for traditional expatriates when levels of compensation were significantly higher in the host country than in the home country, local-plus is currently being applied independently of the differences in the level of compensation between home and host countries.

The localisation system simply means that the expatriate receives a salary that is consistent with the salary levels in their posting destination, or where they were already living and working. In short, localisation for the person involved implies the removal or absence of 'expatriate' status in terms of company policy, which includes allowances and premiums (McNulty 2015).

As we have seen, the local-plus and localisation compensation systems are an alternative to the balance sheet approach. Their advocates contend that they are better suited to the new global mobility scenario in the highly globalised twenty-first century. In this respect, although it is easy to argue that they reduce costs and facilitate repatriation, the extent to which they manage to redress the other three shortcomings is more debatable.

- *Are they fairer?* The new compensation systems do not appear to create problems of fairness among HCNs, as expatriates ultimately end up blending in with local staff (McNulty, 2015). Nevertheless, if the firm uses the local-plus or localisation systems in parallel with the balance sheet arrangement, the issue of the perception of injustice shifts onto new incoming employees from abroad when they compare themselves to the expatriates who continue to be paid according to the traditional arrangement. This perception may be a cause of greater staff turnover.
- *So does this help to retain international staff?* As we have already mentioned, the new compensation systems eliminate the repatriation stage. We may therefore assume that they remove a problem. But this is not the case. Although retaining international staff when they return from their posting may be less of an issue (unless they return to a comparatively less attractive context), it aggravates the problem of retaining staff while they are actually on their international assignment. Throughout the entire posting the firm has to deal with local competition. These new compensation systems mean that employees' opportunity cost is greatly reduced, and they will therefore be more willing to swap their allegiance more readily than if they were subject to the traditional balance sheet system. This, therefore, clearly increases the firm's risk of losing employees with a high overall potential (McNulty, 2014).
- *Do these new systems foster cultural integration?* We should remember that the traditional system was an obstacle to the cultural integration of expatriates. The new compensation systems will clearly mean diminishing this obstacle, as international assignees are less likely to be considered expatriates and might blend in more with the local workforce.

Overall, the new systems for compensating international assignees have some advantages (e.g., they foster cultural integration and reduce costs), but they are not without their drawbacks. One of these we would like to highlight involves the risk of a larger turnover of high value added staff (qualified personnel who accept an international posting). For international staff, the opportunity cost of leaving the firm is very low both in terms of salary (they do not receive the traditionally high pay packages) and emotionally (psychological contract), as they do not create an employment relationship, whereby they are obliged to give more because they receive more.

5.4 Trends in International Compensation

Following an analysis of the possible ways of compensating international postings, we shall now highlight what firms are actually doing in this area. There are three core tendencies: (1) reducing costs, (2) increasing the range of approaches to compensation and (3) focusing more on the value of assignments.

5.4.1 More Cost Control

According to KPMG (2016), 40 per cent of the companies they surveyed consider that expatriates are overpaid. However, there is nothing new about this view of expatriation as being very costly. Quite the opposite, it is an opinion that has been regularly reflected in all the surveys conducted over the past twenty years. Indeed, a survey by Brookfield Global Relocation Services (2015) indicates that 23 per cent of companies report that the cost of these postings is the main challenge they face within the field of global mobility.

The increasing use of the local plus or localisation approach can be interpreted as a way of reducing expatriation costs. Another initiative has been to increase the number of short-term postings and commuter assignments (i.e., employees who work in a foreign country but who return home with some frequency) involved in working abroad (Bonache, 2006). These are two more economical solutions, as they do not involve – or they do so to a lesser extent – many of the costly items included in the compensation package of many long-term assignments (e.g., education or partner allowance).

A third way of reducing costs has involved examining traditional items of expenditure (differentials of goods and services, incentives for mobility, taxes, and allowances) and looking for ways of applying cuts to each one of them. When we compare the data on the conditions of expatriation, there is a noticeable increase in the number of companies that, for example, reduce costs by: (1) merging all the incentives and allowances into a single item (with a lower allocation than the sum of their separate amounts), (2) paying allowances as lump-sums, paying part upfront and the rest when the assignment has been successfully completed (with the ensuing cost saving in the event of non-completion), (3) using tax equalisation (the employee pays neither more nor less tax than they would have paid in the home country) as opposed to a tax protection policy (employee pays no more than they would have paid in the home country, but may pay less in certain situations), or (4) making alternative downward adjustments in other differentials such as cost of living or housing. All-in-all, over a period of 20 years, those companies that remunerate their expatriates using the balance sheet approach have seen their average costs fall in comparison with their home-country counterparts (Reynolds, 1997; Mercer, 2015).

5.4.2 Salary Differentiation among Expatriates (and its Legitimation)

Despite the advantages of some international compensation systems, we have stressed that no arrangement is without its difficulties, which are due to the numerous goals that the system seeks to meet. Some understand or restrict the purpose of the system to simply being an instrument for attracting and motivating employees to accept an international posting in order to enable the firm to compete globally. But this general objective must be accompanied by more specific ones, such as cost control, facilitating repatriation, or upholding equity across groups of employees (Bonache, 2006; Bonache & Zárraga-Oberty, 2020). This is an extremely challenging issue because it is almost impossible to achieve all these objectives at the same time. For example, the objective of attracting staff can be readily achieved by offering a generous pay package although, as we have seen, such a policy may have a number of negative consequences: it incurs high costs for the firm in terms of both gross and management expenses, it leads to inequity perceptions among HCNs, and it may make repatriation more difficult.

The tension between conflicting objectives results in internal differentiation between groups of expatriates (AIR Inc, 2010, 2011; Bitten, 2001; Bonache & Zárraga-Oberty, 2017, 2020), in which, depending on the group involved, some objectives will be prioritised over others. For executive postings, the balance-sheet approach with high premiums and benefits is normally used (Phillips & Fox, 2003). The aim here is to set a reference salary (normally the salary is paid to the expatriates in their home country), and add a series of adjustments to maintain their purchasing power abroad (i.e., goods and services differentials, housing allowances, and tax equalization), along with sundry premiums (e.g., assignment premium, performance bonuses, 'lost income' reimbursement for the 'trailing' partner) to incentivise international mobility (Suutari & Tornikoski, 2001). This system makes assignments financially very attractive for employees, albeit at the cost of impeding the achievement of other objectives, such as costs, equity, and cultural integration. These other objectives, however, can be pursued through alternative systems, such as local-plus or localisation (McNulty, 2015), and can be applied to other expatriates (e.g., self-initiated expatriates), who in most cases will be compensated according to the salary conditions in the host country (localisation), or in others, also according to the host country, but increased by a series of allowances (e.g., transport, housing, children's schooling). In short, it is common today to encounter a broad range of formal arrangements (Yan et al., 2002), with the same company applying both contractual relationships (i.e., those based on long-term service and loyalty) and transactional ones (project-based), as well as very attractive compensation packages for some expatriates, and more modest ones for others (see Table 5.1).

Table 5.1 *Type of assignment and compensation approach*

Length	Reason of assignment	Typical Compensation Approach
Long assignments (two to five years)	Key employee Developmental transfers	Balance sheet + high premiums + benefits
Short assignments	High potentials	'Local plus' or localization approach
	Know-how/expertise transfer	Home based + allowances and/or incentives
Definitive	One-way transfer	Localization approach
	Locally hired foreigner Job posting	'Local plus' or localization approach
Contingent	Project work	

How can this internal differentiation in salary conditions between expatriates be justified? It is obvious that it cannot be explained in terms of needs, as these should be the same, for example, for both a key executive and a veteran employee with children who are relocated abroad. What justifies an unequal allocation of compensation is their respective contributions. This requires calling upon the merit-based equity norm, whereby rewards should be proportional to contributions. It is the reference norm, and also the most representative one within the sphere of MNCs (Toh & DeNisi, 2003). The person assigned to an executive position is valued as crucial, requiring the company to offer an attractive salary and the substantial benefits traditionally associated with expatriate positions. This preference has a moral sense: it is understood to be the most legitimate way of distributing rewards, particularly in Western thinking, where it is considered unfair to compensate individuals on an equal basis when their inputs or contributions are unequal.

This way of legitimising differences both promotes and justifies a series of relative comparisons in which individuals will be comparing their respective inputs and outputs. It is highly likely that this process will create problems of inequity (e.g., between expatriate groups subject to very different conditions), although it is often assumed to be the price that has to be paid if the organisation is to compete globally in a cost-effective manner (Toh & DeNisi, 2003).

5.4.3 More Focus on the Value of Assignments

As we have seen, companies have paid a great deal of attention to costs. This explains the very slow growth in the number of management expatriates, and their replacement with other options that are more economical and satisfactory, not only for the parent company but also for the subsidiary. In theory at least, if an assignment's value added is not readily apparent, it is highly unlikely to take place (McNulty, De Cieri, & Hutchings, 2009; Farndale, Scullion, & Sparrow, 2010).

5.5 A Future Research Agenda

So far, we have focused on the advantages and disadvantages of different systems to compensate an international assignment. Though discussion of these systems will continue to attract the attention of practitioners, there are a number of more strategic topics which should also attract academics' interest and guide future research in this area. We will classify these topics in the context of two main areas: (1) the determinants of expatriate compensation, and (2) the effects of different expatriate compensation systems. Below is a brief analysis of these topics as well as the theories that support their investigation.

5.5.1 The Determinants of Expatriate Compensation

The organizational context. The organizational context must be considered as an essential contingency factor in the design and implementation of expatriates' compensation packages. In contrast to the early assumption from the literature that the type of organisation is irrelevant to compensation decisions (Edstrom & Galbraith, 1977), a recent qualitative interpretive study (Bonache & Zárraga-Oberty, 2020) on the challenge of designing expatriation pay in a workers' cooperative has highlighted the impact of the organisational context on the way that compensation is understood and managed. As opposed to the conventional view analysed in this chapter, which involves supporting the business by meeting multiple and conflicting objectives (e.g., satisfying expatriates' needs and expectations, controlling costs, ensuring equity with local employees, facilitating repatriation), the challenge is understood in the cooperative as redesigning the policy so that its organizational identity is respected and upheld. The debates that are normally the focus of attention in the literature (e.g., how can we attract staff to an expatriate assignment without it becoming too costly? How can we avoid a situation of inequity with local staff? How can we ensure the return is not seen as a pay-cut?) are not the ones discussed by cooperative members nor do they even feature on their agendas. Instead, they are dominated by discussions on how to achieve a remuneration policy that while being competitive is still consistent with the cooperative's social mission and (democratic) decision-making process. The tension between financial and social performance, which characterises a large part of the literature on social enterprises, also appears in relation to this specific HRM policy. Once the challenge is understood, the way of managing it and the compensation decisions adopted are also very different to the conventional approach (see Bonache and Zárraga-Oberty, 2020). Clearly, we need more qualitative interpretive research on how the type of organisation, including non-governmental organisations, political organisations, armed forces, charities, not-for-profit corporations, etc., may follow a very different logic from the one that we have represented in the rest of this chapter for conventional multinational companies.

Control and monitoring needs. Agency theory (Gomez-Mejia, Berrone, & Franco-Santos, 2014) offers a useful perspective on analysing how the need to control executive decisions impacts compensation packages. This theory is relevant to situations that have a principal-agent structure. The HQs-expatriate relationship corresponds to a principal-agent structure: HQ (the principal) delegates work and responsibilities to expatriates (the agent). In this type of relationship, there is a risk that the 'agency problem' may arise. This refers to the possibility that agents will pursue their own interests, which may diverge from the interests of the principal. This is a real possibility in the multinational arena. For example, in a subsidiary located in a culturally different environment, it is possible for an expatriate to enjoy excellent work conditions while making very little effort. His resulting poor performance can then be excused by attributing it to the lack of fit of the company's procedures to the local culture. Incentive alignment is a traditional device used to address the agency problem. This is defined as the extent to which the reward structure is designed to induce managers to make decisions that are in the best interests of the principal (Gomez-Mejia et al., 2014). Properly designed, the reward structure promotes self-monitoring as it provides performance incentives that encourage agents to minimise opportunism and promote their alignment with the principal's interests. Through these performance incentives, expatriates, pursuing their own goals, will also be pursuing the goal of the headquarters (HQs). From an agency perspective, future research could analyse how different configurations of the expatriate incentives (i.e., the proportion of bonuses and long term incentives versus salary and benefits, the short and long time horizon of incentives, the quantitative and qualitative criteria used to trigger rewards) respond to the intentions of the multinational to solve the agency problem and procure an appropriate alignment of interests between the company and expatriates.

Strategic position of the expatriate. While in the literature it is usual to refer to long-term corporate expatriates as a homogenous group of employees, a closer look at the strategic position they can occupy abroad allows us to make some distinctions that have important implications for international compensation strategies. Just as in other categories of employees, long-term corporate expatriates can perform different sorts of jobs. Specifically, we can discern between 'star' and 'guardian' positions (Baron & Kreps, 1999; Bonache & Noethen, 2014). This distinction is based on the possible effects on total company performance of the individual outcomes of the employees who occupy these positions. Star jobs are those in which a bad performance is not particularly critical, but a good performance is very beneficial for the company. A long-term corporate expatriate performing a star job would be a manager who runs a subsidiary that has very little dependence on HQ (e.g., its products, brand image, procedures) and where what is essential is developing new projects highly tailored to the local market. Guardian jobs are those in which an exemplary performance will be of little consequence for the company's accomplishments, but a bad performance will cause a disaster. A guardian job for a long-term corporate expatriate would be that of representing the firm to important host country's external constituencies, the reputation of the firm being a valuable asset. Subsidiary managers in the financial industry typically fall within this category.

5.5.2 Effects of Compensation Packages

Cross-cultural research on expatriates' satisfaction with their compensation. As has been mentioned earlier, MNCs commonly design different compensation systems for different types of expatriates. It would be reasonable to expect that this would lead to different levels of satisfaction among expatriates regarding their compensation. The evidence on this point is, however, non-existent. The influence of nationality on expatriates' attitudes toward their salaries is another important, and complementary, topic to examine. Some studies analyse the cross-cultural and motivational utility of various compensation strategies on managers and the workforce at large (Lowe, Milliman, De Cieri, & Dowling, 2002). Their goal was to compare pay practices or preferences for pay practices across cultures. For example, when compared to individualist cultures, collectivist countries have been found to place more value on seniority. They see compensation according to needs as being fairer. Drawing on these studies, it would be illustrative to conduct in-depth academic cross-cultural research analysing the motivational utility of various compensation strategies on expatriates from different nationalities. Such research would aim at providing some clues for companies as to which expatriate compensation strategy is most likely to be a good match for the values of a particular culture.

The issue of transaction costs. It is very common to say that expatriates are very expensive. Some studies (Bonache & Pla-Barber, 2005) based on transaction cost theory have nonetheless questioned the general validity of this affirmation. In particular, they consider a series of costs which, although omitted in the traditional literature on expatriation, should be taken into account when making decisions to recruit expatriates or local managers in an MNC's subsidiaries, such as the costs incurred by the recruitment, training, and assessment of the subsidiary's technical and management staff. For example, whenever the foreign subsidiary is a new venture or located in environments that are culturally very different, these costs may be very high, with the result that the overall cost of using HCNs may be higher than the salary costs incurred through deploying expatriates. This explains the apparent contradiction whereby firms in a business context defined by the need to reduce expenditure may continue to make intensive use of such an apparently costly solution as expatriation. If expats really do add value to the organization, they may be a more efficient option and offset the high costs incurred by their deployment. In any case, measuring the return-on-investment from global assignments remains an onerous challenge for organizations. Without a doubt, determining when the transaction costs of using expatriates are lower than those of using local managers is of interest and deserves more attention from the literature.

Justice perceptions and other theoretical views. As mentioned earlier, a number of empirical studies on the determinants and effects of salary inequity among local employees and expatriates have been published (Oltra et al., 2013). It would be interesting to extend this type of research to comparisons among expatriates belonging to different categories, including those described in Chapters 1 and 7. In this sense, while equity theory is the traditional reference used to analyse organizational justice, other approaches regarding justice are also possible. One possible and complementary alternative is Rawl's theory of justice (see Bonache, 2004, for an analysis of this theory as applied to HRM). According to this theory, different work arrangements for expatriates and local employees will be fair in cases where (1) the groups have the same basic labour rights and opportunities, (2) greater rewards correspond to greater merits, and (3) the greater rewards of the expatriates group (the most favoured group) improve those of the less favoured group of local employees. Theoretical and empirical research on the topic using this (or other) theoretical frameworks may be very instructive.

Impact on competitive advantage. More research is also needed on the effects of expatriate compensation systems on firms' competitive advantages. In this regard, and contrary to the basic assumption underlying much of the research on traditional compensation literature, competitive advantage cannot be attained if companies simply implant a 'state of the art' compensation package. As is well-explained by the resource-based view of the firm, a competitive advantage must come from a resource that is valuable, rare, and difficult to imitate (Barney, 2001). Accordingly, instead of focusing on standard compensation packages, competitive advantage will come from crafting compensation and reward systems to create employment relationships that extract the value of firm-specific resources. We have no information about the way in which expatriate packages can be designed to create a shared mindset, extract tacit knowledge among expatriates and repatriates, encourage innovation, creativity and responsiveness, and stimulate the development of productive relationships among people. Investigation along this line would undoubtedly be of great academic and professional interest.

5.6 Conclusions

The remuneration of international staff is no trivial matter. For over half a century now, the balance sheet approach has been used as the basis for calculating the most suitable compensation for both the individual and the company. Nevertheless, when judged according to the goals it aspires to accomplish, this system has a series of shortcomings that are becoming increasingly apparent, and which need to be resolved by HRM departments. Local-plus and localisation are alternative approaches for compensating expatriates which, despite providing certain advantages, are not without their own problems and difficulties. Given the lack of an 'ideal system', companies have been distinguishing between types of postings, with different conditions and approaches for each one of them. This is not the only feature defining the current landscape of international compensation. Other trends include implementing different initiatives to reduce expatriation costs and analysing the expatriate's added value for a company. Examining how the Covid-19 crisis and other contextual and organisational variables affect the way in which the challenge of designing an expatriation package is understood and addressed, and analysing the impact of expatriate compensation on a number of individual and organisational outcomes, are research areas deserving of attention from scholars.

References

Adams, J. S. 1965. Inequity in social exchange. In L. Berkowitz (ed.), *Advances in Experimental Social Psychology*, 2: 267–299. New York: Academic Press.

AIR Inc. 2010. *Diverse Expatriate Populations – Alternative Remuneration Packages*. New York: AIR Inc.

AIR Inc. 2011. *Local-Plus: Tips, Tools and Trends*. New York: AIR Inc.

Barney, J. B. 2001. Resource-based theories of competitive advantage: a ten-year retrospective on the resource-based view. *Journal of Management*, 27(6): 643–650.

Baron, J. N. & Kreps, D. M. 1999. HRM in emerging companies. *Strategic Human Resources*. New York: Wiley.

Bitten, J. 2001. Compensation strategies for international assignments: alternatives to the balance sheet. *HR Professional*, 18(2): 29–31.

Bonache, J. 2004. Towards a re-examination of work arrangements: an analysis from Rawls' theory of justice. *Human Resource Management Review*, 14(4): 395–408.

Bonache, J. 2005. Job satisfaction among expatriates, repatriates and domestic employees: the perceived impact of international assignments on work-related variables. *Personnel Review*, 34(1): 110–124

Bonache, J. 2006. The compensation of expatriates: a review and a future research agenda. In G. Stahl & I. Bjorkman, *Handbook of Research in International Human Resource Management*: 158–175. Cheltenham: Edward Elgar Publishing.

Bonache, J. & Noethen, D. 2014. The impact of individual performance on organizational success and its implications for the management of expatriates. *The International Journal of Human Resource Management*, 25(14): 1960–1977.

Bonache, J. & Pla Barber, J. 2005. When are international managers a cost effective solution? The rationale of transaction cost economics applied to staffing decisions in MNCs. *Journal of Business Research*, 58(10): 1320–1329.

Bonache, J., Sanchez, J. I., & Zárraga-Oberty, C. 2009. The interaction of expatriate pay differential and expatriate inputs on host country nationals' pay unfairness. *The International Journal of Human Resource Management*, 20(10): 2135–2149.

Bonache, J. & Stirpe, L. 2012. Compensating global employees. In G. K. Stahl, I. Björkman, & S. Morris, (eds.), *Handbook of Research in International Human Resource Management* (2nd ed.): 162–182. Cheltenham: Edward Elgar Publishing.

Bonache, J. & Zárraga-Oberty, C. 2017. The traditional approach to compensating global mobility: criticisms and alternatives. *The International Journal of Human Resource Management*, 28(1): 149–169.

Bonache, J. & Zárraga-Oberty, C. 2020. Compensating Global Mobility in a Workers' Cooperative: an interpretive study, in *Journal of World Business*, in Press.

Brookfield, 2015. Global Relocation Trends Survey Report. Woodridge, IL.

Caligiuri, P. & Bonache, J. 2016. Evolving and enduring challenges in global mobility. *Journal of World Business*, 51(1): 127–141.

Chen, C. C., Choi, J., & Chi, S. C. 2002. Making justice sense of local-expatriate compensation disparity: mitigation by local referents, ideological explanations, and interpersonal sensitivity in China-foreign joint ventures. *Academy of Management Journal*, 45(4): 807–826.

Chen, G., Ployhart, R. E., Thomas, H. C., Anderson, N., & Bliese, P. D. 2011. The power of momentum: a new model of dynamic relationships between job satisfaction change and turnover intentions. *Academy of Management Journal*, 54(1): 159–181.

Dickover, G. F. 1957. Employee relations in foreign operations. In *Case Studies in Foreign Operations*: International Management Association: 118–133.

Edström, A. & Galbraith, J. R. 1977. Transfer of managers as a coordination and control strategy in multinational organizations. *Administrative Science Quarterly*, 22(2): 248.

Farndale, E., Scullion, H., & Sparrow, P. 2010. The role of the corporate HR function in global talent management. *Journal of World Business*, 45(2): 161–168.DOI:10.1016/j.jwb.2009.09.012.

Festing, M. & Perkins, S. 2008. Rewards for internationally mobile employees. In M. Dickmann, C. Brewster, & P. Sparrow (eds.), *International Human Resource Management: A European Perspective*: 150–173. Oxon: Routledge.

Festinger, L. 1954. A theory of social comparison processes. *Human Relations*, 7: 117–140.

Gomez-Mejia, L. R., Berrone, P., & Franco-Santos, M. 2014. *Compensation and Organizational Performance: Theory, Research, and Practice*. Abingdon: Routledge.

Gupta, A. K. & Govindarajan, V. 2002. Cultivating a global mindset. *The Academy of Management Executive*, 16(1): 116–126.

Harvey, M. G. 1993a. Designing a global compensation system: the logic and a model. *Colombia Journal of World Business*, 28: 56–72.

Harvey, M. G. 1993b. Empirical evidence of recurring international compensation problems. *Journal of International Business Studies*, 24 (4): 785–799.

Kahneman, D. & Tversky, A. 1984. Choices, values and frames. *American Psychologist*, 39(4): 341–350.

KPMG 2016. Global Assignment Policies and Practices. Publication number: 133764-G.

Leung, K., Zhu, Y., & Ge, C. 2009. Compensation disparity between locals and expatriates: moderating the effects of perceived injustice in foreign multinationals in China. *Journal of World Business*, 44(1): 85–93.

Lowe, K. B., Milliman, J., De Cieri, H., & Dowling, P. J. 2002. International compensation practices: a ten-country comparative analysis. *Human Resource Management: Published in Cooperation with the School of Business Administration, The University of Michigan and in alliance with the Society of Human Resources Management*, 41(1): 45–66.

McNulty, Y. 2014. The opportunity costs of local-plus and localization approaches to expatriate compensation. In L. Berger and D. Berger (eds.), *The Compensation Handbook* 6th ed. Columbus: McGraw-Hill Education.

McNulty, Y. 2015. Employing novel compensation approaches to compete for expatriate talent. In L. Berger and D. Berger (eds.), *The Compensation Handbook: A State-of-the-Art Guide to Compensation Strategy and Design* 6th ed.: 503–518. Columbus: McGraw-Hill Education. ISBN-13: 978–0071836999. Reprinted in: Mendenhall, M., G. Oddou, G. Stahl, & R.S. Reiche (eds.). (2016). Readings and Cases in International HRM and OB (5th ed.), in press.

McNulty, Y., De Cieri, H., & Hutchings, K. 2009. Do global firms measure expatriate return on investment? An empirical examination of measures, barriers and variables influencing global staffing practices. *International Journal of Human Resource Management*, 20(6): 1309–1326.

Mercer 2015. *Worldwide Survey of International Assignment Policies and Practices*. Geneva: Mercer.

Nowak, C. & Linder, C. 2016. Do you know how much your expatriate costs? An activity based cost analysis of expatriation. *Journal of Global Mobility*, 4(1): 88–107.

Oltra, V., Bonache, J., & Brewster, C. 2013. A new framework for understanding inequalities between expatriates and host country nationals. *Journal of Business Ethics*, 115(2): 291–310.

O'Really, M. 1996. Expatriate pay: the state of the art. *Compensation and Benefits Review*, 12(1): 54–60.

Paik, Y., Parboteeah, K. P., & Shim, W. 2007. The relationship between perceived compensation, organizational commitment and job satisfaction: the case of Mexican workers in the Korean Maquiladoras. *International Journal of Human Resource Management*, 18(10): 1768–1781.

Phillips, L. & Fox, M. A. 2003. Compensation strategy in transnational corporations. *Management Decision*, 41(5): 465–476.

Reiche, B. S., Kraimer, M. L., & Harzing, A. W. 2011. Why do international assignees stay? An organizational embeddedness perspective. *Journal of International Business Studies*, 42(4): 521–544.

Reynolds, C. 1997. Expatriate compensation in historical perspective. *Journal of World Business*, 32(2): 118–132.

Shaffer, M. A, Harrison, D., & Gilley, M. 1999. Dimensions, determinants, and differences in the expatriate adjustment process. *Journal of International Business Studies*, 30(3): 557–581.

Stahl, G. K., Miller, E., & Tung, R. 2002. Toward the boundaryless career: a closer look at the expatriate career concept and the perceived implications of an international assignment. *Journal of World Business*, 37: 216–227.

Suutari, V. & Tornikoski, C. 2000. Determinants of expatriate compensation–Findings among expatriate members of SEFE. *Finnish Journal of Business Economics*, 49(4): 517–539.

Suutari, V. & Tornikoski, C. 2001. The challenge of expatriate compensation: the sources of satisfaction and dissatisfaction among expatriates. *The International Journal of Human Resource Management*, 12(3): 389–404.

Toh, S. M. & DeNisi, A. 2003. Host country national reactions to expatriate pay policies: a model and implications. *Academy of Management Review*, 28(4): 606–621.

Tornikoski, C., Suutari, V., & Festing, M. 2014. Compensation package of international assignees. *The Routledge Companion to International Human Resource Management*, 289.

Welch, C. L., Welch, D. E., & Tahvanainen, M. 2008. Managing the HR dimension of international project operations. *The International Journal of Human Resource Management*, 19(2): 205–222.

Yan, A., Zhu, G., & Hall, D. T. 2002, International assignments for career building: a model of agency relationships and psychological contracts. *Academy of Management Review*, 27(3): 373–391.

6 Repatriation and Career Development

FLORA F. T. CHIANG, EMMY VAN ESCH, THOMAS A. BIRTCH

6.1 Introduction

What is repatriation and why is it important? Repatriation refers to the final phase of an international assignment in which the expatriate returns and reintegrates or repatriates into his or her originating employing organisation or country (Chiang et al., 2018). Individuals can repatriate from a number of different types of international assignments (see Figure 6.1). For example, an individual returning from an assigned posting and an individual returning from a self-initiated international assignment both are considered repatriates. Whereas assigned expatriate repatriation typically follows the completion of a specific time-based task or organisational goal, self-initiated expatriate repatriation typically follows the fulfilment of one's own personal or career development goals. International assignments can also be of either a short (less than twelve months) or long duration (e.g., two or more years) depending on need and the complexity of the assignment (Chiang et al., 2018; Harrison, Shaffer, & Bhaskar-Shrinivas, 2004; Shaffer et al., 2012). Although other forms of global mobility exist (see Chapter 7), the main focus of this chapter is placed on assigned and self-initiated expatriates given their more pronounced effects and implications (Chiang et al., 2018).

As organisations expand and strengthen their presence overseas, their need for international assignees typically grows (Brookfield, 2015; Ernst & Young, 2014). A recent survey (KPMG, 2018) suggests that more than 90 per cent of multinational enterprises (MNEs) currently use long-term assigned expatriates. However, some changes are clearly taking place. For example, efforts by organisations to reduce costs and promote talent retention have led to a rise in permanent transfers and indefinite length assignments (KPMG, 2018). Short-term assignments and self-initiated expatriation have also grown in

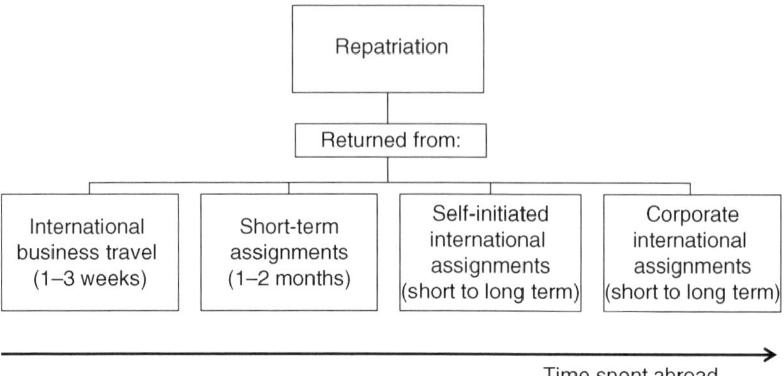

Figure 6.1 Examples of different types of international assignments

popularity (Harrison, 2016). Nevertheless, traditionally assigned expatriates continue to be widespread and are expected to remain at or near half of all international positions for the foreseeable future (Harrison, 2016). Moreover, not only do organisations view international assignments as vital to the stability and control of their foreign operations but also to their knowledge transfer efforts (McCall & Hollenbeck, 2002; Riusala & Suutari, 2004). In particular, repatriation is increasingly being recognised by MNEs as an opportunity to harness newly acquired skills, perspectives, and knowledge essential to their competitive advantage, making understanding the dynamics and implications of the repatriation process imperative to business success.

However, repatriation is not free from problems. In fact, a range of issues, including those associated with re-adjustment, retention, repatriation systems, practices and policies, and others, can have a profound influence on organisations and individual repatriates (Bossard & Peterson, 2005; Linehan & Scullion, 2002). For example, research suggests that upwards of 38 per cent of repatriates leave their employing organisation within a year of returning home (Bolino, Klotz, & Turnley, 2017). High levels of repatriate turnover are costly to organisations not only in terms of lost productivity and employee replacement but also in terms of losses associated with training and development (Kulkarni, Lengnick-Hall, & Valk, 2010; Lazarova & Caligiuri, 2001) and international know-how, skills, knowledge, and networks that repatriates acquired and developed while abroad (Cho, Hutchings, & Marchant, 2013; Kraimer et al.,

2012). A high rate of repatriate turnover may also pose a competitive risk to organisations because repatriates often take up positions in competing firms bringing their newly acquired skills, knowledge, and networks to the benefit of their new employer (Kraimer et al., 2012). Repatriate turnover has also been shown to affect employee morale and adversely impact the willingness of other employees to participate in international assignments (Cho et al., 2013; Kraimer et al., 2012).

6.2 Repatriation and Career Development

What career resources and competencies can repatriates develop as a function of living and working abroad? An international assignment provides assignees with opportunities to acquire new experiences, knowledge, ideas, and business practices and to learn from local suppliers and clients, foreign cultures and national markets, which can facilitate the development of new and valuable career resources and competencies (Lazarova & Tarique, 2005; Stevens et al., 2006). These career resources and competencies can be categorised as: 'knowing how', 'knowing whom', and 'knowing why' (DeFillippi & Arthur, 1994).

6.2.1 Knowing How

Knowing how career resources and competencies refer to job-related knowledge, skills, and competencies (DeFillippi & Arthur, 1994). International assignments enable repatriates to develop both general competencies, such as explicit knowledge, implicit experiences, technical expertise, and soft skills, and career-specific competencies, such as intercultural skills, cultural intelligence, a global business mind-set and perspective, and even foreign language skills (Cao, Hirschi, & Deller, 2012; Dickmann & Harris, 2005; Suutari & Mäkelä, 2007). These general and career-specific international competencies are beneficial to the individual repatriate's career development and success (e.g., accumulating career capital in Dickmann & Doherty, 2008; preparing for a senior position and increasing marketability in Haslberger & Brewster, 2009; and the organisation's competitive advantage in Lazarova & Cerdin, 2007; Mäkelä & Brewster, 2009; Oddou, Osland, & Blakeney, 2009; Stevens et al., 2006). Yet, most MNEs neither have a system in place for identifying and utilising the competencies that repatriates have gained during their international assignment (Brookfield, 2015) nor do they have performance- or talent-management processes formally tied to repatriation (Harrison, 2016).

6.2.2 *Knowing Whom*

Knowing whom career resources and competencies refer to the networks that individuals engage with that can aid in their career development (DeFillippi & Arthur, 1994). International assignments enable repatriates to develop new contacts both within and outside the organisation, contacts that are characterised by geographic, cultural, social, and professional diversity and would not be possible if people remain in their home country (Mäkelä & Suutari, 2009). Such international networks can be beneficial to both the organisation and the individual repatriate. For example, in the case of the organisation, networks can aid in the development of transnational capabilities essential to coordinate and control multiple globally dispersed units of the MNE (Cerdin & Le Pargneux, 2009; Yan, Zhu, & Hall, 2002) whereas in the case of the repatriate, networks can help them to develop skills through shared experiences (Cerdin & Le Pargneux, 2009) and to acquire intercultural skills and knowledge (Cao et al., 2012).

6.2.3 *Knowing Why*

Knowing why career resources and competencies refer to individuals' values, identity, and motivation, and embody understanding how and why individuals obtain meaning from their work and career (DeFillippi & Arthur, 1994), including the goals and motivation (extrinsic and intrinsic) associated with an international assignment (Doherty, Dickmann, & Mills, 2011; Suutari & Brewster, 2003). Understanding the underlying motivation for an international assignment helps organisations develop a more appropriate repatriation plan and better manage repatriate expectations. Developing a greater sense of self-awareness also helps repatriates improve understanding of their personal strengths and weaknesses, work and career values, and aspirations (Suutari & Mäkelä, 2007) and align their values, preferences, and larger life and career goals.

6.2.4 *Different Perspectives on Repatriation and Career Development*

What is career development? Career development represents an international assignee's personal and professional career outcomes acquired, developed, and accumulated over time (Arthur, Hall, & Lawrence, 1989). When repatriates have worked in their home country and at least one foreign country, they are pursuing a global career – a career that 'spans two or more countries' (Baruch & Reis 2016: 14), or one that 'encompasses a succession or collection of multiple international assignments' (Suutari, Tornikoski, & Mäkelä, 2012: 3456). According to career stage theory (Super, 1957), individuals experience four stages of career development, namely exploration (below 24 years of age), establishment (between the ages of 25 and 44), maintenance (between the ages of 45 and 64), and disengagement (above the age of 65). As a consequence, individuals are likely to possess different career concerns and priorities at different stages of their career (Brookfield, 2015). For example, with most repatriates falling within the establishment and maintenance stages of career development, these groups are more likely to focus on consolidating career choices and maintaining what they have already established versus those in the exploration stage, which are more likely to be in a period of self-examination and be more concerned with clarifying career interests and directions (Reichers, 1986).

How do different career perspectives help us understand the challenges of returning home? Some might argue that returning home should be the easiest or least problematic stage of an international assignment. However, as mentioned earlier, a significant percentage of repatriates leave their employing organisations within a very short time (e.g., several months to a year) after repatriating (Bolino et al., 2017; Brookfield, 2015). To improve our understanding of the (difficult) repatriation experience and its implications for career development, the international human resource management literature offers two main perspectives: (1) the traditional bounded career perspective and (2) the more recent or emerging proactive career perspective (see Table 6.1).

6.2.5 *Bounded Career Perspective*

The more traditional repatriate literature takes a 'bounded' view of career development in which a career is characterised by relatively

Table 6.1 *Perspectives on repatriation and career development*

Perspective	Implications for organisations
Bounded career	Organisations should emphasise helping repatriates avoid and cope with problems associated with different aspects of re-adjustment (i.e., general, interaction, and work).
Proactive career	Organisations should emphasise helping repatriates understand their motives for an international assignment and how to prepare for and be proactive in planning and managing their career.

stable organisational structures (see Sullivan, 1999) and defined in terms of a repatriate's relationship with the employing organisation. Career progression is derived from hierarchical advancement within a company in order to obtain greater extrinsic rewards (Rosenbaum, 1979) and the employer-employee relationship is characterised by the exchange of loyalty for job security (Rousseau, 1989; Sullivan & Baruch, 2009; Suutari & Mäkelä, 2007). This traditional perspective draws upon uncertainty reduction theory and describes repatriates as passive individuals who do not actively direct their own careers towards the best available career opportunities (i.e., dissatisfaction-maladjustment; Lazarova & Cerdin, 2007).

Repatriate turnover is said to result from problems associated with re-adjustment (Lazarova & Cerdin, 2007), conceptualised as a three-dimensional construct consisting of general, interaction, and work re-adjustment (Black & Gregersen, 1991). In terms of general re-adjustment, repatriates may find that their self-conceptualisations and identity have changed upon returning, perceiving themselves as different people than the ones that left because of the new perspectives, experiences, skills, and interests they have gained. They may also feel that their new perspectives, experiences, skills, and interests are not valued by others in their home country. Moreover, the repatriates' family members (e.g., partner, children), who often accompany them on an international assignment, may similarly find it difficult to settle back into life in their home country, further reinforcing the belief that their personal lives have been adversely affected by the international assignment (Black & Gregersen, 1991). As a result, many repatriates feel as though they no longer fit into their home country and, interestingly, experience a more intense culture shock upon returning home than they experienced when moving abroad (Bossard & Peterson, 2005; Linehan & Scullion, 2002). In terms of interaction re-adjustment, repatriates may find that their communication style has changed upon returning and that they have developed new social customs that influence the nature of interpersonal dynamics (Gregersen & Black, 1996). In terms of work re-adjustment, repatriates may feel dissatisfied with their job, team, or organisation upon returning (Suutari & Brewster, 2003). For example, the repatriate may wish to put his or her newly acquired skills and knowledge to use but instead experience disappointment when these inputs are not valued or needed by the home organisation. Additionally, repatriates may feel disappointed that their colleagues do not appreciate or show interest in their adventures abroad. It is also possible that the repatriate's previous job duties have changed; previous team members have been reshuffled; original supervisors, peers, and subordinates have moved on or advanced in their careers; or the business has been reorganised, leaving the repatriate feeling alienated from co-workers and causing other adverse effects, such as job dissatisfaction and increased turnover intention (Bossard & Peterson, 2005; Brookfield, 2015; Linehan & Scullion, 2002; Suutari & Brewster, 2003). Thus, according to the bounded career perspective, to make returning home or repatriating easier and turnover less likely, there is a need for MNEs to help repatriates avoid the problems associated with all three types of re-adjustment, that is, general, interaction, and work.

6.2.6 *Proactive Career Perspective*

Recent changes in the environment such as technological advancement, increased globalisation and workforce diversity, increased life spans and changing family structures (e.g., increased number of dual-career couples, single working parents) have changed the traditional organisational structure and employer-employee relationship (Sullivan & Baruch, 2009). Such changes have also meant that self-initiated international assignments are becoming more common, making the traditional bounded perspective less relevant because individuals are now acting as their own agents and taking responsibility for their own careers.

In response, scholars have adopted a longer-term career development perspective, moving away from the traditional 'bounded' career perspective to a more proactive boundaryless career perspective (Arthur & Rousseau, 1996) or protean career perspective (Hall, 2004; Hall & Moss, 1998). These emerging career perspectives argue that repatriate turnover is likely the result of problems associated with career opportunities (Hyder & Lövblad, 2007; Kraimer, Shaffer, & Bolino, 2009; Lazarova & Cerdin, 2007; Stahl et al. 2009) as opposed to re-adjustment problems, especially when there is a perception that better employment opportunities may exist in the external labour market. Evidence suggests (KPMG, 2018) that external labour market competitiveness (pull factor) and the lack of appropriate job opportunities within one's organisation after repatriation (push factor) represent two primary drivers of repatriate turnover. In the case of the 'boundaryless career' perspective (Arthur & Rousseau, 1996), the literature mainly focuses on the changing nature of global job markets (Eby, Butts, & Lockwood, 2003; Hall, 2004) and career opportunities beyond the boundary of a single organisation. Assignees pursuing a boundaryless career often navigate the changing environment and are open to physical and/or psychological movement. In contrast, the literature on the protean career perspective (Hall, 1976) mainly focuses on internal careers (Eby et al., 2003; Hall, 2004) and career opportunities that are in line with one's own interests and values (values-driven).

Both the boundaryless and protean career orientations advance the idea of rational choice and individual agency. Repatriates are perceived as active and proactive agents who manage their own career during the repatriation stage (Lazarova & Cerdin, 2007), including seeking out the best available career opportunities for further professional development which may be within or outside the organisation (Baruch, 2006; Lazarova & Tarique, 2005). In other words, according to these perspectives, it is the individual not the organisation that is in control of career development and an international assignment is viewed as a means of acquiring new career resources and competencies (Haslberger & Brewster, 2009). At the same time, individuals, especially millennials (Brookfield, 2015), are more willing to change employers to work for a series of organisations or make lateral career moves across organisations and countries (Banai & Wes, 2004; Baruch, Altman, & Tung, 2016). In this sense, an international assignment is often viewed as a way of fostering not only one's career prospects within the sending organisation but also as a means of creating new opportunities outside one's employing organisation (Haslberger & Brewster, 2009; Lazarova & Tarique, 2005). Such employees are typically characterised as having lower levels of organisational commitment (Lazarova & Tarique, 2005), making them more susceptible to leaving an organisation when the external job market is favourable (Stahl et al., 2009; Suutari & Brewster, 2003) or when they are dissatisfied with perceived opportunities for career advancement with their current employer (Brookfield, 2015; Kraimer et al., 2009; Lazarova & Cerdin, 2007; Reiche, Kraimer, & Harzing, 2011; Stahl et al., 2009). Hence, both boundaryless and protean career orientations are not favourable to organisations, particularly in terms of repatriate retention (Cerdin & Le Pargneux, 2009). It is therefore important to long-term repatriate retention that MNEs consider implementing mutually beneficial career and talent development programmes and strategies. Thus, as the proactive career perspectives implies (i.e., boundaryless and protean), to make returning home or repatriating easier and turnover less likely, MNEs must closely monitor repatriates' career concerns at different stages of their career and help them to manage their career development over the longer term.

6.3 Repatriation Success

How is repatriation success measured? 'Repatriation success' is measured differently by the organisation than it is by the individual repatriate. Making such a determination also depends upon who is evaluating repatriation success as well as what objectives and/or subjective measures are being considered (Judge et al., 1995).

6.3.1 Organisational Perspective on Repatriation Success

The more traditional bounded career literature tends to evaluate repatriation success from the perspective of the organisation. For example, success is based on evaluations of observable task and work goal attainment (i.e., objective success, Judge et al., 1995), meaning that repatriation is considered successful when key organisational objectives performed by a repatriate have been achieved (e.g., Furuya et al., 2009; Yan et al., 2002). Another extensively studied objective indicator of success is repatriate retention (Cerdin & Le Pargneux, 2009).

Moreover, two subjective indicators at the individual level are also frequently considered: re-adjustment and job success (Cerdin & Le Pargneux, 2009). Whilst, as discussed previously, re-adjustment is typically measured using three factors (i.e., general, interaction, and work, Black & Gregersen, 1991), job success is determined according to job satisfaction (Cerdin & Le Pargneux, 2009; Yan et al., 2002) and job commitment (Chi & Chen, 2007; Stevens et al., 2006). Other objective variables may also be used, including promotions and pay increases (Cerdin & Le Pargneux, 2009; Yan et al., 2002).

6.3.2 Individual Perspective on Repatriation Success

The proactive career literature tends to focus on the individual repatriate when assessing 'repatriation success'. This stream of literature argues that repatriation is successful when assignees' individual objectives attached to their repatriation have been achieved. One frequently used indicator is career success, which reflects repatriates' 'positive psychological or work-related outcomes or achievements one has accumulated as a result of one's work experiences' (Judge et al., 1995: 3). In this sense, career success is largely based on repatriates' feelings of accomplishment and career satisfaction (i.e., subjective success, Judge et al., 1995). Commonly studied outcomes include job satisfaction and career satisfaction, or feelings of success relative to one's own goals and expectations (Cerdin & Le Pargneux, 2009). Another measure often used is development success, which typically assesses long-term career growth or continued development opportunities, including experienced learning, challenging job assignments, increased responsibilities (Yan et al., 2002); new knowledge, skills, and abilities; and one's marketability upon return (Cerdin & Le Pargneux, 2009). Development success can also be measured in terms of network building because international assignments enable assignees to develop a network of new contacts both within and outside the organisation which can help them to develop their knowledge, skills, and abilities (Cerdin & Le Pargneux, 2009). Indirectly, these individual objectives are also highly relevant to organisational success. Network building, for example, is important to developing transnational capabilities which facilitate the coordination and control within and across multiple units of the MNE (Cerdin & Le Pargneux, 2009; Yan et al., 2002). At the same time, global knowledge and competencies acquired have the potential to contribute to the creation of new organisational knowledge and capabilities that can contribute to a firm's competitive advantage (Lazarova & Cerdin, 2007; Mäkelä & Brewster, 2009; Oddou et al., 2009).

6.4 Managing the Repatriation Process

What can be done to improve the process of repatriating? Implementing an effective repatriation strategy should be high on the agenda of every MNE. However, evidence suggests that most organisations do not have a formal repatriation strategy in place (Brookfield, 2015). In fact, most post-assignment interventions are currently primarily financial in nature (KPMG, 2018). So, what steps can be taken to better manage the repatriation process and, ultimately, repatriates' career development? We discuss below a number of challenges that need to be considered when attempting to improve the repatriation process and its outcomes (see Table 6.2).

6.4.1 Individual-level Challenges

International assignments are uncertain and challenging. They require individuals to devote time and effort to adapting to and coping with unforeseen problems. Coping refers to repatriates' 'efforts to master demands (conditions of harm, threat or challenge) that are appraised (or perceived) as exceeding or taxing his or her resources' (Monat & Lazarus, 1991: 5). In general, there are two types of coping strategies, problem-focused and emotion-focused, with the former attempting to act on the stressor and the latter attempting to manage the emotions associated with the stressor (Feldman & Tompson, 1993; Herman & Tetrick, 2009). Some evidence suggests that problem-focused strategies may be more beneficial to re-adjustment than emotion-focused strategies (Feldman & Tompson, 1993; Herman & Tetrick, 2009). Organisations should therefore provide support that helps repatriates develop problem-focused coping strategies a priority, such as offering training about the common pitfalls that may be encountered during repatriation and how to deal with them (Herman & Tetrick, 2009). By contrast, emotion-focused coping interventions could include pre-repatriation

Table 6.2 *Challenges and implications to organisations*

Challenges	Implications for organisations
Individual-level	
✓ Coping strategies	✓ Promote both problem- and emotion-focused coping strategies
✓ Identity	✓ Promote embeddedness in home communities during time abroad
✓ Expectations	✓ Help repatriates develop more realistic expectations before and after repatriating
✓ Personal characteristics: personality and motivation	✓ Select/train proactive assignees ✓ Select/train highly motivated assignees ✓ Select assignees who have a high learning orientation
Interpersonal and team-level	
✓ Ability/motivation to transfer knowledge ✓ Social categorisation ✓ Interaction frequency	✓ Demonstrate behaviours and practices that promote trust and shared cognitive ground ✓ Develop reintegration and relationship building practices to foster social interactions and knowledge sharing
Organisation-level	
✓ HRM practices and policies ✓ Psychological contract ✓ Job factors ✓ Career opportunities	✓ Build a supportive HRM system ✓ Survey and manage on-going employment relationship and expectations ✓ Communicate job demand and need expectations ✓ Develop career repatriation policy and programme
Country-level	
✓ Cultural distance ✓ Social and economic development	✓ Provide additional support to assignees returning from countries with greater differences, fore example, cultural, social, and economic ✓ Collect data

visits to the home country, settling-in time off, and repatriation counselling services that aim to reduce stress and facilitate re-adjustment (Feldman & Tompson, 1993).

Moreover, international assignments can influence one's identity (Hyder & Lövblad, 2007; Kraimer et al., 2012). Research has shown that repatriates who were highly embedded in their prior host communities are more likely to develop an international identity (Kraimer et al., 2012). For some repatriates, this newly developed identity may fade over time after returning home, while for others it may be more resilient, which can make fitting in upon return harder and re-adjustment difficulties more likely (Haslberger & Brewster, 2009). Accordingly, organisations should do more to keep international assignees embedded in their home-country communities during their time abroad, such as mentorship programmes that require an assignee to maintain regular contact with a home-country based mentor. Tasks that require more frequent contact with home-based co-workers may also help to reduce assignees feelings of isolation and foster deeper connections (e.g., updates about home-country environment and colleagues) (Carraher, Sullivan, & Crocitto, 2008). Expatriates should be encouraged to maintain regular contact with as many co-workers and managers as possible while abroad to ensure a good 'landing' upon return (Clegg, 2016).

Research indicates that managing expectations is also essential to the repatriation process with repatriates whose expectations are met tending to be more satisfied (Vidal, Valle & Aragón, 2008). Yet, repatriates' expectations are often higher than an organisation can meet, which leads to disappointment and re-adjustment difficulties (Doherty & Dickmann, 2009; Shen & Hall, 2009). Most employees who accept an international assignment expect to be rewarded upon return with, for instance, greater career advancement opportunities, opportunities to use newly acquired international experiences and skills, and higher levels of support from the organisation and their colleagues (Suutari & Brewster 2003). Upon return, however, repatriates often fail to receive the expected pay and career opportunities and advancement, even though their colleagues may have already been promoted, leaving them to feel less satisfied with the repatriation process (Ren et al. 2013). Even for self-initiated repatriates, although their motives for international assignment are more for personal development, when they perceive that their future career interests and personal growth are unsatisfactory within a company they are more likely to quit (Vaiman, Haslberger, & Vance, 2015). Such findings imply that organisations should do more to help repatriates develop more realistic expectations about their return from an international assignment (Kulkarni et al., 2010; Suutari & Brewster, 2003), including offering appropriate briefings during an international assignment and encouraging interactions with individuals who have had repatriation experience in the firm (Carraher et al., 2008).

Repatriates' personalities may also affect their attitudes toward the international assignment and hence their ability to re-adjust upon returning. Research indicates that a proactive personality (i.e., high extraversion, conscientiousness, emotional stability, agreeableness and openness) drives proactive behaviour (e.g., social networking and information seeking), which in turn, has been shown to reduce turnover intention and re-adjustment problems (Lazarova & Cerdin, 2007; O'Sullivan, 2002). Moreover, research also suggests that a repatriate with a higher level of motivation is also more likely to marshal personal resources to overcome challenges and is found to be positively related to desirable repatriation outcomes, such as knowledge transfer (Hyder & Lövblad, 2007; Paik, Segaud, & Malinowski, 2002). These findings have important implications for the selection criteria that organisations use to identify and designate individuals for international assignments. Choosing appropriate candidates should not only focus on their cross-cultural suitability to work overseas (Dowling, Festing, & Engle, 2013) but also on whether they have the right mix of personality traits (e.g., proactive personality), motivations (e.g., extrinsic or intrinsic), and attitudes (e.g., highly motivated and willingness to learn) for an international assignment. Yet, currently most MNEs do not assess and select candidates based on such criteria (Brookfield, 2015). Given the above shortcomings, repatriates themselves should then be more proactive in managing their own repatriation process and career development. As Unruh and Cabrera (2013: 136) assert '[y]ou can't rely on your company to expand your global horizons ... a do-it-yourself mind-set is key'.

6.4.2 Interpersonal and Team-level Challenges

Repatriates may be 'new' and considered as 'out-group' by their home-office colleagues when they return. Research indicates that repatriates' ability and motivation to interact with their colleagues helps build interpersonal trust and shared cognitive ground, which are instrumental to knowledge transfer (Mäkelä & Brewster, 2009; Oddou et al.,

2009). To help repatriates to 're-integrate' into the workforce, organisations can promote communication and social interaction which may include encouraging assignees to blog about their experiences both during and after the international assignment, postings that can be shared via internal social media and commented on by others throughout the organisation. Repatriates' profiles could also be displayed by organisations to highlight the skills and experiences they have accumulated, thereby not only increasing their credibility but opportunities for their expertise to be harnessed (Molinsky & Hahn, 2016). Informal talks and discussions by repatriates (e.g., brown bag lunches) showcasing their overseas experiences are also likely to help foster social interaction and increase the repatriate's motivation to share additional knowledge with local colleagues. Such practices are also likely to help rebuild repatriates' relationships and enhance their credibility, all of which can bolster employee commitment.

6.4.3 Organisation-level Challenges

Research has shown that human resources management (HRM) systems and practices are important for effective repatriation. While non-supportive HRM systems are associated with dissatisfaction and maladjustment, supportive HRM systems (e.g., reorientation programmes, repatriation training seminars, pre-return briefings) are associated with positive repatriation outcomes (Kraimer et al., 2009; Kulkarni et al., 2010; Stahl et al., 2009; Vidal et al., 2008). Consequently, MNEs should focus on developing supportive interventions, such as home-based mentoring (Linehan & Scullion, 2002) and professional career management (Vidal et al., 2008). Companies such as Motorola and Maersk provide formal mentors at both ends of an international assignment: people to whom assignees can turn to when they encounter problems or need career advice, connections that also keep them informed about their home country/organisation to alleviate anxiety associated with 'out-of-sight, out-of-mind'. Adidas offers contracts to those on fixed-term international assignments, guaranteeing them the right to return and offering help to find their next position upon repatriation (Clegg, 2016). In addition, practices which enable repatriates to use their newly acquired skills and knowledge (Furuya et al., 2007), access local resources and networks while abroad (Linehan & Scullion, 2002), and learn about promotion opportunities (Kraimer et al., 2009) are all vital to the repatriation process and career development.

In addition, research has demonstrated that perceived psychological contract fulfilment is associated with repatriate commitment and retention (Chi & Chen, 2007) and that perceived psychological contract breach and turnover intention are stronger during repatriation than at any other time during the employment relationship (Haslberger & Brewster, 2009). Because perceived psychological contract breaches are related to negative outcomes (e.g., employee attitudes, such as mistrust, job dissatisfaction, organisational commitment, turnover intention, and work behaviours, such as job performance, organisational citizenship behaviours: see the meta-analytic study by Zhao et al., 2007), organisations need to be cognisant of what they promise to assignees even if such promises (e.g., promotion) are made in good faith. In other words, organisations should be cautious about over-promising what might happen following an assignment. To help overcome such challenges, the conventional approach of relocating expatriates overseas with rich expatriation packages is being revisited by companies such Samsung and Walmart which are now offering short-term assignments (e.g., 6 months) in their effort to develop assignees' global know-how and experiences earlier in their careers without encountering the many challenges associated with relocating from long-term assignments (Geissler, Kuhn, & McGinn, 2011). Short-term assignments also have the added benefit of helping to reduce repatriates' career uncertainty.

Finally, a job's nature in the host office is often different from the home office. For example, expatriate job assignments are often strategic in nature versus back home where they are usually more operational oriented (Clegg, 2016), suggesting that MNEs need to clearly communicate such differences to repatriates. However, most MNEs do not have a formal career repatriation strategy or policy linked to career management (Brookfield, 2015). In fact, according to consultancy reports, two-thirds of companies do not have a global mobility programme that is aligned with their organisation's overarching talent management strategy (KPMG, 2018).

A structured and systematic career repatriation programme should therefore be in place from the beginning of an international assignment through the repatriation process. However, many multinational employers '[have lost] expensively developed talent through lack of forward planning' (Clegg, 2016). Additionally, MNEs should monitor expatriates' performance and development to ensure that the skills and competencies they acquire overseas are transferable to the home country as well as to identify more appropriate re-entry positions that might exist.

To better prepare repatriates for their return, the home sponsors should also initiate contact with the returnee in advance of their return to discuss the reintegration process. Open and frank communication between the repatriate and home sponsor(s) is important. During these interactions potential repatriates can express their interests and expectations and provide an update about their new skills, knowledge and experiences. At the same time, the sponsors can provide information about the types of career opportunities available in the home office, or possibly even opportunities for future international assignments. For example, Tesco has a career repatriation policy offering repatriates a choice to either extend their current assignment or choose from other new assignments. Finally, MNEs should also organise a formal re-orientation and de-briefing programme for repatriates upon their return. Organisations that manage their repatriates successfully usually have advanced planning and structures in place for the repatriation stage. For example, six months before an individual is scheduled to return home, Honda initiates an active matchmaking process to locate a suitable job for the repatriate and conducts a debriefing interview to capture lessons the repatriate has learned from the assignment (Black & Gregerson, 1999). Having effective career development pathways also differentiates organisations from one another, not only in terms of retaining repatriates but also in attracting high quality repatriates from other organisations. Making repatriation an integral part of an organisation's knowledge management process is also likely to foster knowledge sharing and reinforce the value of international assignments.

6.4.4 Country-level Challenges

A host country environment may differ significantly from the home country environment. Country factors, such as cultural distance, can have a significant impact on repatriation outcomes. For example, the greater the cultural distance between the home and host country, the more difficult the re-adjustment process may become due to 'reverse culture shock' (Gregersen & Stroh, 1997). This suggests that organisations should offer additional support for repatriates returning from countries with a greater cultural distance. Besides cultural differences, repatriates may also be affected by different levels of economic and social development between the home versus host country. In some cases, repatriation may be more favourable because repatriates view their home country as 'the next land of opportunity where they can build their careers and realize their dreams' (Guo, Porschitz, & Alves, 2013: 41) or have a larger number of job opportunities (Kulkarni et al., 2010). Although repatriating from an emerging (host) economy to a more developed (home) economy may create fewer re-adjustment problems than the reverse (Harrison et al., 2004), in terms of career development, due to differences in the availability of job opportunities, it may be more difficult for repatriates to obtain comparable or advanced positions back in one's home country (Clegg, 2016). A lack of appropriate jobs available in the home country is considered a top reason for many repatriates leaving their employing organisations upon return (KPMG, 2018). Regrettably, recent research also reveals that 78 per cent of organisations are unable to determine why they are losing repatriates to competitors because they do not collect data on the reasons for repatriate turnover (Clegg, 2016).

6.5 Conclusions

How do different types of international assignments influence the repatriation process? What types of career resources and competencies are associated with repatriation? Will an international assignment make or break one's career? How can the benefits of an international assignment be maximised and the pitfalls minimised? This chapter highlights the importance of repatriation to organisations and individuals engaged in or considering an international assignment. It also delineates how the bounded- and proactive-career perspectives inform our understanding of repatriation and career development. In addition to identifying some of the key challenges facing repatriation, we suggest a number of possible interventions that organisations and repatriates can take to help facilitate the repatriation process and improve the likelihood of success.

Although a number of studies have examined the relationship between contextual antecedents and repatriation outcomes, including contextual factors such as interpersonal, team, organisational and country characteristics, future research could extend this stream of work by investigating topics such as interpersonal relationships at work (interpersonal characteristics), work group composition (team characteristics), organisational structure (organisational characteristics), and economic and social development of home and host countries (home and host country characteristics). By contrast, few studies have investigated the relationship between individual antecedents and repatriation outcomes, suggesting that many questions remain unexplored. For example, do coping strategies influence readjustment or vice versa? How do repatriates deal with identity (self-concept) changes upon return? In what ways can MNEs manage their repatriates' expectations to better facilitate the repatriation process and generate positive outcomes? Do motivation processes contribute to repatriation outcomes and, if so, how and under what circumstances? How do personality traits relate to repatriation outcomes? Are extraversion, openness to experience, self-efficacy, positive affectivity, cultural flexibility, and a willingness to communicate as important traits for repatriates as they are for expatriates? An improved understanding of these repatriation topics will contribute not only to organisations wishing to build and retain global competencies and talent but also to the personal and professional development of individual repatriates (Chiang et al., 2018). In addition, it is important to note that most prior research has focused on either the expatriation or repatriation phase of international assignments in isolation. Instead of viewing expatriation and repatriation as two separate processes, future studies should examine both phases as an integrated process to provide a more holistic understanding of the international assignment process as a whole (Chiang et al., 2018). For now, repatriation remains an under-researched stage of the international assignment process in need of greater scholarly and practitioner's attention.

References

Arthur, M. B. & Rousseau, D. M. 1996. *The Boundaryless Career: A New Employment Principle for a New Organizational Era*. New York: Oxford University Press.

Arthur, M. B., Hall, D. T., & Lawrence, B. S. 1989. Generating new directions in career theory: the case for a transdisciplinary approach. In M. B. Arthur,

D. T. Hall, & B. S. Lawrence (eds.), *Handbook of Career Theory*: 7–25. Cambridge: Cambridge University Press.

Banai, M. & Wes, H. 2004. Boundaryless global careers: the international itinerants. *International Studies of Management and Organization*, 34(3): 96–130.

Baruch, Y. 2006. Career development in organizations and beyond: balancing traditional and contemporary viewpoints. *Human Resource Management Review*, 16(2): 125–138.

Baruch, Y., Altman, Y., & Tung, R. L. 2016. Career mobility in a global era: advances in managing expatriation and repatriation. *Academy of Management Annals*, 10(1): 841–889.

Baruch, Y. & Reis, C. 2016. How global are boundaryless careers and how boundaryless are global careers? Challenges and a theoretical perspective. *Thunderbird International Business Review*, 58(1): 13–27.

Black, J. S. & Gregersen, H. B. 1991. When Yankee comes home: factors related to expatriate and spouse repatriation adjustment. *Journal of International Business Studies*, 22(4): 671–694.

Black, J. S. & Gregersen, H. B. 1999. The right way to manage expats. *Harvard Business Review*. https://hbr.org/1999/03/the-right-way-to-manage-expats.

Bolino, M. C., Klotz, A. C., & Turnley, W. H. 2017. Will refusing an international assignment derail your career? *Harvard Business Review*. https://hbr.org/2017/04/will-refusing-an-international-assignment-derail-your-career.

Bossard, A. B. & Peterson, R. B. 2005. The repatriate experience as seen by American expatriates. *Journal of World Business*, 40(1): 9–28.

Brookfield 2015. Global Relocation Trends: 2015 Survey Report. Chicago: Brookfield Global Relocation Services.

Cao, L., Hirschi, A., & Deller, J. 2012. Self-initiated expatriates and their career success. *Journal of Management Development*, 31(2): 159–172.

Carraher, S. M., Sullivan, S. E., & Crocitto, M. M. 2008. Mentoring across global boundaries: an empirical examination of home-and host-country mentors on expatriate career outcomes. *Journal of International Business Studies*, 39(8): 1310–1326.

Cerdin, J.-L. & Le Pargneux, M. 2009. Career and international assignment fit: toward an integrative model of success. *Human Resource Management*, 48(1): 5–25.

Chi, S. C. S. & Chen, S. C. 2007. Perceived psychological contract fulfilment and job attitudes among repatriates: an empirical study in Taiwan. *International Journal of Manpower*, 28(6): 474–488.

Chiang, F. F., van Esch, E. Birtch, T. A., & Shaffer, M. A. 2018. Repatriation: what do we know and where do we go from here. *International Journal of Human Resource Management*, 29(1): 188–226.

Cho, T., Hutchings, K., & Marchant, T. 2013. Key factors influencing Korean expatriates' and spouses' perceptions of expatriation and repatriation. *International Journal of Human Resource Management*, 24 (5): 1051–1075.

Clegg, A. 2016. Expatriate employees struggle to readjust to old lives. *Financial Times*. www.ft.com/content/7e77b478-a1da-11e6-aa83-bcb58d1d2193.

DeFillippi, R. J. & Arthur, M. B. 1994. The boundaryless career: a competency-based perspective. *Journal of Organizational Behavior*, 15(4): 307–324.

Dickmann, M. & Harris, H. 2005. Developing career capital for global careers: the role of international assignments. *Journal of World Business*, 40(4): 399–408.

Dickmann, M. F. & Doherty, N. 2008. Exploring the career capital impact of international assignments within distinct organizational contexts. *British Journal of Management*, 19(2): 145–161.

Doherty, N. T. & Dickmann, M. 2009. Exploring the symbolic capital of international assignments. *International Journal of Human Resource Management*, 20(2): 301–320.

Doherty, N. T., Dickmann, M., & Mills, T. 2011. Exploring the motives of company-backed and self-initiated expatriates. *International Journal of Human Resource Management*, 22(3): 595–611.

Dowling, P. J., Festing, M., & Engle, A. D. 2013. *International Human Resource Management: Managing People in a Multinational Context*, 6th ed. Mason: Thomson.

Eby, L. T., Butts, M., & Lockwood, A. 2003. Predictors of success in the era of the boundaryless career. *Journal of Organizational Behavior: International Journal of Industrial, Occupational and Organizational Psychology and Behavior*, 24(6): 689–708.

Ernst & Young 2014. *Strategic Global Mobility: Unlocking the Value of Cross-border Assignments*. www.ey.com/Publication/vwLUAssets/ey-global-mobility-cross-border-assignments-value/#FILE/ey-HBR-Report.pdf.

Feldman, D. C. & Tompson, H. B. 1993. Expatriation, repatriation, and domestic geographical relocation: an empirical investigation of adjustment to new job assignments. *Journal of International Business Studies*, 24(3): 507–529.

Furuya, N., Stevens, M. J., Oddou, G., Bird, A., & Mendenhall, M. E. 2007. The effects of HR policies and repatriate self-adjustment on global competency transfer. *Asia Pacific Journal of Human Resources*, 45(1): 6–23.

Furuya, N., Stevens, M. J., Bird, A., Oddou, G., & Mendenhall, M. 2009. Managing the learning and transfer of global management competence: antecedents and outcomes of Japanese repatriation effectiveness. *Journal of International Business Studies*, 40(2): 200–215.

Geissler, C., Kuhn, L., & McGinn, D. 2011. Developing Your Global Know-How. *Harvard Business Review*. https://hbr.org/2011/03/developing-your-global-know-how.

Gregersen, H. B. & Black, J. S. 1996. Multiple commitments upon repatriation: the Japanese experience. *Journal of Management*, 22(2): 209–229.

Gregersen, H. B. & Stroh, L. K. 1997. Coming home to the Arctic cold: antecedents to Finnish expatriate and spouse repatriation adjustment. *Personnel Psychology*, 50(3): 635–654.

Guo, C., Porschitz, E. T., & Alves, J. 2013. Exploring career agency during self-initiated repatriation: a study of Chinese sea turtles. *Career Development International*, 18(1): 34–55.

Hall, D. T. 1976. *Careers in Organizations*. Glenview: Scott, Foresman.

Hall, D. T. 2004. The protean career: a quarter-century journey. *Journal of Vocational Behavior*, 65(1): 1–13.

Hall, D. T. & Moss, J. E. 1998. The new protean career contract: helping organizations and employees adapt. *Organizational Dynamics*, 26(3): 22–37.

Harrison, M. 2016. *The Decline of the Traditional Expat? Employee Conditions Abroad*. www.eca-international.com/insights/articles/may-2016/the-decline-of-the-traditional-expat.

Harrison, D. A., Shaffer, M. A., & Bhaskar-Shrinivas, P. (2004). Going places: roads more and less traveled in research on expatriate experience. *Research in Personnel and Human Resources Management*, 23: 199–247.

Haslberger, A. & Brewster, C. 2009. Capital gains: expatriate adjustment and the psychological contract in international careers. *Human Resource Management*, 48(3): 379–397.

Herman, J. L. & Tetrick, L. E. 2009. Problem-focused versus emotion-focused coping strategies and repatriation adjustment. *Human Resource Management*, 48(1): 69–88.

Hyder, A. S. & Lövblad, M. 2007. The repatriation process–a realistic approach. *Career Development International*, 12(3): 264–281.

Judge, T. A., Cable, D. M., Boudreau, J. W., & Bretz R. D.Jr 1995. An empirical investigation of the predictors of executive career success. *Personnel Psychology*, 48(3): 485–519.

KPMG 2018. 2018 *Global Assignment Policies and Practices Survey*. https://home.kpmg/xx/en/home/insights/2016/10/global-assignment-policies-and-practices-survey-2016.html.

Kraimer, M. L., Shaffer, M. A., & Bolino, M. C. 2009. The influence of expatriate and repatriate experiences on career advancement and repatriation retention. *Human Resource Management*, 48(1): 27–48.

Kraimer, M. L., Shaffer, M. A., Harrison, D. A., & Ren, H. 2012. No place like home? An identity strain perspective on repatriate turnover. *Academy of Management Journal*, 55(2): 399–420.

Kulkarni, M., Lengnick-Hall, M. L., & Valk, R. 2010. Employee perceptions of repatriation in an emerging economy: the Indian experience. *Human Resource Management*, 49(3): 531–548.

Lazarova, M. & Caligiuri, P. 2001. Retaining repatriates: the role of organizational support practices. *Journal of World Business*, 36(4): 389–401.

Lazarova, M. & Cerdin, J. L. 2007. Revisiting repatriation concerns: organizational support versus career and contextual influences. *Journal of International Business Studies*, 38(3): 404–429.

Lazarova, M., & Tarique, I. 2005. Knowledge transfer upon repatriation. *Journal of World Business*, 40(4): 361–373.

Linehan, M. & Scullion, H. 2002. Repatriation of European female corporate executives. International *Human Resource Management Journal*, 13(2): 254–267.

Mäkelä, K. & Brewster, C. 2009. Interunit interaction contexts, interpersonal social capital, and the differing levels of knowledge sharing. *Human Resource Management*, 48(4): 591–613.

Mäkelä, K. & Suutari, V. 2009. Global careers: a social capital paradox. *International Journal of Human Resource Management*, 20(5): 992–1008.

McCall, M. W. & Hollenbeck, G. P. 2002. *Developing Global Executives*. Cambridge: Harvard Business School Press.

Molinsky, A. & Hahn, M. 2016. 5 tips for managing successful overseas assignments. *Harvard Business Review*. https://hbr.org/2016/03/5-tips-for-managing-successful-overseas-assignments.

Monat, A. & Lazarus, R. S. (eds.) 1991. *Stress and Coping*. An Anthology, 3rd ed. New York: Columbia University Press.

Oddou, G., Osland, J. S., & Blakeney, R. N. 2009. Repatriating knowledge: variables influencing the 'transfer' process. *Journal of International Business Studies*, 40(2): 181–199.

O'Sullivan, S. 2002. The protean approach to managing repatriation transitions. *International Journal of Manpower*, 23(7): 597–616.

Paik, Y., Segaud, B., & Malinowski, C. 2002. How to improve repatriation management: are motivations and expectations congruent between the company and expatriates? *International Journal of Manpower*, 23(7): 635–648.

Reiche, B. S., Kraimer, M. L., & Harzing, A. W. 2011. Why do international assignees stay? An organizational embeddedness perspective. *Journal of International Business Studies*, 42(4): 521–544.

Reichers, A. E. 1986. Conflict and organizational commitment. *Journal of Applied Psychology*, 71(3): 508–514.

Ren, H., Bolino, M. C., Shaffer, M. A., & Kraimer, M. L. 2013. The influence of job demands and resources on repatriate career satisfaction: a relative deprivation perspective. *Journal of World Business*, 48(1): 149–159.

Riusala, K. & Suutari, V. 2004. International knowledge transfers through expatriates. *Thunderbird International Business Review*, 46(6): 743–770.

Rosenbaum, J. E. 1979. Tournament mobility: career patterns in a corporation. *Administrative Science Quarterly*, 24(2): 220–241.

Rousseau, D. M. 1989. Psychological and implied contracts in organizations. *Employee Responsibilities and Rights Journal*, 2(2): 121–139.

Shaffer, M. A., Kraimer, M. L., Chen, Y. P., & Bolino, M. C. 2012. Choices, challenges, and career consequences of global work experiences: a review and future agenda. *Journal of Management*, 38(4): 1282–1327.

Shen, Y. & Hall, D. T. 2009. When expatriates explore other options, retaining talent through greater job embeddedness and repatriation adjustment. *Human Resource Management*, 48(5): 793–816.

Stahl, G. K., Chua, C. H., Caligiuri, P., Cerdin, J. L., & Taniguchi, M. 2009. Predictors of turnover intentions in learning-driven and demand-driven international assignments: the role of repatriation concerns, satisfactions with company support, and perceived career advancement opportunities. *Human Resource Management*, 48(1): 89–109.

Stevens, M. J., Oddou, G., Furuya, N., Bird, A., & Mendenhall, M. 2006. HR factors affecting repatriate job satisfaction and job attachment for Japanese managers. *International Journal of Human Resource Management*, 17(5): 831–841.

Sullivan, S. E. 1999. The changing nature of careers: a review and research agenda. *Journal of Management*, 25(3): 457–484.

Sullivan, S. E. & Baruch, Y. 2009. Advances in career theory and research: a critical review and agenda for future exploration. *Journal of Management*, 35(6): 1542–1571.

Super, D. E. 1957. *The Psychology of Careers*. New York: Harper.

Suutari, V. & Brewster, C. 2003. Repatriation: empirical evidence from a longitudinal study of careers and expectations among Finnish expatriates. *International Journal of Human Resource Management*, 14(7): 1132–1151.
Suutari, V. & Mäkelä, K. 2007. The career capital of managers with global careers. *Journal of Managerial Psychology*, 22(7): 628–648.
Suutari, V., Tornikoski, C., & Mäkelä, L. 2012. Career decision making of global careerists. *International Journal of Human Resource Management*, 23(16): 3455–3478.
Unruh, G. C. & Cabrera, A. 2013. Join the global elite. *Harvard Business Review*, 91(5): 135–139.
Vaiman, V., Haslberger, A., & Vance, C. M. 2015. Recognizing the important role of self-initiated expatriates in effective global talent management. *Human Resource Management Review*, 25(3): 280–286.
Vidal, M. E. S., Valle, R. S., & Aragón, M. I. B. 2008. International workers' satisfaction with the repatriation process. *International Journal of Human Resource Management*, 19(9): 1683–1702.
Yan, A., Zhu, G., & Hall, D. T. 2002. International assignments for career building. *Academy of Management Review*, 27(3): 373–383.
Zhao, H., Wayne, S., Glibkowski, B. C., & Bravo, J. 2007. The impact of psychological contract breach on work-related outcomes: a meta-analysis. *Personnel Psychology*, 60(3): 647–680.

PART II

Different Types of Expatriates and Stakeholders

7 *Short-term Assignees, International Business Travellers, and International Commuters*

CHRIS BREWSTER, MICHAEL DICKMANN, VESA SUUTARI

7.1 Introduction

People can work internationally without being classified as expatriates or migrants. This chapter explores these alternative options, focusing, in particular, on three of the main alternative 'other' ways of arranging international work: short-term assignments (STAs), international business travel (IBTs), and international commuting (McNulty & Brewster, 2019). While expatriates are people who go to work in another country on a temporary basis but for a number of years and migrants are people who go to work in another country expecting to settle down there (McNulty & Brewster, 2019), the 'other' ways of working in another country tend to be shorter and, crucially, do not involve relocating 'home' or taking the family, if there is one, with them.

As is always necessary, we note the fungibility of the categories we explore and we discuss that briefly as follows: international business travellers are sometimes already expatriates, and some international commuters do not retain a permanent home in their own country; people who start as short-term assignees may be asked to stay on and become expatriates, and so on. But the categories indicate important classes of people who have to date received much less research attention than expatriates or migrants, even though there are substantial numbers in each group.

Each of the three major categories of 'other' international work – STAs, IBT, and international commuting – can be either organisationally initiated or can be self-initiated and we note these variations as we explore the topic. Common to all three main alternative types of international work is that the period of time they spend outside the home country is relatively short: during the working day only or varying from a few days to one year (Mäkelä, Saarenpää, & McNulty, 2017) – if it is longer than that, of course, they meet the criteria for 'expatriation'. Serious research on this large group of international workers is limited; some of the best information and reports that we have about 'other' international workers and the opportunities and challenges that they and their employers face have to be taken from the consulting field. Scholarly work is, as we shall show, only slowing catching up.

From the organisational perspective, consultancy reports predict that while long-term expatriation is forecast to stay at about current levels, or to grow only slowly, these other kinds of work are expected to grow by more than half over the next few years (KPMG, 2017). It seems that similar patterns can be found in all regions of the world (Cartus, 2018; Johnson, 2017). For the organisation these could be cost-effective ways of working that fit business requirements. The one-off, up-front costs are more attractive than commitment to costs over a long period of time (Air Inc, 2018; Johnson, 2017). Expatriation is expensive for organisations and they are continually seeking ways to reduce the costs of getting work done internationally, while trying to gain some, though necessarily not all, of the benefits of expatriation. 'Other' international workers are normally cheaper than expatriates, staying on home country salaries, with fewer additional benefits and perks. Because assignments are short, families do not accompany them, and that is cheaper for the employer. In addition, administration is more straightforward, and hence cheaper, because in most cases no international tax liabilities are created (Duxbury, 2018). In nearly all cases, the employment contract remains in the home country and is administered under its terms and conditions (Mäkelä et al., 2017).

Yet these cheaper 'other' international assignments have some (though not all) of the benefits of expatriation. They can bring needed skills to a specific location (Mäkelä et al., 2017; Minbaeva & Michailova, 2004), they are flexible, (Air Inc, 2012; Brookfield Global Relocation Services, 2009) and they fit with operational requirements. In addition, the use of, for example, commuter assignments may be safer than expatriation to a dangerous territory (Welch & Worm, 2006)

One consequence is that much of these 'other' forms of international work are outside the purview of the Global HRM function, where the specialists are responsible for expatriation, and the local HRM function, where the specialists may know about and be trying to integrate migrants. Neither has responsibility for the other forms of international work, which are largely controlled by line managers: the organisation as a whole may not even have a clear view of how many people they have in each of these categories.

For the people who are on short-term assignments, or travelling frequently or commuting, these patterns may be convenient or safer, or they may just be part of the way their job is done and, perhaps, always has been done. We explore the advantages and disadvantages of each form of work for each of the key stakeholders as we address them in turn.

7.2 Short-term Assignees

7.2.1 Overview

Though empirical research has been scarce, there has been increasing discussion in the literature about short-term assignments (Collings, McDonnell & McCarter, 2015; Harvey et al., 2010; Mäkelä et al., 2017; Suutari & Brewster, 2009). Such assignments are typically defined as lasting less than a year (Collings et al., 2015) though in practice they commonly last less than half a year, due to the tax, insurance and social security implications of longer assignments (Collings et al., 2015; Suutari et al., 2013).

While many organisations aim to reduce the number of long-term assignments the use of STAs appears to be increasing, though our evidence is still quite limited and relies largely on consultancy reports. For example, a survey by Mercer (2016) reported that organisations are more likely to deploy STAs than long term assignees; and a report by ECA International (2016) found the use of STAs was already 22 per cent of all assignments, compared to 14 per cent in 2008, and was increasing further. There are academic studies reporting similar increases (Kang, Shen, & Benson, 2016).

7.2.2 Motives and Barriers

These increases have taken place due to reasons such as better transportation and communication systems, wider organisational networking, more flexible intra-organisational coordination of global units, and cost containment initiatives (Harvey et al., 2010). STAs are often used for problem solving on specific issues that do not require longer term expatriation (Collings et al., 2015). Typical work has been found to relate to tasks such as construction projects, spreading changes, managing projects, and expanding the company's market (Salleh & Koh, 2013). STAs are often thus involved in project work that is required for some months but then ceases. They allow temporary access to specialised talent that requires the moving of people to other countries (Hocking, Brown & Harzing, 2004). Sending a skilled person to fix a problem will be considerably quicker and easier than training up local staff or trying to resolve a problem at a distance (Meyskens et al., 2009; Tahvanainen et al., 2005). STAs can also be utilised in management development programmes (Salleh & Koh, 2013). In that respect, STAs at headquarters for foreign subsidiary unit employees, or, 'inpatriation' – from an ethnocentric viewpoint – offer technical training and learning about the corporate culture (Harvey et al., 2010; Reiche, Harzing & Kraimer, 2009). At the same time, inpatriates can bring host country knowledge into the headquarters. Overall, STAs can become an important source of information relevant to developing relationships in global networks and can, thus, facilitate knowledge sharing across borders (Harvey et al., 2010; Minbaeva & Michailova 2004).

At the same time, employee interests also support the growth of short-term assignments: they are much easier for assignees and their families. Though the absence of assignees for a period can disturb their family's daily life for anything up to several months, the partners can still continue their own careers and children can continue their schooling uninterrupted (Dickmann, Suutari, & Wurtz 2018: 13). Furthermore, and again from the organisational perspective, since partners or families typically stay at home, the costs involved with these 'extra' people – which are significant– are much lower than in the case of long-term expatriation (Starr & Currie 2009; Tahvanainen et al., 2005).

For assignees, STAs can offer a change of routine (Crowley-Henry & Heaslip, 2014). They can provide the opportunity of working in and getting to know about another country – although some individuals, sometimes called FIFO, or fly-in-fly-out contractors (Blackman et al., 2014), are 'off-shore' or in remote locations. In all cases they offer self-development opportunities (Starr & Currie 2009). Adjustment occurs on a positively skewed distribution, with most learning taking place in the first few months (Haslberger, Brewster, & Hippler, 2014), so short-term assignees may get similar developmental benefits to many long term expatriates. Therefore, STAs can be a form of training (Crowne & Engle 2016), particularly in inpatriate assignments, and they can develop managerial skills (Crowley-Henry & Heaslip, 2014), project skills (Suutari et al., 2013), and offer the possibility to experience new cultures and business practices (Harvey et al., 2010; Reiche et al., 2009). STAs may be a useful way to give young potentials international work experience (Mayrhofer & Scullion 2002; Starr & Currie 2009; Suutari et al., 2013) that such people often value (Collings et al., 2015). For people from emerging economies, they can be a good way of getting their first international experience and of polishing their English.

Though the research evidence on STAs is limited, both from the individual and organisational angles, the existing research has already covered STA experience from several perspectives. For example, Starr and Currie (2009) analysed the role of the family in the STA process, Crowne and Engle (2016) studied the cross-cultural adaptation stress of assignees, and Starr (2009) explored the 'repatriation' experiences of such assignees. There have also been several studies from the organisational perspective such as studies by Salleh and Koh (2013) that analysed the purposes of STAs, and Crowley-Henry and Heaslip (2014) who focused on the use of STAs in the military sector. Several case studies have examined human resource management processes around STAs: Tahvanainen, Welch, and Worm (2005) investigated the use and management of STAs and Suutari et al. (2013) reported on development processes related to the management of different alternative assignment types within one MNC.

7.2.3 *Management of STAs*

Although we have noted several reasons for the increased use of STAs within companies, there are also some disadvantages for the employing organisation and for the assignees. The management challenges involve administrative issues connected with the individual's taxation and social security issues, particularly if the assignment lasts longer than six months (Collings et al., 2015; Tahvanainen et al., 2005). In some countries the need for visas and work permits, especially in locations where the company does not yet have an affiliate, can create problems (Collings et al., 2015; Tahvanainen et al., 2005). There are also problems of allocating responsibility. Many STAs are costed within the budget of the line manager and often managed by them with little support from the IHRM department (Brewster, Harris, & Petrovic, 2001). There can therefore be problems of co-ordination and of appropriate compensation. However, there are some signs that companies are developing explicit STA policies and practices including stringent reward rules (Dickmann, 2016).

It can be difficult for STAs to become integrated into the local workplace and host community, hence they find it harder to develop effective relationships with local colleagues and customers (Tahvanainen et al., 2005). Since they have little time to adjust to local ways of doing things, those in non-technical jobs, in particular, may find that individual adjustment problems cause challenges for the well-being and performance of the whole group (Suutari et al., 2013). The partner and family may not move abroad during the STA, but the absence of the assignee impacts family life in other ways, adding extra burdens to the partner and the children, and can lead to family stress and difficulties in work-life balance (Meyskens et al., 2009; Starr & Currie 2009; Tahvanainen et al., 2005). It is relatively easy to communicate with the family in the era of Skype, FaceTime, WhatsApp, Kick, Facebook, and other social media sites (Bonache et al., 2018), but no technology can replace the actual presence of the complete family. In turn, without family responsibilities, the expatriate can focus on their work: short term assignees typically put in long hours at the plant or in the office. This may lead to problems of stress and fatigue (Tahvanainen et al., 2005). Short-term assignees typically live in hotels or, for more remote locations (oil rigs, pipelines, etc.), in company provided dormitories or similar accommodation. Once off work, particularly in countries where they cannot speak the language and in less-developed countries, there is little to do other than go back to their sleeping quarters. For some the result will be boredom, heavy drinking and/or depression (Wurtz, 2018); others will find themselves taking risks they would not do when they were at home with their family.

In order to succeed in the management of short-term expatriation, many multinationals have been developing their STA policies and practices. For example, Mäkelä, Saarenpää and McNulty (2017) argue that consultancy reports indicate that STAs may be more systematically managed than is apparent from the extant research evidence. There is limited case study evidence examining the issue from the perspective of human resource management (Tahvanainen et al., 2005; Suutari et al., 2013). In practice, the role of line managers is, however, often central in the process and the follow-up of assignments, the costs involved or the overall success of assignments (Collings et al., 2015; Dickmann, 2015). The lack of basic monitoring of these assignments means that learning becomes difficult and many of the challenges involved in working abroad are left to assignees themselves to deal with.

The selection of assignees appears to be mostly informal, involving little bureaucracy, even if HRM specialist may be aware that a more formalised selection process would avoid an over-reliance on line managers' personal contacts (Kang et al., 2016; Suutari et al., 2013; Tahvanainen et al., 2005). This over-reliance on personal contacts can also lead to a critical shortage of internationally experienced project staff. Still, our evidence on selection processes is very limited (Collings et al., 2015).

The administrative issues related to STAs may be dealt with by IHRM or global mobility units (Collings et al., 2015), while taxation and alignment to immigration regulations are frequently outsourced to mobility service providers (Dickmann, 2016). With regard to STAs lasting less than six months, salary payment and associated taxes, insurances and pension arrangements typically remains in the home company and country, the home country salary forms the basis for compensation for more than three quarter of STAs (Dickmann, 2016). The assignee typically continues on the same contract that they were on at home (Kang et al., 2016). Sometimes the company's travel policy may form a basis for additional rewards (Tahvanainen et al., 2005) and they thus get a per diem: a (tax free) daily allowance and a hardship allowance when needed (Collings, Scullion, & Morley, 2007). For assignments over six months, more detailed contracts can be organised, and in many countries such contracts are required also in the host country (Suutari et al., 2013).

7.2.4 Future Research Avenues

Clearly, given their numbers and importance we need to know more about STAs. We know little about their selection. There has been almost no research on the requirements for training among other types of assignees than long-term assignees (Collings et al., 2007).

Training of STAs is still often limited due to the restricted time for preparation, the costs of training, and a lack of understanding of the need for training (Suutari et al., 2013). Such a lack of preparation may have negative impacts for both organisations and individuals (Collings et al., 2015). It may hinder the integration of assignees with the local workforce, restrict their adaptation to local practices, and limit the performance of the assignees (Tahvanainen et al., 2005). Sometimes, if cultural distance is higher between the home and host country, some training may be provided, though even here it is on a voluntary basis and only available if the timing works out (Kang et al., 2016). In the case of more difficult environments, some training about travel, and health and safety in foreign countries may be given (Collings et al., 2007). If an STA is itself used as a tool for professional or managerial development, nominating a mentor with defined responsibilities, more careful planning of such assignments, and in-depth evaluation of learning are also seen as necessary (Suutari et al., 2013).

Given that the training of assignees is rare, it is not surprising to find that the further step of family support is even less often offered (Tahvanainen et al., 2005), but again we have little empirical evidence. The organisations that do provide support typically grant additional family leave and finance flights home (Dickmann, 2016). In those few cases where the STA lasts longer, the family may accompany the assignee and the company may pay the related costs (Tahvanainen et al., 2005). In a case reported by Suutari et al (2013), the company had started arranging visits and providing informal guidance for the whole family in order to reduce the problems involved.

We have little data about what happens after the assignment. Given that such individuals are away for less time than long-term assignees, repatriation should be easier, but we lack empirical evidence (Tahvanainen et al., 2005). Nevertheless, it has been reported that repatriation and integration back home may still not be without problems (Starr, 2009). STAs were found to sometimes build expectations about upward mobility and new jobs after the international mobility experience and may get disappointed when such expectations are not met. Whether such experiences impact on intentions to leave deserves further research attention (Collings et al., 2015).

Not all STAs lead to repatriation and continued employment in the organisation. In some cases, assignees may be recruited specifically for the role – this is typical for specialists in information technology, in resource exploration, or in short-term expatriation to dangerous environments. At the end of the contract such assignees often leave the organisation.

7.3 International Business Travellers

7.3.1 Overview

An international business traveller, or as they are sometimes called a 'frequent flyer', is someone 'for whom business travel is an essential component of their work' (Welch & Worm, 2006: 284). Crucially, IBTs do not relocate, differentiating them from STAs and other forms of assignees. And they normally travel to several different countries and on less regular patterns, which sets them apart from international commuters. The duration of their visits is defined by the goals of their work and they may be involved with a range of teams in different countries (Collings et al., 2015).

The last decades have seen an increase in international business travel (Brookfield GMAC, 2013; DeFrank, Konopaske, & Ivancevich, 2000; Hovhannisyan & Keller, 2015) and it has been common to assume that this trend will continue. The value of the global business travel market is already well over #1 trillion and forecast to grow to #1.3 trillion by 2023 (Allied Market Research, 2018). Many authors have pointed to patterns of globalisation and the increased need for cooperation, innovation, and trust across units that operate in different countries. While some of these factors are clearly right, we are currently witnessing a strong societal trend emerging that may limit this growth. Global warming and the need to reduce carbon emissions have become central in the political and environmental discourse of many societies and the pressure to limit one's carbon footprint is increasing. While this has yet to manifest itself in less international travel it remains a distinct possibility that many MNCs may take drastic actions to use more virtual means of business meetings and coordination. This may decrease costs and their carbon footprints further while alleviating some of the pressures on IBTs to travel as frequently as before.

There are different perspectives that can be used to explore the issues involved in IBTs. We have chosen to use a perspective that focuses predominantly on individual, organisational, and family

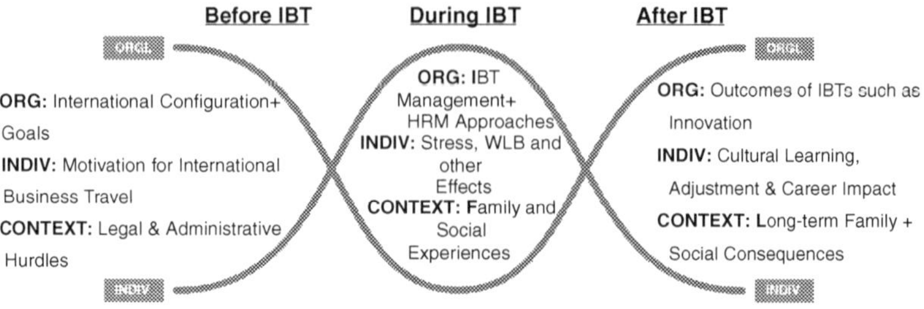

Figure 7.1 The double helix of IBTs – combining perspectives

characteristics. As with other expatriation models (Harris, Brewster, & Sparrow, 2003) it employs a temporal view and takes account of the mutual dependency of international workers and their employers. Given, however, that international travel may be part of a normal career pattern in a multinational organisation we have developed a double helix framework that indicates that the endings might also be new beginnings in another position that equally involves international travel.

Work as an IBT is distinct from work as an expatriate who relocates to a foreign country. The pressures on expatriates have been depicted through the expatriation cycle (Harris et al., 2003). While a mutual dependence between organisation and individuals obviously exists for IBTs, its nature is distinct. Expatriates depend most on their organisation when they are moving abroad – for household shipping, schooling, accommodation, health provision, etc. – and when they are returning from abroad (predominantly for the physical relocation and for gaining a 'good' job in the next location). For IBTs this dependency has different nuances (the focus is on travel arrangements, security, and health implications) and it is more evenly stretched in time and in relation to all their travel activities. Thus, the organizational support needed is distinct. The family – which does not move abroad – is affected in a different way. In addition, the learning that IBTs are likely to accumulate is less single foreign location specific and may include some more transferable skills and insights (Baruch et al., 2013). The double helix of IBTs depicts the interplay and complex interdependencies between individuals, organisations, and the wider context.

7.3.2 Motives and Barriers

Why do organisations use IBTs? It is argued that the costs of business travel are lower than traditional expatriation and that the flexibility of their use – IBTs can work in a variety of locations, on diverse projects, etc. – is superior (Collings et al., 2015). In addition, they may support the integration of organisational culture and the achievement of common standards. IBTs can have similar control and coordination as well as knowledge transfer roles to other forms of international work assignments (Edström & Galbraith, 1977; Harvey et al., 2010). In addition, face-to-face meetings and (physical) joint work is still often seen as beneficial for trust-building and to cement personal relationships amongst the key stakeholders in projects or more permanent work teams (Beaverstock et al., 2010; Davidson & Cope, 2003; Mäkelä & Brewster, 2009). Little is known about how IBTs are selected for their jobs and whether it is linked to strategic goals. Operationally, however, Demel and Mayrhofer (2010) suggest that multinationals should improve their selection mechanisms to go beyond technical expertise and cultural insights and skills. They suggest that physical fitness, persistence, resilience and self-discipline should also be assessed given some of the challenges outlined below.

The organisational drivers that may guide the use of IBTs in MNCs include cost, cultural and operational issues, in that IBTs are seen as a more cost-effective variant of international work than traditional expatriation while still allowing cultural coordination and operational integration. The effects of IBTs within specific business configurations (Bartlett & Ghoshal, 2002) in relation to control and coordination, innovation, cost, leadership development, and knowledge transfer (Dickmann & Müller-Camen, 2006) have not been explored holistically. Nevertheless, work has emerged that looks at some sub-section of these issues. For instance, Hovhannisyan and Keller (2015) find that increased business travel is correlated with an increase in patenting in organisations. There is also some indication that IBT costs are lower than those of traditional expatriation (Collings et al., 2015) although tracking these costs is difficult and not well executed (Dickmann, 2018). Crucially, cost is not equal to value and MNCs are traditionally weak in assessing value in global mobility (McNulty, De Cieri, & Hutchings, 2009; Renshaw, Parry, & Dickmann, 2018).

IBTs themselves might be driven by a mixture of factors that determine their willingness to work abroad while wanting to keep their 'home base'. People with a global mindset and an international career orientation are seen to be more likely to accept or seek cross-border business travel (Kedia & Mukherji, 1999; Phillips et al., 2014). Conversely, if they were to decline to travel this might harm their career prospects (Shaffer et al., 2012) as travelling might be seen as a 'must for career development' (Demel & Mayrhofer, 2010: 305). However, there may be a range of further considerations that guide the decision to undertake frequent international business travel, including health, learning, having a respite, monetary and family elements (Beaverstock et al., 2010; Demel & Mayrhofer, 2010; Westman & Etzion, 2002; Westman, Etzion, & Chen, 2009b). Concerns about the security of the host location if the family were to relocate, for the career of the partner (for instance avoiding the dual career problem of long-term expatriation), or for the non-interruption of the education of children, are likely to be substantial in shaping individuals' motivation to become an IBT (Dickmann & Baruch, 2011).

The IBT literature has explored the individual experience of the global worker in detail, identifying a range of negative effects. More than two decades ago Rogers (1998) found that international travel often results in physical and psychological health issues. Striker et al. (1999) identified risk factors that led to stress amongst World Bank IBTs. Working abroad for some time, separated from one's family and often on schedules that are very crowded and dynamic may lead to job, social, and emotional worries. For instance, IBTs would worry about the impact of their absence on their family, social links, and work upon return. DeFrank, Konopaske, and Ivancevich (2000) point out that international travel may be associated with emotional upset and even in some cases physical illness. While any solo travel is associated with being away from loved ones and friends, international journeys often imply differences in time zones, languages, culture, safety contexts, customs, and business practices – all of which place higher demands on IBTs. In addition, physical effects such as an unbalanced diet, more food and alcohol intake and other health concerns are frequently associated with international travel (Demel & Mayrhofer, 2010). Thus, compared to domestic trips, IBTs feel more mental and physical strain (Baker & Ciuk, 2015) and they can experience loneliness and burnout (Collings et al., 2015). They also suffer work-family conflict and sleeping problems (Mäkelä et al., 2014).

Where IBTs perceive an imbalance between their efforts and resulting rewards, this can increase work to life conflict (Mäkelä, Kinnunen, & Suutari, 2015). However, positive effects are also possible. For instance, in the same study it was found that a low effort-reward imbalance can support work to life enrichment if coupled with a pronounced international career orientation.

Clearly, IBT affects not only organisations and their staff but also impacts a wide variety of other stakeholders such as the family and friends of the cross-border traveller. It is not only global workers who suffer from increased stress but also their partners, especially if they had young children, if travel plans are changed frequently, or if their partners (in the case of female partners) were young (Espino et al., 2002). The work-family interface in IBTs seems to be affected predominantly by the range of key factors outlined earlier: the length of absence, control of the global worker of the travel schedule, predictability of travel periods and organisational support measures (Baker & Ciuk, 2015). In international work the boundaries of family and work are blurred (Caligiuri et al., 1998; Lazarova, Westman, & Shaffer, 2010) and this general observation regarding expatriates is likely to extend to IBTs, too. It is, therefore, no surprise that IBTs themselves had a range of negative feelings when travelling 'too much' – they could not attend important family gatherings, other key events in the lives of their children and partners, or were not available when a crisis happened (DeFrank et al., 2000; Demel & Mayrhofer, 2010; Espino et al., 2002). Their partners echoed these negative impressions. While negative effects have been explored in more depth there are a range of potential positive effects of international business travel that could be more thoroughly investigated. These include the effects of absence on the time that partners and families are able to spend together (e.g., the 'golden weekend or holidays'), the insights and other positive spill-over effects that IBTs can bring back into their families (Mäkelä et al., 2014; Westman et al., 2009a) or the effects of IBTs on host unit teams.

IBTs are not traditional expatriates so that some of the expected outcomes of their international work are different. Given that they are less embedded in a foreign host culture and that they generally work less time abroad their cultural experiences are different and the likely cultural adjustment to one host culture is lower (Baruch et al., 2013).

While their cross-cultural agility (Caligiuri, 2012) may well be high as they have to adjust to potentially many countries and host contexts, so their cultural learning is likely to be different. Demel and Mayrhofer (2010) found IBTs had some negative and some highly positive expectations in relation to the outcomes of their international work on future careers. The positive expectations included gaining valuable professional, project, and personal experiences, building useful networks abroad and acquiring a strong and positive reputation that would allow them greater choice of career possibilities.

A large range of negative and some positive work-family and work-life spill-over effects from international business travel have been outlined previously. It is clear that the absence from one's family and social network has some major short-term effects in terms of stress, feeling of loneliness, and worry. Amongst the longer-term effects are 'burn-out' and enduring family tension. In addition, because IBTs are likely to have highly unpredictable patterns relating to when they are 'at home' their whole social network and activities may suffer long-term damages. Saarenpää (2017) outlines an extensive range of negative work-family balance issues – exploring these holistically in the long-term would aid our understanding of how to manage IBTs and how to select them greatly (Demel & Mayrhofer, 2010).

7.3.3 Management of IBTs

Because international business travel is part and parcel of certain jobs in multinational enterprises, the information on tailored HRM approaches is sparse. Very few organisations have their HRM or GM departments involved in setting separate policy guidelines for cross-border travellers. Where the international trips are especially long – extended business trips that often trigger compliance issues – about a quarter of larger firms have dedicated policy approaches (Dickmann, 2018: 83). Enterprises also occasionally have different reward approaches where IBTs may get some extra remuneration. However, the likelihood that IBTs attract a mobility premium, cost of living, hardship or home leave allowance is lower for IBTs than for short-term, long-term, or commuter assignments (Dickmann, 2018: 88). In addition, it seems that HRM support practices such as cross-cultural training are predominantly aimed at other forms of international working – ignoring IBTs (Harvey et al., 2010; Mäkelä et al., 2015). This is not to argue that organisations should not devise special policies or practices for IBTs. It is known, for instance, that where IBTs have more control over their resources and trip numbers, this is associated with travellers having higher vigour (Westman, Etzion, & Chen, 2009a); and efficient and safe travel arrangements as well as the opportunity to rest after a stay abroad are related to higher IBT satisfaction (Beaverstock et al., 2010). An early article listed a range of organisational and individual activities that could help to manage traveller stress (DeFrank et al., 2000: 67).

Given that cross-border business travel is associated with many professional career paths in multinational enterprises and seen as 'part of the job', it is highly likely that global mobility departments are not involved in the selection and management of IBTs. In fact, in many cases GM professionals complain about having insufficient data about travel patterns (some might get these via their travel agencies) and see major tax and compliance risks (Brookfield GMAC, 2013). Assuring legal compliance, for example, that IBTs have the right working visa and that all corporate and individual taxes are being paid, can be highly complex.

Beyond the legal context, there are a number of destination factors that organisations might factor into their IBT strategies. The emerging literature on expatriation to hostile environments (Bader, Schuster, & Dickmann 2019; Pinto, Bader, & Schuster, 2017; Posthuma et al., 2017) explores some of the physical and psychological risks of working in dangerous contexts. While it seems likely that some of these insights might be transferred to IBTs (e.g., risk management approaches, training) some authors have suggested that multinationals might reduce their expatriate numbers in favour of increased use of IBTs (Mäkela, Kinnunen, & Suutari, 2015).

7.3.4 Future Research Avenues

The management literature on IBTs is even more sparse than the literature on short-term assignees. Overall, we know little about either the management or the personal problems of IBTs. More evidence about the existence and effects of specific work arrangements, career and development patterns as well as performance and reward implications specifically for IBTs would be a welcome addition to our understanding of these global workers. There are also issues with the assessment of the value of international business travel, particularly where it has a managerial or control function: is the impact of someone with little understanding of the local context, pressured to take quick decisions after a short visit, and then to fly off and leave local managers to deal with the fall-out, always going to be positive? The lack of understanding of the effects of IBTs on local teams and units, global configurations and particular business goals are hampering an assessment of IBT value and would provide an exciting area for further investigation.

More research is needed on the outcomes for the individuals concerned. What problems do they face and how might they be alleviated? Are the positive expectations some IBTs have (Demel & Mayrhofer, 2010) likely to come to fruition and what would influence long-term career patterns of current or former IBTs? Westman et al. (2009b) argue that the positive impact of international travel such as improved business learning; individual growth; career impact of IBTs; and getting to know new cultures, nations, and regions has rarely been studied.

7.4 International Commuters

7.4.1 Overview

International commuters live in one country and work in another. Although there may be millions of such people, there is almost no research about them. For them, their journey to work involves crossing the border between the two countries. There are two different categories of international commuters: one is people who simply prefer to live in their home country and work in the neighbouring state; and one involves living in one country that is not home and commuting to one, or to others, that are also not home. We explore each in turn.

For commuters living at home, the decision to adopt a lifestyle of international commuting is usually taken by them, a self-initiated decision, it might be called, and their employer is either unconcerned with the decision or neutral about it (Mäkelä et al., 2017). Hence, they are unlikely to provide financial or any other support for the arrangement. For these people, as for domestic commuters (Sandow, 2014), travelling is simply a necessary part of their working lives. These kinds of arrangement are common in Europe, because of the number of countries in a relatively small land space and where, within the

European Union, there are no restrictions on cross-border employment. France, for example, has land borders with eight other countries and many people prefer to live in France, where taxes are lower and work, for example, in Switzerland. People living in southern Sweden commute to Copenhagen by crossing the bridge that connects Sweden and Denmark, travelling across every weekday morning and back every evening. Crossing from the Czech Republic to Austria may involve less than a 15-minute car journey to work (Mäkelä et al., 2017).

Other commuters do not live at home. In some intergovernmental agencies, in aid organisations, and in religious groups, the work may be in turbulent, war-torn, or physically dangerous conditions. These people are expatriates in both the country that they and, sometimes, their family live in, and they are also international commuters, travelling regularly between that state and another.

Here, too, there will be employees from the shipping industry, with entire families relocating, usually from poorer countries such as Indonesia or Bangladesh to places such as Singapore or Hong Kong where the families can live in a nearby and attractive location (Dickie & Dwyer, 2011), where work is available and where the family earners can commute to their work on ships or oil rigs.

7.4.2 Motives and Barriers

When cities are close together, albeit across a national border, people can easily be mobile between the countries involved (Huber & Nowotny, 2013). The choice of this form of international commuting may simply be a personal or family preference, but often the life-style, or living standards, in the home country are beneficial to the commuter, while the better work and higher salaries are available in the country where they work. Hence, for example, there are Uruguayans commuting to work in Brazil and Malaysians commuting to work in Singapore. It is particularly frequent for those in the unskilled workforce (domestic helpers, tradesmen, construction workers) commuting daily, weekly, or monthly between two countries in order to earn a living. Their salaries are higher where they work, and they can live better on the money they make in their own country.

For the countries themselves (where the commuter works) there can be benefits such as cheaper labour and increased tax receipts, while the neighbouring state (where the commuter lives) loses those gains but does have the costs of community and social services, schooling and policing, etc. Accordingly, some states have spent heavily on transportation or reduced road tolls to improve systems and reduce travelling times to make such commuting easier (Knowles & Matthiessen, 2009).

In few cases, international commuting based on living at home may be employer initiated. For instance, a company may promote a manager to a position where they are responsible for dealing with suppliers from three adjacent states. The manager continues to live at home but travels regularly to the other states to conduct their work, perhaps on a half-weekly, weekly, or bi-weekly rotation. The employer will be expected to pay for their travel and subsistence and perhaps to provide additional time off or extra leave to compensate for the commuting. Workers in industries such as oil and gas, typically travel to their country of work, or to their rig in international waters, on a monthly basis, working for 30 days on the rig and then having 30 days at home. Flight crew in the airlines or shipping employees will have work patterns matching the required transportation schedules (Mäkelä et al., 2017).

For the workers in less comfortable circumstances the main motives concern safety. Bodies such as the United Nations categorise locations around the world – some are categorised as 'non-family', meaning that the organisation feels that it is too dangerous to place the worker's family in that country (Cartus, 2012). In such cases, the family may be left behind, whereas in other cases families may relocate with the worker to a nearby country deemed to be safer, with the employee commuting on a regular basis to the state which they are trying to help (Fee & McGrath-Champ, 2017; Mäkelä et al., 2017: 277).

7.4.3 Management of International Commuters

For the commuters living at home there may be very little additional management involved: for them, their travel to work just happens to include crossing a national border (non-visibly in the EU for example, and often unattended as between, say, France and Switzerland). Their employer has no more interest in their journey to work than anyone else's journey to work.

There are, however, some limitations and considerations that do not necessarily apply to other international work forms. The international commuter may live in a country where the organisation does not have formal operations. For instance, a UK firm may not operate in Poland but may have some staff who work in a German factory just across the Polish border. On normal days these Polish workers commute to their German place of work. However, on those occasions where they have a 'home-office day' they run the risk that the Polish authorities might regard this as establishing an office in Poland. Thus, legal and tax compliance issues would arise, and companies would be well advised to not allow working from home for these international commuters.

For those employers motivated by concern for their employees' welfare, management becomes a key issue. By making such arrangements they have acknowledge the dangers involved and accepted an obligation of responsibility. Unfortunately, while we are beginning to get a better understanding of the management of expatriates in dangerous environments (Bader, Schuster, & Dickmann 2019; Pinto, Bader, & Schuster, 2017; Posthuma et al., 2017), we have little knowledge of the issues involved in managing international commuting in such cases.

7.4.4 *Future Research Avenues*

Given our almost total absence of information about international commuters, the research requirements are plain. We need to separate out the two main categories of commuters and then, in each case, to explore the motivation and management of these arrangements, and their negative and positive outcomes for individuals, families, organisations, and colleagues. There is a rich research agenda here.

7.5 Conclusions

Overall, it seems that 'other' kinds of international working are growing faster than the more familiar forms of expatriation. Due to such growth and our lack of research evidence around such forms of mobility, we need further understanding of the special nature of such mobility. In Table 7.1, we compare the characteristics of the three types of international mobility we have discussed. Table 7.1 collects together the key points in what literature we have. A major research problem is that in many cases there is no central repository within organisations about these categories of worker. Because some of these types of international working (such as international commuting in the European Union) are organised by and controlled by individuals, and

Table 7.1 *Comparing the main other types of international work*

	STAs	IBTs	International commuting
Common features	No relocation of 'home' Family does not usually travel: less family impacts than in long-term expatriation and less costs for the company Salary/tax/etc. all based on home location		
Length of international work	Short-term stay, usually one to six months. In some project kind of works, the work may involve many STAs	Usually just one or a few days Many jobs involve frequent travelling	Regular, periodic travelling between two locations
Main individual motivations	Nature of work Development opportunities International work experience Career development A change of routine	Nature of work International travel possibilities Career development	New work possibilities Salary increases Convenience for commuter
Main organizational motivations	Problem solving Staffing problems Project work Management development Knowledge transfer Control and coordination Separation from family	Integration Flexibility Knowledge transfer Innovation Control and coordination Relationship building Separation from family	Flexibility Staffing problems Project work Management development Separation from family

Individual challenges	Adjustment Intensive work Stress and fatigue Freetime possibilities	Impacts on personal life Stress of travel Health issues	Travel stress Danger
Organisational challenges	Taxation and social security issues Visa and work permits Responsibility allocation (line and HRM) Control	Travel arrangements Legal compliance (e.g., Visa) Safety issues	Risk of corporate establishment of business if commuter works from home in a country where organization is not incorporated
Future research avenues	Long-term individual effects of STAs Impact on families Cost/benefit analysis Repatriation Management of STAs	Variety of types of international travel Long-term effects of travel Cost/benefit analysis How long can someone do this?	Due to overall lack of research, more research is needed both from individual and organization angles

many of the other kinds (short-term contracts, frequent travel, etc.) are organised and controlled by individual line managers and financed directly from their budgets, the human resource management specialists may not even know how many of these types of international workers the organisation has, never mind understand their issues and their potential. This makes research difficult. It may also be that some characteristics posed for certain type might also be relevant for other types, but those have not been raised in the literature. Further research is thus needed to fully understand the characteristics of these types of international work.

As noted throughout the chapter, our knowledge of such workers is generally thin: there is much that we do not know. These are areas of international mobility where the opportunities for further research appear fruitful, ultimately advancing not just our academic knowledge but also informing organisations, policy-makers as well as STAs, IBTs, and cross-border commuters and their families of the likely benefits and potential threats to their careers and lives.

Based on our review and discussion on future research avenues related with each type of international work in the text, we have suggested some areas for further research in Table 7.1. Even where we have evidence, it often comes from just one or very few, often limited, studies. We thus have little information about different types of employees, and certain types of organisations or country contexts. It is difficult to generalise findings to other types of situation and we need further research to validate the observations. There is a fruitful research field here.

References

Air Inc. 2012. *Giving Your Managers Wings: Flexible Mobility Policies that Work*. New York, NY: Air Inc.

Allied Market Research 2018. Business Travel Market by service, industry, traveler – Global opportunity analysis and industry forecast. www.alliedmarketresearch.com/business-travel-market.

Bader, B., Schuster, T., & Dickmann, M. 2019. Managing people in hostile environments: Lessons learned and new grounds in HR research. *International Journal of Human Resource Management*. DOI:10.1080/09585192.2018.1548499.

Baker, C. & Ciuk, S. 2015. Keeping the family side ticking along: an exploratory study of the work-family interface in the experiences of rotational assignees and frequent business travellers. *Journal of Global Mobility*, 3(2): 137–154.

Baruch, Y., Dickmann, M., Altman, Y., & Bournois, F. 2013. Exploring international work: types and dimensions of global careers. *International Journal of Human Resource Management*, 24(12): 2369–2393.

Bartlett, C. A. & Ghoshal, S. 2002. *Managing across Borders: The Transnational Solution*. Boston: Harvard Business Press.

Beaverstock, J., Derudder, J., Faulconbridge, J., & Witlox, F. 2010. *International Business Travel in the Global Economy*. Surrey: Ashgate Publishing Ltd.

Blackman, A., Welters, R., Murphy, L., Eagle, L., Pearce, M., Pryce, J., Lynch, P., & Low, D. 2014. Workers' perceptions of FIFO work in North Queensland, Australia. *Australian Bulletin of Labour*, 40(2): 180.

Bonache, J., Brewster, C., Suutari, V., & Cerdin, J.-L. 2018. The changing nature of expatriation. *Thunderbird International Business Review*, 60(6): 815–821. DOI.org/10.1002/tie.21957.

Brewster, C., Harris, H., & Petrovic, J. 2001. Globally mobile employees: Managing the mix. *Journal of Professional HRM*, 25: 11–15.

Brookfield Global Relocation Services. 2009. *International Mobility: Introducing flexibility into policy structures*. Woodridge, IL: Brookfield Global Relocation Services.

Brookfield GMAC. 2013. *Global Relocation Trends: 2013 Survey Report*. Bun Ridge, IL, USA: Brookfield.

Caligiuri, P. 2012. *Cultural Agility: Building a Pipeline of Successful Global Professionals*. John Wiley & Sons.

Caligiuri, P. M., Hyland, M. M., Joshi, A., & Bross, A. S. 1998. Testing a theoretical model for examining the relationship between family adjustment and expatriates' work adjustment. *Journal of Applied Psychology*, 83(4): 598.

Cartus. 2012b. *Managing Expats in 'Unsafe' Locations*. Wilmington, NC: Cartus.

Cartus. 2018. *Biggest Challenges Survey Report*. Danbury, CT: Cartus.

Collings, D., McDonnell, A., & McCarter, A. 2015. Types of international assignees. In D. Collings, G. Wood, & P. Caligiuri (eds.). *Routledge Companion to International Human Resource Management*: 259–275. London: Routledge.

Collings, D. G., Scullion, H., & Morley, M. J. 2007. Changing patterns of global staffing in the multinational enterprise: challenges to the conventional expatriate assignment and emerging alternatives. *Journal of World Business*, 42(2): 198–213.

Crowley-Henry, M. & Heaslip, G. 2014. Short-term assignments. Military perspectives and implications for international human resource management. *European Management Journal*, 32: 752–760.

Crowne, K. A. & Engle, R. 2016. Antecedents of cross-cultural adaptation stress in short-term international assignments. *Organization Management Journal*, 13(1): 32–47.

Davidson, R. & Cope, B. 2003. *Business Travel: Conferences, Incentive Travel, Exhibitions, Corporate Hospitality and Corporate Travel.* New York: Pearson Education.

DeFrank, R., Konopaske, R., & Ivancevich, J. 2000. Executive travel stress: perils of the road warrior. *Academy of Management Executive*, 14: 58–71.

Demel, B. & Mayrhofer, W. 2010. Frequent business travelers across Europe: career aspirations and implications. *Thunderbird International Business Review*, 52(4): 301–311.

Dickie, C. & Dwyer, J. 2011. A 2009 perspective of HR practices in Australian mining. *Journal of Management Development*, *30*(4), 329–343.

Dickmann, M. 2015. Programme Management and Technology, Chapter 5. In M. Dickmann (ed.), *Strategic Global Mobility & the Talent Management Conundrum*: 88–99. The RES Forum Annual Report 2015, London: RES Forum.

Dickmann, M. 2016. *Beyond Uniformity – A World of Opportunity.* The RES Forum Annual Report 2016, London: RES Forum.

Dickmann, M. 2018. *Global Mobility of the Future – Smart, Agile, Flawless and Efficient*: 157. The RES Forum Annual Report, London: RES Forum, Harmony Relocation Network and Equus Software.

Dickmann, M. & Baruch, Y. 2011. *Global Careers.* London: Routledge.

Dickmann, M. & Müller-Camen, M. 2006. A typology of international human resource management strategies and processes. *International Journal of Human Resource Management*, 17(4): 580–601.

Dickmann, M., Suutari, V., & Wurtz, O. (2018). The multiple forms and shifting landscapes of global careers. In Dickmann, M., Suutari, V. & Wurtz, O. (eds.), *The Management of Global Careers. Exploring the Rise of International Work.* Cham: Palgrave Macmillan.

Duxbury, A. 2018. *Commuter Assignments – the Consequences beyond the Financial Cost.* London: ECA International.

ECA International. 2016. The decline of the traditional expatriate. www.eca-international.com/insights/articles/may-2016/the-decline-of-the-traditional-expat.

Edström, A. & Galbraith, J. R. 1977. Transfer of managers as a coordination and control strategy in multinational organizations. *Administrative Science Quarterly*: 248–263.

Espino, C., Sundstrom, S., Frick, H., Jacobs, M., & Peters, M. 2002. International business travel: Impact on families and travellers. *Occupational and Environmental Medicine*, 59(3): 309–322.

Fee, A. & McGrath-Champ, S. 2017. The role of human resources in protecting expatriates: insights from the international aid and development sector. *International Journal of Human Resource Management*, 28(14): 1960–1985.

Harris, H., Brewster, C., & Sparrow, P. 2003. *International Human Resource Management*. London: CIPD Publishing.

Harvey, M., Mayerhofer, H., Hartmann, L., & Moeller, M. 2010. Corralling the 'horses' to staff the global organization of 21st century. *Organization Dynamics*, 39(3): 258–268.

Haslberger, A., Brewster, C., & Hippler, T. 2014. *Managing Performance Abroad: a New Model for Understanding Expatriate Adjustment*. London: Routledge.

Hocking, B. J., Brown, M., & Harzing, A. W. 2004. A knowledge transfer perspective of strategic assignment purposes and their path-dependent outcomes. *International Journal of Human Resource Management*, 15 (3): 565–586.

Hovhannisyan, N., & Keller, W. 2015. International business travel: an engine of innovation? *Journal of Economic Growth*, 20(1): 75–104.

Huber, P. & Nowotny, K. 2013. Moving across borders: Who is willing to migrate or to commute? *Regional Studies*, 47(9): 1462–1481.

Johnson, L. 2017. *Smart Moves: Companies Look to Lower the Cost of Global Mobility*. Danbury, CT: Crown World Mobility.

Kang, H., Shen, J., & Benson, J. 2016. Not all expatriates are the same: Non-traditional South Korean expatriates in China. *International Journal of Human Resource Management*, 28(13): 1842–1865.

Kedia, B. L. & Mukherji, A. 1999. Global managers: Developing a mindset for global competitiveness. *Journal of World Business*, 34(3): 230–251.

Knowles, R. & Matthiessen, C. 2009. Barrier effects of international borders on fixed link traffic generation: The case of Øresundsbron. *Journal of Transport Geography*, 17(3): 155–165.

KPMG. 2017. *Global Assignment Policies and Practices Survey*. Geneva: KPMG.

Lazarova, M., Westman, M., & Shaffer, M. A. 2010. Elucidating the positive side of the work-family interface on international assignments: A model of expatriate work and family performance. *Academy of Management Review*, 35(1): 93–117.

Mäkelä, K. & Brewster, C. 2009. Interunit interaction contexts, interpersonal social capital, and differing levels of knowledge sharing. *Human Resource Management*, 48(4): 591–614.

Mäkelä, L., Bergbom, B., Tanskanen, J., & Kinnunen, U. 2014. The relationship between international business travel and sleep problems via work-family conflict. *Career Development International*, 19(7): 794–812.

Mäkelä, L., Kinnunen, U., & Suutari, V. 2015. Work-to-life conflict and enrichment among international business travelers: The role of international career orientation. *Human Resource Management*, 54(3): 517–531.

Mäkelä, L., Saarenpää, K., & McNulty, Y. 2017. International business travelers, short-term assignees and international commuters. In Y. McNulty & J. Selmer (eds.), *Research Handbook of Expatriates*: 276–294. London: Edward Elgar.

Mayrhofer, W. & Scullion, H. 2002. Female expatriates in international business: Empirical evidence from the German clothing industry. *International Journal of Human Resource Management*, 13: 815–836.

McNulty, Y. & Brewster, C. 2019. *Working Internationally: Expatriation, Migration and Other Global Work*. Cheltenham: Edward Elgar.

McNulty, Y., De Cieri, H., & Hutchings, K. 2009. Do global firms measure expatriate return on investment? An empirical examination of measures, barriers and variables influencing global staffing practices. *International Journal of Human Resource Management*, 20(6): 1309–1326.

Mercer 2016. *Exploring Smarter Global Mobility Strategies*. London: Mercer. https://mobilityexchange.mercer.com/Insights/mobility-guides.

Meyskens, M., Von Glinow, M., Werther, W., & Clarke, L. 2009. The paradox of international talent: alternative forms of international management. *International Journal of Human Resource Management*, 20(6): 1439–1450.

Minbaeva, D. & Michailova, S. 2004. Knowledge transfer and expatriation in multinational corporations: The role of disseminative capacity. *Employee Relations*, 26(6): 663–679.

Phillips, J. M., Gully, S. M., McCarthy, J. E., Castellano, W. G., & Kim, M. S. 2014. Recruiting global travelers: the role of global travel recruitment messages and individual differences in perceived fit, attraction, and job pursuit intentions. *Personnel Psychology*, 67(1): 153–201.

Pinto, L. H. F., Bader, B., & Schuster, T. 2017. Dangerous settings and risky international assignments. *Journal of Global Mobility*, 5(4): 342–347.

Posthuma, R. A., Ramsey, J. R., Flores, G. L., Maertz, C., & Ahmed, R. O. 2017. A risk management model for research on expatriates in hostile work environments. *International Journal of Human Resource Management*, 30(11): 1822–1838.

Reiche, B. S., Harzing, A-W, & Kraimer, M. 2009. The role of international assignees' social capital in creating inter-unit intellectual capital: A cross-level model. *Journal of International Business Studies*, 40(3): 509–526.

Renshaw, P. S. J., Parry, E., & Dickmann, M. 2018. Seconded national experts and global mobility – Extending the paradigm. *Thunderbird International Business Review*, 60(6): 897–909.

Rogers, H. L. 1998. *A Survey of the Travel Health Experiences of International Business Travelers*. Calgary: University of Calgary (unpublished PhD thesis).

Saarenpää, K. 2017. *Stretching, adapting and negotiating: International business travel and its influence on work-family interaction*. PhD, University of Vaasa, Finland.

Salleh, N. & Koh, J. 2013. Analysing the functions of short-term expatriate assignments. *Procedia – Social and Behavioral Sciences*, 107: 34–42.

Sandow, E. 2014. Til work do us part: The social fallacy of long-distance commuting. *Urban Studies*, 51(3): 526–543.

Shaffer, M., Kraimer, M., Chen, Y-P., & Bolino, M. 2012. Choices, challenges, and career consequences of global work experiences: a review and future agenda. *Journal of Management*, 38(4): 1282–1327.

Starr, C. 2009. Repatriation and short-term assignments: an exploration into expectations, change and dilemmas. *International Journal of Human Resource Management*, 20(2): 286–300.

Starr, T. & Currie, G. 2009. 'Out of sight, but still in the picture': Short-term international assignments and the influential role of family. *International Journal of Human Resource Management*, 20(6): 1421–1438.

Striker, J., Luippold, R., Nagy, L., Liese, B., Bigelow, C., & Mundt, K. 1999. Risk factors for psychological stress among international business travellers. *Occupational and Environmental Medicine*, 56(4): 245–252.

Suutari, V. & Brewster, C. 2009. Beyond expatriation: Different forms of international employment. In P. Sparrow (ed.), *Handbook of International Human Resource Management: Integrating people, process and context*: 131–150. Chichester, UK: Wiley.

Suutari, V., Brewster, C., Riusala, K., & Syrjakari, S. 2013. Managing non-standard international experience: evidence from a finish company. *Journal of Global Mobility*, 1(2): 118–138.

Tahvanainen, M., Welch, C., & Worm, V. 2005. Implications of short-term international assignments. *European Management Journal*, 23(6): 663–673.

Welch, D. E., & Worm, V. (2006). International business travellers: A challenge for IHRM. In G. K. Stahl & I. Bjorkman (Eds.), Handbook of research in international human resource management. Cheltenham, UK: Edward Elgar.

Westman, M. & Etzion, D. 2002. The impact of short overseas business trips on job stress and burnout. *Applied Psychology: An International Review*, 51(4): 582–592.

Westman, M., Etzion, D., & Chen, S. 2009a. The crossover of exhaustion and vigor between international business travelers and their spouses. *Journal of Managerial Psychology*, 24: 269–284.

Westman, M., Etzion, D., & Chen, S. 2009b. Crossover of positive experiences from business travelers to their spouses. *Journal of Managerial Psychology*, 24(3): 269–284.

Wurtz, O. 2018. Expatriation, alcohol and drugs: antecedents and consequences of substance use in expatriation. *Journal of Global Mobility*, 6(3/4): 316–334.

8 Self-initiated Expatriates

SEBASTIAN STOERMER, FABIAN JINTAE FROESE, VESA PELTOKORPI

8.1 Introduction

Skilled individuals with professional qualifications increasingly decide to relocate temporarily and work in foreign countries (Doherty, Dickmann, & Mills, 2011; Froese, 2012; Suutari, Brewster, Mäkelä, Dickmann, & Tornikoski, 2018). These individuals, referred to as self-initiated expatriates (SIEs) (Froese & Peltokorpi, 2013; Lee, 2005; Peltokorpi, 2008; Peltokorpi & Froese, 2009; Selmer & Lauring, 2014; Tharenou, 2013), are estimated to make up the majority of the overall expatriate population (Shao & Al Ariss, 2020; Stoermer, Davies, & Froese, 2017). In contrast to assigned expatriates (AEs), sent from headquarters to work in a foreign subsidiary for a set period of time to achieve an organisational goal (Harrison, Shaffer, & Bhaskar-Shrinivas, 2004: 203), the key distinguishing characteristic of SIEs is that their expatriation is not company-backed (Inkson, Arthur, Pringle, & Barry, 1997; Suutari & Brewster, 2000) and less driven by career concerns. SIEs tend to place more emphasis on the desire to spend some time living in a certain country of their choice and to initiate a change of scenery (Doherty et al., 2011; Selmer & Lauring, 2012; Suutari & Brewster, 2000; Thorn, 2009). For organisations, SIEs are a welcomed and valuable addition to the available talent pool and can be hired to fill shortage of skilled labour and to buy-in expertise with the aim of facilitating intra-organisational knowledge transfer and learning processes (Tang, Chang, & Cheng, 2017; Tharenou, 2013; Vaiman & Haslberger, 2013; Vaiman, Haslberger, & Vance, 2015).

Although the traditional research on expatriates has implicitly or explicitly focused on AEs (Selmer & Lauring, 2013), research on SIEs has started to gain momentum in the past two decades and evolved into its own field of inquiry (Dickmann, Suutari, Brewster, Mäkelä, Tanskanen, & Tornikoski, 2018; Doherty, 2013). One stream of this research has also compared the career experiences, trajectories, and cross-cultural adjustment between SIEs and AEs (Froese & Peltokorpi, 2013; Jokinen, Brewster & Suutari, 2008; Peltokorpi & Froese, 2009; Suutari & Brewster, 2000; Suutari et al., 2018). Another stream of research has further increased the clarity of the SIE-concept (Al Ariss & Crowley-Henry, 2013; Andresen, Bergdolt, Margenfeld, & Dickmann, 2014; Cerdin & Selmer, 2014), and the motivations that lead individuals to self-initiate expatriation (Cerdin & Pargneux, 2010; Froese, 2012; Inkson et al., 1997; Selmer & Lauring, 2010; Thorn, 2009). Due to the considerable increase of the literature on SIEs and the growing importance of SIEs as a source of talent (Cerdin & Selmer, 2014), the purpose of this chapter is (1) to provide a concise overview of the extant knowledge on SIEs; (2) to outline relevant areas of research that warrant further attention; and (3) to derive recommendations for individuals entrusted with human resource management (HRM) on how to attract and retain SIEs.

The remainder of this chapter is organised as follows. In the next section, we will review the literature on the conceptual definition(s) pertaining to SIEs and illustrate how SIEs differ from AEs and other types of globally mobile individuals. We then outline the relevant literature dealing with the specific characteristics and challenges/advantages of the SIE-situation. Here, we cover vital aspects, such as SIE demographics, motivation, cross-cultural adjustment to the host country, and career experiences and career capital accumulation. In the discussion section, we synthesise the most pressing implications for the management of SIEs and future research, and conclude with a brief summary.

8.2 SIEs – Definition and Differentiation

In the expatriate literature, SIEs were first mentioned in an article by Inkson et al. (1997) describing common practice among university graduates in Australia and New Zealand to work and travel abroad for a certain time and then return home (Inkson & Myers, 2003). Since then, various different SIE-related terms and definitions have emerged, such as self-initiated foreign work experience (SFE) (Suutari & Brewster, 2000), self-initiated foreign workers (Harrison et al., 2004), and self-initiated foreign expatriates (SEs) (Biemann & Andresen, 2010). In addition to inconsistent terms and definitions of SIEs, there has been confusion on the defining features that constitute self-initiated expatriation and how SIEs are distinguished from other expatriate types, sojourners, and migrants (Al Ariss & Crowley-Henry, 2013; Andresen et al., 2014; Cerdin & Selmer, 2014; McNulty & Brewster, 2017; Peltokorpi & Froese, 2012). SIEs were often defined as individuals who decide by themselves to live and work in foreign countries (Peltokorpi & Froese, 2009). To differentiate SIEs from migrants, Peltokorpi and Froese (2012) suggested that SIEs should harbour at least some thoughts of returning back to their home country. However, many SIEs eventually become migrants planning to remain indefinitely in the host country (Al Ariss & Crowley-Henry, 2013).

Despite the initial (and to some extent continuing) vagueness about what the SIE-categorisation entails, several scholars have developed criteria for defining SIEs (Cerdin & Selmer, 2014; McNulty & Brewster, 2017; Peltokorpi & Froese, 2012). Among the most notable efforts, Cerdin and Selmer (2014) developed a taxonomy consisting of four criteria: (1) self-initiated international relocation; (2) regular employment intentions; (3) intentions of a temporary stay; and (4) skilled/professional qualifications. The first criterion relates to whether the expatriate or the employing organisation initiated the international relocation. If individuals have been deployed by their employer to carry out an international assignment, they should be considered AEs. The same applies to individuals who proactively initiated their expatriation within the boundaries of their organisation, because they still remain employees of their home country company and usually receive support during the expatriation cycle. In contrast, individuals who move on their own accord without organisational support from the home country should be considered SIEs. This may also include individuals who self-dependently acquired their job in the host country before relocation and who received relocation support from the new employer in the host country. In addition, following criterion two, SIEs take up regular employment in the host country or at least have the intention to do so. Application of this criterion helps to distinguish SIEs from students or trailing partners who have no intention to become employed in the host country (Cerdin & Selmer, 2014). Third, while SIEs can in some cases obtain the citizenship of the host country, the intention of a temporary stay during the initiation of the relocation is what differentiates SIEs from migrants, who usually plan to settle permanently in the host country. Fourth, SIEs need to have certain skills/professional qualifications that allow them to find a job in the host country. However, Andresen et al. (2014) do not consider criteria three and four essential for SIEs and adopt a much broader understanding of the SIE-concept.

In summary, the criteria provided by Cerdin and Selmer resonate to a great extent with the other available differentiation schemes found in the literature (McNulty & Brewster, 2017; Peltokorpi & Froese, 2012), suggesting that SIEs (1) seek employment abroad self-dependently; (2) are employed in the host country; (3) intend to stay for a limited time; and (4) are skilled professionals. However, scholars still appear to have different opinions of how to categorise SIEs and debate exists regarding the differentiation from migrants (Al Ariss & Crowley-Henry, 2013; Andresen et al., 2014; Cerdin & Selmer, 2014).

8.3 SIEs – Who They Are

SIEs have been estimated to account for a substantial and increasing number of the globally mobile workforce (Shao & Al Ariss, 2020; Vaiman & Haslberger, 2013). However, estimating a precise SIE head-count is a difficult task because reports about temporary worker migration as provided by the OECD and other large-scale studies are not without caveats and data coverage might not be exhaustive. Also, in part due to different definitions of SIEs and classifications of migration statistics of temporary workers, it is difficult to make an exact estimation of the SIE-population. Nevertheless, the accumulated research on SIEs has provided valuable information on the individuals constituting the SIE-population and helped to triangulate the demographic profiles of SIEs.

Regarding gender, the SIE-population is estimated to have a more even share of males and females as compared to the male-dominated AE-population – which is estimated to be approximately 75 per cent males (e.g., Brookfield Global Relocation Services, 2016). Based on an analysis of large-scale studies (e.g., Napier & Taylor, 2002; Thorn, 2009), Tharenou (2010) estimated that approximately half of the SIE-population is female. She reasoned that women may self-initiate expatriation to circumvent male-bias in selection processes for company-backed overseas assignments. Then again, some female spouses become SIEs in an attempt to follow their husbands while maintaining their careers. Similar numbers reflecting a nearly even share of male and female SIEs are found in several studies (Andresen, Biemann & Pattie, 2015; Cerdin & Pargneux, 2010; Chen & Shaffer, 2017; Suutari & Brewster, 2000).

In terms of age and organisational rank, research suggests that SIEs start their overseas working experience at a younger age than AEs (Biemann & Andresen, 2010; Cerdin & Pargneux, 2010; Suutari & Brewster, 2000). SIEs tend to work in lower levels in organisational hierarchy (Froese & Peltokorpi, 2013; Jokinen et al., 2008) and since self-initiated expatriation is not subject to intra-organisational selection processes (Cerdin & Selmer, 2014; Peltokorpi & Froese, 2012), it might fit better into the life stage of younger individuals. This assumption is in line with Inkson et al.'s (1997) account of overseas experience as a time for young university graduates to go abroad for travel and work.

With regards to marital status and number of children, research suggests that SIEs are often singles (or, at least not married) and have no or fewer children than AEs (Cerdin & Pargneux, 2010; Suutari & Brewster, 2000; Suutari et al., 2018), which could have facilitated their motivation to expatriate without organisational support (Kim & Froese, 2012). Furthermore, a study suggests that married expatriates with children were less motivated to be geographically mobile unless circumstances rendered no other alternative (Crowley-Henry, 2007). Of course, these research findings can be confounded with the age differences between AEs and SIEs.

Referring to education level, several studies consistent with Cerdin's and Selmer's (2014) taxonomy suggest that SIEs are well-educated. For example, this tendency is reflected in studies focusing on SIE-academics (Chen & Shaffer, 2017; Froese, 2012; Richardson & McKenna, 2002; Richardson & Mallon, 2005; Selmer & Lauring, 2010), and other skilled groups of SIEs such as accountants, IT-experts, managers, and lawyers (Lee, 2005; Suutari & Taka, 2004; Tharenou & Caulfield, 2010). Perhaps for this reason, Haslberger and Vaiman (2013: 4) characterised self-initiated expatriation with 'high skill level'. However, research suggests that there are no major differences between AEs and SIEs in terms of education level – most hold at least a graduate degree (Dorsch, Suutari & Brewster, 2013).

In terms of country of origin, early studies focused mainly on SIEs originating from Anglo-American and Western European countries (e.g., Biemann & Andresen, 2010; Cerdin & Pargneux, 2010;

Dickmann et al., 2018; Inkson et al., 1997; Richardson & McKenna, 2002; Suutari & Brewster, 2000; Suutari & Taka, 2004; Tharenou & Caulfield, 2010; Thorn, 2009). In the light of this bias on Western industrialised countries, research on SIEs and AEs has some similarities. More recent studies on SIEs have also expanded the scope to SIEs from emerging markets such as China (Shao & Al Ariss, 2020), and less developed countries such as Lebanon (Al Ariss & Özbilgin, 2010) or Sri Lanka (Chathurani, Froese & Bader, 2019). Considering the 'push-pull model' in the migration literature (Cerdin, Abdeljalil-Diné, Brewster, 2014), we expect that a substantial number of the present SIE population moves from developing countries to industrialised countries, because industrialised countries tend to provide better career opportunities for highly educated and mobile individuals. In general, the accumulated research suggests that SIEs come from various countries and move in various directions. This is somewhat in contrast to AE who are mainly assigned from industrialised countries to other industrialised and major emerging markets such as China (e.g., Brookfield Global Relocation Services, 2016).

As for duration of host country stay, scholars have argued that SIEs stay longer – on average between six to eight years – whereas AEs' stay often ranges between two to five years (Cerdin & Selmer, 2014; Peltokorpi & Froese, 2012). As already noted, AEs by definition are sent from headquarters to work in a foreign subsidiary for a given period of time to achieve an organisational goal (Harrison et al., 2004). In contrast, SIEs have more flexibility to determine the duration of their stay in the host country. Perhaps for this reason, studies show that SIEs remain longer in host countries than AEs (Peltokorpi, 2008). Turning to further explanatory factors underlying duration of stay, a recent study (Meuer et al., 2019) focused on the influence of embeddedness, which relates to individuals' perceptions of how strongly there are enmeshed in the host country (e.g., Tharenou & Caulfield, 2010). Meuer et al. showed that community embeddedness (i.e., non-work-related links, fit, and sacrifices) is more important for explaining the repatriation intentions of AEs than of SIEs, whereas on-the-job embeddedness (i.e., work-related links, fit, and sacrifices) is more important for explaining the repatriation intentions of SIEs compared to AEs.

Taken together, previous research has not provided any definite numbers capturing the global SIE population. Nevertheless, accumulated studies allow us to infer some rough trends suggesting that the SIE population is (1) more balanced in terms of gender than AEs; (2) younger than AEs; (3) less bounded by family obligations than AEs; (4) well-educated; (5) highly diverse in terms of country of origin; and (6) stay abroad longer than AEs. While substantial research has identified typical characteristics, most previous SIEs studies have used convenience samples that do not necessarily present the overall SIE population. Large-scale data is still missing to provide a representative account of SIE characteristics, particularly on a global scale.

8.4 SIEs – Motivations for Going Abroad

Research suggests some notable differences in SIEs' and AEs' motivations for going abroad (Andresen et al., 2015; Cerdin & Pargneux, 2010; Doherty et al., 2011; Inkson et al., 1997; Jokinen et al., 2008; Selmer & Lauring, 2010; Suutari & Brewster, 2000; Thorn, 2009). While AEs often accept overseas assignments for career-related reasons (Cerdin & Pargneux, 2010; Doherty et al., 2011), studies suggest the subordinate role of (immediate) career motives for SIEs. In a qualitative study, Inkson et al. (1997) analysed the accounts of New Zealand SIEs to explore the reasons that make them relocate. They found that SIEs placed great importance on collecting cultural experience, were highly curious, and considered their time abroad as a means to grow as a person. A similar picture was drawn in one of the most comprehensive endeavours by Thorn (2009) who collected data from more than 2,600 New Zealand SIEs spread across 93 host destinations. The study revealed that the opportunity to travel was the most important motive followed by getting to know the home country of the partner, which relates to the fact that many SIEs are married to host country nationals (Froese, 2012; Vance, 2005). In Thorn's study (2009), better remuneration was the most important economic concern, ranked as the third important overall motive.

From interviews among British SIE academics, Richardson and McKenna (2002) derived four metaphors that capture the main motives for self-initiated expatriation: explorer; refugee; mercenary; and architect. The explorer, the mercenary and the architect leave their home country in order to gain something in the other country (interesting cultural experience, financial rewards or career-building, respectively). A 'refugee' is mostly interested in leaving the country he or she presently works in. Relatedly, the seminal qualitative study by Richardson and Mallon (2005) developed a set of five themes that underlie SIE-motivation to move abroad. The most salient themes in their qualitative analysis related to adventure/travel, family, and change of scenery (e.g., being bored with life in the home country). Subordinate themes were financial reasons and career enhancement – for example, in terms of improving one's resume by adding an international profile. Delving further into the motivational differences between SIEs and AEs, one stream of research has examined varying conceptions of careers between SIEs and AEs. Focusing on career anchors (Schein, 1990) – a combination of perceived areas of competence, motives, and values relating to professional work choices – Cerdin and Le Pargneux (2010) found that dedication to a cause and lifestyle considerations were more pronounced in SIEs than AEs.

Further, protean (Hall, 2004) and boundaryless career orientations (Arthur, 1994) have been used in research on SIE motives to move abroad. Individuals with a protean/boundaryless career orientation take charge of their own careers, emphasise freedom and personal growth, and de-emphasise objective success criteria, such as salary or position, for the sake of personal goals. They are more committed to their profession as compared to their organisation and attach great relevance to being satisfied with work (Hall, 2004). Likewise, the boundaryless career concept takes account of the development that nowadays careers are less likely to unfold within a single organisational context and that individuals become increasingly independent from traditional organisational career principles (Arthur, 1994). The research on SIE-motivation has portrayed SIEs as protean/boundaryless careerists (e.g., Cao, Hirschi & Deller, 2012; Ceric & Crawford, 2016: Crowley-Henry, 2007; Howe-Walsh & Schyns, 2010; Inkson, 2006) conveying the notion that SIEs tend to pursue a boundaryless career in which they move between organisations and countries; whereas AEs usually follow an organisational career (Biemann & Andresen, 2010). Yet, in their empirical study, Andresen et al. (2015) showed that while SIEs can be regarded as protean/boundaryless careerists no significant differences to AEs exist.

Another aspect influencing SIEs' motivations to relocate are home and host country characteristics. In this stream of research, scholars have often relied on the 'push-pull' model (Bierbrauer & Pedersen, 1996; Massey & Espinosa, 1997) to delineate factors that draw SIEs to certain locations and make them leave their home country. These motives range from better employment conditions in the host country labour market to family considerations, such as having extended family in the host location (e.g., Froese, 2012; Thorn, 2009). For example, job markets – at home and abroad – have been shown to affect SIEs' decision to move abroad (Jokinen et al., 2008; Tharenou, 2010). Further, Doherty et al.'s (2011) study compared a set of pull factors and their influence on the decision to relocate between SIEs and AEs. Interestingly, their findings suggest that SIEs placed significantly more relevance on aspects related to the host culture, the perceived ability to adapt, and the reputation of the host country.

Taken together, the above evidence suggests that SIEs (1) assign high importance to gaining cultural experience; (2) don't consider career enhancement as the top priority; (3) are protean/boundaryless careerists; and (4) allocate greater value to host country characteristics in their decision to move abroad. Most studies in this domain are qualitative. While these studies have identified key motivating factors, quantitative studies are needed to validate and establish the generalisability of findings.

8.5 SIEs – Host Country Adjustment

Because individuals moving abroad are often confronted with a novel and unfamiliar cultural environment in host countries, cross-cultural adjustment is one of the most important antecedents of successful international relocation (Bhaskar-Shrinivas et al., 2005). Cross-cultural adjustment refers to the degree to which expatriates are psychologically comfortable and familiar with different aspects of a foreign environment (Black, 1988). One strand of the literature suggests that the construct has three sub-dimensions: general adjustment, work adjustment, and interaction adjustment. General adjustment is the degree of psychological comfort with regard to the host culture environment, such as climate, food, health care, housing conditions, and shopping; work adjustment is the degree of comfort regarding different expectations, performance standards, and work values; and interaction adjustment is comfort associated with interacting with HCNs inside and outside of work (Black, 1988).

To date, research has focused predominately on the antecedents of SIEs' cross-cultural adjustment. Looking at the role of personality of

SIE academics in Denmark, Selmer and Lauring (2014) found significant interrelations between dispositional affectivity and all three adjustment facets. Dispositional affectivity is a personality trait comprised of two dimensions – positive and negative affectivity – delineating an individuals' general propensity to respond positively or negatively to environmental stimuli (Watson, Clark & Carey, 1988). More specifically, the findings suggest that positive affectivity has a positive effect on all three facets of adjustment; whereas negative affectivity relates negatively to the three adjustment facets. Emphasising the importance of personality and cultural intelligence, the study by Huff, Song and Gresch (2014) investigated SIE teachers in Japan. Their findings indicate a positive relationship between motivational cultural intelligence and all three adjustment facets. In addition, two of the Big Five personality traits, that is intellect (openness to experience) and neuroticism, showed significant relationships with interaction adjustment. As such, neuroticism had a negative association with interaction adjustment; whereas intellect related positively to interaction adjustment. Furthermore, investigating multi-wave data, Fu et al. (2017) showed that organisational socialisation tactics facilitated SIE-teachers' social integration and learning in the Hong Kong workplace, which in turn facilitated interaction and work adjustment. Another study of SIE-teachers in Korea shows that whereas host country language proficiency and social interaction frequency with HCNs had a more positive influence on general and interaction adjustment facets, English use in the workplace, congruent communication, and conflict styles were more relevant to work adjustment (Froese, Peltokorpi & Ko, 2012). Elucidating the role of family-related variables for SIE-academics' adjustment in East Asia, Davies, Kraeh and Froese (2015) found that SIE academics who were married to locals experienced the steepest increase in overall cross-cultural adjustment over time. Drawing on person-environment (PE) fit theory (Jansen & Kristof-Brown, 2006), Nolan and Morley (2014) tested how correspondence between SIE needs and organisational supplies, and SIE abilities and job demands affected their cross-cultural adjustment. The authors found that a good fit between SIE abilities and job demands facilitated work adjustment; whereas needs-supply fit facilitated interaction adjustment. Furthermore, Cao et al. (2012) argued that a protean career orientation influences cross-cultural adjustment positively. The positive interrelation between protean career orientation and overall cross-cultural adjustment were corroborated in a subsequent empirical study (Cao, Hirschi & Deller, 2013).

While both SIEs and AEs can face similar culture-related challenges adjusting to the host country environment, SIEs can encounter additional challenges because they often work in lower positions and start working in an entirely novel organisational context (McDonnell & Scullion, 2013). Peltokorpi and Froese conducted two studies comparing AEs and SIEs in Japan. In their first study (Peltokorpi & Froese, 2009), SIEs reported higher general and interaction adjustment. However, the levels of work adjustment were similar between AEs and SIEs. In their second study, Froese and Peltokorpi (2013) centred on the causes that could explain the different levels of adjustment. Their results suggest that SIEs were more adjusted to interactions with locals due to better Japanese language proficiency and longer stays in Japan. Also, Japanese language proficiency and duration of stay in Japan mediated the effects of expatriate type on interaction adjustment. Interestingly, despite scoring higher on interaction adjustment, SIEs were not adjusted to work under a Japanese supervisor. Indeed, the mediation analysis of Froese and Peltokorpi (2013) show that supervisor national background carried an indirect effect in the association between expatriate type and job satisfaction, and accounted for lower levels of job satisfaction with SIEs.

In terms of outcomes of cross-cultural adjustment, Tang et al. (2017) investigated a sample of SIEs in Vietnam. The authors found a positive link between work adjustment and SIE knowledge sharing in the workplace. Furthermore, the study of SIEs in Germany by Cao et al. (2013) provided evidence that overall cross-cultural adjustment leads to higher career and life satisfaction as well as increased host country stay intentions. The study by Selmer, Lauring, Normann and Kubovcikova (2015) focused on how adjustment informs a host of pivotal work outcomes for SIE academics. Inter alia, they found that each of the three adjustment facets was positively correlated with job performance and job satisfaction. Likewise, time needed to establish proficiency on the job was negatively correlated with adjustment facets. In addition, the authors provided evidence that relationships varied between SIEs working for local or foreign universities. Moreover, the study by Froese et al. (2012) suggested a strong negative relationship between work adjustment and SIEs' turnover intentions across a sample of SIE teachers in South Korea.

Taken together, the above research on SIEs suggests that (1) cross-cultural adjustment is influenced by SIEs' cultural intelligence, personality, and host country language proficiency; (2) that cross-cultural adjustment facilitates stay intentions, job/career satisfaction, and job performance; and (3) higher levels of adjustment to the cultural environment and interaction with locals are more likely to be found among SIEs. However, since the focus in research on SIEs has been on cross-cultural adjustment as an outcome itself, more studies are needed to consolidate the effects of cross-cultural adjustment facets on pertinent work outcomes, such as job performance or knowledge sharing. Research could also expand its focus and centre on variables such as voluntary turnover. Further, while SIEs and AEs differ on several dimensions, little is also known about the unique situation of SIEs since scholars have often replicated prior research from AEs to SIEs. In terms of methodology, prior research was mainly confined to qualitative and cross-sectional quantitate data. As a next step, we recommend more research relying on longitudinal research designs.

8.6 SIEs – Careers

A stream of research has examined SIEs' career experiences and outcomes (Al Ariss & Özbilgin, 2010; Biemann & Andresen, 2010; Dickmann et al., 2018; Doherty, Richardson & Thorn, 2013; Inkson et al., 1997; Jokinen et al., 2008; Lee, 2005; Myers & Pringle, 2005; Richardson & Mallon, 2005; Rodriguez & Scurry, 2014). In general, SIEs are found to benefit from their international experience. In the case of younger SIEs, who set out to explore foreign cultures and to use their experience abroad to learn and develop, Inkson et al. (1997) found that SIEs returned to their home countries with a clearer outline of their career goals and felt more self-confident and self-reliant. In another study on New Zealand SIEs, Myers and Pringle (2005) stated that self-initiated expatriation provided individuals with accelerated career development opportunities and that especially female SIEs, because of their longer stays and more profound (work) experiences, accumulated more career capital than male SIEs. In this regard, key career qualities found in the study by Myers and Pringle were self-confidence, focus and career aspirations, interpersonal relations, and cross-cultural skills. Likewise, in Richardson and Mallon's study (2005) on SIE-academics, a pattern emerged reflecting that the interviewed individuals associated their international experience with an increased employability in the internationalised academic job market.

Comparing the development of career capital between Finnish SIEs and AEs, Jokinen et al. (2008) focused on three types of career capital: knowing-how, knowing-why, and knowing-whom. Overall, their findings suggest that both AEs and SIEs associated their foreign experience with an increase in career capital across the three types of career capital. AEs and SIEs perceived that their social skills, their self-awareness of personal values and interests, and knowledge of key decision-makers in their organisation had increased as part of their foreign experience (Jokinen et al., 2008). In terms of differences, the study showed higher increases in AEs' knowing-whom career capital. Furthermore, using time-lagged data to examine the development of career capital, Dickmann et al., (2018) collected information from a group of Finnish AEs and SIEs in 2004 and 2012. Similar to Jokinen et al. (2008), they focused on changes in knowing-how, knowing-why, and knowing-whom, career capital. In summary, their study provided evidence that both AEs and SIEs perceived an overall increase in their career capital due to their expatriation experience; however, AEs gained significantly more knowing-whom and knowing-why career capital compared to SIEs. In another study relying on the same data, Suutari et al. (2018) compared the career satisfaction, promotion and job changes of SIEs and AEs. The found no differences in terms of career satisfaction and promotion, but found that AEs changed their jobs more often than SIEs.

While the above evidence suggests generally positive effects of foreign work experience on SIEs' careers, SIEs are also found to encounter challenges in the foreign workplace. Using a sample of SIEs in Singapore, Lee (2005) examined the impact of perceived underemployment – perceptions of working in an inferior, lesser, or lower quality type of employment with little opportunities to utilise one's skills – finding negative effects on SIEs' job satisfaction, identification with work, and career satisfaction. In the same study, antecedents to perceived underemployment were a lack of job autonomy, a poor fit between SIEs' skills and job demands, low variability in tasks, and unfulfilled promises made by the organisation. Furthermore, a study by Al Ariss and Özbilgin (2010) on career experiences of Lebanese SIEs in France suggests the existence of structural constraints that impeded the utilisation of SIEs' skills. Their study raised awareness on issues of downward career mobility related to self-initiated expatriation. In a related manner, Hildisch, Froese and Toh (2015) found evidence for the existence of discrimination of SIEs in Asia-Pacific and detrimental effects on retention outcomes.

While some SIEs seek to stay abroad and eventually become naturalised (Al Ariss & Crowley-Henry, 2013), repatriation is an important concern for most SIEs. In one of the few longitudinal studies on SIEs, Tharenou and Caulfield (2010) examined the factors that promote and inhibit repatriation. The findings show that career and community embeddedness acted as pull factors to stay in host country; whereas national identity, family encouragement to return, perceptions of better living conditions in the home country, and pressing situational factors (e.g., pregnancy and illness of a family member) acted as push factors to leave. The long-term career consequences of SIEs' repatriation have not been comprehensively investigated given that this requires longitudinal research designs. Nonetheless, the small-scale qualitative study by Begley, Collings and Scullion (2008) on the readjustment experiences of self-initiated repatriates to Ireland suggests that SIEs face greater stress and upheaval when returning to the home labour market than AEs, who remain in the same company.

In summary, the above evidence suggests that self-initiated expatriation is (1) associated with increased career capital; (2) not completely devoid of issues related to underemployment or structural barriers; (3) likely to get terminated/extended by push- and pull-factors; (4) presumably linked to more difficulties when it comes to re-adjusting to work after repatriating. Because prior research was mainly limited to subjective career perceptions, we know little about other objective career outcomes such as promotions and pay rise and little about the long-term consequences of self-initiated expatriation.

8.7 Conclusions

Changing demographics and globalisation have led to increased opportunities for skilled individuals to pursue international careers, and many SIEs have taken up these opportunities. In line with these changes, substantial research has been devoted to analyse the situation of SIEs (e.g., Froese, 2012; Jokinen et al., 2008; Peltokorpi & Froese, 2009). This chapter has reviewed the burgeoning literature on SIEs. Based on a comprehensive screening of the extant literature, we grouped prior research into five topics. Early research sought to define the concept of SIEs and describe the characteristics of SIEs, the first two topics we discussed in this chapter. This line of inquiry reached a certain level of saturation as it has created some clarity about the definition and characteristics of SIEs. We see more research opportunities in the other areas: motivation, adjustment and success, and career development. For these three areas, Table 8.1 summarises key findings, future research avenues, and practical implications for the management of SIEs.

A substantial body of research has focused on the motivations of SIEs and identified differences between AEs and SIEs (e.g., Andresen et al., 2015; Cerdin & Pargneux, 2010; Doherty et al., 2011; Froese, 2012). We encourage future research to investigate how these differences affect other relevant outcomes, such as job performance; knowledge sharing; and voluntary turnover, preferably in a longitudinal fashion. Longitudinal designs would also reveal whether and how motivations change and how SIEs respond to such changes. For organisations, it would be important to consider the motivation of SIEs in their HRM practices. Given the boundaryless career understanding of many SIEs, organisations may consider international careers for their SIEs, such as relocation to other countries and rotations into other functions to offer learning opportunities. For aspiring SIEs, it would be important to obtain realistic job previews so that jobs would match their expectations.

Similar to the research on AEs (Bhaskar-Srinivas et al., 2005), a large portion of prior SIE research has investigated the antecedents of cross-cultural adjustment and, to a lesser extent, its outcomes (e.g., Cao et al., 2013; Davies et al., 2015; Froese et al., 2012). While previous SIE research has largely replicated and confirmed previous research on AEs, it is time for more contextualised research considering the unique situation of SIEs. For example, future research could examine the role of culture-specific knowledge and motivation of SIEs. Further, SIE research could consider other important outcome variables. In terms of methodology, we need more robust research designs, including longitudinal research. Based on previous research, organisations are recommended to provide more support to SIEs so that they can thrive. As SIEs do not receive the support and status that AEs do, they need to develop their own skills, resources and supporters to succeed in the foreign

Table 8.1 *Summary and implications for research and practice*

Topic	Key findings	Future research	Practical implications
Motivation	– SIEs are adventure-seeking – pay less attention to career enhancement – pursue boundaryless careers; interested in host-country, for example, culture	– Longitudinal research – Link motivation with relevant outcomes	– Organisations: consider SIE-motivation in the recruitment, motivation, and retention management – Individuals: try to obtain realistic preview
Adjustment and success	– adjustment improves work attitudes – cultural intelligence and organisational support important – SIEs tend to be better adjusted than assigned expatriates	– Consider different outcomes – Consider the unique situation of SIEs – Longitudinal research	– Organisations: provide support to SIEs – Individuals: Carefully select host country and employer, learn cultural skills
Career development	– increased career capital – on-the-job challenges – push-pull factors – repatriation challenges	– Investigate different career outcomes – Investigate long-term career consequences – Consider other stakeholders	– Organisations: offer idiosyncratic career paths – Individuals: carefully select target country, focus on learning and development

country. It would be important for them to carefully select a host country where they benefit from certain advantages, for example, prior existing network, language abilities, highly sought-after skills.

Career and career development have been a key topic in SIE research (e.g., Al Ariss & Özbilgin, 2010; Biemann & Andresen, 2010; Dickmann et al., 2018), as it is an important concern for SIEs. Beyond research on subjective career perceptions, we need more research on objective career outcomes, also considering long-term consequences. It would also be interesting to consider other stakeholders, such as HCN colleagues and partners, in this process. Organisations employing SIEs could consider individually tailored HRM practices to better motivate SIEs. SIEs, in turn, should carefully select host countries that would be beneficial for their careers and focus their efforts on learning to maintain their employability.

References

Al Ariss, A. & Crowley-Henry, M. 2013. Self-initiated expatriation and migration in the management literature: Present theorizations and future research directions. *Career Development International*, 18(1): 78–96.

Al Ariss, A. & Özbilgin, M. 2010. Understanding self-initiated expatriates. Career experiences of Lebanese self-initiated expatriates in France. *Thunderbird International Business Review*, 52(4): 275–285.

Andresen, M., Bergdolt, F., Margenfeld, J., & Dickmann, M. 2014. Addressing international mobility confusion – developing definitions and differentiations for self-initiated and assigned expatriates as well as migrants. *International Journal of Human Resource Management*, 25(16): 2295–2318.

Andresen, M., Biemann, T., & Pattie, M. W. 2015. What makes them move abroad? Reviewing and exploring differences between self-initiated and assigned expatriation. *International Journal of Human Resource Management*, 26(7): 932–947.

Arthur, M. B. 1994. The boundaryless career: A new perspective for organizational inquiry. *Journal of Organizational Behavior*, 15(4): 295–306.

Begley, A., Collings, D. G., & Scullion, H. 2008. The cross-cultural adjustment experiences of self-initiated repatriates to the Republic of Ireland labour market. *Employee Relations*, 30(3): 264–282.

Bhaskar-Shrinivas, P., Harrison, D. A., Shaffer, M. A., & Luk, D. M. 2005. Input-based and time-based models of international adjustment: Meta-analytic evidence and theoretical extensions. *Academy of Management Journal*, 48(2): 257–281.

Biemann, T. & Andresen, M. 2010. Self-initiated foreign expatriates versus assigned expatriates. *Journal of Managerial Psychology*, 25(4): 430–448.

Bierbrauer, G. & Pedersen, P. 1996. Culture and migration. In G. Semin & K. Fiedler (eds.), *Applied Social Psychology*: 399–422. London: Sage.

Black, J. S. 1988. Work role transitions: A study of American expatriate managers in Japan. *Journal of International Business Studies*, 19(2): 277–294.

Brookfield Global Relocations Services 2016. *Global Mobility Trends Survey*. http://globalmobilitytrends.bgrs.com/assets2016/downloads/Full-Report-Brookfield-GRS-2016-Global-Mobility-Trends-Survey.pdf accessed 25 April 2019.

Cao, L., Hirschi, A., & Deller, J. 2012. Self-initiated expatriates and their career success. *Journal of Management Development*, 31(2): 159–172.

Cao, L., Hirschi, A., & Deller, J. 2013. The positive effects of a protean career attitude for self-initiated expatriates: Cultural adjustment as a mediator. *Career Development International*, 18(1): 56–77.

Cerdin, J.-L., Abdeljalil-Diné, M., & Brewster, C. 2014. Qualified immigrants' success: Exploring the motivation to migrate and to adjust. *Journal of International Business Studies*, 45(2): 151–168.

Cerdin, J.-L. & Le Pargneux, M. 2010. Career anchors. A comparison between organization-assigned and self-initiated expatriates. *Thunderbird International Business Review*, 52(4): 287–299.

Cerdin, J.-L. & Selmer, J. 2014. Who is a self-initiated expatriate? Towards conceptual clarity of a common notion. *International Journal of Human Resource Management*, 25(9): 1281 1301.

Ceric, A. & Crawford, H. J. 2016. Attracting SIEs. Influence of SIE motivation on their location and employer decisions. *Human Resource Management Review*, 26(2): 136–148.

Chathurani, I., Froese, F. J., Bader, K., 2019. Relocation with or without you: An attachment theory perspective on expatriate withdrawal. *Academy of Management Best Paper Proceedings*. https://doi.org/10.5465/AMBPP.2019.12

Chen, Y. P. & Shaffer, M. A. 2017. The influences of perceived organizational support and motivation on self-initiated expatriates' organizational and community embeddedness. *Journal of World Business*, 52(2): 197–208.

Crowley-Henry, M. 2007. The protean career: Exemplified by first world foreign residents in Western Europe? *International Studies of Management & Organization*, 37(3): 44–64.

Davies, S., Kraeh, A., & Froese, F. J. 2015. Burden or support? The influence of partner nationality on expatriate cross-cultural adjustment. *Journal of Global Mobility*, 3(2): 169–182.

Dickmann, M., Suutari, V., Brewster, C., Mäkelä, L., Tanskanen, J., & Tornikoski, C. 2018. The career competencies of self-initiated and assigned expatriates. Assessing the development of career capital over time. *International Journal of Human Resource Management*, 29(16): 2353–2371.

Doherty, N. 2013. Understanding the self-initiated expatriate. A review and directions for future research. *International Journal of Management Reviews*, 15: 447–469.

Doherty, N., Dickmann, M., & Mills, T. 2011. Exploring the motives of company-backed and self-initiated expatriates. *International Journal of Human Resource Management*, 22(3): 595–611.

Doherty, N., Richardson, J., & Thorn, K. 2013. Self-initiated expatriation: Career experiences, processes and outcomes. *Career Development International*, 18(1): 6–11.

Dorsch, M., Suutari, V., & Brewster, C. 2013. Research on self-initiated expatriation: History and future directions. In M. Andersen, A. Al Ariss, & M. Walther (eds.) *Self-initiated Expatriation: Individual, Organizational, and National Perspectives*: 42–56. Routledge: London.

Froese, F. J. 2012. Motivation and adjustment of self-initiated expatriates. The case of expatriate academics in South Korea. *International Journal of Human Resource Management*, 23(6): 1095–1112.

Froese, F. J., Peltokorpi, V., & Ko, K. A. 2012. The influence of intercultural communication on cross-cultural adjustment and work attitudes: Foreign workers in South Korea. *International Journal of Intercultural Relations*, 36(3): 331–342.

Froese, F. J. & Peltokorpi, V. 2013. Organizational expatriates and self-initiated expatriates: Differences in cross-cultural adjustment and job satisfaction. *International Journal of Human Resource Management*, 24(10): 1953–1967.

Fu, C., Hsu, Y.-S., A. Shaffer, M., & Ren, H. 2017. A longitudinal investigation of self-initiated expatriate organizational socialization. *Personnel Review*, 46 (2): 182–204.

Hall, D. T. 2004. The protean career. A quarter-century journey. *Journal of Vocational Behavior*, 65(1): 1–13.

Harrison, D. A., Shaffer, M. A., & Bhaskar-Shrinivas, P. 2004. Going places: Roads more and less traveled in research on expatriate experiences. *Research in Personnel and Human Resources Management*, 23: 199–247.

Haslberger, A., and Vaiman, V. 2013. Self-initiated expatriates: A neglected source of the global talent flow. In V. Vaiman & A. Haslberger (eds.), *Talent Management of Self-Initiated Expatriates: A Neglected Source of Global Talent*: 1–18. Palgrave Macmillan: Hampshire.

Hildisch, K., Froese, F. J., & Toh, S. M. 2015. Foreigners welcome? Discrimination and turnover of self-initiated expatriates in Asia. Paper presented at the annual meetings of the Academy of International Business, Bangalore, India, and European Academy of Management, Warsaw, Poland.

Howe-Walsh, L. & Schyns, B. 2010. Self-initiated expatriation. Implications for HRM. *International Journal of Human Resource Management*, 21(2): 260–273.

Huff, K. C., Song, P., & Gresch, E. B. 2014. Cultural intelligence, personality, and cross-cultural adjustment. A study of expatriates in Japan. *International Journal of Intercultural Relations*, 38: 151–157.

Inkson, K. 2006. Protean and boundaryless careers as metaphors. *Journal of Vocational Behavior*, 69(1): 48–63.

Inkson, K., Arthur, M. B., Pringle, J., & Barry, S. 1997. Expatriate assignment versus overseas experience: Contrasting models of international human resource development. *Journal of World Business*, 32(4): 351–368.

Inkson, K. & Myers, B. A. 2003. 'The big OE'. Self-directed travel and career development. *Career Development International*, 8(4): 170–181.

Jansen, K. J., & Kristof-Brown, A. 2006. Toward a multidimensional theory of person-environment fit. *Journal of Managerial Issues*, 18(2): 193–212.

Jokinen, T., Brewster, C., & Suutari, V. 2008. Career capital during international work experiences. Contrasting self-initiated expatriate experiences and assigned expatriation. *International Journal of Human Resource Management*, 19(6): 979–998.

Lee, C. H. 2005. A study of underemployment among self-initiated expatriates. *Journal of World Business*, 40(2): 172–187.

Kim, J. & Froese, F. J. 2012. Expatriation willingness in Asia: The importance of host-country characteristics and employees' role commitments. *International Journal of Human Resource Management*, 23: 3414–3433.

Massey, D. & Espinosa, K. 1997. What's driving Mexico-U.S. migration? A theoretical, empirical, and policy analysis. *American Journal of Sociology*, 102(4): 939–999.

McDonnell, A. & Scullion, H. 2013. Self-initiated expatriates' adjustment: A neglected terrain. In V. Vaiman & A. Haslberger (eds.), *Talent management of self-initiated expatriates*, 136–155. London: Palgrave Macmillan.

McNulty, Y. & Brewster, C. 2017. Theorizing the meaning(s) of 'expatriate'. Establishing boundary conditions for business expatriates. *International Journal of Human Resource Management*, 28(1): 27–61.

Meuer, J., Troster, C., Angstmann, M., Backes-Gellner, & Pull, K. 2019. Embeddedness and the repatriation intention of assigned and self-initiated expatriates. *European Management Journal*, 37(6): 784–793.

Myers, B. & Pringle, J. K. 2005. Self-initiated foreign experience as accelerated development. Influences of gender. *Journal of World Business*, 40(4): 421–431.

Napier, N. K. & Taylor, S. 2002. Experiences of women professionals abroad: Comparisons across Japan, China and Turkey. *International Journal of Human Resource Management*, 13(5): 837–851.

Nolan, E. M. & Morley, M. J. 2014. A test of the relationship between person–environment fit and cross-cultural adjustment among self-initiated expatriates. International Journal of Human Resource Management, 25 (11): 1631–1649.

Peltokorpi, V. 2008. Cross-cultural adjustment of expatriates in Japan. *International Journal of Human Resource Management*, 19(9): 1588–1606.

Peltokorpi, V., & Froese, F. 2009. Organizational expatriates and self-initiated expatriates. Who adjusts better to work and life in Japan? *International Journal of Human Resource Management*, 20(5): 1096–1112.

Peltokorpi, V. & Froese, F. 2012. Differences in self-initiated and organizational expatriates' cross-cultural adjustment. In M. Andersen, A. Al Ariss, and M. Walther (eds.), *Self-initiated Expatriation: Individual, Organizational, and National Perspectives*: 104–118. Routledge: London.

Richardson, J. & Mallon, M. 2005. Career interrupted? The case of the self-directed expatriate. *Journal of World Business*, 40(4): 409–420.

Richardson, J. & McKenna, S. 2002. Leaving and experiencing. Why academics expatriate and how they experience expatriation. *Career Development International*, 7(2): 67–78.

Rodriguez, J. K. & Scurry, T. 2014. Career capital development of self-initiated expatriates in Qatar. Cosmopolitan globetrotters, experts and outsiders. *International Journal of Human Resource Management*, 25(7): 1046–1067.

Schein, E. H. 1990. *Career Anchors: Discovering Your Real Values*. San Diego, CA: Pfeiffer & Company.

Selmer, J. & Lauring, J. 2010. Self-initiated academic expatriates: Inherent demographics and reasons to expatriate. *European Management Review*, 7(3): 169–179.

Selmer, J. & Lauring, J. 2012. Reasons to expatriate and work outcomes of self-initiated expatriates. *Personnel Review*, 41(5): 665–684.

Selmer, J. & Lauring, J. 2013. Self-initiated expatriate academics: Personal characteristics and work outcomes. In V. Vaiman & A. Haslberger (Eds.), *Talent management of self-initiated expatriates*, 181–201. London: Palgrave Macmillan.

Selmer, J. & Lauring, J. 2014. Mobility and emotions. *International Studies of Management & Organization*, 44(3): 25–43.

Selmer, J., Lauring, J., Normann, J., & Kubovcikova, A. 2015. Context matters: Acculturation and work-related outcomes of self-initiated expatriates employed by foreign vs. local organizations. *International Journal of Intercultural Relations*, 49: 251–264.

Shao, J. J. & Al Ariss, A. 2020. Knowledge transfer between self-initiated expatriates and their organizations: Research propositions for managing SIEs, *International Business Review*, 29(1). DOI:10.1016/j.ibusrev.2019.101634.

Stoermer, S., Davies, S., Froese, F. J. 2017. Expatriate cultural intelligence, embeddedness and knowledge sharing: A multilevel analysis. *Academy of Management Best Paper Proceedings*. https://doi.org/10.5465/AMBPP.2017.155.

Suutari, V. & Brewster, C. 2000. Making their own way: International experience through self-initiated foreign assignments. *Journal of World Business*, 35(4): 417–436.

Suutari, V., Brewster, C., Mäkelä, L., Dickmann, M., & Tornikoski, C. 2018. The effect of international work experience on the career success of expatriates. A comparison of assigned and self-initiated expatriates. *Human Resource Management*, 57(1): 37–54.

Suutari, V. & Taka, M. 2004. Career anchors of managers with global careers. *Journal of Management Development*, 23(9): 833–847.

Tang, A. D., Chang, M.-L., & Cheng, C.-F. 2017. Enhancing knowledge sharing from self-initiated expatriates in Vietnam. The role of internal marketing and work-role adjustment in an emerging economy. *Asia Pacific Business Review*, 23(5): 677–696.

Tharenou, P. 2010. Women's self initiated expatriation as a career option and its ethical issues. *Journal of Business Ethics*, 95(1): 73–88.

Tharenou, P. 2013. Self-initiated expatriates: An alternative to company-assigned expatriates? *Journal of Global Mobility*, 1(3): 336–356.

Tharenou, P. & Caulfield, N. 2010. Will I stay or will I go? Explaining repatriation by self-initiated expatriates. *Academy of Management Journal*, 53(5): 1009–1028.

Thorn, K. 2009. The relative importance of motives for international self-initiated mobility. *Career Development International*, 14(5): 441–464.

Vaiman, V. & Haslberger, A. 2013. *Talent Management of Self-Initiated Expatriates. A Neglected Source of Global Talent*. London: Palgrave Macmillan.

Vaiman, V., Haslberger, A., & Vance, C. M. 2015. Recognizing the important role of self-initiated expatriates in effective global talent management. *Human Resource Management Review*, 25(3): 280–286.

Vance, C.M. 2005. The personal quest for building global competence: A taxonomy of self-initiating career path strategies for gaining business experience abroad. *Journal of World Business*, 40(4): 374–385.

Watson, D., Clark, L. A., & Carey, G. 1988. Positive and negative affect and their relation to anxiety and depressive disorders. *Journal of Abnormal Psychology*, 97(3): 346–353.

9 Skilled Migrant Careers

JELENA ZIKIC, VIKTORIYA VOLOSHYNA

9.1 Introduction

One of the main challenges in the current literature on skilled migrant integration is understanding how distinct this population is from other groups of global careerists, such as expatriates, for example. Skilled migrants are often defined as individuals who bring credentials and experience from other countries who permanently settle and work in the host country have often been described as 'forgotten' and 'invisible men and women' (Bell, Kwesiga, & Berry, 2010). Thus far, one of the main differentiating features tends to be the intended length of stay that is the permanency of this decision. Migrants typically move with an idea of making their host country home for them and their families for the future. Moreover, in many migrant-welcoming countries, such as Canada, migrants initiate their migration journey into their home country through a lengthy process of application for immigration visas and thus their decision and the process of transition starts from home. Finally, another major distinction in most cases is the proactive nature as well as the independent character of their move. That is, most migrants arrive in the host country without any guarantee of work, not having many or any local relationships, so they have to proactively search for work and navigate the local labour market. This chapter will focus on skilled migrants, in particular, and their work and life trajectories in the new host country (see Figure 9.1). The chapter is organised in three major sections: (1) exploring individual level factors in skilled migrant adaptation and coping, (2) social capital and skilled migrant trajectories in the host country, and (3) organisational pathways towards migrant integration.

9.2 Individual Level Factors in Skilled Migrant Adaptation and Coping

One of the major challenges and most commonly researched topics related to skilled migrant careers in the host country has been their

Figure 9.1 Skilled migrants' work and life trajectories in the host country.

inability to secure employment commensurate to their level of education. This phenomenon is often described as underemployment or career downshifting. It has been studied in the context of regulated and unregulated professions; that is those who are regulated by local professional associations/bodies vs. those who do not have such barriers to practice. Typically, the research finds that skilled migrants in regulated professions such as doctors, lawyers, engineers, and teachers experience much more serious barriers to entry to the point that they suffer emotionally, and may experience strong form of professional identity threat due to occupational closure in those tightly controlled regulated fields (e.g., Zikic & Richardson, 2016). On the other hand, skilled migrants in unregulated professions, such as sales and marketing managers, financial analysts, or IT specialists, also face barriers often typical of anyone seeking work in the host country. This group of unregulated professionals is more challenged by issues such as having inadequate language/communication skills, seeking local social networks, and/or lacking full understanding of the local business norms.

Thus, some of the most common issues addressed in the literature today are these individual level barriers, whether related to credential recognition or what is commonly called ‘human capital translation’. Career challenges are also just one possible difficulty; migrants may also experience social and professional isolation, lack of belongingness, and inability to fully identify and acculturate locally. Questions revolve around not only migrants’ ability to manage these challenges but also how local context, society, and structures may affect their ability to cope. Thus, individual level issues must be understood in the context of local culture, organisation, and society overall.

Questions also focus on migrant’s motivation to migrate and integrate as well as their readiness to cope with variety of challenges experienced locally. Researchers pointed that a combination of rational and irrational factors draws skilled migrants into developed industrial countries (Haug, 2008). For example, rational choice and human capital theory proposed that economic and demographic factors motivate migration, since level of skills and qualification is strongly connected with the opportunities for finding a job and with the level of income in the country of destination (Haug, 2008). However, Boneva and Frieze (2001; 2006) noted that individuals might also be driven by the specific sets of personality characteristics, such as openness to experience (Canache et al., 2013), power motivation, and work-family values that initiate migratory behaviour pushing individuals to leave their country of origin. Among other factors leading to migration, researchers highlighted the presence of networks contributing to the skilled migrants’ expectations regarding help and desire to settle in certain countries/regions (Epstein, 2008).

As mentioned above, one of the common individual level barriers is language and communication. Language and culture, for example, are the most significant factors through which individuals define their similarity and differences in relation to others and these serve as the basis for group formation and differences. At the same time, social categorisation processes and stereotyping behaviours may determine action against groups seen as dissimilar (Bonache, Brewster, & Suutari, 2007; Bonache, Langinier, & Zárraga-Oberty, 2016; Harvey et al., 2005; Ogbonna & Harris, 2006); thus, in the case of skilled migrants vs. locals one may observe language, cultural, and human capital (foreign vs. local) differences as the most salient basis for differentiation. Moreover, beyond basic language skills, skilled migrants often struggle with mastering the tacit forms of communication skills, such as confidence, tact, fluency, modesty, interaction skills, and effective face to face techniques (Mahmud, Alam, & Hartel 2014). As a result, locals and migrants may easily encounter communication difficulties due to these culturally differing communication norms. In fact, communication competence overall is seen as one of the key indicators of employment success in today knowledge economy (e.g., Dugdale et al., 2005). Most local employers find that communication skills remain the biggest barrier for skilled migrants in terms of fitting into the local workplace, irrespective of their professional background (Derwing & Munro, 2009). In the context of these communication challenges, accents also are associated with prejudice and negative stereotypes by the native speakers (Derwing, 2003; Lippi-Green, 1997). Accordingly, non-native speakers are also likely to be viewed as less competent individuals as their accents can make it difficult to understand them, exchange information, and learn about each other (Bresnahan et al., 2002; Lindemann, 2003). Moreover, when skilled migrants become aware of these language differences, some may be more reluctant to share their ideas, or even lose self-confidence: in meetings and interviews, for example (Harrison, Harrison, & Shaffer, 2019; Lauring & Klitmoller, 2017). As a result, communications challenges remain one of the major barriers in skilled migrant/local relationships.

In addition to language skills, migrant vs. non-migrant identity (i.e., including both surface and deep level characteristics) will become an important and salient basis for categorisation and easily identified social category as the source of social identity. It has been shown more recently that 'immigrant status' is a complex and deeply ingrained social category' (Bell et al., 2010), easily perceived by local society and local organisations. Migrants are likely to identify with their 'migrant identity' based on their unique life and organisational experiences in the host country. For example, migrants share experiences of the liability of foreignness and employment challenges related to navigating the local labour market (e.g., DiBenigno & Kellogg, 2014; Zikic & Richardson, 2016), thus constantly seeking to learn local business norms as well as showcasing their value and uniqueness to local colleagues.

The liability of foreignness namely hazards of discrimination and unfamiliarity with skilled migrants' foreign human capital (Fang et al., 2013; Luo & Mezias, 2002) also affects how migrants experience and cope with potential devaluation of their foreign credentials. While foreign degrees are often the basis for being welcomed to the local economy as skilled migrants, local employers often have doubts about its applicability and relevance in relation to the local standards, local customers and market in general (Mahmud, Alam, & Hartel, 2014). Moreover, due to devaluation of migrants' foreign skills and experience at the time of hiring and selection, skilled migrants often end up working at lower levels compared to their original qualifications, experiencing career downshifting and underemployment (Bauder & Cameron, 2002; Chiswick & Miller, 2012; Zikic, Bonache, & Cerdin, 2010). This lack of legitimacy afforded to the foreign credentials and experience can lead to reluctance and doubts in interactions with local co-workers and supervisors (Almeida, Fernando, & Sheridan, 2012); it may lead to questioning of migrants' fit and suitability to actively contribute and participate in various meetings, collaborations, local business networks, etc. Moreover, for many skilled migrants in highly regulated professions, this devaluation or even their inability to re-enter their professions affects their sense of self and professional identity and may lead to major consequences for the person such as identity struggle, feelings of loss, and even depression (Zikic & Richardson, 2016).

Finally, while skilled migrants may need many individual resources such as resilience and proactivity to cope with many of the challenges listed above (e.g., communication difficulties, learning a new language, translating their human capital, dealing with accreditation difficulties), another key individual dimension in managing migrant lives and careers is their motivation to address these challenges as well as integrate and become part of local organisations. For example, some migrants arrive with a fear of losing a lot by coming to the host country and these individuals may have the lowest motivation to integrate, while those with the highest motivation to integrate typically believed that they have a lot to gain by migrating to the host country (Cerdin, Abdul-Dine, & Brewster, 2014). Similarly, skilled migrants' initial framing and expectations may even determine the effectiveness of organisational integration policies (Cerdin et al., 2014) as well as how they view employment and tenure in local organisations (Dietz et al., 2015).

Another source of evidence regarding skilled migrants' motivation is found in the cross-cultural psychology literature. Frieze, Hansen, and Boneva (2006) report that some immigrants may have higher motivation to leave their home country as well as adjust and succeed locally and this is based on what they describe as a 'migrant personality'. These individuals are more likely to leave their home country in search of better opportunities, and they often have higher achievement and power motivation (Boneva & Frieze, 2001; Frieze et al., 2006) to adapt locally. For example, they may experience heightened need to support their families especially during settlement and adaptation in the host country (De Castro, Gee, & Takeuchi, 2008). Similar findings were reported by Zikic et al. (2010) who studied skilled migrants in three different countries. Zikic et al. (2010) concluded that some migrants do in fact exhibit very strong motivation to adapt. This group was said to have an 'embracing' career orientation in the host country, to be driven by the force of their subjective career and even to be challenged by the objective career barriers they were experiencing. A majority of skilled migrants however were described as 'adaptive' in their new career orientation (Zikic et al., 2010), that is being proactive in their adaptation efforts, while still cognisant of the barriers along the way. A small group of skilled migrants in this study, however, was defined as 'resisting' and these individuals could not mobilise sufficient career motivation and psychological mobility to deal with objective barriers in the labour market. Thus, a majority of skilled migrants fall into the embracing and adaptive category and this motivation may be an asset to organisations; the resisting group is a much smaller group and due to this, orientation will be less likely to engage with the job market at all, thus unlikely to come in contact with the employers. Together, the findings reviewed in this section lend support to the multifaceted nature of individual resources and how they may impact the adaptation, settlement, and careers of migrants. However, all individual level factors are intertwined with organisational, professional, social, and even more broadly societal characteristics where migrants settle.

9.3 Social Capital and Skilled Migrant Trajectories in the Host Country

A second major area of research addresses the social aspect of the migrant experience, namely the ability to obtain local social capital that will assist in learning and integrating. It is important to clarify that under social capital we consider several types of relationships (e.g., family, friendships, and professional relationships). The main challenge faced by skilled migrants is that, after they move to a new country, most of their network of contacts is simply obsolete, as their networks typically reside in their home country. Instead, many newcomers will resort to what is typically seen as the logical coping strategy, namely looking for similar others for advice and support upon arrival. Thus, they will seek social support which helps skilled migrants to more successfully face the challenges associated with settling into the local society (Hobfoll et al., 1994). In general, social support can provide immediate resources, such as understanding, information, and encouragement in the face of difficulties, and thus also creates feelings of safety (Schweizer, Schnegg, & Berzborn, 1998; Walker, Wasserman, & Wellman, 1994). This is particularly relevant in the case of migrants, due to various issues such as identity challenges and lack of established social networks and relationships in the course of their migration (De Leon Siantz, 1997; Turchick Hakak, Holzinger, & Zikic, 2010). As a result, migrants often gravitate towards their own ethnic community which can provide comfort and support. In other cases, this strategy can be especially challenging as it may lead to survival jobs that often detract one from their original career path (Lubbers, Molina, & McCarty, 2007).

Moreover, typically, migrant newcomers form a minority in local communities and organisations, and will seek to become part of homophilous networks (Ibarra, 1993): that is, they become part of the networks of similar others. Yet, these networks typically do not involve high-status contacts since the similar others who are present in organisations are usually not in positions of authority (Turckick Hakak et al., 2010). Moreover, these subgroups of skilled migrants may be seen as highly distinctive from majority members in organisations. And while connecting to others who may be facing similar difficulties in their transition locally can be encouraging and lead to formation of strong ties, and provide emotional support, these subgroups may also be seen as forming a 'clique' structure (Brass et al., 2004). These cliques may be somewhat marginalised, and even cut off from the mainstream of information, and may also seem insular to the majority employees. On the flipside, there is also some evidence that by being on the outskirts of the social networks, these employees may have more opportunities to span structural holes and even increase creativity of local units (Burt, 2004; Harrison et al., 2019)

Thus, while the ties to the ethnic community and formation of homophilous networks may provide social support that acts as a buffer for many other challenges they face in their adaptation to a new country; these types of connections may not be enough in terms of migrants' career needs. Instead, recent work on the role of local social support also finds that skilled migrants may do best when they are able to obtain both types of support, not only homophilous but also heterophilous ties (i.e., with members of the local community) (Zikic & Voloshyna, 2018). In fact, those migrants who managed to integrate most effectively both in terms of their career as well as outside of work and later even gave back to the local community were those that merged both types of ties. Specifically, when skilled migrants not only leveraged contacts and networks from their own communities but also successfully explored, and proactively connected to, local communities and contacts in the host country, they achieved best results. Thus, a mix of ties, blended between those from one's country of origin and locals is likely to lead to most effective adaptation and even career outcomes (Bhaskar-Shrinivas et al., 2005). Overall, what is known is that social networks can both constrain as well as facilitate skilled migrant experiences. Thus, we must understand deployment of social capital (perhaps, for example, drawing on ethnic networks) vs. accumulation of new local contacts. In this context, Al Ariss and Syed (2011) find accumulation of local social capital to be challenging, while deployment of social capital is influenced by factors such as gender and ethnicity.

In the context of relying on ethnic networks, it is also known that these contacts can sometimes be one avenue for achieving career success in the local economy, for example when they assist newcomers in starting their own business (Salaff et al., 2003). Thus, a lack of local social capital and an inability to obtain employment in local organisations can force immigrants to turn to entrepreneurship. Empirical evidence suggests that skilled migrants form a large proportion of the population of the founders of successful businesses (Neville et al., 2014) and, therefore, research describes several explanations of this propensity for immigrants to become business owners. For example, business ownership is usually higher among skilled migrants who are more educated. In addition, empirical evidence shows that skilled migrants' propensity to take a risk positively contributes to their ability to develop successful enterprises (El-Assal, 2018). Another explanation could be found in selection and discrimination processes in local organisations that can also contribute to higher level of entrepreneurship among skilled migrants (Vandor & Franke, 2016). In this case it is said that migrants may feel 'frustrated in their goals to join the mainstream society', and as a result they find it easier to draw on the enclave for social capital at different stages of building a business. Thus, some skilled migrants depend on social networks to establish their own businesses in the local economy (Blustein, 2017); for example, 27.5 per cent of US entrepreneurs are skilled migrants and, in addition, about 'one-fourth of all technology and engineering companies started in the US between 2006 and 2012 had at least one immigrant co-founder' (Vandor & Franke, 2016).

Finally most recently, researchers described another fruitful avenue assisting skilled migrant integration through obtaining local social capital, has been mentoring programmes between local professionals and skilled migrant newcomers (Zikic, 2018; Zikic & Sondhi, 2015). These types of relationships have been linked to potential job search and career assistance from local experts in the field. Moreover, when newcomers are able to connect and associate themselves with locals, some of the major challenges of adaptation and re-establishing their careers may be alleviated. In reviewing literature on the relationships between migrants and locals, whether prior to organisational entry or after, it turns out that focusing on the dyadic relationships between skilled migrants and locals may be the most important diversity integration mechanism, one that has been little understood so far (Zikic, 2018). Much of the literature seems to present locals vs. migrants as two opposing sides and provides evidence of discrimination, whether overt or covert depending on the social and national context (Turchick Hakak & Al Ariss, 2013). Moreover, typically the two groups may also feel threatened by each other as skilled migrants' (newcomers) desire to obtain much needed recognition for their foreign human capital may be met by local colleagues' doubts and even feeling threatened, thus fearing for their established status and not knowing newcomers' abilities (Tartakovsky & Walsh, 2016).

However, by proposing to integrate these two seemingly opposing perspectives and focusing on the quality of the migrant/local relationships, via interventions such as mentoring, we highlight the importance of combining the conflicting nature of this relationship through focusing on what they have in common and how to achieve successful collaboration between the two. For example, both sides are seeking to achieve the same basic needs at work (for belongingness and competence), as well as meeting organisational goals, for example. As a result, recent conceptual work proposes creating and fostering opportunities for high quality connections (Heaphy & Dutton, 2008) between foreign (i.e., skilled migrant) and local workforces (Zikic, 2018). Thus, we expect that through high-quality connections between skilled migrants and locals, both groups will obtain much needed opportunities for social connection, knowledge exchange, and learning from each other that will in turn: (1) ease their relational challenges and reduce uncertainty, (2) allow for a more balanced understanding of relational threats vs. benefits, and (3) enhance satisfaction of both belongingness and uniqueness needs. In fact, it is said that dyadic relationships (e.g., with co-workers, superiors, subordinates) are said to be the foundation of how individuals feel about themselves in the context of work and even the basis of their overall success in local organisations (Harrison et al., 2019). As the most common type of work relationships, we propose that local organisations should focus their attention on improving the quality of these dyadic relationships, with special attention given to relationships and communication between skilled migrants and local employees.

9.4 Organisational Pathways towards Migrant Integration

A third major area of research regarding skilled migrant careers has been migrant integration into local organisations. Again, this topic has a dualistic character whereby the rhetoric and the onus is placed on the migrants themselves to 'integrate', to fit into the local business culture and the society overall. However, much less is known about local efforts to manage this type of diversity and assist integration into local organisations (e.g., Harrison et al., 2019). Some of the current research describes potential benefits related to skilled migrant entry and integration, specifically in the context of foreign human capital being one aspect of the unique competitive advantage (Zikic, 2015). Yet, much of the diversity literature still finds many related barriers that prevent both skilled migrants as well as local individuals and organisations, from leveraging this unique form of human capital. On occasion, the barriers are related to individual level issues, as described earlier. Other times barriers are much more systemic and thus harder to address as they centre at the level of the organisational system, culture, local norms, and also societal attitudes.

The most common scenario, in the context of skilled migrants working alongside local employees, is that migrants will be judged as belonging to the 'out-group' at least based on several obvious characteristics. Skilled migrants as organisational insiders are clearly 'newcomers' who come from another country, also they are often but not always, demographically dissimilar, and typically end up in lower status positions or underemployed compared to their qualifications and experience. These differences in comparison with locals are often said to create a 'perfect storm' of 'otherness' (Muhr, 2008). There is research to suggest that due to some of these aspects of 'otherness' skilled migrants may be discriminated against at the point of entry into local organisations (Banerjee, Reitz, & Oreopoulos, 2017; Almeida et al., 2015). For example, Almeida et al. (2012) found out that instead of considering a wider pool of candidates, including skilled migrant applicants, employers often rely on well-known networks and sources that will lead to hiring from a narrow pool of candidates with qualifications, work experiences, and attributes similar to the already existing employee base. There is also evidence for a variety of challenges in terms of skilled migrant entry into local workforces, resulting from a lack of HRM know-how (for example, procedures specifically dealing with skilled migrant diversity), as well as inefficient and faulty systems and screening procedures. As a result, organisations are advised to review whether they in fact have an 'inclusive recruitment strategy', a recruitment philosophy that focuses on skills, as opposed to country of origin, or other candidate characteristics (Mourtada, 2010); similarly, creating barrier-free job advertisements and ensuring job descriptions do not exclude any qualified candidates.

On the other hand, much less is known about the actual experiences of skilled migrants as organisational insiders. Some speculate that, based on our understanding of diversity in general, where dissimilarity may breed contempt and especially by sounding and looking different (Creese & Kambere, 2003), migrants may receive a more negative treatment in organisations too. For example, their status as described above may lead to stigmatisation by the dominant group and they could be seen as less worthy members of local organisations, thus receive less support from co-workers or even be trusted less (Harrison et al., 2019). Some recent research supports these ideas that likely due to this perceived 'otherness', migrants may be susceptible to lower overall success as members of local organisations (Fang et al., 2013; Turchick Hakak et al., 2010) such as unfavourable performance reviews, less training and fewer promotions, etc. Similarly, there is evidence that foreign-sounding names and even physical characteristics of migrants in the United States of America, for example, negatively impact their wages (Hersch, 2008; Oreopoulos, 2011). Finally, migrants may encounter antagonism simply based on the competition for valuable and often limited organisational resources as well as skilled migrants being seen as a potential threat due to their foreignness, so 'less deserving' of these resources.

These issues between migrants and locals have been captured by the threat-benefit model (Tartakovsky & Walsh, 2016). In this model the authors discuss how at the same time locals may perceive migrants as both beneficial and threatening for the receiving society. They may be perceived as threatening in terms of competition for resources and possibly incompatibile with the local society, while at the same time migrants may also be perceived as benefiting local society by filling vacant jobs and bringing cultural diversity to the local society. Thus, how migrants are perceived by local organisations and the resulting challenges are also closely related to the overall attitude towards migrants in the local society more broadly (Tartakovsky & Walsh, 2016). Specifically, macro factors at the societal level, such as anti-immigration attitudes, may impact how organisational insiders feel and interact with skilled migrants inside local organisations and perhaps even intensify the challenges skilled migrants may face as insiders (Syed, 2008). Thus, while the three challenges discussed above distance locals and skilled migrants and impede their collaboration and integration, the threat-benefit paradigm, specifically its emphasis on the benefits, may assist in understanding how local organisations may frame and further discuss these challenges. For example, while organisations can acknowledge the potential feelings of threat by some employees, it is imperative to highlight the benefits of having skilled migrants locally and in this way create a more positive context for integration to take place. This can be done as part of diversity management training and cross-cultural intervention programmes. By diversity management is meant managerial actions aimed at either increasing diversity and inclusion or promoting amicable, productive working relationships within local organisations (Jonsen, Maznevski, & Schneider, 2011). Thus, understanding and incorporating threat-benefit rhetoric into local organisations' diversity management training, for example and programmes focusing on cross-cultural topics will produce a more balanced view of skilled migrants, while limiting extreme perceptions of threat and recognising the value and uniqueness that skilled migrants bring to the local organisation and the local society overall.

In further focusing on the 'how' of integration, Zikic (2015) applies the resource-based view of the firm as a theoretical lens to understand how skilled migrant career capital, in particular, may be the source of competitive advantage. Thus, skilled migrants may be diverse in many ways, but their uniqueness comes from the diversity of their career capital (i.e., motivation for migration, human and social capital). However, in understanding how this population can be the source of competitive advantage it is important to know the conditions or contingencies; specifically, knowing the existing internal and external context and cultural values of a particular organisation in order to judge its readiness and need to invest in creating, promoting and benefit from skilled migrant diversity (Almeida et al., 2012). Thus, the integration of skilled migrants requires consideration of influences related to factors already inherent in the local organisation, for example, the presence of diversity champions, or individuals who play a key role in promoting and creating a culture that leverages on diversity (Thomas, 2004) (e.g., modelling positive diversity values, at the top management team level, Guillaume et al., 2013). In addition to understanding organisational culture and internal support, one must also assess the external environment, for example the diversity of the community, its customers, as well as already existing organisational diversity that may influence the firm's orientation towards skilled migrant diversity.

Finally here, Zikic (2015) recommends that local employers seek to establish networks in order to better tap into the skilled migrant talent pool (Malik, Manroop, & Singh, 2017); for example, through creating various partnerships between local employers, policymakers, immigrant community agencies, and professional associations (Habib, 2011). These initiatives can be geared towards educating local leaders and employers about the value of skilled migrant career capital, as well as helping design specific procedures and more efficient ways of assessing and attracting foreign human capital. Greater cultural understanding and integration of skilled migrant newcomers may also help in creating improved team collaborations leading to more creative solutions at work (Janssens & Brett, 2006).

Therefore, skilled migrants do not exist in isolation of local colleagues. In order to understand how skilled migrants cope with these contrasting needs amid local obstacles, their perspective must be understood, together with that of local colleagues with whom they must collaborate and work closely together with. Local employees are already established organisational insiders, eager to emphasise their already achieved belongingness and unique contributions to the local organisation. As a result, immigrant organisational integration is defined here as a joint effort between local organisations (local employees) and skilled migrants to create a context where at each stage of the integration process (from entry to later stages), both parties have the ability to contribute free of barriers, and to experience belongingness in every aspect of organisational life. Effective integration between skilled migrants and local employees will allow each group to grow their careers, and in this process feel respected and recognised for each other's uniqueness. Overall, effective integration of skilled migrants has the potential to benefit both entities: (1) as skilled migrants and locals collaborate through productive working relationships, local employers and the host country can leverage migrants' foreign capital towards enhanced competitive advantage (Zikic, 2015); and (2) effective integration can enhance migrants' career success, well-being, and their overall prosperity in the host country.

9.5 Conclusions

This review provides evidence for the multifaceted nature of skilled migrant integration into local organisations and local societies. Three major themes served as an organising framework: the individual, social, and organisational domains of migrant life (summarized in Figure 9.1). Clearly in each domain we see the migrants as the focal point, both in terms of their human, social, and motivational capital as well as their role in the local labour market or local organisations. Skilled migrants are an integral part of many global economies and their pathways into those economies may also be distinct based on local laws, and the broader national context (Turchick Hakak & Al Ariss 2013), labour policies and the general climate related to how migrants are portrayed in the local discourse (the threat vs. benefit paradigm).

Overall, one of the major dichotomies in research on migrants so far is the need to understand both local as well as migrant perspective in the process of integration. Specifically, questions arise about the responsibility of the local society (e.g., local employees) vs. migrants' own proactivity and ability to integrate and adapt, and 'fit' locally. Much of the research portrays the migrants as 'vulnerable' or even 'oppressed' actors (e.g., Esses et al., 2010), however, it is important to strike a balance in terms of understanding migrant expectations/ motivations to integrate as well as what local society may have to offer in regards to settling and trying to re-start their careers. While some countries may be known to be migrant receiving economies (with well-developed migrant settlement and integration models), there is still a need to understand both overt as well as covert factors related to discrimination from organisational entry (e.g., organisational gatekeepers) to broader integration into local community and society overall. Overall, skilled migrants are equally seen as very resilient and proactive individuals (Voloshyna & Zikic, 2018; Frieze et al., 2006) who take major career risks as a result of their cross-national moves in the hopes of better lives and career opportunities. Thus, a more nuanced portrayal and acknowledgement of local vs. migrant perspectives is needed in the hopes of obtaining a more holistic and valid understanding of skilled migrant transitions and local integration.

Much of the research focuses on the time when the migrant is already in the host country, yet it is important to understand that pre-arrival expectations and connections also play an important role in adaptation. In this context, social networks, whether local or ethnic, have received much attention and their influence on migrant pathways in local economies is a powerful one. Again, there is a dichotomy between finding local mentoring connections that can ease migrant integration into local organisations and ethnic connections that may instead reinforce migrants' desire towards entrepreneurial careers. Thus, the role played by a variety of social factors has powerful impact on migrant integration locally. Similarly, it is important to understand that migrant social and career experiences in the host country must also be understood in the context of intersectionality of ethnicity, religion, sex, age, and physical abilities among other determinants (Al Ariss et al., 2012).

Finally, the third aspect of migrant experience that requires much more research is related to how migrants navigate local organisations. Much of the existing research focuses on the pre-entry stage, focusing on migrants as 'outsiders' to local organisations, mainly navigating on the periphery of the labour market. In this context, the literature often takes the 'normalising' approach in that it is expected that the migrant must find a way to somehow 'fit into' local organisations and as a result the migrant is expected to 'fix' some aspects of the self (e.g., take extra training, downshift in their career, improve communication/language skills). In much of the literature, the onus to adapt and succeed in the new country is often put on the migrants, thus if they experiences challenges then they must be 'deficient' in some ways and need to adapt to the local norms and conditions. This one-sided view must be expanded in future research by allowing for local perspectives and a deeper understanding of the role of gatekeepers (e.g., HRM professionals, line managers, local leaders). Thus, we propose one avenue for merging these opposing sides by focusing on fostering high quality dyadic relationships as the basic building blocks that can buffer the feelings of threat, lower discrimination, and accentuate the benefits related to welcoming and integrating skilled migrants into local economies.

References

Almeida, S., Fernando, M., & Sheridan, A. 2012. Revealing the screening: organizational factors influencing the recruitment of immigrant professionals. *International Journal of Human Resource Management*, 23(9): 1950–1965.

Almeida, S., Fernando, M., Hannif, Z., & Dharmage, S. C. 2015. Fitting the mould: the role of employer perceptions in immigrant recruitment decision-making. *International Journal of Human Resource Management*, 26(22): 2811–2832.

Al Ariss, A. & Syed, J. 2011. Capital mobilization of skilled migrants: a relational perspective. *British Journal of Management*, 22(2): 286–304.

Al Ariss, A., Koall, I., Özbilgin, M., & Suutari, V. 2012. Careers of skilled migrants: towards a theoretical and methodological expansion. *Journal of Management Development*, 31(2): 92–101.

Banerjee, R., Reitz, J. G., & Oreopoulos, P. 2017. Do Large Employers treat Racial Minorities More Fairly? A new analysis of Canadian field experiment data. Research Report. https://munkschool.utoronto.ca/wp-content/uploads/2017/01/Which-employers-discriminate-Banerjee-Reitz-Oreopoulos-January-2017.pdf.

Bauder, H. and Cameron, E. 2002. Cultural Barriers to Labour Market Integration: Immigrants from South Asia and the Former Yugoslavia. Working Paper Series No. 02–03. Vancouver Center of Excellence. Retrieved from http://mbc.metropolis.net/assets/uploads/files/wp/2002/WP02-03.pdf.

Bell, M. P., Kwesiga, E. N., & Berry, D. P. 2010. Immigrants: the new 'invisible men and women' in diversity research. *Journal of Managerial Psychology*, 25(2): 177–188.

Bhaskar-Shrinivas, P., Harrison, D. A., Shaffer, M. A., & Luk, D. A. 2005. Input-based and time-based models of international adjustment: meta-analytic evidence and theoretical extensions. *Academy of Management Journal*, 48: 257–281.

Blustein, D. L. 2017. The psychology of working: a new perspective for career development. *Career Planning & Adult Development Journal*, 33 (2): 60–68.

Bonache, J., Brewster, C., & Suutari, V. 2007. Preface: knowledge, international mobility, and careers. *International Studies of Management & Organization*, 37(3): 3–15.

Bonache, J., Langinier, H., & Zárraga-Oberty, C. 2016. Antecedents and effects of host country nationals negative stereotyping of corporate expatriates. A social identity analysis. *Human Resource Management Review*, 26(1): 59–68.

Boneva, B. S. & Frieze, I. H. 2001. Toward a concept of a migrant personality. *Journal of Social Issues*, 57(3): 477–491.

Brass, D. J., Galaskiewicz, J., Greve, H. R., & Tsai, W. 2004. Taking stock of networks and organizations: a multilevel perspective. *Academy of Management Journal*, 47(6): 795–817.

Bresnahan, M. J., Ohashi, R., Nebashi, R., Liu, W. Y., & Shearman, S. M. 2002. Attitudinal and affective response toward accented English. *Language & Communication*, 22(2): 171–185.

Burt, R. S. 2004. Structural holes and good ideas. *American Journal of Sociology*, 110(2): 349–399.

Canache, D., Hayes, M., Mondak, J. J., & Wals, S. C. 2013. Openness, extraversion and the intention to emigrate. *Journal of Research in Personality*, 47(4): 351–355.

Cerdin, J. L., Abdul-Diné, M., & Brewster, C. 2014. Qualified immigrants' success: exploring the motivation to migrate and to integrate. *Journal of International Business Studies*, 45(2): 151–168.

Chiswick, B. R. & Miller, P. W. 2012. Negative and positive assimilation, skill transferability, and linguistic distance. *Journal of Human Capital*, 6 (1): 35–55.

Creese, G. & Kambere, E. N. 2003. What colour is your English?. *Canadian Review of Sociology/Revue canadienne de sociologie*, 40(5): 565–573.

De Castro, A. B., Gee, G. C., & Takeuchi, D. 2008. Relationship between job dissatisfaction and physical and psychological health among Filipino immigrants. *Workplace Health & Safety*, 56(1): 33–40.

De Leon Siantz, M. L. 1997. Factors that impact developmental outcomes of immigrant children. *Immigration and the family: Research and policy on US immigrants*, 149–161.

Derwing, T. 2003. What do ESL students say about their accents? *Canadian Modern Language Review*, 59(4): 547–567.

Derwing, T. M. & Munro, M. J. 2009. Putting accent in its place: rethinking obstacles to communication. *Language Teaching*, 42(4): 476–490.

DiBenigno, J. & Kellogg, K. C. 2014. Beyond occupational differences: the importance of cross-cutting demographics and dyadic toolkits for collaboration in a US hospital. *Administrative Science Quarterly*, 59(3): 375–408.

Dietz, J., Joshi, C., Esses, V. M., Hamilton, L. K., & Gabarrot, F. 2015. The skill paradox: explaining and reducing employment discrimination against skilled immigrants. *International Journal of Human Resource Management*, 26(10): 1318–1334.

Dugdale, A., Daly, A., Papandrea, F., & Maley, M. 2005. Accessing e-government: challenges for citizens and organizations. *International Review of Administrative Sciences*, 71(1): 109–118.

El-Assal, K. 2018. Enhancing success. Canada's Immigrant Entrepreneurs and International Trade. www.conferenceboard.ca/temp/07e32c6a-ef9d-4be9-966e-d39bee2b6426/9692_Enhancing%20Success_RPT.pdf.

Epstein, G. S. 2008. Herd and network effects in migration decision-making. *Journal of Ethnic and Migration Studies*, 34(4): 567–583.

Esses, V. M., Deaux, K., Lalonde, R., & Brown, R. 2010. Psychological perspectives on immigration. In K. Deaux, V. Esses, R. Lalonde, & R. Brown (Eds.), Immigrants and hosts: perceptions, interactions, and transformations. *Journal of Social Issues*, 66(4): 635–647.

Fang, T., Samnani, A. K., Novicevic, M. M., & Bing, M. N. 2013. Liability-of-foreignness effects on job success of immigrant job seekers. *Journal of World Business*, 48(1): 98–109.

Frieze, I. H., Hansen, S. B., & Boneva, B. 2006. The migrant personality and college students' plans for geographic mobility. *Journal of Environmental Psychology*, 26(2): 170–177.

Guillaume, Y. R., Dawson, J. F., Woods, S. A., Sacramento, C. A., & West, M. A. 2013. Getting diversity at work to work: what we know and what we still don't know. *Journal of Occupational and Organizational Psychology*, 86(2): 123–141.

Habib, M. 2011. Helping immigrant workers fit in. *The Globe and Mail.* Retrieved April 5, 2019, from www.theglobeandmail.com/report-on-business/careers/career-advice/helping-immigrant-workers-fit-in/article596170/.

Harrison, D. A., Harrison, T., & Shaffer, M. A. 2019. Strangers in strained lands: learning from workplace experiences of immigrant employees. *Journal of Management*, 45(2): 600–619.

Harvey, M., Novicevic, M. M., Buckley, M. R., & Fung, H. 2005. Reducing inpatriate managers' 'liability of foreignness' by addressing stigmatization and stereotype threats. *Journal of World Business*, 40(3): 267–280.

Haug, S. 2008. Migration networks and migration decision-making. *Journal of Ethnic and Migration Studies*, 34(4): 585–605.

Heaphy, E. D. & Dutton, J. E. 2008. Positive social interactions and the human body at work: linking organizations and physiology. *Academy of Management Review*, 33(1): 137–162.

Hersch, J. 2008. Skin color, immigrant wages, and discrimination. In *Racism in the 21st Century*: 77–90. Springer, New York, NY.

Hobfoll, S. E., Dunahoo, C. L., Ben-Porath, Y., & Monnier, J. 1994. Gender and coping: the dual-axis model of coping. *American Journal of Community Psychology*, 22(1): 49–82.

Ibarra, H. 1993. Personal networks of women and minorities in management: a conceptual framework. *Academy of Management Review*, 18(1): 56–87.

Janssens, M. & Brett, J. M. 2006. Cultural intelligence in global teams: a fusion model of collaboration. *Group & Organization Management*, 31(1): 124–153.

Jonsen, K., Maznevski, M. L., & Schneider, S. C. 2011. Special review article: diversity and its not so diverse literature: an international perspective. *International Journal of Cross-Cultural Management*, *11*(1), 35–62.

Lauring, J. & Klitmøller, A. 2017. Inclusive language use in multicultural business organizations: the effect on creativity and performance. *International Journal of Business Communication*, 54(3): 306–324.

Lindemann, S. 2003. Koreans, Chinese or Indians? Attitudes and ideologies about non-native English speakers in the United States. *Journal of Sociolinguistics*, 7(3): 348–364.

Lippi-Green, R. 1997. What we talk about when we talk about Ebonics: why definitions matter. *The Black Scholar*, 27(2): 7–11.

Lubbers, M. J., Molina, J. L., & McCarty, C. 2007. Personal networks and ethnic identifications: the case of migrants in Spain. *International Sociology*, 22(6): 721–741.

Luo, Y. & Mezias, J. M. 2002. Liabilities of foreignness: concepts, constructs, and consequences. *Journal of International Management*, 8(3): 217–221.

Mahmud, S., Alam, Q., & Härtel, C. 2014. Mismatches in skills and attributes of immigrants and problems with workplace integration: a study of IT and engineering professionals in Australia. *Human Resource Management Journal*, 24(3): 339–354.

Malik, A. R., Manroop, L., & Singh, P. (2017). Self-initiated international career transition: a qualitative case study of Pakistani immigrants to Canada. *European Business Review*, 29(5), 584–602.

Mourtada, R. 2010. Firms that don't automatically reject foreign education or experience can gain an edge in the race for talent. *The Globe & Mail*. Retrieved September 7, 2020, from http://triec.ca/broadening-the-talent-poo-2/.

Muhr, S. L. 2008. Othering diversity–a Levinasian analysis of diversity management. *International Journal of Management Concepts and Philosophy*, 3(2): 176–189.

Neville, F., Orser, B., Riding, A., & Jung, O. 2014. Do young firms owned by recent immigrants outperform other young firms? *Journal of Business Venturing*, 29(1): 55–71.

Ogbonna, E. & Harris, L. C. 2006. The dynamics of employee relationships in an ethnically diverse workforce. *Human Relations*, 59(3): 379–407.

Oreopoulos, P. 2011. Why do skilled immigrants struggle in the labor market? A field experiment with thirteen thousand resumes. *American Economic Journal: Economic Policy*, 3(4): 148–71.

Salaff, J. W., Greve, A., Siu-Lun, W., & Ping, L. X. L. 2003. Ethnic entrepreneurship, social networks, and the enclave. In *Approaching Transnationalisms*: 61–82. Springer, Boston, MA.

Schweizer, T., Schnegg, M., & Berzborn, S. 1998. Personal networks and social support in a multiethnic community of southern California. *Social networks*, 20(1): 1–21.

Syed, Y. 2008. Employment prospects for skilled migrants: a relational perspective, *Human Resource Management Review*, 18: 28–45.

Tartakovsky, E. & Walsh, S. D. 2016. Testing a new theoretical model for attitudes toward immigrants: the case of social workers' attitudes toward asylum seekers in Israel. *Journal of Cross-Cultural Psychology*, 47(1): 72–96.

Turchick Hakak, L. & Al Ariss, A. 2013. Vulnerable work and international migrants: a relational human resource management perspective.

International Journal of Human Resource Management, 24(22): 4116–4131.

Turchick Hakak, L., Holzinger, I., & Zikic, J. 2010. Barriers and paths to success: Latin American MBAs' views of employment in Canada. *Journal of Managerial Psychology*, 25(2): 159–176.

Thomas, D. A. 2004. Diversity as strategy. *Harvard business review*, 82(9): 98–98.

Vandor, P. & Franke, N., 2016. Why are Immigrants More Entrepreneurial. https://hbr.org/2016/10/why-are-immigrants-more-entrepreneurial.

Voloshyna V. & Zikic, J. 2018. Do I stay or do I go: understanding career boundary preferences through social ties and the role of trust. Organizing for Resilience, LAEMOS Conference, Buenos-Aires, Argentina.

Walker, M., Wasserman, S., & Wellman, B. 1994. Statistical Models for Social Support Networks, Advances in Social Network Analysis, Research in the Social and Behavioral Sciences. In S. Wasserman & J. Galaskiewicz (eds.), *Advances in Social Networks. Research in the Social And Behavioural Sciences*: 53–79. Thousands Oaks, California: Sage.

Zikic, J. 2015 Skilled migrants' career capital as a source of competitive advantage: implications for strategic HRM. *International Journal of Human Resource Management*, 26(10): 1360–1381.

Zikic, J. 2018 Becoming insiders: Dyadic Relational Framework Towards Improves migrant-local integration outcomes. Paper presented at the JMS conference: Diversity Perspective on Management: Towards more complex conceptualizations of diversity in management studies. Boston, USA.

Zikic, J., Bonache, J., & Cerdin, J. L. 2010. Crossing national boundaries: a typology of qualified immigrants' career orientations. *Journal of Organizational Behavior*, 31(5): 667–686.

Zikic, J. & Richardson, J. 2016. What happens when you can't be who you are: Professional identity at the institutional periphery. *Human Relations*, 69(1): 139–168.

Zikic, J. & Sondhi, G. 2015. Mentoring Partnerships: Building Successful Exchange Relationships, Practitioner Report, Toronto Region Immigrant Employment Council.

Zikic, J. & Voloshyna V. 2018. Exploring individual level resilience: The role of migrant career capital in achieving career success post migration. Organizing for Resilience, LAEMOS Conference, Buenos-Aires, Argentina.

10 *Women and Global Mobility*

HELEN DE CIERI

10.1 Introduction

Globalisation has facilitated the spread and awareness of dramatic changes in societal values and legislation, and there have been major shifts in women's participation in the global workforce. Gender diversity in management and leadership is associated with better organisational performance and reputation (Brieger et al., 2019; Hoobler et al., 2018; Jeong & Harrison, 2017). However, women continue to be under-represented in management and leadership roles worldwide, including in global mobility, and the current situation is a long way from global gender equality (Eden & Gupta, 2017). This warrants attention because understanding the factors that affect women and the implications for individuals and their employers is important for the advancement of research and management of global mobility.

There is debate about whether research on women in management should: (a) focus on women; (b) include diverse genders and sexualities; or (c) view gender as one category in the broader field of workforce diversity and inclusion. On one hand, scholars who study diversity and inclusion (e.g., Roberson, 2019; Shore, Cleveland & Sanchez, 2018) emphasise that diversity in the global workforce includes not simply the binary categories of men and women but also diverse genders and sexualities, as well as attributes such as ethnicity, age, culture, and religion (Mor Barak 2017; Kim & Von Glinow, 2017). Managing issues that affect women at work can be seen as part of workplace inclusion, which refers to the processes that ensure everyone is accepted, respected, and able to contribute to organisational success (Shore et al., 2018). Without doubt, diversity and inclusion research has enriched our understanding of gender and of the importance of inclusion in workplaces and in society. On the other hand, scholars whose research focuses on gender have cautioned that broadening the discussion to all forms of diversity and inclusion may divert attention from, and dilute efforts to address, concerns that are specific to women (Broadbridge & Simpson, 2011). For more detailed discussions about gender and management research, see Broadbridge and Simpson (2011) and Bullough, Moore and Kalafatoglu (2017). In this chapter, we focus on women in global mobility and hope to offer some insights that will inform research and practice both targeted for women in global mobility and inclusive for a diverse workforce. We argue for the importance of both targeted and inclusive policies, processes and practices, and suggest that these are complementary rather than mutually exclusive.

10.1.1 The Global Context for Women

Research and management of women in global mobility is a small yet important component of the larger context for gender equality worldwide. The World Health Organisation defines gender as the socially constructed characteristics of men and women, such as norms, roles, behaviour, and attributes, that a particular society considers appropriate for men and women (www.who.int). Gender equality means that: 'women and men enjoy the same rights and opportunities across all sectors of society, including economic participation and decision-making, and [...] the different behaviours, aspirations and needs of women and men are equally valued and favoured' (United Nations Conference on Trade and Development, 2016: 31). According to the Global Gender Gap Report 2018, 'although many countries have achieved important milestones towards gender equality ..., there remains much to be done' (World Economic Forum, 2018: v).

However, as Syed and Van Buren (2014: 252) discuss, 'what gender equality means in practical terms is a subject of considerable debate, and especially so when considering how cultures and societies differ'. There are ongoing tensions between principles of equality that might be thought of as universal and local views of gender and equality. The prevention of gender inequality and strategies to deal with the negative effects of inequality will vary across national contexts and require understanding of societal and institutional differences (Syed & Van Buren, 2014; Triana et al., 2019).

Women represent half the population in most countries and the participation of women in higher education and in the workforce has risen in almost all regions of the world (World Economic Forum,

2018). Worldwide, there is increasing representation of women in managerial roles and women constitute just over 40% of managers, professionals, and technicians (International Labour Office, 2016), which is the group where most research on globally mobile employees has been focused. Although there has been progress in recent years, women remain under-represented in political and business leadership positions worldwide (Bullough et al., 2012; Peus, Braun & Knipfer, 2015). A recent global survey found that women represent 29% of senior management roles and 15% of chief executive officers (Grant Thornton, 2019). Globally, around 25% of all companies do not have a woman in a senior management role (Catalyst, 2019). Studies continue to show that women remain under-represented in globally mobile work.

10.1.2 Women and Global Mobility

As Michailova and Hutchings (2016: 349) have shown 'the IB [international business] literature has paid, and continues to give, little consideration to gender generally and much less to women specifically'. The same can be said for the field of global mobility, where research to date on women in global mobility has been somewhat fragmented, despite valuable contributions.

Women participate in all forms of global mobility, which includes various types of work that involve international travel, such as expatriation, international business travel, global project teams (Meyskens et al., 2009), and migration for employment purposes (Bierwiaczonek & Waldzus, 2016). We adopt a broad definition of an expatriate by including employees who are sent abroad by an organisation, usually for between one to five years (Cerdin & Brewster, 2014), as well as self-initiated expatriates who find their own employment opportunities and undertake international work experiences for a limited or undefined duration (Andresen et al., 2014). Many expatriates are employed by multinational enterprises (MNEs), yet other expatriates include volunteers, particularly in the aid and development sector (Bhatta et al., 2009), diplomats (Dunn et al., 2015), and/or military personnel (Beder, Coe & Sommer, 2011).

Within the research on global mobility, much of the attention has been narrowly focused on long-term company assigned expatriates who 'have typically been senior managers, Western, males in their late 40s or early 50s, with an accompanying female spouse and children' (McNulty & Hutchings, 2016: 699). Some research has focused on women who are expatriate partners, often non-working individuals who are dependent on their partner for the right to remain in a country (e.g., De Cieri, Dowling & Taylor, 1991; Doherty, Richardson & Thorn, 2013). Adler (1984) asked: 'Where are the women in international management?' raising awareness of the large gender disparity, specifically with regard to expatriate assignments, based on a survey of major North American firms where only 3% of their expatriates were women. In the mid-1980s, countries like the United States of America saw important developments such as legislation for equal employment opportunity and affirmative action – and increasing participation of women in the labour force. Such developments led Adler (1984) to predict a rise in the representation of women in international assignments. In the 1990s, the numbers crept up so that women represented 12–15% of all expatriate managers (Caligiuri, Joshi & Lazarova, 1999). Altman and Shortland (2008) reported that the 2000s saw a further increase in the engagement of women in international assignments. Current surveys indicate that women constitute around 25% of the global expatriate population (Brookfield Global Relocation Services, 2016).

In recent decades, research in the management field has broadened to include self-initiated expatriates (e.g., Doherty et al., 2013; Wechtler, 2018), international business travellers (e.g., Mäkelä et al., 2017), and migrants (Colakoglu, Yunlu & Arman, 2018). The situation for women varies across different types of global mobility. It is interesting to note that women appear to be more prevalent among self-initiated expatriates than among corporate-initiated expatriates (Doherty et al., 2013). This may be because self-initiated expatriates include occupations and industries that have higher representation of women, such as healthcare workers, teachers, and academics.

There is increasing awareness that globally mobile women include highly skilled professionals who represent a valuable source of human capital (Kemp & Rickett, 2018). However, studies of highly skilled migrants have found that female migrants experience more difficult transitions than do male migrants, due to a range of factors including visa processes that tend to give preference to male-dominated occupations, and women having less access to professional social networks and taking more responsibility for childcare (Salaff & Greve, 2004). The career of a female migrant will be more negatively affected by migration than will a male migrant's career (Salaff & Greve, 2004; Colakoglu et al., 2018).

Although management researchers have paid more attention to high-status professionals in global mobility, the global talent pool is diverse in gender, age, family status and occupation (see McNulty & Hutchings, 2016; Paisley & Tayar, 2016), and social status (Haak-Saheem & Brewster, 2017). It is important to recognise that gender parity is an important concern across all layers of the workforce and for all women whose work and lives are affected by the global economy (Metcalfe & Rees, 2010). Globalisation is empowering for some, yet disempowering and impoverishing for others, particularly unskilled women in developing countries (Guillén, 2001). Extreme forms of gender inequality and exploitation may be evidenced and experienced by women who are in low-skilled work such as 'hidden expatriates' (Haak-Saheem & Brewster, 2017) and sex trafficking (Laite, 2017). While a full discussion of women in all types of global mobility is beyond the scope of this chapter, we hope to contribute to awareness of the range of experiences.

10.2 A Framework of Factors Affecting Women in Global Mobility

Building on previous research on women in the workforce and women's career advancement (Metz & Kumra, 2019; Ragins & Sundstrom, 1989), four levels of factors that affect women in global mobility can be identified: (1) societal and institutional; (2) organisational; (3) interpersonal; and (4) individual (see Figure 10.1). These factors may act either as barriers that hinder women's global mobility or as facilitators for women. It is important to note that some factors such as stereotypes permeate multiple levels: 'stereotypes operate at the social systems level and thereby influence the lower levels' (Peus et al., 2015: 56). Also, there will be interactions between factors at different levels. For example, in influential early research, Caligiuri and Cascio (1998) identified four categories of antecedents for the success of female expatriates: (1) organisational support; (2) host nationals' attitudes towards women expatriates; (3) family support; and (4) personality traits.

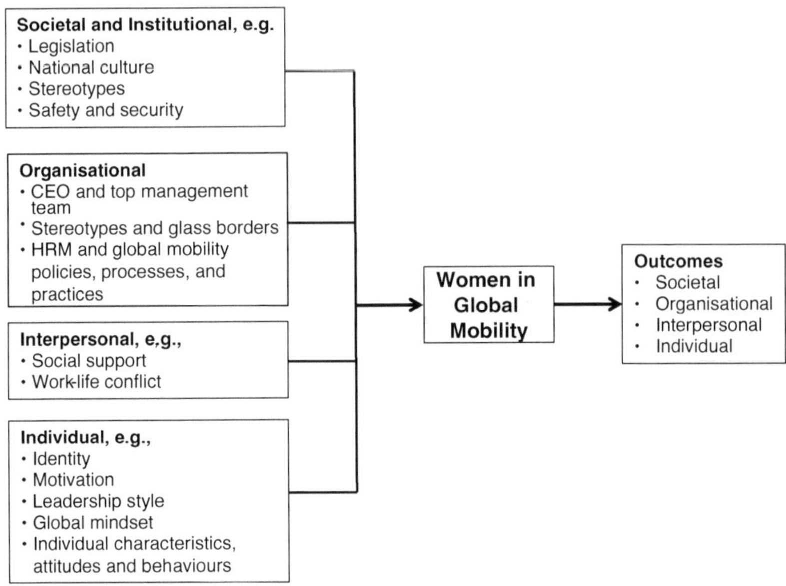

Figure 10.1 Framework for women in global mobility

Our framework also identifies important outcomes at each level for women in global mobility.

10.2.1 Societal and Institutional Factors

Societal and institutional factors include the legal, cultural, political, economic, and technological characteristics in each country that create the context for gender equality (Brieger et al., 2019; Eden & Gupta, 2017; Peus et al., 2015; World Economic Forum, 2018). The extent, causes, and characteristics of gender inequality within countries have direct implications for women's employment, career advancement, and opportunity to participate in global mobility. Institutional theory (DiMaggio & Powell, 1983) offers an explanation of how institutions such as legal frameworks set the rules and legitimise actions, creating isomorphic pressure so that organisations and individuals will seek to conform in order to prosper and survive (Kostova & Zaheer, 1999). Institutional and societal support is necessary in order for actors such as women in leadership roles to have legitimacy; increasing the representation of women in leadership roles requires societal and institutional change (Bullough et al., 2012; Lewellyn & Muller-Kahle, 2019). It is important to note that a country's stage of economic development does not seem to play a key role in determining the percentage of women in senior official or managerial positions (Michailova & Hutchings, 2016). For example, in China the participation rate of women in the workforce is much higher than the global average, which can be largely attributed to the legacy of state socialism and recent government reforms (Cooke, 2005; Woodhams, Xian & Lupton, 2015).

Legislation. In many countries, important progress has been made in legislative reform for gender equality. Many governments have implemented equal opportunity and anti-discrimination laws, and most countries have equal opportunity laws that specifically include gender as a protected attribute (Michailova & Hutchings, 2016; Mor Barak, 2017). In addition, several countries have implemented legislative reforms to improve women's workforce and managerial participation. For example, countries such as Iceland, Finland, Norway, and Sweden have implemented laws specifying quotas, and penalties for lack of compliance, for the gender diversity of corporate boards (Lewellyn & Muller-Kahle, 2019; Sojo et al., 2016). However, currently only six countries in the world (Belgium, Denmark, France, Latvia, Luxembourg, and Sweden), offer women and men equal rights via laws that affect women throughout their working lives (World Bank Group, 2019). In many countries, laws are influenced by patriarchal cultures that place restrictions on the roles and opportunities for women to participate in the workforce (e.g., Bullough et al., 2012; de Klerk & Verreyne, 2017). Legislation plays a critical role in gender equality, yet the legal framework is not sufficient to bring about the social change required for gender equality.

National culture. Societal barriers for women seeking global mobility might include religions or traditional norms, national culture, and stereotypes (Mor Barak, 2017; Triana et al., 2019). For example, de Klerk and Verreyne (2017: 479) discuss the barriers caused by norms that hinder women managers, particularly in emerging economies. Changing mindsets about gender, work, and family roles and efforts to make it easier for both men and women to engage in career and family is a complex and large-scale societal issue (Puchmüller & Fischlmayr, 2017). Comparative and cross-cultural research such as the Global Leadership and Organizational Behavior Effectiveness

Project (GLOBE, House et al., 2004) has led to a stream of research investigating which national societal or cultural characteristics either facilitate or hamper women's career advancement (e.g., Bullough & Sully de Luque, 2015).

Stereotypes. Scholars in the management and leadership fields have discussed the systemic discrimination that has led to gender imbalance in leadership roles, which has been explained as a 'lack of fit' model (Heilman, 2012) or a 'think manager, think male' mindset (Kossek, Su & Wu, 2017). According to Heilman (2012), stereotypes or preconceptions that a manager looks and behaves in ways that are typically associated with men will lead people to underestimate the managerial potential of women and others who do not fit the stereotype. Due to this underestimation, women may be excluded from opportunities such as managerial and leadership opportunities. With regard to global mobility, the 'think international manager, think male' mindset (Festing, Kornau, & Schäfer, 2014) may be exacerbated by stereotypes held about cultural expectations within countries, linked to negative reactions by host country nationals towards female expatriates, and explain why women are so under-represented in international assignments.

Valuable contributions to understanding societal and institutional factors have been made by a growing stream of research conducted in Middle Eastern contexts, with studies including explorations of employment opportunities for Middle Eastern women (e.g., Hutchings, Metcalfe & Cooper, 2010) and the work experiences of foreign women in the Middle East (e.g., Kemp & Rickett, 2018). Alhejji et al. (2016) examined MNEs in Saudi Arabia and found that although formal institutional factors such as laws and government policy encourage gender equality, there are powerful factors, particularly cultural norms and traditions, that may hamper efforts towards gender equality. Similarly, Stalker and Mavin's (2011) interviews with self-initiated expatriates in the United Arab Emirates identified ongoing cultural and institutional constraints on workplace participation for both local and foreign women, although they predicted that social changes will transform future work settings.

Safety and security. The global context for work has become more risky, or at least we are more aware of safety and security hazards such as terrorism, geopolitical tensions, and hostile environments (Bader & Schuster, 2015). Some occupational groups are more likely to be engaged in hazardous global work, such as aid and development workers, military personnel or war journalists, and some safety and security concerns are particularly important for women. For example, Bhatta et al.'s (2009) study of risks and problems encountered by volunteers overseas found no gender differences with regard to outcomes such as likelihood of suffering post-traumatic stress disorder, yet identified rape and sexual violence as a category of trauma to which aid workers and particularly women might be vulnerable in high-risk locations such as war zones.

10.2.2 Organisational Factors

Many employers worldwide make substantial investment in gender equality and workplace inclusion (Groysberg & Connolly, 2013; Wentling, 2004). In business terms, it makes sense for all qualified employees to have equal opportunity to engage in work; discrimination against any segment of the human resource pool is in neither the individuals' nor the employer's interests (Hoobler et al., 2018).

CEO and top management team mindset. According to upper echelon theory, demographic characteristics and cognitive biases of the CEO and top management team are likely to be reflected in the firm's culture and organisational characteristics (Hambrick & Mason, 1984). Hence, the mindsets of the top management team will influence the firm's approach and outcomes relevant to gender equality, and there may be both overt and subtle power relations and mechanisms that hinder women in global mobility (Athanasopoulou et al., 2018; London, Bear, Cushenbery & Sherman, 2018). Studies have shown that decision makers may be influenced by biases or stereotypes that lead them to view women as less competent than men (Heilman, 2012; Tinsley & Ely, 2018).

Stereotypes and glass borders. Research evidence of barriers for women's career advancement in global mobility is quite consistent and the pace of change is slow (Chrobot-Mason et al., 2019). Women face barriers to their global career advancement that men do not encounter (e.g., Linehan & Scullion, 2008; Tzeng, 2006). It should be understood that this is not due to some inherent factor present, or deficient, in individuals. Rather, the key barrier for women has been described as the 'think international manager, think male' mindset (Festing et al., 2014) already noted as a societal factor, or an enduring form of the 'glass ceiling' for women (Caligiuri & Tung, 1998) identified in global mobility as a 'second layer' of glass ceiling (Insch, McIntyre & Napier, 2008) or 'glass border' (Linehan & Walsh, 1999). All of these terms refer to stereotypes held by decision makers and senior management about female managers and their interest in and suitability for global mobility. Such stereotypes may lead women to have less access to the resources, such as job feedback, mentors, and challenging work assignments that would help them to advance in their careers (Chrobot-Mason et al., 2019). Several researchers have investigated the importance of managerial attitudes in influencing women's participation in global mobility. For example, Paik and Vance (2002) found that managers' unfounded selection biases influenced expatriate selection decisions to the detriment of female candidates. Gender stereotypes also have negative consequences for men. Collins and Bertone (2017) reported that men who are expatriate partners may experience isolation and loss of self-esteem due to their lower social status as a non-working partner rather than as a 'breadwinner'.

HRM and global mobility policies, processes and practices. Numerous studies have shown that policies, processes, and practices to facilitate women's participation in global mobility span all areas of HRM and global mobility, including leadership development, talent management, and training; recruitment and selection; remuneration; flexible work arrangements; and occupational safety and health. It is clear that no single HRM initiative will fully address inequality. A strategic and comprehensive approach is required to manage the global workforce and specifically to manage global mobility for women.

Many employers have recognised the benefits of improving representation of women at senior levels in the organisation and have introduced targets for gender balance on boards and at senior management levels, even in countries where there is no governmental/institutional requirement for gender equality on boards (Sojo et al., 2016). Smith and Parrotta (2018) present empirical evidence that suggests an important way to increase female representation on boards is for employers to implement policies and initiatives that improve the pipeline for women progressing through managerial positions to reach leadership roles. In addition to targets, HRM strategies could include opportunities for women to develop networks with senior managers who are likely to offer support for their career advancement (Bullough et al., 2017; Shortland, 2018), and mentoring and coaching programmes (Linehan & Scullion, 2008).

For women interested in global mobility, formal performance reviews and talent management processes offer important opportunities to flag their interest. Leadership development programmes can offer a way to combat gendered world-views and stereotypes in workplaces (Madsen & Scribner, 2017), and to improve women's participation in global mobility. Training programmes for women, their managers, and co-workers can be valuable initiatives to reduce stereotyping and to improve cross-cultural sensitivity and skills (Tung, 2008). Training programmes offered before international assignments in many MNEs already include topics such as diversity and inclusion and legal obligations; however, there is room for more targeted attention to women's global mobility. Shortland and Perkins (2019: 110) also suggest that 'formalised, transparent expatriate career management supports women's access to expatriation'. As an example of career development policies tailored for the Chinese context, Woodhams et al. (2015) recommend work-life policies for flexible work hours, mentoring, the use of collective learning techniques and collaborative methods such as team coaching, to be consistent with local cultural values of high collectivism.

An enduring issue relevant to the impact of globalisation is that of pay inequality across and within countries; on average, women work for lower pay than their male counterparts, even when women advance in their careers and occupy senior positions (see Blau & Kahn, 2017). The evidence over the past three decades shows gender inequality in pay has decreased yet persisted, and discrimination accounts for a substantial proportion of the gender pay gap (Blau & Kahn, 2017; Rubery & Koukiadaki, 2016; World Economic Forum, 2018). Given the widespread and endemic nature of gender pay inequity across industries and countries, it seems naïve to assume there is no inequity among globally mobile workers. Despite this, there appears to have been very little, if any, research focused on gender pay inequity in global mobility.

Flexible work arrangements include part-time work, job-share arrangements, changes in work schedules, changes in work location (such as working from home), as well as access to parental and carer leave, and childcare. Although flexible work arrangements and corporate-funded childcare emerged as a 'Western' concept (Puchmüller & Fischlmayr, 2017), flexibility is becoming more widespread and many employees, not only women, increasingly seek flexible arrangements (Brumley, 2014; Távora & Rubery 2013). Where formal childcare is commonly available and widely used, it can facilitate women's participation in the paid workforce, and attitudes towards childcare tend to be more positive (Hegewisch & Gornick 2011). However, there are differences across countries. In developing economies, informal and family-based childcare is likely to be available at lower cost. In contrast, in developed countries there tends to be more reliance on formal childcare. The introduction of parental and carer leave, including paid leave for fathers, has been led by the Nordic countries (Távora & Rubery 2013). In addition to positive initiatives, the removal of barriers such as workplace policies that require women to stop working upon marriage and pregnancy, and the right to paid leave with job security, are critical steps for women's workforce participation, given that women are overwhelmingly the primary carers for children in many societies (Brumley, 2014). There has been valuable scholarly discussion of the work-life interface for expatriates (e.g., Lazarova, Westman & Shaffer, 2010) and some examination of women's experiences associated with global mobility, work-life and domestic responsibilities (e.g., Bergström Casinowsky, 2013). However, there appears to have been little, if any, empirical research focused on flexible work arrangements for globally mobile workers.

The organisational context and type of global mobility are likely to be important factors for women, so policies, processes, and practices should be flexible to cater for differences. For example, where women are unaccompanied expatriates, working and living alone in a male-dominated workplace may be an isolating and lonely experience. In such circumstances, organisational supports such as social networks and HRM practices designed to attract and retain more women in the worksite could be particularly helpful (Shortland, 2018). For dual career couples, organisational supports could include resources such as discussion and preparation before an international assignment, as well as a mentor, and support for childcare (Fischlmayr & Puchmüller, 2016).

Occupational safety and health (Cruz Rios, Chong & Grau, 2017) is a critically important aspect of women's global mobility. Adler (1984) noted that safety concerns in some host country locations were one of the reasons used to explain managers' reluctance to send women on international assignments. International travel and work have always posed risks such as travel-related stress, affective disorders, cardiovascular disease, sleep disturbance, trauma exposure, or substance abuse (Anderzén & Arnetz, 1997; Eriksson et al., 2001; Jensen & Knudsen, 2017; Richards & Rundle, 2011; Wurtz, 2018). Collings et al. (2007) point out the implications of ill-health for MNE performance and for the international worker's family and suggest that 'MNCs must be aware of these potential issues and proactively develop HR policies accordingly'. However, the majority of studies in this area have focused at the individual level on stress and coping (e.g., Andresen, Goldmann & Volodina, 2018; Kollinger-Santer & Fischlmayr, 2013); there has been relatively little discussion of the management of safety and health in global mobility – and even less for women.

Research has recently begun to investigate the experience of workplace sexual harassment and discrimination experienced by women on international assignments (Bader et al., 2018), despite the implementation of legislation and workplace policies designed for prevention, protection and punishment. Bader et al.'s (2018) results are consistent with domestic research and show that women expatriates experience more harassment and discrimination than do men. Rather than deter women from global mobility, MNEs should emphasise supportive HRM practices such as awareness training, reporting of unacceptable behaviour, and development of inclusive organisational climates (Bader et al., 2018; Roberson, 2019).

Employers carry a duty of care to take responsibility for protecting their employees from hazards and risks (Claus & McNulty, 2015). Duty of care typically includes ensuring that appropriate management plans are in place for matters such as crisis and disaster management and should facilitate women's global mobility. For globally mobile workers, specific areas for attention might include access to risk assessments of host locations as well as access to information and training to ensure their safety and health (Quigley, Claus & Dothan, 2015).

10.2.3 Interpersonal Level Factors

Interpersonal factors refer to the quality and characteristics of social supports and relationships that women in global mobility have with managers, co-workers, family, and friends.

Social support. Social support refers to the informational, emotional, and instrumental resources that are available to an individual and contribute to the individual's ability to cope with stress (Cohen, 2004). Puchmüller and Fischlmayr (2017) examined the types of social support available to female international business travellers of various nationalities with dual-career families. Their interviews identified support at all levels – government, organisational, interpersonal, and individual – that would help women to juggle their responsibilities for career, travel, partner, and family, although the specific types of support that were available and desired varied by nationality. Other researchers have suggested that female executive repatriates can offer social support and act as role models and mentors to other women who wish to undertake international assignments (Alhejji et al., 2016; Linehan & Scullion, 2008). While the importance of social support networks is recognised in many societies, the context varies between countries. For example, in China, 'existing evidence suggests that women, more so than men, tend to enter their managerial careers by a route dependent on personal/family network, or "Guanxi"' (Cooke, 2005: 158).

Shen and Jiang (2015) examined factors that affect Chinese female expatriates' performance and found that prejudice from host country nationals had a significant negative relationship, while the expatriate's self-efficacy had a significant positive relationship with female expatriate performance. These authors also found that perceived organisational support played a moderating role where the female expatriate faced prejudice from host country nationals. It should be noted that Shen and Jiang (2015) focused on female expatriates and it would be interesting for future research to compare the circumstances for women and men. Varma and Russell (2016) demonstrated that perceived organisational support can play an important role in global mobility and they discuss how employers might dismantle pre-, during, and post-assignment barriers for women who are potential expatriates.

Work-life conflict. Several studies have shown that women in dual-career couples encounter work-life conflict related to their opportunity for, and experience of, global mobility (Kollinger-Santer & Fischlmayr, 2013). In a study conducted with Finnish expatriates, Mäkelä et al. (2017) found that in dual-career couples women experienced more work-life conflict than did men. Fischlmayr and Puchmüller's (2016) interviews with women who are in dual-career couples and are international business travellers found that these women maintain major caretaking roles such as organising childcare even when they are absent from home. This is consistent with other research (e.g., Bergström Casinowsky, 2013) that has shown globally mobile women and men both feel guilty due to their absence but men are less likely to be engaged in home-life while travelling for work.

10.2.4 Individual Level Factors

There has been a substantial body of research focused on factors at the individual level that are influential for women's global mobility. Studies have 'evolved' from a focus on women as expatriate spouses (e.g., De Cieri et al., 1991), through identifying barriers to women's international careers (e.g. Tzeng, 2006), to more sophisticated analyses exploring the complexities of work, relationships and travel for culturally diverse, globally mobile women (e.g., Puchmüller & Fischlmayr 2017).

Identity. Much of the research focused on individual factors has been underpinned by identity theory (Ashforth & Mael, 1989), which conceptualises the self as a social construct that is 'a collection of identities that reflects the roles that a person occupies in the social structure' (Terry, Hogg & White, 1999: 226). Engaging in role-appropriate behaviour reinforces or validates one's role status. However, we all have multiple identities associated with work, age, gender, and so on, and conflicts may arise between the expectations that are seen as appropriate in each of these roles. For a globally mobile woman, her identity roles may conflict, for example, where the expectations of her work role conflict with expectations associated with her familial role (Janssens, Cappellen & Zanoni, 2006).

Some worthwhile research has examined the intersection between gender and other identities such as sexuality, age, and ethnicity. Intersectionality theory (Crenshaw, 1989) explains that simultaneous membership in multiple social groups that are stigmatised or disadvantaged leads to greater social inequality. For example, lesbian expatriates may encounter a double layer of discrimination where there are social stigmas associated with being female and homosexual (Gedro, 2010). As Paisley and Tayar (2016) have discussed, identification as a lesbian, gay, bisexual, or transgender (LGBT) expatriate in some countries and cultural contexts may be difficult and even dangerous.

Although these studies have focused on discrimination experienced in host countries, global mobility might also provide an escape from a restrictive institutional context in one's parent country.

Motivation. Several studies have investigated differences between men and women with respect to their motivation for global assignments. There is now a substantial body of research showing that women are motivated to participate in global mobility, although there are complex dynamics underlying decisions to expatriate (Caligiuri et al., 1999). Shortland (2016) found that the key motivator for women to take up an expatriate assignment was career advancement, although family and financial matters were factors that influenced their decision. Motivations appear to vary across types of global mobility. Wechtler (2018) analysed online diaries of single, childless female self-initiated expatriates and identified motivations for global mobility, including the potential for escape and identity reconstruction, which are distinct from the motivations found among assigned expatriates. Valk et al. (2014) interviewed women in India working in science and technology and reported that key motivators for these women to participate in global mobility were: exposure to foreign cultures, work opportunities specifically for international collaboration in science, and personal and professional development. Overall, the research findings do not suggest there are gender differences in factors that motivate individuals to expatriate, although Stoermer et al. (2017) found that men were more willing than women to relocate to dangerous destinations.

Leadership style. To some extent, the research focus in global mobility reflects research on women in management, by moving 'beyond looking for whether women 'fit' normative expectations of 'leader'/'manager' at work to explicitly acknowledging how social roles, such as motherhood, that are unique to women have real consequences for their work lives' (Joshi et al., 2015: 1463). In the 1970s and 1980s, studies of women in global mobility were focused on Western perspectives, particularly on expatriates from North America (e.g., Adler, 1984). There has also been a substantial body of research on this topic in Europe (e.g., Festing et al., 2014; Kollinger, 2005). More recently, studies have been conducted in the Middle East (e.g., Harrison & Michailova, 2012; Shaya & Abu Khait, 2017; Stalker & Mavin, 2011), and Asia (e.g., Shen & Jiang, 2015). In an interesting study, Peus et al. (2015) interviewed women managers in Asia (China, India, Singapore) and the United States of America to investigate cross-cultural differences in leadership styles and critical success factors. They found larger differences within Asia (particularly between China and India) than differences between Asia and the USA. Some scholars have introduced diverse perspectives, such as Syed and Van Buren's (2014) analysis of Islamic views of women's employment. Africa and Latin America are still under-represented in studies of women in leadership and global mobility (Madsen & Scribner, 2017).

Global mindset. Studies have demonstrated that a global mindset is a valuable individual factor for success in global mobility, although some gender differences have been found. For example, Javidan, Bullough and Dibble (2016) examined gender differences in global mindsets in over 1,000 managers from 74 countries. They found that women were more likely to have mindsets that are open to diversity, with higher levels of cross-cultural empathy and diplomacy. In contrast, men were more likely to have higher global leadership self-efficacy with regard to global business savvy, cosmopolitan outlook, and interpersonal impact.

Individual characteristics, attitudes, and behaviours. Some studies have examined gender differences in attitudes and behaviours associated with global mobility. Lee, Chua, Miska and Stahl (2017) examined gender differences in turnover intentions among company-initiated expatriates. While they found no gender difference in the level of turnover intention, women were more likely to be influenced by their level of satisfaction with company support during expatriation. In contrast, men were influenced not only by company support but also by opportunities for career advancement.

In sum, the body of research suggests the importance of looking beyond simple explanations of gender differences to investigate the context and mechanisms that will influence individual attitudes and behaviours.

10.2.5 Outcomes of Women's Global Mobility

As we have discussed there are many factors that may either facilitate or hinder global mobility for women. There are also important outcomes for individuals, employers, and society, of increasing the participation of women in global mobility.

Societal outcomes. To identify societal outcomes of women's participation in global mobility, we must view global mobility as part of the global context for equality. Where a country's institutions are more supportive of gender equality, and gender equality is encouraged, women's representation in leadership roles will increase (Brieger et al., 2019; Jeong & Harrison, 2017). There are potential benefits for societal performance overall, as equality and inclusion can contribute to poverty reduction and improvements in national development (McKinsey Global Institute, 2018). For example, '[a]dvancing women's equality in the countries of Asia Pacific could add [US]$4.5 trillion to their collective annual GDP by 2025, a 12 percent increase over the business-as-usual trajectory' (McKinsey Global Institute, 2018: 1).

Organisational outcomes. Gender diversity in management and leadership is associated with organisational outcomes such as better performance and reputation (Brieger et al., 2019; Hoobler et al., 2018). A meta-analysis of 146 studies in 33 countries found that greater representation of women in upper management levels has a net long-term benefit for firms, although the relationship is complex (Jeong & Harrison, 2017). As one example of this complexity, in a recent study in the South Korean context Siegel, Pyun and Cheon (2019) show that where MNEs hire more local women as managers, the firm's profitability and productivity improved in the local market. Women are marginalised in managerial ranks in South Korea, so foreign MNEs have the advantage of being outsiders and can benefit by employing talented women who have been overlooked by local firms. However, Siegel et al. (2019: 393) also noted the potential for a negative backlash from local 'regulators, customers, business partners, and/or male employees'.

Interpersonal outcomes. Global mobility typically entails changes in one's work and non-work spheres, and affects individuals and their relationships in many different ways. Beyond the work sphere, global mobility can lead to positive new opportunities linked to travel but there can be negative consequences such as work-life conflict and separation from family (Bergström Casinowsky, 2013). There may be complex and sometimes traumatic implications of global mobility, as graphically described in the cases discussed in McNulty's (2015) study of the causes and consequences of divorce for expatriate women and men.

Individual outcomes. The outcomes of global mobility at the individual level include work-related attitudes and behaviour such as job satisfaction and successful job performance as well as personal outcomes such as health and well-being. Globally mobile work provides opportunities for individuals to gain career advancement into global leadership positions and to build cross-cultural knowledge and skills (Dickmann & Harris, 2005). The overwhelming evidence to date shows that women are successful in global mobility, even in host countries that might be perceived as unwelcoming for women (van der Boon, 2003). Overall, it seems likely that factors other than host country attitudes will influence whether women are effective expatriates. Company and managerial support, and the personal competencies of the female assignee, all play important roles in expatriate success (Caligiuri & Lazarova, 2002). Several researchers (e.g., Gustafson, 2014; Ren et al., 2015) have identified positive outcomes and potential benefits of global mobility for individual well-being.

The impact of global mobility on a range of outcomes relevant to individuals' adjustment, stress, health, and well-being has received considerable research attention (e.g., Andresen et al., 2018; Jensen & Knudsen, 2017). Expatriates are likely to experience more stress than do domestic employees. Other types of global mobility such as short-term assignments and frequent flyer work are likely to be stressful as they are characterised by most of the challenges and none of the perks or generous compensation of traditional long-term expatriation (Tahvanainen, Welch & Worm, 2005). Stressful outcomes of global mobility, particularly for women, have been shown to result from changes in family responsibilities (e.g., Bergström Casinowsky, 2013). Wurtz (2018) surveyed expatriates and expatriate-supervisor dyads to examine the implications of stress associated with global mobility for the use and abuse of alcohol and drugs. This study supported previous research that has shown men are more likely than women to respond to stress with substance abuse. While this has contributed valuable knowledge, more research is needed to investigate contexts and factors that will facilitate positive experiences for women in global mobility (Madsen & Scribner, 2017).

10.3 Research Directions

Our review of the literature on women and global mobility has summarised current knowledge and identified some important gaps and areas in need of attention to improve understanding of the experiences of women and their participation in global mobility.

Numerous theoretical perspectives have been applied to research on women in global mobility. These range from theories that explain contextual forces, such as institutional theory (DiMaggio & Powell, 1983); organisational perspectives such as upper echelon theory (Hambrick & Mason, 1984); gender-based theory such as stereotyping (Heilman, 2012); interpersonal factors such as social support (Cohen, 2004); and individual-level theories that explain attitudes and behaviours, such as social identity theory (Ashforth & Mael, 1989). This is by no means a comprehensive list of theoretical perspectives that may apply to women in global mobility. Most of the theoretical frameworks applied in research to date are not specific to gender or to global mobility, which may limit the research questions being addressed. There is opportunity for future research to apply new theoretical frames and build theory to explain phenomena relevant to women in global mobility.

The literature reviewed in this chapter has focused to some extent on antecedents of women's participation in global mobility. Future research could build more sophisticated analyses by identifying moderators and mediating relationships, as well as by further exploring the outcomes of women's participation in global mobility. There have been increasing efforts to build cross-level research of women in global mobility and we encourage future studies to explore the connections and interactions between the four levels of factors (societal, organisational, interpersonal, and individual). Overall, the focus of research is moving from barriers for women to identifying ways in which organisations can accommodate difference in aspiration, preference, and motivation across the globally mobile workforce.

Future research on women and global mobility could be shaped in several ways:

1. Applying relevant theoretical perspectives and developing new theoretical frames;
2. Bringing together knowledge from different fields such as anthropology, gender studies, health, international human resource management, and psychology;
3. Designing cross-level research to investigate the inter-relationships between societal and institutional, organizational, interpersonal, and individual influences and outcomes;

4. Utilising innovative and rigorous research design and methods, particularly to test interventions to advance women's careers, and using longitudinal studies; and
5. Building comparative studies of inclusive and gender-specific practices that account for contextual differences in national culture, industry, and organisational characteristics.

Some directions for future research and illustrative research questions are suggested in Table 10.1.

Table 10.1 *Suggestions for future research directions*

Theoretical framing	Illustrative research questions
Institutional	How are societal and institutional forces associated with women's participation in global mobility? How do MNEs manage where societal and institutional forces conflict with their policies on gender equality and social inclusion?
Comparative and cross-cultural studies	How do gender stereotypes in different countries affect women's career advancement and global mobility? How do attitudes towards gender equality shape attitudes towards other forms of diversity (e.g., religion, ethnicity, age)?
Diversity and inclusion management	What are the facilitators and obstacles for inclusive global mobility practices? What drives their success or failure? How can inclusive workplace cultures be developed without diluting the efforts to address gender-specific concerns?
Leadership and gender	How is gender leadership identity formed in leadership programmes? What actions could be taken by leaders to share power and encourage women's career advancement in global mobility? What combination of leadership opportunities are needed for current and future women leaders in global mobility?

Table 10.1 (*cont.*)

Theoretical framing	Illustrative research questions
	How can we evaluate the impact of leadership development programmes on women's participation in global mobility?
Global talent management	To what extent do global mobility and talent management conflict with, or support, social inclusion and gender equality?
Careers	How can women's career pathways be understood across different cultural contexts? What are the individual and contextual factors associated with the career success of women in different forms of global mobility (expatriates, migrants, international business travellers)? What are the implications of global mobility at different stages of one's career and life?
Human resource management	How do global mobility policies, processes, and practices address gender equality? What is the situation for gender pay equity among globally mobile women? How do MNEs manage their duty of care for globally mobile workers? What are the implications for health and safety among globally mobile women?
Flexibility and work-life	What types of flexible work arrangements are available and used by women in global mobility? To what extent can flexible approaches to global mobility respond to employees' non-work interests and responsibilities?
Social support	What types of social supports may be most effective to facilitate women's global mobility? What are the cross-cultural differences in social supports that facilitate women's global mobility? How can we explain the extent to which work and non-work relationships, both positive and negative, impact women' leadership emergence and development in global mobility?

Table 10.1 (*cont.*)

Theoretical framing	Illustrative research questions
Gender in management	What actions could be taken by men to 'undo' gender in global mobility?
Intersectionality	How does intersectionality (e.g., gender and race) play out in the globally mobile workforce?
Positive psychology and thriving	How might interventions such as stress management or mindfulness training contribute to women's thriving in global mobility?

10.4 Practical Implications

In the following sections 10.4.1–10.4.4 give recommendations, we offer recommendations at societal, organisational, interpersonal, and individual levels.

10.4.1 Recommendations for Policy-Makers

To advance gender equality in the work context we need government policies and workplace programmes that can address long-standing barriers and deliver gender equality (Eden & Gupta, 2017; Lewellyn & Muller-Kahle, 2019). Specific initiatives and implementations are likely to vary across cultures and contexts (Syed & Van Buren, 2014), and efforts to implement gender equality initiatives will be most effective where key decision makers within the country see the connection to 'enhanced legitimacy and the standing of the country internationally' (Alhejji et al., 2016: 156).

Recommendations for interventions by governments and at societal level that could address women's under-representation in leadership and thus contribute to greater participation by women in global mobility include:

1. Impose requirements for public reporting of representation of women in leadership roles and set targets or quotas for women in government and corporate boards.
2. Implement initiatives to encourage women's participation in the paid workforce and to address unpaid care work.

3. Improve access to digital technology and take action to encourage girls and women to engage in scientific education and careers.
4. Collaborate with other governments and with MNEs on regional solutions to 'broaden the global female talent pool or at least encourage good management practices and accountability to facilitate female empowerment' (Athanasopoulou et al., 2018: 633).

10.4.2 Recommendations for Employers

Promoting gender equality requires changes to be made to strategic and structural conditions in organisations that shape the conditions of work for all employees (Rubery & Koukiadaki, 2016). It is important for managers and individuals to recognise that the role and conceptions of gender will vary across national and societal contexts, requiring application of global policies to be balanced with nuanced understanding of local conditions. Targeted policies are important to address problems that apply to women, such as the gender pay gap, while complementary inclusive policies are important to address the multiple forms of diversity in the global workforce (Groysberg & Connolly, 2013; Rubery & Koukiadaki, 2016). Equality of opportunity in global mobility requires a strategic approach towards inclusive workplaces that will bring benefits for women and for the diverse workforce (Roberson, 2019; Tinsley & Ely, 2018). The management of global mobility will be most successful where there is a combination of targeted and inclusive policies, processes, and practices. Many recommendations can be offered for employers, including:

1. Assess the current state of global mobility management to identify areas of strength and areas for improvement, by: auditing current policies, processes and practices; conducting focus groups with employees or surveying employee attitudes; measuring absenteeism and turnover; and benchmarking within the organisation and with other organisations. Seek to identify any differences that might indicate inequity between demographic sub-groups of the workforce.
2. Ensure recruitment and selection processes are free from bias and discrimination with regard to any protected attribute of diversity

(e.g., gender, age, ethnicity). Decision-making about international assignments should be evidence based. Unconscious bias and unfounded assumptions should be identified and removed from decision-making processes.

3. Make flexible work arrangements available and encourage their uptake. Flexible work arrangements should facilitate a larger resource pool of employees who are qualified and willing to engage in global work. Managers should be educated to support flexible work arrangements.
4. Safety and health risks should be assessed, prevented, monitored, and managed for all globally mobile work. Jobs and working conditions could be modified or re-designed to ensure work is healthy and safe. Reporting and recording of safety and health incidents could include gender information to allow analysis of gender differences.
5. Provide a supportive and inclusive work environment. All forms of discrimination, harassment, bullying, and violence should be prevented in the workplace. Safety and health issues should be included in global mobility planning and pre-assignment training. This might include training and policies to ensure respectful behaviour in the workplace. Effective mechanisms should be in place for the prevention, reporting, and management of negative acts such as sexual harassment.
6. Training for globally mobile workers should include awareness of stress and coping strategies. Leaders, line managers, and HRM specialists should be trained to provide support. Organisational resources such as employee assistance programmes should be accessible.
7. Leadership development programmes should challenge restrictive constructs of gender, systemic bias, and stereotypes, in order to shift mental models to facilitate women's advancement into leadership roles.
8. Hold managers accountable for gender equality and inclusion. Provide information, resources, and diversity and inclusion training programmes for leaders, supervisors, and all organisational members.
9. Implement positive interventions, such as stress management and mindfulness training, to contribute to women's thriving in global mobility.

10.4.3 Recommendations for Leaders and Managers

Some research in the management field has focused on offering advice to women, which seems to reflect an assumption that somehow the women need to be 'fixed'. However, the evidence is that it is systemic, structural changes and cultural attitudes of those working with women, particularly those in powerful roles, that could make the most difference (London et al., 2018; Tung, 2008). Recommendations for leaders and managers include:

1. Be involved in the development and implementation of policies, processes, and practices to improve gender equality and inclusion.
2. Help women to build social networks and find mentors, particularly for women managers in emerging economies.
3. Lead by example and be a role model for other leaders and managers in supporting women in global mobility.
4. Be an ally for women in your workplace. Actively tackle myths, biases, and stereotypes that managers may have about women in global mobility.

In the literature on gender equality there is relatively little advice directed at men. Kelan (2018) addresses this by identifying how men can do, and undo, gender to support gender equality in workplaces, and this advice is equally helpful for global mobility. Although Kelan (2018) identifies these as actions to be taken by men, they are relevant to anyone in a position of power to influence and lead change (also see London et al., 2018):

1. Instead of creating connection with other men and excluding women, men could specifically sponsor and include women in work meetings and events.
2. Rather than men distancing themselves from women, for example by undermining a female colleague or by being hostile to women, men could be visibly supportive of women.
3. Instead of seeking to impress others by self-promoting and 'peacocking', men could display humility and listen to women's voices.
4. Where men may display 'heroism', for example by undermining flexible work arrangements and insisting on presenteeism that disadvantages those with non-work responsibilities, they could instead demonstrate dedication to their families and show their vulnerability.

10.4.4 Recommendations for Women

While recognising that many women face structural and relational constraints that limit their choices with regard to employment and career advancement (Chrobot-Mason et al., 2019), some suggestions can be offered at an individual level.

1. Whether a local or expatriate woman, explore opportunities for collaborative learning, particularly to share knowledge by offering mentoring and coaching to the next generation of women.
2. Develop social capital by building networks and seeking out supportive structures such as a coach or mentor for future career development. Develop strategies to generate contacts that will lead to international work.
3. Participate in training, workshops, and programmes that aim to increase women's leadership abilities and leader identity.
4. Know your rights and share the responsibility to work in respectful and inclusive ways.
5. Take active ownership of your career and explore opportunities for development and develop your own leadership style.
6. Understand your own strengths, be pro-active in your own career, and identify specific steps to be taken before, during, and after an international assignment.
7. Manage your health and wellbeing through healthy activities and stress management techniques.

10.5 Conclusions

It is in the best interests of scholars, managers, employees, and communities to make sense of and understand the complexities in research and practice relevant to women in global mobility. While there has been progress for women in global mobility, there are enduring problems, challenges, and opportunities for researchers, managers, and individuals to address. We share a responsibility to debate and investigate, monitor and measure, and to work on solutions. Learning from issues that are specific to women will help us to work with all forms of diversity and to build more inclusive organisations.

References

Adler, N. J. 1984. Women in international management: where are they? *California Management Review*, 26(4): 78–89.

Alhejji, H., Ng, E. S., Garavan, T. & Carbery, R. 2016. The impact of formal and informal distance on gender equality approaches: the case of a British MNC in Saudi Arabia. *Thunderbird International Business Review*, 60(2): 147–159.

Altman, Y. & Shortland, S. 2008. Women and international assignments: taking stock – a 25-year review. *Human Resource Management*, 47(2): 199–216.

Anderzén, I. & Arnetz, B. B. 1997. Psychophysiological reactions during the first year of a foreign assignment: results of a controlled longitudinal study. *Work & Stress*, 11: 304–318.

Andresen, M., Bergdolt, F., Margenfeld, J. & Dickmann, M. 2014. Addressing international mobility confusion – developing definitions and differentiations for self-initiated and assigned expatriates as well as migrants. *International Journal of Human Resource Management*, 25: 2295–2318.

Andresen, M., Goldmann, P. & Volodina, A. 2018. Do overwhelmed expatriates intend to leave? The effects of sensory processing sensitivity, stress, and social capital on expatriates' turnover intention. *European Management Review*. 15: 315–328.

Ashforth, B. E. & Mael, F. 1989. Social identity theory and the organization. *Academy of Management Review*, 14: 20–39.

Athanasopoulou, A., Moss-Cowan, A., Smets, M. & Morris, T. 2018. Claiming the corner office: female CEO careers and implications for leadership development. *Human Resource Management*, 57: 617–639.

Bader, B. & Schuster, T. 2015. Expatriate social networks in terrorism-endangered countries: an empirical analysis in Afghanistan, India, Pakistan, and Saudi Arabia. *Journal of International Management*, 21(1): 63–77.

Bader, B., Stoermer, S., Bader, A. K. & Schuster, T. 2018. Institutional discrimination of women and workplace harassment of female expatriates Evidence from 25 host countries. *Journal of General Management*, 6(1): 40–58.

Beder, J., Coe, R. & Sommer, D. 2011. Women and men who have served in Afghanistan/Iraq: coming home. *Social Work in Health Care*, 50(7): 515–526.

Bergström Casinowsky, G. 2013. Working life on the move, domestic life at standstill? Work-related travel and responsibility for home and family. *Gender, Work & Organization*, 20: 311–326.

Bhatta, P., Simkhada, P., van Teijlingen, E. & Maybin, S. 2009. A questionnaire study of voluntary service overseas (VSO) volunteers: health risk and problems encountered. *Journal of Travel Medicine*, 16: 332–337.

Bierwiaczonek, K. & Waldzus, S. 2016. Socio-cultural factors as antecedents of cross-cultural adaptation in expatriates, international students, and migrants: a review. *Journal of Cross-Cultural Psychology*, 47: 767–817.

Blau, F. D. & Kahn, L. M., 2017. The gender wage gap: extent, trends, and explanations. *Journal of Economic Literature*, 55(3): 789–865.

Brieger, S. A., Francouer,C. Welzel, C. & Ben-Amar, W. 2019. Empowering women: the role of emancipative forces in board gender diversity. *Journal of Business Ethics*, 155: 495–511.

Broadbridge, A. & Simpson, R. 2011. 25 years on: reflecting on the past and looking to the future in gender and management research. *British Journal of Management*, 22(3): 470–483.

Brookfield Global Relocation Services, 2016. *Global Mobility Trends Survey*, Brookfield Global Relocation Services, New York, NY. http://globalmobilitytrends.bgrs.com/.

Brumley, K. M. 2014. 'Now, we have the same *rights* as men to keep our jobs': gendered perceptions of opportunity and obstacles in a Mexican workplace. *Gender, Work & Organization*, 21(3): 217–230.

Bullough, A., Kroeck, K. G., Newburry, W., Kundu, S. K. & Lowe, K. B. 2012. Women's political leadership participation around the world: an institutional analysis. *Leadership Quarterly*, 23: 398–411.

Bullough, A., Moore, F. & Kalafatoglu, T. 2017. Research on women in international business and management: then, now, and next. *Cross-Cultural & Strategic Management*, 24(2): 211–230.

Bullough, A. & Sully de Luque, M. 2015. Women's participation in entrepreneurial and political leadership: the importance of culturally endorsed implicit leadership theories. *Leadership*, 11(1): 36–56.

Caligiuri, P. M. & Cascio, W. F. 1998. Can we send her there? Maximizing the success of western women on global assignments. *Journal of World Business*, 33(4): 394–416.

Caligiuri, P. & Lazarova, M. 2002. A model for the influence of social interaction and social support on female expatriates' cross-cultural adjustment. *International Journal of Human Resource Management*, 13: 761–772.

Caligiuri, P. M., Joshi, A. & Lazarova, M. 1999. Factors influencing the adjustment of women on global assignments. *International Journal of Human Resource Management*, 10: 163–179.

Caligiuri, P. M. & Tung, R. L. 1998. Comparing the success of male and female expatriates from a US-based multinational company. *International Journal of Human Resource Management*, 10: 763–782.

Catalyst. (2019). *Women CEOs of the S&P 500*. www.catalyst.org/knowledge/women-sp-500-companies.

Cerdin, J.-L. & Brewster, C. 2014. Talent management and expatriation: bridging two streams of research and practice. *Journal of World Business*, 49(2), 245–252.

Chrobot-Mason, D., Hoobler, J. & Burno, J. 2019. Lean in versus the literature: an evidence-based examination. *Academy of Management Perspectives*, 33(1): 110–130.

Claus, L. & McNulty, Y. 2015. Editorial: duty of care obligations of employers to protect the health, safety, security and wellbeing of employees. *European Journal of International Management*, 9(6): 667–672.

Cohen, S. 2004. Social relationships and health. *American Psychologist*, 59 (8): 676–684.

Colakoglu, S., Yunlu, D. G. & Arman, G. 2018. High-skilled female immigrants: career strategies and experiences. *Journal of Global Mobility*, 6 (3/4): 258–584.

Collings, D. G., Scullion, H. & Morley, M. J. 2007. Changing patterns of global staffing in the multinational enterprise: challenges to the conventional expatriate assignment and emerging alternatives. *Journal of World Business*, 42: 198–213.

Collins, H. E. & Bertone, S. 2017. Threatened identities: adjustment narratives of expatriate spouses. *Journal of Global Mobility*, 5(1): 78–92.

Cooke, F. L. 2005. Women's managerial careers in China in a period of reform. *Asia Pacific Business Review*, 11: 149–162.

Crenshaw, K. 1989. Demarginalizing the intersection of race and sex: a black feminist critique of antidiscrimination doctrine, feminist theory, and antiracist politics. *University of Chicago Legal Forum*, 8: 139–167.

Cruz Rios, F., Chong, W. K. & Grau, D. 2017. The need for gender-specific occupational safety analysis. *Journal of Safety Research*, 62: 53–62.

De Cieri, H., Dowling, P. J. & Taylor, K. F. 1991. The psychological impact of relocation on expatriate partners. *International Journal of Human Resource Management*, 2: 377–414.

De Cieri, H., Sheehan, C., Costa, C., Fenwick, M. & Cooper, B. K. 2009. International talent flow and intention to repatriate: an identity explanation. *Human Resource Development International*, 12(3): 243–261.

de Klerk, S. & Verreynne, M.-L. 2017. The networking practices of women managers in an emerging economy setting: negotiating institutional and social barriers. *Human Resource Management Journal*, 27(3): 477–501.

Dickmann, M. & Harris, H. 2005. Developing career capital for global careers: the role of international assignments. *Journal of World Business*, 40(4): 399–408.

DiMaggio, P. J. & Powell, W. W. 1983. The iron cage revisited: institutional isomorphism and collective rationality in organizational fields. *American Sociological Review*, 48(2): 147–160.

Doherty, N., Richardson, J. & Thorn, K. 2013. Self-initiated expatriation and self-initiated expatriates. *Career Development International*, 18: 97–112.

Dunn, R., Williams, R., Kemp, V., Patel, D. & Greenberg, N. 2015. Systematic review: deployment length and the mental health of diplomats. *Occupational Medicine*, 65: 32–38.

Eden, L. & Gupta, S. F. 2017. Culture and context matter: gender in international business and management. *Cross-Cultural & Strategic Management*, 24(2): 194–210.

Ely, R. J., Ibarra, H. & Kolb, D. M. 2011. Taking gender into account: theory and design for women's leadership development programs. *Academy of Management Learning and Education*, 10: 474–493.

Eriksson, C. B., Van de Kemp, H., Gorsuch, R., Hoke, S. & Foy, D. W. 2001. Trauma exposure and PTSD symptoms in international relief and development personnel. *Journal of Traumatic Stress*, 14(1): 205–212.

Festing, M., Kornau, A. & Schäfer, L. 2014. Think talent – think male? A comparative case study analysis of gender inclusion in talent management practices in the German media industry. *International Journal of Human Resource Management*, 26: 707–732.

Fischlmayr, I. C. & Puchmüller, K. M. 2016. Married, mom and manager – how can this be combined with an international career? *International Journal of Human Resource Management*, 27: 744–765.

Gedro, J. 2010. The lavender ceiling atop the global closet: human resource development and lesbian expatriates. *Human Resource Development Review*, 9: 385–404.

Grant Thornton, 2019. *Women in Business. Building a Blueprint for Action*. www.grantthornton.global/en/insights/women-in-business–2019/.

Groysberg, B. & Connolly, K. 2013. Great leaders who make the mix work. *Harvard Business Review*, September: 68–76.

Guillén, M. 2001. Is globalization civilizing, destructive or feeble? A critique of five key debates in the social science literature. *Annual Review of Sociology*, 27: 235–260.

Gustafson, P. 2014. Business travel from the traveller's perspective: stress, stimulation and normalization. *Mobilities*, 9(1): 63–83.

Haak-Saheem, W. & Brewster, C. 2017. 'Hidden' expatriates: international mobility in the United Arab Emirates as a challenge to current understanding of expatriation. *Human Resource Management Journal*, 27(3): 423–439.

Hambrick, D. C. & Mason, P. A. 1984. Upper echelons: the organization as a reflection of its top managers. *Academy of Management Review*, 9(2): 193–206.

Harrison, E. C. & Michailova, S. 2012. Working in the Middle East: Western female expatriates' experiences in the United Arab Emirates. *International Journal of Human Resource Management*, 23: 625–644.

Hegewisch, A. & Gornick, J. C. 2011. The impact of work-family policies on women's employment: a review of research from OECD countries. *Community, Work and Family*, 14(2): 119–138.

Heilman, M. E. 2012. Gender stereotypes and workplace bias. *Research in Organizational Behavior*, 32: 113–135.

Hoobler, J. M., Masterson, C. R., Nkomo, S. M. & Michel, E. J. 2018. The business case for women leaders: meta-analysis, research critique, and path forward. *Journal of Management*, 44(6): 2473–2499.

House, R. J., Hanges, P. J., Javidan, M., Dorfman, P. W. & Gupta, V. 2004. *Culture, Leadership and Organizations: The GLOBE Study of 62 Societies*. Thousand Oaks, CA: Sage.

Hutchings, K., French, E. & Hatcher, T. 2008. Lament of the ignored expatriate. An examination of organisational and social network support for female expatriates in China. *Equal Opportunities International*, 27(4): 372–391.

Hutchings, K., Metcalfe, B. & Cooper, B. K. 2010. Exploring Arab Middle Eastern women's perceptions of barriers to, and facilitators of, international management opportunities. *International Journal of Human Resource Management*, 21 (1): 61–83.

Insch, G. S., McIntyre, N. & Napier, N. K. 2008. The expatriate glass ceiling: the second layer of glass. *Journal of Business Ethics*, 83: 19–28.

International Labour Office, 2016. *Women at Work: Trends 2016*. Geneva: International Labour Office.

Janssens, M., Cappellen, T. & Zanoni, P. 2006. Successful female expatriates as agents: positioning oneself through gender, hierarchy, and culture. *Journal of World Business*, 41(2): 133–48.

Javidan, M., Bullough, A. & Dibble, R. 2016. Mind the gap: gender differences in global leadership self-efficacies. *Academy of Management Perspectives*, 30 (1): 59–73.

Jensen, M. T. & Knudsen, K. 2017. A two-wave cross-lagged study of business travel, work–family conflict, emotional exhaustion, and psychological health complaints. *European Journal of Work and Organizational Psychology*, 26: 30–41.

Jeong, S.-H. & Harrison, D. A. 2017. Glass breaking, strategy making, and value creating: meta-analytic outcomes of women as CEOs and TMT members. *Academy of Management Journal*, 60(4): 1219–1252.

Joshi, A., Neely, B., Emrich, C., Griffiths, D. & George, G. 2015. Gender research in AMJ: an overview of five decades of empirical research and calls to action. *Academy of Management Journal*, 58(5): 1459–1475.

Kelan, E. 2018. Men doing and undoing gender at work: a review and research agenda. *International Journal of Management Reviews*, 20: 544–558.

Kemp, L. J. & Rickett, B. 2018. The lived experiences of foreign women: influences on their international working lives. *Gender Work & Organization*, 25: 343–360.

Kim, K. & Von Glinow, M. A. 2017. Contextual determinants in disclosing one's stigmatized identity during expatriation. The case of lesbian and gay self-initiated expatriates. *Journal of Global Mobility*, 5(3): 317–338.

Kittler, M. G. & Faeth, P. C. 2017. How do you fear? Examining expatriates' perception of danger and its consequences. *Journal of Global Mobility*, 5 (4): 391–417.

Kollinger, I. 2005. Women and expatriate work opportunities in Austrian organizations. *International Journal of Human Resource Management*, 16 (7): 1243–60.

Kollinger-Santer, I. & Fischlmayr, I. C. 2013. Work life balance up in the air – Does gender make a difference between female and male international business travelers? *Zeitschrift für Personalforschung*, 27 (3): 195–223.

Kossek, E. E., Su, R. & Wu, L. 2017. 'Opting out' or 'pushed out'? Integrating perspectives on women's career equality for gender inclusion and interventions. *Journal of Management*, 43: 228–254.

Kostova, T. & Zaheer, S. 1999. Organizational legitimacy under conditions of uncertainty: the case of the multinational enterprise. *Academy of Management Review*, 24(1): 64–81.

Laite, J. 2017. Between Scylla and Charybdis: women's labour migration and sex trafficking in the early twentieth century. *International Review of Social History*, 62(1): 37–65.

Lazarova, M., Westman, M. & Shaffer, M. A. 2010. Elucidating the positive side of the work-family interface on international assignments: a model of expatriate work and family performance. *Academy of Management Review*, 35(1): 93–117.

Lee, H.-J., Chua, C. H., Miska, C. & Stahl, G. 2017. Looking out or looking up: gender differences in expatriate turnover intentions. *Cross-Cultural & Strategic Management*, 24(2): 288–309.

Lewellyn, K. B. & Muller-Kahle, M. I. 2019. The corporate board glass ceiling: the role of empowerment and culture in shaping board gender diversity. *Journal of Business Ethics*, https://doi.org/10.1007/s10551-01 9–04116-9

Linehan, M. & Scullion, H. 2008. The development of female global managers: the role of mentoring and networking. *Journal of Business Ethics*, 83: 29–40.

Linehan, M. & Walsh, J. S. 1999. Senior female international managers: breaking the glass border. *Women in Management Review*, 14(7): 264–272.

London, M., Bear, J. B., Cushenbery, L. & Sherman, G. D. 2018. Leader support for gender equity: understanding prosocial goal orientation, leadership motivation, and power sharing. *Human Resource Management Review*, 29(3): 418–427.

Madsen, S. R. & Scribner, R. T. 2017. A perspective on gender in management. The need for strategic cross-cultural scholarship on women in management and leadership. *Cross-Cultural & Strategic Management*, 24(2): 231–250.

Mäkelä, L., Lämsä, A.-M., Heikkinen, S. & Tanskanen, J. 2017. Work-to-personal-life conflict among dual and single-career expatriates. *Journal of Global Mobility*, 5(3): 301–316.

McKinsey Global Institute, 2018. *The Power of Parity: Advancing Women's Equality in Asia Pacific*, McKinsey Global Institute: www.mckinsey.com/mgi.

McNulty, Y. 2015. Till stress do us part: the causes and consequences of expatriate divorce. *Journal of Global Mobility*, 3: 106–136.

McNulty, Y. & Hutchings, K. 2016. Looking for global talent in all the right places: a critical literature review of non-traditional expatriates. *International Journal of Human Resource Management*, 27 (7): 699–728.

Metcalfe, B. D. & Rees, C. 2010. Gender, globalization and organization. Exploring power, relations and intersections. *Equality, Diversity and Inclusion*, 29(1): 5–22.

Metz, I. & Kumra, S. 2019. Why are self-help books with career advice for women popular? *Academy of Management Perspectives*. 33(1): 82–93.

Meyskens, M., Von Glinow, M. A., Werther, W. B. Jr. & Clarke, L. 2009. The paradox of international talent: alternative forms of international assignments. *International Journal of Human Resource Management*, 20: 1439–1450.

Michailova, S. & Hutchings, K. 2016. Critiquing the marginalised place of research on women within international business. Where are we now and where should we be going? *Critical Perspectives on International Business*, 12(4): 348–368.

Mor Barak, M. E. 2017. *Managing Diversity. Toward a Globally Inclusive Workplace*. (4th edn.) Thousand Oaks, CA: Sage.

Paik, Y. & Vance, C. M. 2002. Evidence of back-home selection bias against US female expatriates. *Women in Management Review*, 17(2): 68–79.

Paisley, V. & Tayar, M. 2016. Lesbian, gay, bisexual and transgender (LGBT) expatriates: an intersectionality perspective. *International Journal of Human Resource Management*, 27: 766–780.

Peus, C., Braun, S. & Knipfer, K. 2015. On becoming a leader in Asia and America: empirical evidence from women managers. *Leadership Quarterly*, 26: 55–67.

Puchmüller, K. & Fischlmayr, I. 2017. Support for female international business travellers in dual-career families. *Journal of Global Mobility*, 5 (1): 22–42.

Quigley, R. L., Claus, L. & Dothan, M. 2015. Medical requests for assistance from globally mobile populations: contrasting international assignees from different sectors. *European Journal of International Management*, 9(6): 712–736.

Ragins, B. R. & Sundstrom, E. (1989). Gender and power in organizations: a longitudinal perspective. *Psychological Bulletin*, 105: 51–88.

Ren, H., Yunlu, D. G., Shaffer, M. & Fodchuk, K. M. 2015. Expatriate success and thriving: the influence of job deprivation and emotional stability. *Journal of World Business*, 50: 69–78.

Richards, C. A. & Rundle, A. G. 2011. Business travel and self-rated health, obesity, and cardiovascular disease risk factors. *Journal of Occupational and Environmental Medicine*, 53: 358–363.

Roberson, Q. M. 2019. Diversity in the workplace: a review, synthesis, and future research agenda. *Annual Review of Organizational Psychology and Organizational Behavior*, 6: 69–88.

Rubery, J. & Koukiadaki, A. 2016. *Closing the Gender Pay Gap: A Review of the Issues, Policy Mechanisms and International Evidence.* International Labour Office – Geneva: ILO.

Salaff, J. W. & Greve, A. 2004. Can women's social networks migrate? *Women's Studies International Forum*, 27(2): 149–162.

Shaya, N. & Abu Khait, R. 2017. Feminizing leadership in the Middle East. Emirati women empowerment and leadership style. *Gender in Management: An International Journal*, 32(8): 590–608.

Shen, J. & Jiang, F. 2015. Factors influencing Chinese female expatriates' performance in international assignments. *International Journal of Human Resource Management*, 26: 299–315.

Shore, L. M., Cleveland, J. M. & Sanchez, D. 2018. Inclusive workplaces: a review and model. *Human Resource Management Review*, 28(2): 176–189.

Shortland, S. 2016. The purpose of expatriation: why women undertake international assignments. *Human Resource Management*, 55(4): 655–678.

Shortland, S. 2018. Female expatriates' motivations and challenges: the case of oil and gas. *Gender in Management: An International Journal*, 33(1): 50–65.

Shortland, S. & Perkins, S. J. 2019. Great expectations? Female expatriates' perceptions of organisational performance and development reviews in supporting access to international assignments. *Career Development International*, 24(2): 110–126.

Siegel, J., Pyun, L. & Cheon, B. Y. 2019. Multinational firms, labor market discrimination, and the capture of outsider's advantage by exploiting the social divide. *Administrative Science Quarterly*, 64(3): 370–397.

Smith, N. & Parrotta, P. 2018. Why so few women on boards of directors? Empirical evidence from Danish companies in 1998–2010 *Journal of Business Ethics*, 147: 445–467.

Sojo, V. E., Wood, R. E., Wood, S. A. & Wheeler, M. A. 2016. Reporting requirements, targets, and quotas for women in leadership. *The Leadership Quarterly*, 27: 519–536.

Stalker, B. & Mavin, S. 2011. Learning and development experiences of self-initiated expatriate women in the United Arab Emirates. *Human Resource Development International*, 14(3); 273–290.

Stoermer, S., Davies, S. E., Bahrisch, O. & Portniagin, F. 2017. For sensation's sake: differences in female and male expatriates' relocation willingness to dangerous countries based on sensation seeking. *Journal of Global Mobility*, 5(4): 374–390.

Syed, J. & Van Buren, H. J. III. 2014. Global business norms and Islamic views of women's employment. *Business Ethics Quarterly*, 24(2): 251–276.

Tahvanainen, M., Welch, D. & Worm, V. 2005. Implications of short-term international assignments. *European Management Journal*, 23: 663–673.

Távora, I. & Rubery, J. 2013. Female employment, labour market institutions and gender culture in Portugal. *Journal of European Social Policy*, 22(1): 63–76.

Terry, D. J., Hogg, M. A. & White, K. M. 1999. The theory of planned behaviour: self-identity, social identity and group norms. *British Journal of Social Psychology*, 38: 225–244.

Tinsley, C. H. & Ely, R. J. 2018. What most people get wrong about men and women. *Harvard Business Review*, May-June: 114–121.

Triana, M. C., Jayasinghe, M., Pieper, J. R., Delgado, D. M. & Li, M. 2019. Perceived workplace gender discrimination and employee consequences: a meta-analysis and complementary studies considering country context. *Journal of Management*, 45(6): 2419–2447.

Tung, R. L. 2004. Female expatriates: the model global manager? *Organizational Dynamics*, 33 (3): 243–253.

Tung, R. L. 2008. Do race and gender matter in international assignments to/from Asia Pacific? An exploratory study of attitudes among Chinese and Korean executives. *Human Resource Management*, 47(1): 91–110.

Tzeng, R. 2006. Gender issues and family concerns for women with international careers. Female expatriates in Western multinational corporations in Taiwan. *Women in Management Review*, 21(5): 376–392.

United Nations Conference on Trade and Development [UNCTAD], 2016. *Development and Globalization: Facts and Figures*, UNCTAD, Geneva.

Valk, R., Van der Velde, M., Van Engen, M. & Godbole, R. 2014. International career motives, repatriation and career success of Indian women in Science & Technology. *Journal of Global Mobility*, 2(2): 203–233.

van der Boon, M. 2003. Women in international management: an international perspective on women's ways of leadership. *Women in Management Review*, 18(3): 132–146.

Varma, A. & Russell, L. 2016. Women and expatriate assignments. Exploring the role of perceived organizational support. *Employee Relations*, 38(2): 200–223.

Wechtler, H. 2018. 'Life if elsewhere.' A diary study of female self-initiated expatriates' motivations to work abroad. *Career Development International*, 23(3): 291–311.

Wentling, R. M. 2004. Factors that assist and barriers that hinder the success of diversity initiatives in multinational corporations. *Human Resource Development International*, 7, 165–180.

Woodhams, C., Xian, H. & Lupton, B. 2015. Women managers' careers in China: theorizing the influence of gender and collectivism. *Human Resource Management*, 54(6): 913–931.

World Bank Group, 2019. *Women, Business and the Law. A Decade of Reform*. Washington, DC: International Bank for Reconstruction and Development / The World Bank.

World Economic Forum, 2018. *The Global Gender Gap Report 2018*. Geneva: World Economic Forum.

Wurtz, O. 2018. Expatriation, alcohol and drugs: antecedents and consequences of substance use in expatriation. *Journal of Global Mobility*, 6(3/4): 316–334.

11 Global Families

MARGARET A. SHAFFER, MIN (MAGGIE) WAN

11.1 Introduction

As the world economy becomes more intertwined and trade barriers decline, the global mobility of human talent has increased. Despite the high costs of international assignees and the increased variety of global employees (Shaffer et al., 2012), multinational firms around the world continue to send expatriates and their families to live and work in foreign countries. These assigned expatriates are sent by their employer to live and work in a foreign country for at least one year to complete a specific task, with the expectation that they will repatriate to the home country (Harrison et al., 2004). As barriers restricting the movement of human resources have also decreased, an increasing number of expatriates are self-initiated employees who generally sponsor their own relocation and that of their family to a foreign country (Suutari & Brewster, 2000). The majority of assigned and self-initiated expatriates (commonly referred to as expatriates in the rest of this chapter) relocate with family members, who are both a source of support as well as a concern. Indeed, it is the family that is credited for being responsible for most failed international assignments (Brookfield Global Relocation Services, 2016).

Given the critical role of families to expatriate success (Erogul & Rahman, 2017; Haslberger & Brewster, 2008; Webb, 1996), researchers have included family members in studies since the 1980s, and for every decade since then, partner and family adjustment has been a recurrent theme in the expatriate literature (Kraimer, Bolino & Mead, 2016). Drawing on Black, Mendenhall and Oddou's (1991) model of international adjustment, early scholars interested in the role of expatriate families focused on partner adjustment (e.g., Black & Gregersen, 1991a, 1991b; Shaffer & Harrison, 2001), defined in terms of comfort with the general cultural environment (i.e., cultural adjustment) and with interacting with host country nationals (i.e., interaction adjustment). As confirmed by meta-analytic evidence of various anticipatory, individual, job, organisational and nonwork factors associated with expatriate adjustment, partner adjustment is the strongest input to expatriate cultural adjustment and it has a significant influence on both expatriate work and interaction adjustment (Bhaskar-Shrinivas et al., 2005).

Except for a couple of early studies on expatriate family adjustment (e.g., Caligiuri, Hyland, & Joshi, 1998; Caligiuri et al., 1998), research on this topic is more nascent but growing. In fact, there are now two recent reviews of this burgeoning literature that provide good insights into the functioning of the expatriate family (Goede & Berg, 2018; Sterle et al., 2018). In reviewing the literature on expatriate family outcomes, Goede and Berg (2018) developed a multi-level framework of environmental, organisational, and family determinants of various family outcomes before, during, and after the assignment. Interestingly, in their list of individual family characteristics, the adjustment of individual family members is not included. This omission is striking given the predominant focus in the literature on expatriate adjustment and the important role of partner adjustment in this process. Furthermore, only a few scholars have looked at the relationship between partner adjustment and family-related variables (e.g., Ali, Van derZee, & Sanders 2003; Gupta, Banerjee, & Guar 2012; Ramos et al., 2017; Shaffer & Harrison, 2001; Takeuchi et al., 2002; van der Zee, Ali, & Salome 2005; van Erp et al., 2011a, 2011b). Recognising that the expatriate partner is the lynchpin of expatriate success, and wanting to better understand the partner's adjustment to the foreign culture, we chose to conduct an in-depth review of the empirical expatriate partner adjustment literature.

11.2 Review of Empirical Literature on Expatriate Partner Adjustment

To identify manuscripts that included the term 'expatriate partner adjustment', we searched several databases: PsycINFO, Google Scholar, ABI-Inform, and Web of Science. Keywords included 'expatriate' or 'international assignee' plus 'adjustment' and 'spouse', 'partner', 'family', or 'children'. After screening these for papers that conceptualised or assessed expatriate partner adjustment, we ended up with twenty-five empirical articles, including twenty quantitative articles, three qualitative articles, and two mixed method articles.

To facilitate our review of this literature, we identified all significant variables associated with expatriate partner adjustment and well-being (see Table 11.1). For partner adjustment, we differentiated three forms that have dominated the partner adjustment literature: expatriate partner personal adjustment, interaction adjustment, and cultural adjustment. Expatriate partner personal adjustment refers to belonging to or becoming a part of the foreign environment (Shaffer & Harrison, 2001); partner interaction adjustment is defined in terms of relationships or interpersonal interactions with host country nationals; and partner cultural adjustment refers to adaptation to environmental or situational conditions (Black, et al., 1991). We also grouped various indicators of partner well-being (i.e., psychological adjustment, life satisfaction, and overall partner adjustment) to form a fourth category.

In categorising the variables significantly associated with expatriate partner adjustment and well-being, we first separated them into three major categories that represented partner, expatriate, and family aspects. For the partner category, we then identified various personal (i.e., demographic, traits, knowledge/skills/abilities/others, and attitudes/cognitions), relational, organisational, and assignment factors. For the expatriate category, we formed two groupings: personal and job/assignment factors. For the family variables, we separated them based on the source of the rating (i.e., partner or expatriate). Through our analysis of these detected relationships, we observed three major themes: crossover occurrences from partners to expatriates, the relationship between the partner and family dynamics, and under-researched topics relevant to partner adjustment. For each theme, we discuss what we currently know (or don't know), relevant theoretical perspectives to advance our knowledge in these areas and suggestions for future research.

11.2.1 *Partner Adjustment from a Crossover Perspective*

The most consistent relationships we detected have to do with the crossover effects of partner adjustment to expatriate adjustment as well as other expatriate outcomes. Crossover is an inter-individual process that occurs when the experiences of one member of a dyad are transferred to another member (Westman, 2001). For example,

Table 11.1 *Detected relationships with expatriate partner adjustment and well-being*

	Partner personal adjustment	Partner interaction adjustment	Partner cultural adjustment	Partner well-being
Partner variables				
1. Personal factors				
a. Demographic characteristics				
Age (+)		Shaffer & Harrison (2001) Mohr & Klein (2004) Chen & Shaffer (2018)	Mohr & Klein (2004)	
Gender (F > M)			Cole (2011)	
Time on assignment (+)	Simeon & Fujiu (2000) Shaffer & Harrison (2001) Chen & Shaffer (2018)	Shaffer & Harrison (2001) Mohr & Klein (2004) Chen & Shaffer (2018)	Black & Gregersen (1991a) Black & Gregersen (1991b) Shaffer & Harrison (2001) Mohr & Klein (2004) Takeuchi et al. (2007)	
Previous int'l experience (+)			Mohr & Klein (2004)	
Education (+)			Takeuchi et al. (2007)	
Children (+)		Mohr & Klein (2004)		
Children (-)			Mohr & Klein (2004)	

Table 11.1 (*cont.*)

	Partner personal adjustment	Partner interaction adjustment	Partner cultural adjustment	Partner well-being
b. Personal traits				
Cultural empathy (+)		Ali et al. (2003)	Ali et al. (2003)	Ali et al. (2003)
Open-mindedness (+)		Ali et al. (2003)	Ali et al. (2003) van Erp et al. (2014)	Ali et al. (2003)
Social initiative (+)		Ali et al. (2003)	Ali et al. (2003)	Ali et al. (2003) van Erp et al. (2014)
Flexibility (+)		Ali et al. (2003)	Ali et al. (2003)	Ali et al. (2003)
Emotional stability (+)		Ali et al. (2003)	Ali et al. (2003)	Ali et al. (2003) Wiese (2013) van Erp et al. (2014)
Conscientiousness (+)				Wiese (2013)
Openness to experience (+)				Wiese (2013)
Extraversion (+)				Gupta et al (2012)
Social self-efficacy (+)			Shaffer & Harrison (2001)	
Gender-role ideology (+)				Gupta et al. (2012)
c. Knowledge/skills/abilities/others				
Language proficiency (+)		Shaffer & Harrison (2001) Mohr & Klein (2004)	Takeuchi et al. (2002) Mohr & Klein (2004) Takeuchi et al. (2007)	
Marital role value (+)				Bikos & Kocheleva (2012)
Marital role commitment (+)				Bikos & Kocheleva (2012)

Coping – problem focused (+)	Chen & Shaffer (2018)	Chen & Shaffer (2018)	Chen & Shaffer (2018)	
Coping – emotion focused (-)	Chen & Shaffer (2018)	Chen & Shaffer (2018)	Chen & Shaffer (2018)	
Self-initiated training (+)		Black & Gregersen (1991b)		
d. Attitudes/cognitions				
Adjustment – personal (+)		Shaffer & Harrison (2001) Herleman et al. (2008) Cole (2011) Chen & Shaffer (2018)	Shaffer & Harrison (2001) Herleman et al. (2008) Chen & Shaffer (2018)	Herleman et al. (2008)
Adjustment – interaction (+)	Shaffer & Harrison (2001) Herleman et al. (2008) Cole (2011) Chen & Shaffer (2018)		Black & Stephens (1989) Black & Gregersen (1991a) Black & Gregersen (1991b) Shaffer & Harrison (2001) Ali et al. (2003) Mohr & Klein (2004) Herleman et al. (2008) Lauring & Selmer (2015) Mohr & Klein (2004)	Ali et al. (2003) Herleman et al. (2008)

Table 11.1 (*cont.*)

	Partner personal adjustment	Partner interaction adjustment	Partner cultural adjustment	Partner well-being
Adjustment – cultural (+)	Shaffer & Harrison (2001) Herleman et al. (2008) Cole (2011) Chen & Shaffer (2018)	Black & Stephens (1989) Black & Gregersen (1991a) Black & Gregersen (1991b) Shaffer & Harrison (2001) Ali et al. (2003) Mohr & Klein (2004) Herleman et al. (2008) Cole (2011) Lauring & Selmer (2015) Chen & Shaffer (2018)		Ali et al. (2003) Herleman et al. (2008)
Adjustment – role (+)		Mohr & Klein (2004)	Mohr & Klein (2004)	
Well-being (+)	Herleman et al. (2008)	Ali et al. (2003) Herleman et al. (2008)	Ali et al. (2003) Herleman et al. (2008)	
Favourable opinion (+)	Simeon & Fujiu (2000)	Black & Stephens (1989) Black & Gregersen (1991b) Mohr & Klein (2004)		

Assignment duration certainty (+)	Shaffer & Harrison (2001)		Shaffer & Harrison (2001)	
Expectancy/familiarity (+)	Herleman et al. (2008)	Herleman et al. (2008)	Herleman et al. (2008)	Herleman et al. (2008)
Ibasho (+)	Herleman et al. (2008)	Herleman et al. (2008)	Herleman et al. (2008)	Herleman et al. (2008)
Perceived stress (-)	Herleman et al. (2008)		Herleman et al. (2008)	Herleman et al. (2008)
Depression (-)	Herleman et al. (2008)		Herleman et al. (2008)	Herleman et al. (2008)
Feeling different (-)			Lauring & Selmer (2015)	
Feeling welcome (+)		Lauring & Selmer (2015)	Lauring & Selmer (2015)	
Home pacing (-)				van der Zee et al. (2005)
General health (+)				van der Zee et al. (2005)
Voluntariness (+)				Wiese (2013)
Assignment withdrawal cognitions (-)				Wiese (2013)
2. Relational factors				
Social support (+)	Herleman et al. (2008)	Herleman et al. (2008)	Ramos et al. (2017)	Ramos et al. (2017) Wiese (2013)

Table 11.1 (*cont.*)

	Partner personal adjustment	Partner interaction adjustment	Partner cultural adjustment	Partner well-being
HCN support (+)	Shaffer & Harrison (2001)	Black & Gregersen (1991a) Shaffer & Harrison (2001)	Shaffer & Harrison (2001) Malek et al. (2015)	
Breadth of support (+)	Shaffer & Harrison (2001)	Shaffer & Harrison (2001)	Shaffer & Harrison (2001)	
Interactions with HCNs (+)		Black & Gregersen (1991b) Mohr & Klein (2004)		
Social network size (+)	Shaffer & Harrison (2001)	Shaffer & Harrison (2001)	Shaffer & Harrison (2001)	
3. *Organisational factors*				
Support from the company (+)	Simeon & Fujiu (2000)		Malek et al. (2015)	Ali et al. (2003) McNulty (2012) Gupta et al (2012)
Cross-cultural training (-)		Black & Gregersen (1991b)	Black & Gregersen (1991a)	
Cross-cultural training (+)				Gupta et al. (2012)
Pre-move visit (-)		Black & Gregersen (1991b)	Black & Gregersen (1991b)	
Sought spouse opinion (+)		Black & Gregersen (1991b)	Black & Gregersen (1991b)	
Employment assistance (+)		Cole (2011)		

Value of assistance (+)		Cole (2011)		
4. Assignment factors				
Cultural novelty (-)	Shaffer & Harrison (2001) Chen & Shaffer (2018)	Black & Gregersen (1991b) Shaffer & Harrison (2001) Chen & Shaffer (2018)	Black & Gregersen (1991b) Shaffer & Harrison (2001) Mohr & Klein (2004)	Gupta et al (2012)
Living conditions (+)	Shaffer & Harrison (2001)	Black & Gregersen (1991b) Shaffer & Harrison (2001)	Black & Gregersen (1991b)	
Expatriate variables				
1. Personal factors				
Education (+)			Takeuchi et al. (2007)	
Adjustment – work (+)		Black & Stephens (1989) Black & Gregersen (1991)	Black & Stephens (1989) Black & Gregersen (1991) Takeuchi et al. (2002)	Shaffer & Harrison (1998) Bhaskar-Shrinivas et al. (2005)
Adjustment – interaction (+)	Shaffer & Harrison (1998)	Black & Stephens (1989) Black & Gregersen (1991)	Black & Stephens (1989) Black & Gregersen (1991)	Shaffer & Harrison (1998) Bhaskar-Shrinivas et al. (2005)

Table 11.1 (*cont.*)

	Partner personal adjustment	Partner interaction adjustment	Partner cultural adjustment	Partner well-being
Adjustment – cultural (+)	Shaffer & Harrison (1998)	Black & Stephens (1989) Black & Gregersen (1991)	Black & Stephens (1989) Black & Gregersen (1991) Takeuchi et al. (2002) Takeuchi et al. (2007)	Shaffer & Harrison (1998) Bhaskar-Shrinivas et al. (2005)
Adjustment – overall (+)	Shaffer & Harrison (1998) Shaffer & Harrison (2001) Chen & Shaffer (2018)	Shaffer & Harrison (2001) Chen & Shaffer (2018)	Shaffer & Harrison (2001) Mohr & Klein (2004)	
Psychological well-being (+)				van der Zee et al. (2005) van Erp et al. (2011a) van Erp et al. (2011b) van Erp et al. (2014)
Work/job satisfaction (+)		Ali et al. (2003)	Ali et al. (2003) Takeuchi et al. (2002)	Ali et al. (2003)
Affective commitment (+)				Shaffer & Harrison (1998) van Erp et al. (2014)

Normative commitment (+)	Shaffer & Harrison (1998)			Shaffer & Harrison (1998)
Assignment withdrawal cognitions (-)	Shaffer & Harrison (1998)	Black & Stephens (1989)	Black & Stephens (1989) Takeuchi et al. (2002)	Shaffer & Harrison (1998)
Job performance (+)				van Erp et al. (2014)
2. Job/assignment factors				
Assignment completion % (+)				Shaffer & Harrison (1998)
Role conflict (-)			Black & Gregersen (1991a)	
Role ambiguity (-)			Takeuchi et al. (2002) Takeuchi et al. (2007)	
Conflict – work (-)				van Erp et al. (2011a)
Cultural novelty – expatriate (-)			Black & Stephens (1989) Black & Gregersen (1991a)	Shaffer & Harrison (1998)
Family variables				
1. Partner-rated				
Family cohesion (+)			Ali et al. (2003)	Ali et al. (2003)
Family adaptability (+)			Ali et al. (2003)	Ali et al. (2003)
Family communication (+)			Ali et al. (2003)	Ali et al. (2003)
Social support – family (+)			Ramos et al. (2017)	Gupta et al (2012) Ramos et al. (2017)
Social support – partner (+)			Ramos et al. (2017)	Ramos et al. (2017) van der Zee et al. (2005)

Table 11.1 (*cont.*)

	Partner personal adjustment	Partner interaction adjustment	Partner cultural adjustment	Partner well-being
Support – extended family (+)		Shaffer & Harrison (2001)		
Conflict with partner (-)				van Erp et al. (2011a) van Erp et al. (2011b)
Partner distributive justice (+)				van Erp et al. (2011a)
Partner interpersonal justice (+)				van Erp et al. (2011a)
Discussion with expatriate (+)		Black & Gregersen (1991b)		
2. *Expatriate-rated*				
Family/marital commitment (+)				
Nonwork satisfaction (+)	Shaffer & Harrison (1998)		Takeuchi et al. (2002)	Shaffer & Harrison (1998)
Home-work negative spillover (-)				van der Zee et al. (2005)
Conflict with partner (-)				van Erp et al. (2011b)

expatriates whose partners had high levels of personal adjustment were significantly more adjusted in terms of interacting with host country nationals and interfacing with the environment (Chen & Shaffer, 2018; Shaffer & Harrison, 1998, 2001). The influence of partner interaction and cultural adjustment is pervasive, with expatriates benefitting in terms of all three facets (work, interaction, and cultural) of expatriate adjustment when their partners were comfortable with the social and cultural aspects of the assignment (Black & Gregersen, 1991a; Black & Stephens, 1989). Later studies confirmed the strong link between partner cultural adjustment and expatriate work (Takeuchi, Yun, & Tesluk, 2002) and cultural adjustment (Takeuchi et al., 2002; Takeuchi et al., 2007). Mohr and Klein (2004) also reported crossover effects from partner cultural adjustment to expatriate overall adjustment.

Other variables have also been implicated in crossover effects, with expatriate partners facilitating expatriates' experiences on the assignment. For example, expatriate partner well-being has been associated with all three forms of expatriate adjustment (Bhaskar-Shrinivas et al., 2005; Shaffer & Harrison, 1998) and with expatriate psychological well-being (van der Zee et. al., 2005; van Erp et al., 2011a, 2011b, 2014). Various forms of partner adjustment/well-being have also been credited with enhancing a range of expatriate work attitudes, cognitions, and behaviours, including job satisfaction (Ali et al., 2003; Takeuchi et al., 2002), affective commitment (Shaffer & Harrison, 1998; van Erp et al., 2014), normative commitment (Shaffer & Harrison, 1998), assignment retention cognitions (Black & Stephens, 1989; Shaffer & Harrison, 1998; Takeuchi et al., 2002), and expatriate job performance (van Erp et al., 2014). For all of these expatriate outcomes, well-adjusted expatriate partners have proven to be an asset.

In addition to the empirical evidence for crossover effects between expatriates and their partners, scholars have also offered several theoretical arguments to explain the contagion effects that occur in expatriate-partner relationships. For example, the Job Demands-Resources model (Demerouti et al., 2001) is a heuristic model specifying how employees' health impairments, such as burnout, and motivation, such as engagement, are generated by two working conditions: job demands and job resources, separately. Spillover theory (Zedeck, 1992) proposes a permeable boundary existing between one's life roles (e.g., work and family domains), such that the factors from different domains may influence one another. Crossover theory explains how the experiences of one member of a dyad influence those of the other member (Westman, 2001). Integrating these three theories, Lazarova, Westman and Shaffer (2010) proposed a theoretical framework explaining how expatriates' work and family demands and resources determine their work and family role performance through expatriate, partner, and family adjustment and expatriate role engagement. Although the focus of this theoretical model is on expatriate performance, the authors offer two noteworthy contributions to the expatriate partner literature. One has to do with the development of family-role adjustment. Not only do expatriate partners (and expatriates) have to adjust to a foreign environment, they also must adjust to expanded and/or new roles within the family domain. The second contribution is that Lazarova and colleagues (2010) propose different crossover effects for expatriate partners' cultural and family-role adjustment. Specifically, they argue that partner cultural adjustment will cross over to expatriate family role and work role adjustment, and partner family role adjustment will cross over to expatriate family role adjustment. While this approach suggests a more complex interplay between expatriates and partners, to date there is no empirical support for the model.

Another possible avenue for understanding the dynamics between expatriates and their partners is Interdependence theory (Kelley & Thibaut, 1978; Thibaut & Kelley, 1959). According to this theory, interaction between two individuals is a function of two persons' needs, thoughts, and motives in relation to one another such that the (in) congruence of each partner's characteristics jointly influence their personal outcomes (Kelley et al., 2003). For example, it is possible that incongruent levels of partner and expatriate family role adjustment could result in greater levels of work-family conflict for the expatriate. Similarly, if both expatriate and partner are dissatisfied with their marriage, they may be more likely to get a divorce (see McNulty, 2015, for an interesting look at expatriate divorce).

11.2.2 Expatriate Partner Adjustment and Family Dynamics

Given the strong emphasis in the expatriate literature on both expatriate partner adjustment and the family as critical inputs to expatriate success, we were surprised that there was a paucity of research about the influence of partner adjustment on expatriate family dynamics. In fact, only one study reported positive relationships between both partner cultural adjustment and well-being and various family-level variables, including family cohesion, adaptability, and communication (Ali et al., 2003). Even at the individual level, just a few studies reported significant relationships between partner adjustment/well-being and partner-rated family variables such as social support (Gupta et al., 2012; Ramos et al., 2017, Shaffer & Harrison, 2001; van der Zee et al., 2005), partner conflict and justice (van Erp et al., 2011a; 2011b). Expatriate-rated family variables were even scarcer, but some studies did provide support for the beneficial influence of partner adjustment/well-being on expatriate nonwork satisfaction (Shaffer & Harrison, 1998; Takeuchi et al., 2002) and the adverse effects on expatriate negative home/work spill-over (van der Zee et al., 2005) and partner conflict (van Erp et al., 2011b).

One reason for the limited studies linking expatriate partner adjustment and family dynamics may be that researchers have argued for conceptualising the expatriate family as a holistic unit. For example, Caligiuri, Hyland, and Joshi (1998) theorised family dynamics based on an integration of the double ABCX model (Hill, 1949; McCubbin & Patterson, 1982), family systems theory (Minuchin, 1974), and spill-over theory (Zedeck, 1992). In particular, the Double ABCX model illustrates how the stressor elements (aA) yield family adaptation (xX) to these stressors through family adaptive resources (bB) and perceptions of coherence (cC). Family systems theory systematically views family as a unit and suggests that anticipated patterns of interaction that occur in a family system help to maintain the family's equilibrium and the healthy function of each family member. Based on these theories, Caligiuri and colleagues (1998) proposed and found a positive relationship between a set of family factors (cohesion, adaptability, and communication) and family adjustment to living abroad, with this relationship moderated by the family's perception of the global assignment. Further, Haslberger and Brewster (2008) applied the family adjustment and adaptation response (FAAR) model (Patterson,1988) and the theory of work adjustment (Dawis & Lofquist, 1984) to develop an environmental fit model of expatriate family adjustment as a function of the family's capabilities and needs or demands. The FAAR model delineates how the family system applies its capabilities to address its demands, thereby maintaining a balanced functioning of the family. The theory of work adjustment has been used to describe how the correspondence between person factors (e.g., skills or values) and environment factors (e.g., required skills or values) is associated with one's work consequences. While we support these more holistic models, we also encourage researchers to consider multi-level models that include individual family members as well as the family as a unit. In doing so, partner adjustment, as well as the adjustment of children and the expatriate could be incorporated into models of expatriate family adjustment and effective functioning.

Scholars have also suggested that organisations should recognise the importance of the expatriate family as a unit. Based on the theory of stakeholder salience (Mitchell, Agle, & Wood, 1997), which provides a theoretical understanding of who or what really matters to the organisation, Lämsä et al. (2017) proposed that the expatriate family should be considered as a stakeholder of the firm. Relocation for family members represents a tremendous shift in living circumstances, and this can be crucial to the family's adjustment and to expatriates' success. Lämsä and colleagues (2017) highlighted the need for a socially responsible relationship between the company and family to advance the effective functioning of the expatriate family. Again, we would encourage scholars and practitioners to adopt a multi-pronged approach and target the family as a whole, as well as its individual members, each of whom may have unique needs and considerations.

11.2.3 Under-researched Topics Associated with Partner Adjustment

In reflecting on our review of the partner adjustment literature, we noted three topics that we believe deserve greater attention. The first has to do with expatriate children. While the relationship between expatriate and partner adjustment has been well-established, we did not find any evidence that children's adjustment is associated with partner adjustment. Only one study, based on qualitative data from partners, suggested that children are a double-edged sword when it comes to partner adjustment (Mohr & Klein, 2004). On the one hand, children may complicate the partner's forays into the environment, resulting in reduced cultural adjustment. On the other hand, children may also be conduits facilitating interactions with others in the foreign environment, leading to greater interaction adjustment. In testing this in a quantitative study, however, Mohr and Klein (2004) detected no significant differences of any forms of partner adjustment between expatriate partners with or without children. This is similar with null findings from other studies (e.g., Shaffer & Harrison, 1998). It may be that the adjustment of children rather than just their presence is related to expatriate partner adjustment. Although surveying children is challenging, a couple of studies have begun to examine their adjustment (e.g., Rosenbusch & Cseh, 2012; van der Zee, et al., 2007). While researchers did not directly associate children's adjustment with that of the expatriate partner, they did find strong relationships between family characteristics, such as cohesion and flexibility, and children's adjustment. Insofar as it is likely that both children and partners are instrumental in facilitating the assignment success of both expatriates and families, we encourage more in-depth studies of expatriate children to understand their adjustment process as well as their influence on expatriate, partner, and family adjustment.

Another important under-researched topic has to do with the gender of expatriate partners. Of the studies we reviewed, only one reported a significant relationship between gender and partner cultural adjustment, with female partners better adjusted than male partners (Cole, 2011). With the increasing numbers of female expatriates, there is a need to focus also on a growing group of male partners (Haslberger & Brewster, 2008). Although male partners have received much less attention in terms of their difficulties abroad (Selmer & Leung, 2003), some researchers have suggested adding gender dynamics into studies of both expatriates and their trailing partners (e.g., Harris, 2004; Linehan, 2006). One possible theoretical approach to understanding similarities and differences in the adjustment of female and male partners is identity theory (Stryker, 1986). For example, Tharenou (2010) used this theory to argue that the combination of multiple identities – career identity, family identity, and cultural identity – influences expatriation. Similarly, differences in identity (re)formation for female and male expatriate partners could also explain differences in their successful navigation of a foreign environment and their subsequent adjustment.

A final topic that we advocate needs more research attention has to do with organisational support practices and mechanisms that will facilitate expatriate partner adjustment. While company support has been associated with enhanced partner personal (Simeon & Fujiu, 2000) and cultural (Malek, Budhwar, & Reiche, 2015) adjustment, as well as partner well-being (Ali et al., 2003; Gupta et al., 2012;

McNulty, 2012), there is no indication that such support facilitates partner interaction adjustment. Perhaps organisations do not offer training that targets the development and maintenance of effective relationships with host country nationals, or such relationships require more time than is generally allotted to expatriate assignments. Regarding cross-cultural training, the findings are mixed, with Black and Gregersen (1991b) reporting a negative relationship between cross-cultural training and partner cultural adjustment and Gupta et al. (2012) suggesting that such training will facilitate partner well-being. In looking at employment assistance offered by companies and the value of that assistance, Cole (2011) found that these were both related to partner interaction adjustment. Insofar as training and organisational support help to reduce the uncertainty and stress of adjusting to a foreign culture, organisations that offer assistance to expatriate partners will better ensure a positive experience and enhanced adjustment. As Webb (1996) noted, the inclusion of all family members in cross-cultural training is vital. In particular, specific training programmes need to be developed for the unique challenges faced by expatriate partners (e.g., how to get working permit and develop personal career in the other country) and children (e.g., education-related issues).

11.3 Where Do Researchers Go from Here?

Based upon our review of the expatriate partner literature, we propose four directions for future research. First, we encourage scholars to identify the specific mechanisms and boundary conditions that explain the influence of partner adjustment on expatriates' work and nonwork outcomes. Although we noted consistent positive relationships between partner adjustment and expatriates' work performance and adjustment, more empirical evidence is needed to identify the distinct psychological and emotional mechanisms linking these crossover effects (Lazarova et al., 2010). Future research could apply additional theoretical foundations to elucidate the intricate processes linking partners' cross-cultural experiences and expatriates' adjustment and work consequences. For example, the work-home resources model (Ten Brummelhuis & Bakker, 2012), which illustrates how work and home resources influence each other through different theoretical paths, may offer a suitable theoretical framework that facilities our understanding of how partners' adjustment contributes to expatriates' success in their international assignments.

Second, we suggest that the role of expatriate children is a key factor for expatriate scholars to examine. As indicated, research into how children's adjustment determines expatriates' adjustment or work performance is still lacking. Future researchers should pay more attention to children's adjustment and explore the two research questions echoed in the qualitative findings of Mohr and Klein (2004): why is children's adjustment a double-edged sword when it comes to expatriate partners' adjustment? How could we advance the positive effects and buffer the negative effects of children's adjustment in this context? Further, when also considering expatriates' adjustment, we could raise another question: how does the adjustment of expatriates, their partners, and their children intertwine with each other and lead to different positive and negative outcomes for the expatriate family as a whole, as well as for individual family members? Examining these questions theoretically and empirically will enrich the literature and clarify the role of children more thoroughly in global families.

A third future direction is to compare the experiences of male and female expatriates' partners. Future researchers could apply gender-related theories to specify the common challenges for both genders of expatriate partners as well as the gender-specific challenges. Identifying gender-specific challenges is especially critical, as prior research has suggested these differences are significant and calls for more research to address this issue (e.g., Harris, 2004; Linehan, 2006; Selmer & Leung, 2003). Therefore, researchers and practitioners should not neglect the gender-related issues for partners and, in fact, we encourage them to consider these issues across all phases of the assignment, including repatriation.

Fourth, we suggest that future studies should focus more on the family level and examine the well-being, functioning or challenges of the family as a whole. This approach will not only expand our understanding of the global family but it will also contribute to the literature by integrating individual- and family-level factors. We also want to highlight that scholars need to categorise expatriate family well-being in terms of their relocation status. That is, the demands, needed resources, and work and family outcomes for co-located and separated families could be different. For example, families that relocate together on an assignment may need more cross-cultural training during the different stages of expatriation and direct assistance for settling down in the host country. Partners who do not relocate with the expatriate may also benefit from additional support and training so the partner is cognisant of what the expatriate is experiencing, and they have resources that will help them cope with the absence of their partner.

11.4 What Can Organisations Do To Help Expatriate Partners and Families Thrive?

Our review of expatriate partners hints at several practical implications for organisations. First, research confirms the crossover effects of partners' adjustment and well-being on expatriates' adjustment, well-being, job satisfaction and turnover intentions (Chen & Shaffer, 2018; Shaffer & Harrison, 1998). Thus, organisations should invest in supporting expatriate partners to ensure that they effectively adjust to all aspects of the international assignment. Understanding and personalising the support that partners may need is of critical importance, as every situation is different. Some partners are experiencing role changes by quitting jobs in the home country and taking on full responsibility for the family while on assignment; others may be struggling with elder care responsibilities and/or special needs children. By taking into consideration the individual needs of expatriate partners, organisations will be able to better facilitate partners' adjustment and success in living and even possibly working in the foreign country. Advantages will accrue to the organisations in that the positive experiences of expatriate partners will cross over to expatriates and facilitate their satisfaction, productivity, and retention on the assignment and with the organisation.

Second, we encourage organisations to consider the gender differences of expatriate partners when initiating partner and family support programmes. Although the research findings are scarce, our review demonstrates that male and female partners may encounter different gender-related challenges in the host country. For example, male partners may have specific needs when adjusting to living, and possibly working, in another country. This is especially the case when male partners are stay-at-home-parents during the assignment as they may suffer an identity crisis and experience some unique challenges as a minority among expatriate partners (who are mostly female). Organisations need to address these gender-related difficulties of expatriate partners and launch unique workshops, policies, support packages, and even consulting support to ensure that expatriate partners are receiving the right support at the right time. In doing so, organisations are highly likely to help expatriate partners face the challenges of living in a foreign culture, increase their levels of adjustment and further benefit expatriates' adjustment and well-being.

Third, we suggest that organisations take all stakeholders into consideration including the partner and children who relocate with the expatriate as well as extended family members who remain at home but may need extra care. This emphasis on the entire family is important, as organisations will actively evaluate the family's needs as a whole, as well as the specific support that each stakeholder in the family may request or need. Taking the whole family into consideration throughout the initiation and implementation of expatriate family support programmes will improve considerably the efficiency and effectiveness of the assistance, thereby the whole family's functioning and well-being will be enhanced. Consequently, organisations will facilitate positive and successful work and personal experiences for expatriates and their families.

11.5 Conclusions

Based on our review of the expatriate partner adjustment literature, it is clear that expatriate partners are a critical resource in facilitating the success of expatriate assignments. However, despite more than three decades of research on expatriate partner adjustment, there is still much that we do not know about this phenomenon. In addition to further examining various aspects of expatriate partner adjustment, such as identities, gender, and career-related issues, it is also time to focus attention on a wider range of stakeholders in the expatriate process. We agree with scholars who have advocated the adoption of a more holistic approach towards understanding the family, and we encourage researchers to consider all family members, including children, in studies of expatriate family adjustment and functioning.

Because the vast majority of research on the partners and families of global employees focuses on expatriates and the lack of relevant research for the partners of other forms of global employees, we limited our review to the expatriate population. However, with increasing forms of global employees (Shaffer et al., 2012), each of which faces unique challenges regarding families, we also encourage researchers to investigate the partners and other family members of global employees, such as international business travellers and short-term assignees (see Chapter 7). It seems that the partners, and other family members, of these more recent types of global employees have become the new 'forgotten families' of international human resource research and practice.

References

Ali, A., Van der Zee, K. & Sanders, G. 2003. Determinants of intercultural adjustment among expatriate spouses. *International Journal of Intercultural Relations*, 27: 563–580.

Bhaskar-Shrinivas, P., Harrison, D. A., Shaffer, M. & Luk, D. M. 2005. Input-based and time-based models of international adjustment: meta-analytic evidence and theoretical extensions. *Academy of Management Journal*, 48: 257–281.

Bikos, L. H. & Kocheleva, J. 2012. Life role salience dimensions and mental health outcomes among female expatriate spouses in Turkey. *Journal of Career Development*, 40: 107–126.

Black, J.S. & Gregersen, H. B. 1991a. Antecedents to cross-cultural adjustment for expatriates in Pacific Rim assignments. *Human Relations*, 44(5): 497–515.

Black, J. S. & Gregersen, H. B. 1991b. The other half of the picture: antecedents of spouse cross-cultural adjustment. *Journal of International Business Studies*, 22: 461–77.

Black, J. S. Mendenhall, M, & Oddou, G. 1991. Toward a comprehensive model of international adjustment: an integration of multiple theoretical perspectives. *Academy of Management Review*, 16(2): 291–317.

Black, J. S. & Stephens, G. K. 1989. The influence of the spouse on American expatriate adjustment and intent to stay in Pacific Rim overseas assignments. *Journal of Management*, 15: 529–544.

Brookfield Global Relocation Services. 2016. *2015 Global Mobility Trends Survey*. New York, NY: Brookfield.

Caligiuri, P. M., Hyland, M. M. & Joshi, A. 1998. Families on global assignments: applying work/family theories abroad. *Current Topics in Management*, 3(3): 313–328.

Caligiuri, P. M., Hyland, M. M., Joshi, A. & Bross, A. S. 1998. Testing a theoretical model for examining the relationship between family adjustment and expatriates' work adjustment. *Journal of Applied Psychology*, 83(4): 598–614.

Chen, Y-P., Shaffer, M. 2018. The influence of expatriate spouses' coping strategies on expatriate and spouse adjustment: an interdependence perspective. *Journal of Global Mobility*, 6: 20–39.

Cole, N. 2011. Managing global talent: solving the spousal adjustment problem. *International Journal of Human Resource Management*, 22: 1504–1530.

Dawis, R. V. & Lofquist, L. H. 1984. *A Psychological Theory of Work Adjustment: An individual-differences model and its applications.* University of Minnesota Press.

Demerouti, E., Bakker, A. B., Nachreiner, F., & Schaufeli, W. B. 2001. The job demands-resources model of burnout. *Journal of Applied Psychology*, 86(3): 499–512.

Erogul, M. S. & Rahman, A. 2017. The impact of family adjustment in expatriate success. *Journal of International Business and Economy*, 18 (1): 1–23.

Goede, J. & Berg, N. 2018. The family in the center of international assignments: a systematic review and future research agenda. *Managerial Review Quarterly*, 68: 77–102.

Gupta, R., Banerjee, P., & Gaur, J. 2012. Exploring the role of the spouse in expatriate failure: a grounded theory-based investigation of expatriate spouse adjustment issues from India. *International Journal of Human Resource Management*, 23: 3559–3577.

Harris, H. 2004. Global careers: work-life issues and the adjustment of women international managers. *Journal of Management Development*, 23(9): 818–832.

Harrison, D. A., Shaffer, M. A., & Bhaskar-Shrinivas, P. 2004. Going places: roads more and less traveled in research on expatriate experiences. *Research in Personnel and Human Resources Management*, 22: 203–252.

Haslberger, A. & Brewster, C. 2008. The expatriate family: an international perspective. *Journal of Managerial Psychology*, 23(3): 324–346.

Herleman, H. A., Britt, T. W., & Hashima, P. Y. 2008. Ibasho and the adjustment, satisfaction, and well-being of expatriate spouses. *International Journal of Intercultural Relations*, 32: 282–299.

Hill, R. 1949. *Families under Stress*. New York: Harper.

Kelley, H. H., Holmes, J. G., Kerr, N. L., Reis, H. T., Rusbult, C. E., & Van Lange, P. A. M. 2003. *An Atlas of Interpersonal Situations*. New York, NY: Cambridge.

Kelley, H. H. & Thibaut, J. W. 1978. *Interpersonal Relations: A theory of interdependence*. New York: Wiley.

Kraimer, M., Bolino, M., & Mead, B. 2016. Themes in expatriate and repatriate research over four decades: what do we know and what do we still need to learn? *The Annual Review of Organisational Psychology and Organisational Behavior*, 3: 83–109.

Lämsä, A. M., Heikkinen, S., Smith, M., & Tornikoski, C. 2017. The expatriate's family as a stakeholder of the firm: a responsibility viewpoint. *International Journal of Human Resource Management*, 28 (20): 2916–2935.

Lauring, J. & Selmer, J. 2015. Adjustment of spouses of self-initiated expatriates: feeling different vs. feeling welcome. In L. Mäkelä & V. Suutari (eds.), *Work and Family Interface in the International Career Context*: 117–135. Springer, Cham.

Lazarova, M., Westman, M., & Shaffer, M. A. 2010. Elucidating the positive side of the work-family interface on international assignments: a model of expatriate work and family performance. *Academy of Management Review*, 35(1): 93–117.

Linehan, M. 2006. Women in international management, in H. Scullion & D. Collings (eds.), *Global Staffing*: 178–195. London: Routledge.

Malek, M. A., Budhwar, P., & Reiche, B. S. 2015. Sources of support and expatriation: a multiple stakeholder perspective of expatriate adjustment and performance in Malaysia. *International Journal of Human Resource Management*, 26: 258–276.

McCubbin, H. L. & Patterson, J. M. 1982. Family adaptation to crises. In H. L. McCubbin, E. Cauble, & J. M. Patterson (eds.), *Family Stress, Coping, and Social Support*: 26–47. Springfield, IL: Charles C. Thomas.

McNulty, Y. 2012. 'Being dumped in to sink or swim': an empirical study of organisational support for the trailing spouse. *Human Resource Development International*, 15: 417–434.

McNulty, Y. 2015. Till stress do us part: the causes and consequences of expatriate divorce. *Journal of Global Mobility*, 3: 106–136.

Minuchin, S. 1974. *Families and Family Therapy*. Cambridge: Harvard University Press.

Mitchell, R. K., Agle, B. R., & Wood, D. J. 1997. Toward a theory of stakeholder identification and salience: defining the principle of who and what really counts. *Academy of Management Review*, 22(4): 853–886.

Mohr, A. T. & Klein, S. 2004. Exploring the adjustment of American expatriate spouses in Germany. *International Journal of Human Resource Management*, 15: 1189–1206.

Patterson, J. M. 1988. Families experiencing stress: I. The Family Adjustment and Adaptation Response Model: II. Applying the FAAR Model to health-related issues for intervention and research. *Family Systems Medicine*, 6(2): 202–237.

Ramos, H. M. L., Mustafa, M., & Haddad, A. R. 2017. Social support and expatriate spouses' wellbeing: the mediating role of cross-cultural adjustment. *International Journal of Employment Studies*, 25: 6–24.

Rosenbusch, K. & Cseh, M. 2012. The cross-cultural adjustment process of expatriate families in a multinational organisation: a family system theory perspective. *Human Resource Development International*, 15: 61–77.

Selmer, J. & Leung, A. S. 2003. Provision and adequacy of corporate support to male expatriate spouses: an exploratory study. *Personnel Review*, 32 (1): 9–21.

Shaffer, M. A. & Harrison, D. A. 1998. Expatriates' psychological withdrawal from international assignments: work, nonwork, and family influences. *Personnel Psychology*, 51: 87–118.

Shaffer, M. A. & Harrison, D. A. 2001. Forgotten partners of international assignments: development and test of a model of spouse adjustment. *Journal of Applied Psychology*, 86(2): 238–54.

Shaffer, M. A., Kraimer, M. L., Chen, Y. P., & Bolino, M. C. 2012. Choices, challenges, and career consequences of global work experiences: a review and future agenda. *Journal of Management*, 38(4): 1282–1327.

Simeon, R. & Fujiu, K. 2000. Cross-cultural adjustment strategies of Japanese spouses in Silicon Valley. *Employee Relations*, 22: 594–611.

Sterle, M. F., Fontaine, J. R. J., de Mol, J., & Verhofstadt, L. L. 2018. Expatriate family adjustment: an overview of empirical evidence on challenges and resources. *Frontiers in Psychology*, 9: 1–12.

Stryker, S. 1986. Identity theory: developments and extensions. In K. Yardley & T. Honess (eds.), *Self and Identity*: 89–104. New York: Wiley.

Suutari, V. & Brewster, C. 2000. Making their own way: international experience through self-initiated foreign assignments. *Journal of World Business*, 35: 417–136.

Ten Brummelhuis, L. L. & Bakker, A. B. 2012. A resource perspective on the work–home interface: the work–home resources model. *American Psychologist*, 67(7): 545–556.

Takeuchi, R., Lepak, D. P., Marinova, S. V., & Yun, S. 2007. Nonlinear influences of stressors on general adjustment: the case of Japanese expatriates and their spouses. *Journal of International Business Studies*, 38: 928–943.

Takeuchi, R., Yun, S., & Tesluk, P. E. 2002. An examination of crossover and spillover effects of spousal and expatriate cross-cultural adjustment on expatriate outcomes. *Journal of Applied Psychology*, 87: 655–66.

Tharenou, P. 2010. Identity and global mobility. In S. Carr (ed.), *The Psychology of Global Mobility*: 105–123. Springer, New York.

Thibaut, J. W. & Kelley, H. H. 1959. *The Social Psychology of Groups*. New York: Wiley.

Van der Zee, K. I., Ali, A. J., & Haaksma, I. 2007. Determinants of effective coping with cultural transition among expatriate children and adolescents. *Anxiety, Stress, & Coping*, 20: 25–45.

Van der Zee, K. I., Ali, A. J., & Salome, E. 2005. Role interference and subjective well-being among expatriate families. *European Journal of Work and Organisational Psychology*, 14: 239–262.

Van Erp, K. J. P. M., Giebels, E., van der Zee, K. I., & van Duijn, M. A. J. 2011a. Expatriate adjustment: the role of justice and conflict in intimate relationships. *Personal Relationships*, 18: 58–78.

Van Erp, K. J. P. M., Giebels, E., van der Zee, K. I., & van Duijn, M. A. J. 2011b. Let it be: expatriate couples' adjustment and the upside of avoiding conflicts. *Anxiety, Stress, & Coping*, 24: 539–560.

Van Erp, K. J. P. M., van der Zee, K. I., Giebels, E., & Duijn, M. A. J. 2014. *European Journal of Work and Organisational Psychology*, 23: 706–728.

Webb, A. 1996. The expatriate experience: implications for career success. *Career Development International*, 1(5): 38–44.

Westman, M. 2001. Stress and strain crossover. *Human Relations*, 54: 557–591.

Wiese, D. L. 2013. Psychological health of expatriate spouses: a neglected factor in international relocation. *Asian Journal of Counselling*, 20: 1–31.

Zedeck, S. 1992. Introduction: exploring the domain of work/family concerns. In S. Zedeck (ed.), *Work, Families, and Organisations*: 1–32. San Francisco: Jossey Bass.

12 *Roles and Challenges for Global Mobility Departments*

MICHAEL DICKMANN

12.1 Introduction

This chapter explores the pressures that global mobility (GM) is facing, provides insights into the roles of GM departments and develops a refined GM model to successfully cope with mobility challenges. Notwithstanding some of the limitations that diverse contexts, diverging managerial objectives, lacking GM capabilities, and implementation difficulties present, it can be argued that smart, agile, flawless, and efficient GM work (SAFE GM) is at the core of a successful GM department. Smart organizational development and talent management; Agile approaches to embrace a multitude of GM challenges successfully; Flawless design of programme management and compliance approaches; and Efficient ways to structure GM rewards, are leading to a professionalization of global mobility work. Some of the drawbacks to this practice-focussed, managerial approach are explored towards the end of the chapter. Basing the discussion on the general literature on HR roles, and in particular on the ideas of David Ulrich (1997, 1998) it can be held that enacting this SAFE GM framework will strengthen the position of GM departments in their organizations. This chapter addresses the following questions: Why and how do we need to rethink GM to enable it to master its future? What roles do GM professionals enact to refine their work and to make working abroad more attractive?

12.2 HR Department Roles and Their Link to Global Mobility

Global Mobility in its many forms (Baruch, Dickmann, Altman & Bournois, 2013) is growing strongly and there is a substantial interest in exploring the broad phenomena associated with it (McNulty & Selmer, 2017). Interest has focused on individuals and organizations and the context that globally mobile individuals such as company-sponsored and self-initiated assignees are embedded in (Bonache, Brewster & Suutari, 2001; Froese & Peltokorpi, 2013; Suutari & Brewster, 2000). It has also explored macro-level issues such as institutions or macro-talent management (Andresen, Al Ariss & Walther, 2013; Vaiman et al., 2019). Within organizations, research has often focussed on the journey that assignees undertake which has been charted as the expatriate cycle (Harris, Brewster & Sparrow, 2003). Fundamentally, however, the focus is often on how to manage assignees and is reflected in work concentrating on the selection of expatriates (Harris & Brewster, 1999; Caligiuri, 2013), global talent management (Collings, Scullion & Caligiuri, 2018), cultural adjustment (Black & Gregersen, 1991; Davies, Kraeh & Froese, 2015; Haslberger, Brewster & Hippler, 2013), their career journey and management (Andresen et al., 2013; Dickmann, Suutari & Wurtz, 2018), and performance management (Engle, Dowling & Festing, 2008), or repatriation (Lazarova & Cerdin, 2007). However, the roles of global mobility departments have been relatively neglected.

While we have only emerging insights into the structures and roles of GM departments, these are highly interlinked with broad human resource (HR) activities within the organization. There is a long-standing interest in exploring what HR functions do and what roles they have (Beer et al., 1984). It has long been argued that the value added by an HR function depends on the complexity of interaction. Hesketh (2006) argues that these include (in order of diminishing value add): first, corporate governance services (HR strategy, employment relations, strategic workforce planning); second, professional and advisory services (learning management, change management consulting, global mobility); third, employment services (recruitment and selection, training administration); and fourth, more transactional services (payroll administration, relocation services, employment data changes). The reader will notice that GM activities are part of the overall remit of HRM and are predominantly located in the professional and advisory as well as transactional service categories.

One of the most influential authors with respect to the roles and structures of HR departments is David Ulrich. His argument is rooted in the basic observation that all functions in an organization strive to strengthen the competitive position of it. Given the rapid changes in the competitive contexts of firms, it is argued that human capital has become increasingly important to create valuable, non-substitutional, difficult to copy and rare resources (Ambrosini & Bowman, 2009; Barney & Clark, 2007; Sparrow et al., 2010). Therefore, the function of HR, its roles and how it is organized, is crucial for the competitive position of a firm (Becker et al., 1997, Wright, Dunford & Snell, 2001). Ulrich (1998) holds that HR is the key to sustainable competitive advantage.

In particular, Ulrich's ideas on the roles of HR departments have found enthusiastic followers amongst practitioners and have shaped the structural organization of the people function in many firms (Friedman, 2007; CIPD, 2007; Brockbank & Ulrich, 2009). In his writing Ulrich had made a strong case about the dangers of HR working as administrators and showing little leadership in supporting the achievement of strategic business objectives. The call for refocussing HR's operating model towards a model of business partnering has led to many attempts by HR professionals to increase their agility and value to the business. It has also meant that HR experts had to rethink the competencies needed to be successful in their role and to support their employer more effectively (Brockbank & Ulrich, 2009; Caldwell, 2008; Ulrich, 1998).

So what does the 'Ulrich Model' entail? In general, it calls for a reorientation towards closer cooperation with other business functions and a concentration on business-relevant outcomes. This means that HR needs to move out of its cocoon where it concentrated on administrative delivery and people results. The argument is driven by the insight that the value of pure administrative activities is often seen as low (Sparrow et al., 2010) and that errors in non-complex activities can easily lead to a disregard of the function and a loss in reputation. Instead, HR professionals need to understand the more important, often strategic, goals of the organization and develop approaches of how to support the business in achieving these (Brockbank & Ulrich, 2009). In order to do so, Ulrich (1997) initially outlined four roles for HR functions.

Strategic Partner. This role consists of understanding the company's key strategic objectives and how HR can help to achieve them. Thus, HR needs to be aligned to the business strategy in order to acquire,

Figure 12.1 The original Ulrich model, Ulrich, 1997 p. 24

develop, and sustain the right human resource capabilities. Thus, HR professionals need to have the competencies required to diagnose their firm's competitive environment. Based on this diagnosis HR should create and sustain adequate HR policies and practices that support organizational priorities (Ulrich, 1997). If HR leaders manage to do this they are often seen to 'earn a seat at the top table'.

Change Agent. This role consists of building capacity for change in the firm. It is argued that all employees need to accept the necessity of change in highly dynamic industries where the competitive pressures are intense and new developments occur almost on a daily basis. HR professionals need to understand how successful change is delivered, should have the capability to help change leaders to devise communication strategies, should be able to identify change resistance and to deal with change resistors. In addition, they should aim to build trust in order to help change agents to implement change plans successfully (Ulrich, 1997). This role consists of understanding good change management, preparing the organization for change and working together with change leaders.

Employee Champion. This role aims to enhance employee engagement, to build staff capability and to plan work to give individuals the opportunity to use their knowledge and skills. While the role of employee champion is implicitly modelled on the ability, motivation, and opportunity (AMO) framework, it necessitates identifying employee grievances and to deal with these. Ulrich (1997) argues that HR functions need to actively engage with employees. Motivated, committed, and capable individuals are seen to be a cornerstone of dynamic capabilities which would achieve sustained competitive advantage.

Administrative Expert. This role consists of being an efficient and effective administrator, either of internal administrative processes or as the manager of outsourcing relationships. It is clear that HR departments undertake a large number of administrative responsibilities (Dickmann & Tyson, 2005). These should be analysed and, if needed, improved or even totally re-engineered in order to reduce costs and increase administrative effectiveness (Ulrich, 1997).

The drive to decrease administrative costs has often led to the establishment of shared service centres and the development of HR structures that consist of three parts. The first part of this 'three-legged stool' is shared service centres. Shared services deal with many administrative HR issues and are highly process-driven. Given that certain administrative tasks can be clearly defined and that task specialization and information-technology support is normally able to keep costs low, firms have mostly opted to centralize these in shared service centres. However, one of the disadvantages of this structure is that HR personnel working in these centres find it hard to acquire general HR skills and insights and, subsequently, are often faced with career barriers when they want to progress to work on other HR activities (Hird, Sparrow & Marsh, 2010: 32–42). The second leg consists of HR professionals working as HR business partners. Business partners have a primary function to aid the organization in the achievement of its objective and their job description and activities most often include both strategic partner and change agent roles. They are distributed across the organization as sub-units, such as production plants, where they also need HR partnering services. The third leg consists of units that develop specialized HR approaches and tools such as performance management, career and training & development systems. These systems normally benefit from being based on company-wide competency frameworks. These HR professionals are often located in centres of excellence and expertise where they work on capability management (Sparrow et al., 2010, p. 27).

In subsequent years, Ulrich, together with other co-authors such as Brockbank, has further developed this model and has distinguished five reconfigured roles: strategic partner, functional expert, human capital developer, employee advocate, and HR leader (Ulrich & Brockbank,

2005). While this makes much sense for the HR function overall (it is larger and has more need for leadership and development of HR professionals), the roles are either more highly integrated or more clearly delineated – the HR leader role extends into the GM function and may to some extent supersede or supplicate the role of the GM leader. This is particularly the case in terms of development and career decisions within the whole HR team. For the GM field, however, there continues to be a strong relevance of distinguishing strategic and operational dimensions as well as people and process areas. Despite some of the criticism in terms of how to successfully design and implement HR roles based on Ulrich' ideas (Sparrow et al., 2010), the three-legged stool and other business outcome oriented HR approaches are highly popular (CIPD, 2007). How the original Ulrich model has been an inspiration in the realm of GM is outlined below.

I will consider the future of global mobility and the necessary changes using three perspectives. First, the mobility functions as being a substantial partner in creating organizational and international value. Second, I explore implications arising from the broader company context and its stakeholders. These two perspectives are closely aligned to Ulrich's arguments. Third, I want to concentrate on the drivers of global value, the employees and their varying interests and capabilities. Overall, therefore, the perspectives on GM loosely mirror the thrust of the resource-based view of the firm (Barney, 1991) and how it seeks to achieve sustainable competitive advantage through dynamic capabilities (Barney, 2001; Bowman & Ambrosini, 2000).

Information with respect to the roles of GM departments are sparse. Some authors imply roles for GM departments through describing some of the activities that these professionals undertake. The expatriate cycle (Harris et al., 2003) delivers a temporal perspective on expatriate management, depicting an assigned expatriates' journey starting before departure and ending after the assignee returns 'home' or moves to another destination. Dickmann and Baruch (2011) have further refined the expatriation cycle by strengthening the strategic planning and assessment elements of the GM programme as well as integrating the mutual dependency perspective called for by Larsen (2004). Thus, they depict individual and organizational expatriation phases and their interlinkages (see Figure 12.2).

Figure 12.2's strengths lie in depicting the expatriation journey and some of the key, interrelated activities associated with the various

Figure 12.2 A strategic, long-term, and interactive perspective on international work activities
Source: based on Dickmann, 2017.

phases. While it covers a multitude of activities it necessarily has to focus on some of the key expatriation management policies and practices. Crucially, it only indicates that these activities (should) occur but rarely specifies the associated GM goals and their link to wider organizational objectives. Thus, a more nuanced framework of the roles of GM departments and their associated goals is needed.

12.3 GM Department at Cross-Roads: Emerging GM Roles and Their Key Aims

Because the available information in the academic literature is so limited, much of the discussion below is based on data and insights from a large community of GM professionals (https://theresforum .com/)[1]. At the time of writing, The RES Forum was a network of 740 corporations in over 40 countries. It had approximately 1500 members who were all GM professionals, predominantly Head of GM or Head of Global Rewards. The research amongst the RES Forum member has found that in most multinational corporations (MNCs) mobility work is strongly processed and due diligence oriented to the detriment of strategic work or talent management (RES Forum, 2017). In addition, activities that concentrate on understanding the drivers and experiences of expatriation candidates were also rare (RES Forum, 2018). In essence, GM experts seem to concentrate on operational expatriation processes aiming for streamlining these activities to achieve cost savings. In addition, they are fulfilling some strategic work, for instance when GM experts liaise with other functions in relation to the underlying corporate motivations for expatriation (Edström & Galbraith, 1977). However, strategic work elements tend to be underrepresented and certainly GM leaders want to increase these over time (RES Forum, 2018). In addition, the GM people dimension could also be strengthened. While GM staffs are often involved in the selection of international assignees, this continues to be an area where they could become more evidence-guided and more sophisticated (Harris & Brewster, 1999; Caligiuri, 2013; Dowling, Festing, & Engle 2013). Strengthening the strategic and people aspects of GM work could make GM departments more effective and could lead to a higher degree of professionalization. These are some of the roles that would give GM departments a broader, yet more focused purpose, allow it to strengthen the experience of assignees and add to the value creation of GM work. In essence, this would mean that GM departments find themselves in a similar situation as HR departments in the past – they may benefit from analysing the original Ulrich ideas, adapting them to the GM context and their purpose and from implementing these to become more strategic and people-oriented. In short, GM departments are at cross-roads where they need to rethink global mobility.

[1] This section is partially based on The RES Forum Annual Report 2018, especially Chapter 1 by M.Dickmann and C. Debner "Agile Global Mobility: Living the Purpose and Increasing Value".

What do these insights mean in broad terms and how can global mobility be advanced to make it fit for the future? Rethinking global mobility is driven by some key trends and drivers. In the following section I reflect on four fundamental GM roles.

12.3.1 Role 1: Agile Global Mobility Created Through Strategic Advice

GM leaders need to develop agility to align and support their business and HR strategies, to develop value, and to adapt quickly to changing organizational needs. Technological advances, automation, artificial intelligence and robots, the need for new skill sets and dynamic operating models are all expressions of the rapid changes in the business environment (Bader, 2019). These developments make it necessary to find feasible ways to adapt to them and to harness the opportunities for the organization. Constantly changing requirements, which are already varying among different stakeholders, make it necessary to provide flexibility for assignments.

The key value of GM is related to broader business and people management objectives (Dowling, Festing & Engle, 2013; Edstöm & Galbraith, 1977). On a highly strategic level, aligning GM to business and HR strategies in order to enable and support them is highly important. These often embody key objectives such as the control of the business units, cultural integration across borders, knowledge creation, transfer and application, or enabling certain work activities through filling positions. To successfully advance the agility and flexibility of international work in organizations, GM professionals need to fill the role of strategic advisor and to understand the manifold ramifications of their organization's strategy and the diverse GM avenues that could be pursued to realize their MNC's ambition. Figure 12.3 gives an overview of the breadth of GM tasks and recommendations on how to advance GM excellence. The figure outlines all the SAFE areas and depicts the various roles of GM professionals. While agility refers to the strategic advisor role there are spill-over effects into the other quadrants as the other roles would also benefit from the flexibility to master emerging challenges.

In practice, this means that GM professionals have to identify ways how mobility strategies underpin organization-wide

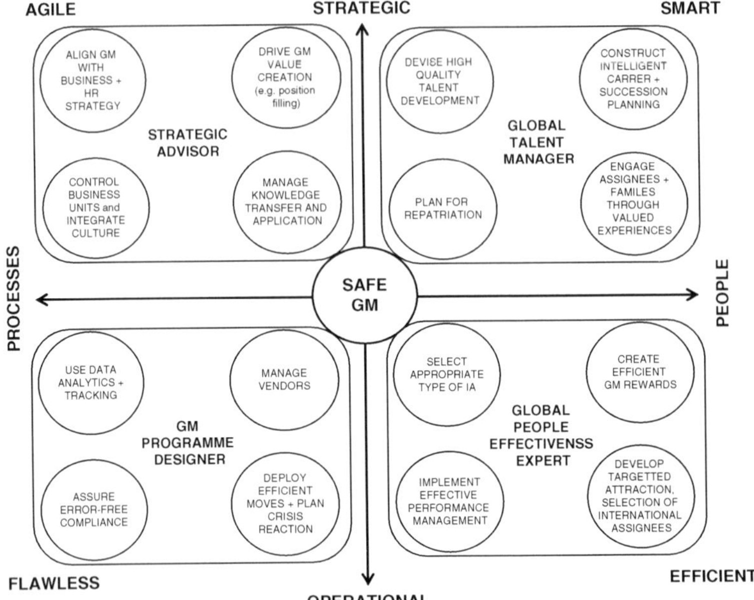

Figure 12.3 SAFE roles of global mobility: managing international work with a purpose

strategies. In addition, GM departments need to develop policies that facilitate agility. This might mean, for instance, to develop 'core flex' approaches and to create flexible governance approaches that incorporate agility in relation to exception management. Agility will also go a long way to future proof GM and may be expressed in other quadrants of Figure 12.3. Younger generations entering the labour market will likely drive a change in more flexible remuneration approaches, which will also have an influence on compensation and benefits in GM. Dealing with agility in GM means to plan for crisis responses, develop scenarios and approaches to refine the corporate reaction to events such as terrorist attacks or natural disasters. This can include, for example, a cost saving scenario or the plans for potential group relocations (e.g., in the light of Brexit). It will be necessary to stay close to the business and its stakeholders to understand their changing needs and future aspirations. The bottom line is to be prepared as much as possible for potential future demands.

12.3.2 Role 2: Smart Global Talent Management and Individualized GM Relationships

Successful GM work is not just smart in the sense of clever; it is also able to create specific, measurable, achievable, results-focused, and time-bound objectives for global workers. The role of the global talent manager will grapple with some of the tensions that are often a challenge in developmental work. Organizations set up talent and career systems and paths that are geared to groups and yet, GM professionals will work with individuals who want a tailored solution in response to their goals and situations. Millennials (and to some extent earlier generations) are already pushing quite hard for an individualization agenda. While the systems aspects always have the potential to display tensions with individualized talent management, developing flexible approaches allows organizations to strive for an agility that is becoming ever more important.

It is important for a firm to reassess its talent recruitment approach; its selection, talent development, performance, potential, GM rewards, and assignment support approaches, in order to manage this situation (RES Forum, 2018; Dowling et al., 2013). Operationalizing a smart global talent management approach may give candidates more certainty in terms of what is expected of them and also a more secure 'pay back' in career terms and development. In addition, providing a good 'deal' in terms of non-monetary assignment factors is known to be attractive to potential assignees (Suutari et al., 2018) and can help to reduce expatriation costs (Dickmann et al., 2008).

The value of a smart global talent management lies in the focus on the intersection of organizational and individual interests. Constructing intelligent careers has shown to be valuable to individuals (Jokinen, Brewster & Suutari, 2008; Mäkelä, Suutari, Brewster, Dickmann & Tornikoski, 2016) and organizations (Inkson & Arthur, 2001). Where organizations engage assignees and their families, devise high quality and useful talent development and plan ahead for repatriation, they are experiencing higher retention figures and better performance (Doherty & Dickmann, 2012; Scullion & Collings, 2006). In addition, their expatriates feel more valued and satisfied with their work abroad.

What are some of the activities necessary to develop smart and individualized GM? There are many roads to Rome but useful activities are centred around understanding and factoring in individual drivers and motivations in the GM attraction, selection, and posting approaches or implementing GM mentor and coaching systems (Dickmann & Doherty, 2008; Hippler, 2009). In addition, it would be useful to truly understand the learning needs of individual assignees (and fit them into the overall development needs of the organization) and to factor these into the career planning for individuals.

12.3.3 Role 3: Flawless Compliance through GM Programme Design

In the past companies have focussed strongly on compliance. The RES Forum data often shows that firms are highly risk averse when it comes to obtaining residence and work visas or when dealing with corporate and individual taxation (RES Forum, 2017). However, compliance is seldom able to substantially improve the employee experience of working abroad. Complying with local tax legislation, remaining in the home social security system as promised, obtaining a work permit, adhering to applicable labour laws, and the existence of an emergency telephone number when needed, normally does not have the potential to make assignees happy, whereas the absence of compliance bears a lot of potential for dissatisfaction. Thus, achieving compliance is simply a hygiene factor.

The value of high quality programme design lies predominantly in two areas. First, being 'flawless' in compliance is highly important because of the multiple risks that come with non-compliance. Firms face stiff fines and stronger regulatory oversight, even down to having their operating permits withdrawn, with a range of further effects on the supply and working patterns of assignees (Anderson, 2007; Sartori, 2010). Second, successful tracking and data analytics, for example, with respect to risk identification, vendor performance, security and crisis arrangement evaluation, movers' satisfaction. is likely to give information that can improve the GM programme, reduce risks and increase satisfaction. This may go some way to senior managers regarding the programme management role as more than simply operational. Where a GM team manages to use data analytics in order to manage risks and improve its GM processes the programme design role has a higher chance of being seen as strategic, thus achieving the effect envisaged by Ulrich (1997) for the HR function as a whole.

Practical approaches in the market to treat compliance for what it really is differ according to the size of the mobility programme. Some of the options are depicted in Figure 12.3 under GM Programme Designer. MNCs with larger programmes should consider whether they can maximize the outsourcing of compliance activities to external partners beyond what they are doing today. It would be useful to identify a dedicated professional, or groups of professionals, with a compliance mindset to be in charge of dealing with external service providers and being knowledgeable about the various aspects of the compliance risk. Good vendor management is obviously important. Being in charge means that these professionals are also positioned in such a way that they can make tactical decisions, for example, on issues and exceptions that would have formerly landed on the desk of the Head of Mobility. In this way, the work is done by the people who are best placed to do it. In a smaller assignment programme, the option to have specialized compliance experts may not be feasible. Specialization is possible only in larger programmes and generalists are typically found where firms have smaller assignment populations. Given that smaller GM programmes have fewer economies of scale, the GM professionals in these companies could seek efficient external partners to whom they could outsource compliance and programme management activities.

12.3.4 Role 4: Efficient Global People Effectiveness Expert

Part of the individualization of the GM role is that of understanding the drivers of individuals who may want to work abroad. Developing an overview of these motivations can help MNCs to improve their global career branding (Point & Dickmann, 2012), to refine selection (Harris & Brewster, 1999) and rewards (Perkins & Festing, 2008). This may enhance their ability to identify the most suitable candidates and to present them with an attractive GM proposition in the shape of job content, talent and career progression, or monetary rewards (RES Forum, 2019).

The obvious value of being a people effectiveness expert is in relation to sending better qualified, culturally sensitive assignees abroad who have the appropriate set of drivers for the objectives of the organization. In addition, this allows the selection of a better matched assignment type, for example, short term or long term assignees, business travellers or cross-border commuters (Baruch et al., 2013). Having superior assignment planning, that builds on individualised candidate information, may also lead to improved performance management in relation to the assignment objectives.

The practical approaches to implement the global people effectiveness role are manifold. They could start in devising a superior global career branding approach that outlines the purpose and advantages of international assignments to internal and external candidates. The actual selection of expatriates can be substantially improved (Harris & Brewster, 1999) through the use of psychometric instruments, competency-based interviews or measures to find out candidates' global work drivers. Thus, going beyond the 'coffee machine selection' to have a more sophisticated and formal approach to global staffing is likely to be highly beneficial (Scullion & Collings, 2011). Designing reward systems that are not 'one size fits all' but are responsive to assignment types, locations, lengths and objectives, can also increase effectiveness and efficiency. The RES Forum reports have begun to delineate the differences in 'assignment packages' that MNCs have implemented (RES Forum, 2017, 2018).

Previously, the case for 'rethinking GM work' has been made and four roles of GM functions were presented in more depth. These had various combinations of strategic and operational management and were often geared to either GM processes or the people dimension in the SAFE framework. The quadrants that were outlined show the primary orientation but this does not mean that the strategic advisor role does not have any operational or people elements. In turn, the GM programme designer role is not simply operational but has also strategic aspects if clever outsourcing provider management or the sophisticated use of data analytics are enacted. In addition, there are many interlinkages between the different roles of GM departments. For instance, if a firm's GM is strategically driven by leadership development and knowledge transfer then the talent manager role is strongly affected. In addition, there are consequences for the selection of assignees and their expatriate package design (Dowling et al., 2013; RES Forum, 2017). While these interactions are real and part of the day-to-day work of GM departments, the framework is necessarily oversimplifying reality. Based on Ulrich, it argues that the key dimensions are strategy/operations and people/processes but there are obviously other elements that are important for GM roles, for example, organizational structure, GM agility and innovation, resources and internal leadership. While these are implicit to some of the roles outlined, they are less explicitly depicted in the SAFE framework. In addition, the roles of other functions and HR areas will also influence the actual roles that GM professionals can play. For instance, if the talent management function has a broad remit that incorporates global talent management it may have many overlaps with GM (Collings et al., 2018). The framework tries to delineate GM work and has to, by necessity, take decisions about what are some of the core contents and processes in the management of global mobility. It will apply to various degrees to large and sophisticated GM departments compared to organizations that have small, emergent GM programmes. Overall, it is hoped that the SAFE framework can guide and inspire GM professionals to rethink and improve their activities. Beyond the four key roles of GM departments there are two further factors to consider if an MNC wants to create a truly attractive and successful expatriation offer.

12.4 Global Mobility with a Compelling Purpose

There is a mutual dependency between assignees and their employers (Larsen, 2004). Organizations highly depend on the quality of their international workers while assignees may find themselves 'high and dry' in certain situations in their host environments, especially in hostile or crisis contexts (Bader & Berg, 2013; Gannon & Paraskevas, 2019). So far, the GM purpose has been predominantly seen through the employer lens and especially incorporates the strategic and operational process dimensions of Figure 12.3.

The value for the organization in determining its key mobility objectives and how GM can support organization-wide strategies have been discussed under the strategic advisor role. However, it is important to go beyond a strategic level to look at the vision of the organization and to long term goals that are attractive to individuals which they can identify with and that give them purpose (Ordoñez de Pablos & Tennyson, 2016; RES Forum, 2018). Working abroad will change the psychological contract of assignees and their expectations (Conway & Briner, 2005; Dowling et al., 2013). In terms of the GM programme designer role, letting people down in terms of compliance or security issues will fundamentally rock their relationship with their employers and will have a detrimental effect on their global work and identification with the organization.

The implications are complex and wide-ranging. The intended role and objective of an assignment will have to be analysed in the sense of delivering purpose to the organization and providing purpose to the individual. Thus, corporate motivations such as knowledge transfer, skills gap filling, control and coordination (Edström & Galbraith, 1977) will need to be aligned to the mindset and motivations of assignees. More broadly, even if the MNC has a purpose statement, it might well make sense to define a team purpose for mobility that is aligned with the company vision and objectives. Some authors in the generational literature argue that purpose is the new currency for creating attraction, retention, and an engaged workforce (Downing, 2006; Ordoñez de Pablos & Tennyson, 2016).

12.5 Global Mobility – Focussing on Assignee Experience

Mobility teams need to engage in the purpose of creating positive assignee experiences. A paradigm shift is already happening in HR and HR transformations. In the past they predominantly focused on cost savings and reducing cycle times. Now they are looking at the effectiveness and, not exclusively, the efficiency of change interventions. Treating compliance as a hygiene factor will support the shift towards purposeful GM that aims to enrich the private and professional lives of assignees.

International assignments are undisputedly one of the most significant experiences employees can have during their careers. It involves their families and creates great learning and developmental opportunities when living and working in other cultural contexts. Where assignees (and their organizations) avoid or overcome the risks associated with working abroad (such as culture shock, work-life imbalance, family separation), it has been shown that their career progression, talent development, and marketability is highly positive (Suutari et al., 2018). This is why Global Mobility needs to focus on employee experiences and how to enhance them.

Assuming a relatively flawless programme design, the experience element of GM is mostly shaped by the people dimension of Figure 12.3. It includes the range of activities that were discussed under the roles of global talent manager and global people effectiveness expert.

To put this into practice would mean taking a closer look at all the interactions that an employee (and their families) experience during their journey along the expatriate cycle. It would further involve checking how positive experiences look and how negative perceptions are created. This also involves an analysis of the assignee experience with the many external service providers.

Furthermore, the host teams and host mentors have a strong impact on how an expatriate feels, adjusts to the local culture, and performs (Toh & DeNisi, 2005; Carraher, Sullivan & Crocitto, 2008). Overall, it would be good to engage as many stakeholders as possible in the search for a good global mobility experience. One step would be to explore what these stakeholders believe has scope for improvement. In practice, mobility departments are often seen as forces onto themselves which operate in separation to other company functions. The argument above strongly implies that GM departments will need to think and live out of their silos, engage with talent management and other stakeholders, understand the purpose and objectives of the assignment, and distinguishing different and alternative forms of global work that are aligned with purpose and that create valued experiences.

12.6 Limitations

This chapter has depicted a simplified, homogenous and idealised picture of what the role of a GM department could entail. It has been deliberately presented this picture in order to draw up the SAFE framework that may inspire global mobility professionals. Nevertheless, this carries a range of limitations.

A simplified approach. MNCs are highly complex organizations that operate by definition on a number of different country contexts. This means that their institutional environments differ and that the environments that expatriates and other global workers face vary. For instance, it may include safe and hostile environments as well as contexts that are more or less welcoming to international workers (Fee, McGrath-Champ & Berti, 2019). This is likely to signify that a one size fits all GM approach does not suit all these different conditions. In addition, the different types of globally mobile workers – for instance including international business travellers or cross-border commuters – can create pressures for many diverse GM approaches (Baruch et al., 2013). While the agile quadrant of the SAFE framework tries to take account of this, the complexity and dynamism in the environment and the manifold demands from individuals, organizations, and institutions may just be too varied to achieve alignment in the various host environments.

A homogenous view. The chapter has treated MNCs as unitary units. However, there are actually many fractions in organizations. We have assumed that there is one vision on the way that MNCs want to achieve competitive advantage neglecting potential differences between local and global goals, counteracting pressures between different business units or potential gaps between the objectives of senior leaders in the MNC and GM managers. In addition, there are some overlaps in some of the functional areas – for example, talent management for all employees versus the smart global talent management role; overall rewards versus local rewards versus global rewards impacting on the efficient people effectiveness expert role – which result in approaches that are potentially beyond the realm of true influence of the GM function and/or necessitate compromises (Dowling et al., 2013). Lastly, the interests of global workers, their line managers and the GM functions may also diverge. Where the line management has strong power it is likely that 'negotiations' with GM professionals result in some adjustment to the intended GM approaches. Thus, enacted practices may diverge from planned ones (Ferner et al., 2004).

An idealised stance. This assumes that GM staff is seeking to pursue extended and more strategic roles as described in the SAFE model and has the required competencies to fulfil these roles. In reality, it has been found that when the HR function embarked on a similar journey following Ulrich's ideas, the interpretation of what this would mean for organizations differed between organizations, the support from other departments and top management within their organizations was often lacking, and the needed competencies for HR practitioners to become more strategic and business focussed were often absent (Sparrow et al., 2010). Given the often quite tactical and specialist roles in GM departments these practical barriers to moving towards a successful formulation and implementation of the SAFE GM approach may also apply. Lastly, it seems to be rare in GM departments to go beyond assessing the cost of global mobility in order to develop a broad value case for specific international assignments and global mobility overall (McNulty, De Cieri, &

Hutchings, 2009; McNulty, 2014; Nowak & Linder, 2016). In the relative absence of well-founded, broad cases for different types of global mobility policies and practices – those that also incorporate benefit considerations and not just cost figures – it will be hard to develop all areas of the SAFE model. The risk is high that some GM departments continue to trouble shoot and to focus purely on operational, short-term issues (Harris et al., 2003; Dowling et al., 2013). Nevertheless, this chapter was written to develop a vision of the GM function's diverse roles that would likely improve the strategic importance and quality of the GM work.

12.7 Conclusions and Learning Points

This chapter has concentrated on the dynamic pressures impacting on GM and is suggesting that agile mobility strategies, structures, and policies enable MNCs to shape the future successfully. For this, GM departments need to move out of their comfort zones and out of their silo mentality. They need to understand organizational and HR strategies and should engage intensively with the business. Based on these pressures, a new SAFE Global Mobility model was developed that depicts key roles and activities emphasizing the purpose and valuable experiences of GM. Notwithstanding the limitations outlined earlier, the chapter contains a range of ideas and recommendations that can improve the GM work of organizations.

The key learning points for GM professionals, formulated as a call to action and bearing in mind the points regarding simplicity, homogeneity, and idealism, include:

1. GM professionals need to understand the massive and rapid changes that define the world of global mobility. Technological advances, automatization, artificial intelligence, new competitive pressures needing new capabilities, and dynamic operating models, create pressures for learning and paradigm shifts.
2. Smart global talent management needs to create tangible results through the management of specific, measurable, achievable, results-focused, and time-bound GM objectives. The value of smart mobility approaches lies in the intersection of organizational and assignee interests. This encourages integration with intelligent career and succession planning.

3. Agile global mobility configurations are constructed through strategic advice. These need to be based on the corporate vision, business, and other strategies and need to be scalable and flexible to react to dynamic competitive developments. In practice, GM professionals have to identify ways how mobility underpins organization-wide strategies.
4. Flawless programme leadership needs to create high quality compliance and vendor relationship management. Flawless programme management mitigates the multiple risks associated with non-compliance. Successful tracking of assignees and sophisticated data analytics can enable GM departments to analyse their activities and improve them even further while increasing client satisfaction.
5. Efficient global people effectiveness approaches need to understand, attract, motivate, and performance manage mobility candidates and assignees. This is enabled through the use of more developed global career branding, more sophisticated mobility selection approaches and instruments, as well as a conscious assignment objective setting and management process.
6. GM professionals should seek to individualize the relationship to assignees through smart global talent management and efficient global people effectiveness approaches. Given the need for superior data for the management of assignees, it can also be used to individualize where expatriates are sent, what form of assignment they go onto, and how they are managed.
7. GM departments need to understand and find shared territory in relation to the purpose of GM work. Beyond using the organizational interest, the purpose needs to incorporate the interests of assignees. This 'mutual purpose' is likely to motivate and energize global workers, resulting in better performance, retention, and commitment.
8. Focus on assignee experience. Staffs increasingly seek meaning in work and life, and good assignee experiences should be valued by expatriates as they are likely to enrich their private and professional lives.

MNCs are embedded in massive change and undertake substantial internal transformations. GM departments and professionals need to understand and shape these changes in order to live their four key roles. Adapting to the new paradigm developed in Figure 12.3 and through the SAFE GM approach, focussing on the purpose and employee experience of working abroad needs sensitive, sophisticated, and agile GM approaches. The road to this is highly complex and will need strong internal support and highly developed strategic and operational capabilities within the GM function. The writer has outlined a strongly practice-focussed chapter and hopes to add to the insights of how to effectively tackle GM challenges in order to take advantage of the manifold opportunities of global work.

References

Ambrosini, V. & Bowman, C. 2009. What are dynamic capabilities and are they a useful construct in strategic management? *International journal of management reviews*, 11(1): 29–49.

Anderson, B. 2007. Battles in time: the relation between global and labour mobilities. *New Migration Dynamics*, 5–24.

Andresen, M., Al Ariss, A., & Walther, M. 2013. *Organizations and Self-Initiated Expatriation*. Abingdon: Routledge.

Andresen, M., Al Ariss, A., & Walther, M. 2013. Introduction: self-initiated expatriation – individual, organizational, and national perspectives. In Andresen, M., Al Ariss, A. and Walther, M. (eds.), *Self-Initiated Expatriation*: 3–10. Abingdon: Routledge.

Bader, B. 2019. A Shiny New World? Global Mobility in the Age of Artificial Intelligence and Robotic Process Automation. RES Forum Quarterly Report, March 2019. London: The RES Forum.

Bader, B. & Berg, N. 2013. An empirical investigation of terrorism-induced stress on expatriate attitudes and performance. *Journal of International Management*, 19(2): 163–175.

Barney, J. B. 1991. Firm resources and sustained competitive advantage. *Journal of Management*, 17(1): 99–120.

Barney, J. B. 2001. Resource-based theories of competitive advantage : a ten-year retrospective on the resource-based view. *Journal of Management* 27 (6): 643–650.

Barney, J. B. & Clark, D. N. 2007. *Resource-based Theory: Creating and Sustaining Competitive Advantage*. Oxford: Oxford University Press.

Baruch, Y., Dickmann, M., Altman, Y., & Bournois, F. 2013. Exploring international work: types and dimensions of global careers. *The International Journal of Human Resource Management, Special Issue on International HRM*, 24(12): 2369–2393.

Becker, B., Huselid, M., Pickus, P., & Spratt, M. 1997. HR as a source of shareholder value: research and recommendations. *Human Resource Management*, 36(1): 39–47.

Beer, M., Spector, B. A., Lawrence, P. R., Quinn Mills, D., & Walton, R. E. 1984. *Managing Human Assets*. Simon and Schuster.

Black, J. S. & Gregersen, H. B. 1991. Antecedents to cross-cultural adjustment for expatriates in Pacific Rim assignments. *Human Relations*, 44(5): 497–515.

Bonache, J., Brewster, C., & Suutari, V. 2001. Expatriation: a developing research agenda. *Thunderbird International Business Review*, 43(1): 3–20.

Bowman, C. & Véronique, A. 2000. Value creation versus value capture: towards a coherent definition of value in strategy – an exploratory study. *British Journal of Management* 11(1): 1–15.

Brockbank, W. & Ulrich, D. 2009. The HR business-partner model: past learnings and future challenges. *People & Strategy*, 32(2): 5–8.

Caldwell, R. 2008. HR business partner competency models: re-contextualising effectiveness. *Human Resource Management Journal*, 18(3): 274–294.

Caligiuri, P. 2013. Developing culturally agile global business leaders. *Organizational Dynamics*, 3(42): 175–182.

Carraher, S. M., Sullivan, S. E., & Crocitto, M. M. 2008. Mentoring across global boundaries: An empirical examination of home-and host-country mentors on expatriate career outcomes. *Journal of International Business Studies*, 39(8): 1310–1326.

CIPD 2007. Survey Report – The Changing HR Function. September. Available at: www.cipd.co.uk/search/searchresults.aspx?PageIndex=1&recommended=False&Query=the+changing+HR+function&PageSize=10&sortby=relevance&doctype=Survey+Report&sitetype=REDESIGN_MAIN.

Collings, D. G., Scullion, H., & Caligiuri, P. M. (eds.) 2018. *Global Talent Management*. London: Routledge.

Conway, N. & Briner, R. B. 2005. *Understanding Psychological Contracts at Work: A Critical Evaluation of Theory and Research*. Oxford: Oxford University Press.

Davies, S., Kraeh, A. & Froese, F. 2015. Burden or support? The influence of partner nationality on expatriate cross-cultural adjustment. *Journal of Global Mobility*, 3(2): 169–182.

Dickmann, M. (2017). International Human Resource Management. In: Wilkinson, A., Redman, T. and Dundon, T. (eds.), *Contemporary Human Resource Management*:258–292, 5th Edition. London: Prentice Hall.

Dickmann, M. & Baruch, Y. 2011. *Global Careers*. London: Routledge.

Dickmann, M. & Doherty, N. 2008. Exploring the career capital impact of international assignments within distinct organisational contexts. *British Journal of Management*, 19(2): 145–161.

Dickmann, M., Suutari, V., & Wurtz, O. 2018. *The Management of Global Careers: Exploring the Rise of International Work*. London: Palgrave Macmillan.

Dickmann, M. & Tyson, S. 2005. Outsourcing payroll – beyond transaction-cost economics. *Personnel Review*, 34(4): 451–467.

Dickmann, M., Doherty, N., Mills, T., & Brewster, C. 2008. Why do they go? Individual and corporate perspectives on the factors influencing the decision to accept an international assignment. *The International Journal of Human Resource Management*, 19 (4): 731–751.

Doherty, N. T. & Dickmann, M. 2012. Measuring the return on investment in international assignments: an action research approach. *The International Journal of Human Resource Management*, 23(16): 3434–3454.

Dowling, P. J., Festing, M., & Engle, A. 2013. *International Human Resource Management*, 6th Edition. London: Cengage Learning.

Downing, K. 2006. Next generation: what leaders need to know about the millennials. *Leadership in Action: A Publication of the Center for Creative Leadership and Jossey-Bass*, 26(3): 3–6.

Edström, A. & Galbraith, J. R. 1977. Transfer of managers as a coordination and control strategy in multinational organizations. *Administrative Science Quarterly*: 248–263.

Engle, A. D., Dowling, P. J., & Festing, M. 2008. State of origin: research in global performance management, a proposed research domain and emerging implications. *European Journal of International Management*, 2(2): 153–169.

Fee, A., McGrath-Champ, S., & Berti, M. 2019. Protecting expatriates in hostile environments: institutional forces influencing the safety and security practices of internationally active organisations. *The International Journal of Human Resource Management*, 30(11): 1709–1736.

Ferner, A., Almond, P., Clark, I., Colling, T., Edwards, T., Holden, L., & Muller-Camen, M. 2004. Dynamics of central control and subsidiary autonomy in the management of human resources: Case-study evidence from US MNCs in the UK. *Organization Studies*, 25(3): 363–391.

Friedman, B. A. 2007. Globalization implications for human resource management Roles. *Employee Responsibilities and Rights Journal*, 19(3): 157–171.

Froese, F. J. & Peltokorpi, V. 2013. Organizational expatriates and self initiated expatriates. differences in cross-cultural adjustment and job satisfaction. *The International Journal of Human Resource Management*, 24(10): 1953–1967.

Gannon, J. & Paraskevas, A. 2019. In the line of fire: managing expatriates in hostile environments. *The International Journal of Human Resource Management*, 30(11): 1737–1768.

Harris, H. & Brewster, C. 1999. The coffee-machine system: how international selection really works. *International Journal of Human Resource Management*, 10(3): 488–500.

Harris, H., Brewster, C., & Sparrow, P. 2003. *International Human Resource Management*. London: CIPD Publishing.

Haslberger, A., Brewster, C., & Hippler, T. 2013. The dimensions of expatriate adjustment. *Human Resource Management*, 52(3): 333–351.

Hesketh, A. J. 2006. *Outsourcing the HR Function: Possibilities and Pitfalls*. London: Corporate Research Forum.

Hippler, T. 2009. Why do they go? Empirical evidence of employees' motives for seeking or accepting relocation. *The International Journal of Human Resource Management*, 20(6): 1381–1401.

Hird, M., Sparrow, P., & Marsh, C. 2010. HR structures: Are they working? In P. Sparrow, M. Hird, A. Hesketh, & C. Cooper (eds.), *Leading HR*: 23–45. Basingstoke: Palgrave Macmillan.

Inkson, K. & Arthur, M. B. 2001. How to be a successful career capitalist. *Organizational Dynamics*, 30(1): 48–61.

Jokinen, T., Brewster, C., & Suutari, V. 2008. Career capital during international work experiences: contrasting self-initiated expatriate experiences and assigned expatriation. *The International Journal of Human Resource Management*, 19(6): 979–998.

Larsen, H. H. 2004. Global career as dual dependency between the organization and the individual. *Journal of Management Development*, 23(9): 860–869.

Lazarova, M. B. & Cerdin, J. L. 2007. Revisiting repatriation concerns: Organizational support versus career and contextual influences. *Journal of International Business Studies*, 38(3): 404–429.

Mäkelä, L., Suutari, V., Brewster, C., Dickmann, M., & Tornikoski, C. 2016. The impact of career capital on expatriates' perceived marketability. *Thunderbird International Business Review*, 58(1): 29–40.

McNulty, Y. 2014. The added value of expatriation: Assessing the return on investment of international assignments. *HRM Practices–Assessing Added Value*. New York, NY: Springer.

McNulty, Y., De Cieri, H., & Hutchings, K. 2009. Do global firms measure expatriate return on investment? An empirical examination of measures, barriers and variables influencing global staffing practices. *The International Journal of Human Resource Management*, 20(6): 1309–1326.

McNulty, Y. and Selmer, J. (eds.) 2017. *Research handbook of expatriates.* London: Edward Elgar Publishing.

Nowak, C. & Linder, C. 2016. Do you know how much your expatriate costs? An activity-based cost analysis of expatriation. *Journal of Global Mobility*, 4(1): 88–107.

Ordoñez de Pablos, P. & Tennyson, R. D. (eds.) 2016. *Handbook of research on human resources strategies for the new millennial workforce.* IGI Global.

Perkins, S. J. & Festing, M. 2008. Rewards for internationally mobile employees. In: P. Dowling, M. Festing & A. Engle *International Human Resource Management*: 172–195. London: Routledge.

Point, S. & Dickmann, M. 2012. Branding international careers: an analysis of multinational corporations' official wording. *European Management Journal*, 30(1): 18–31.

RES Forum 2017. *The RES Forum Annual Report 2017: The New Normal of Global Mobility – Flexibility, Diversity and Data Mastery.* Report authored by M. Dickmann, 122 pages, The RES Forum, Harmony Relocation Network and Equus Software, London. https://theresforum.com/wp-content/uploads/2017/06/RES-Annual-Report-2017-Full-Report-Global-Digital.pdf.

RES Forum 2018. *The RES Forum Annual Report 2018: Global Mobility of the Future – Smart, Agile, Flawless and Efficient.* Report authored by M. Dickmann, 157 pages, The RES Forum, Harmony Relocation Network and Equus Software, London. https://theresforum.com/wp-content/uploads/2018/06/Exec-Summary-RES-Report-2018-RES-FINAL-SINGLE-ONLINE.pdf.

RES Forum 2019. Working Towards 'Top Class': *SMART Global Talent Management and the Employee Value Proposition.* Report authored by M. Dickmann, 18 pages,London: RES Forum Research May 2019. https://theresforum.com/wp-content/uploads/2019/05/RES-Forum-Research-2019-Report.pdf.

Sartori, N. 2010. Corporate governance dynamics and tax compliance. *International Trade & Business Law Review*, 13: 264–278.

Scullion, H. & Collings, D. G. (eds.) 2006. *Global Staffing.* London: Routledge.

Scullion, H., & Collings, D. 2011. *Global Talent Management.* London: Routledge.

Sparrow, P., Hird, M., Hesketh, A., & Cooper, C. 2010. *Leading HR.* Basingstoke: Palgrave Macmillan.

Suutari, V. & Brewster, C. 2000. Making their own way: International experience through self-initiated foreign assignments. *Journal of World Business*, 35(4): 417–436.

Suutari, V., Brewster, C., Mäkelä, L., Dickmann, M., & Tornikoski, C. 2018. The effect of international work experience on the career success of expatriates: a comparison of assigned and self-initiated expatriates, *Human Resource Management*, 57 (1): 37–54.

Toh, S. M. & DeNisi, A. S. 2005. A local perspective to expatriate success. *Academy of Management Perspectives*, 19(1): 132–146.

Ulrich, D. 1997. *Human Resource Champions: The Next Agenda for Adding Value and Delivering Results*. Boston, MA: Harvard Business School Press.

Ulrich, D. 1998. A new mandate for human resources. *Harvard Business Review*, 76(1): 124–134.

Ulrich, D. & Brockbank, W. 2005. *The HR Value Proposition*. Boston, MA: Harvard Business Press.

Vaiman, V., Sparrow, P., Schuler, R., & Collings, D. 2019. *Macro Talent Management in Emerging and Emergent Markets: A Global Perspective*. London: Routledge.

Wright, P. M., Dunford, B. B., & Snell, S. A. 2001. Human resources and the resource based view of the firm. *Journal of Management*, 27(6): 701–721.

Index

Printed in the United States
By Bookmasters